BLOTTED LINES

BLOTTED LINES

EARLY MODERN ENGLISH LITERATURE AND THE POETICS OF DISCOMPOSITION

Adhaar Noor Desai

CORNELL UNIVERSITY PRESS
Ithaca and London

Copyright © 2023 by Adhaar Noor Desai

All rights reserved. Except for brief quotations in a review, this book, or parts thereof, must not be reproduced in any form without permission in writing from the publisher. For information, address Cornell University Press, Sage House, 512 East State Street, Ithaca, New York 14850. Visit our website at cornellpress.cornell.edu.

First published 2023 by Cornell University Press

Library of Congress Cataloging-in-Publication Data

Names: Desai, Adhaar Noor, 1987– author.
Title: Blotted lines : early modern English literature and the poetics of discomposition / Adhaar Noor Desai.
Description: Ithaca [New York] : Cornell University Press, 2023. | Includes bibliographical references and index.
Identifiers: LCCN 2022034300 (print) | LCCN 2022034301 (ebook) | ISBN 9781501769832 (hardcover) | ISBN 9781501769849 (paperback) | ISBN 9781501769856 (epub) | ISBN 9781501769863 (pdf)
Subjects: LCSH: Poetics—History—16th century. | Poetics—History—17th century. | Poetics—History—18th century. | English literature—Early modern, 1500-1700—History and criticism.
Classification: LCC PN1041 .D47 2023 (print) | LCC PN1041 (ebook) | DDC 820.9/003—dc23/eng/20230124
LC record available at https://lccn.loc.gov/2022034300
LC ebook record available at https://lccn.loc.gov/2022034301

For my parents

Contents

Acknowledgments ix

Introduction   1

1. Style: George Gascoigne's "Patched Cote"   28
   Reflection: The Academic Death Penalty   64

2. Invention: Philip Sidney's "Fear of Maybe"   69
   Reflection: Released into Language   104

3. Revision: John Davies of Hereford's "Rough Hewings"   110
   Reflection: Teaching without Judging   149

4. Editing: Anne Southwell's "Extent of Paper"   155
   Reflection: Generous Thinking   195

5. Performance Anxiety: William Shakespeare's "Perfectness"   200
   Reflection: Ars Amateuria   230

Bibliography   237

Index   261

Acknowledgments

The teachers most responsible for helping me become capable of writing this book are Jenny C. Mann and Rayna Kalas. My primary advisers in graduate school and in the years after, Jenny and Rayna have always taken my work so seriously that, despite being daunted by their brilliance, I am never anything but excited to share it with them.

One of the central claims of this book is that modern critical writing, like early modern poetic writing, must be understood as a collaborative effort. At the forefront of my collaborators on this project has been Wendy Beth Hyman, whose marginal comments on every page of early drafts still linger in my memory when I look at the finished product. Wendy's seemingly boundless generosity, coupled with her incisive critical eye, helped me overcome the doubts that plagued this book in its later stages. Debapriya Sarkar organized a working group that gave me an intellectual community in New York City, and I am grateful to her and to Caralyn Bialo, David Hershinow, Laura Kolb, and Lauren Robertson for their feedback and support on an early chapter. Other chapter drafts were read by Jenny Mann, Phil Pardi, and Dianne Mitchell, and portions of early aspects of the book were read, generously and generatively, by Adin Lears, Christian Crouch, Lianne Habinek, Collin Jennings, Jessica Rosenberg, Kate Bonnici, and Jessica Beckman. Maria Sachiko Cecire reviewed early drafts of the book proposal and has been a reliably keen interlocutor throughout the life of this project. The Five College Renaissance Seminar at UMass Amherst, the Columbia University Early Modern Colloquium, and the Columbia Shakespeare Seminar invited me to present my work in progress, and I am so appreciative of the feedback shared by their members.

Patricia Parker, Blair Hoxby, Walter Cohen, Phil Lorenz, Masha Raskolnikov, Andy Galloway, and William J. Kennedy invited me into this discipline. I first felt like a part of a scholarly community thanks to the Early Modern Reading Group at Cornell; thanks, especially, to Shilo

McGiff, who took me under her wing, and to Matthew Bucemi, Molly Katz, Matthew Kibbee, Jonathan Reinhardt, and Sara Schlemm for convincing me that I had found my place and my people. During the final year of writing, I was privileged to join the "Renaissance Project" and to develop my ideas by sharing them with Colleen Ruth Rosenfeld and the rest of the organizing committee: Stephanie Elsky, Wendy Hyman, Kimberly Johnson, Tessie Prakas, and Emily Vasiliauskas. Since becoming an early modernist, I have benefited tremendously from conversations with scholars from across the academy: Faith Acker, Patricia Akhimie, Liza Blake, Claire M. L. Bourne, Emily Coyle, Katherine Cox, Heidi Craig, Hannah Crawforth, Alice Dailey, Callan Davies, Jane Hwang Degenhardt, Allison Deutermann, Jeff Dolven, Ross Duffin, Hillary Eklund, Marissa Greenberg, Roland Greene, Musa Gurnis, Matthew Harrison, John Kuhn, Alexander Lash, Victor Lenthe, Ross Lerner, Erika T. Lin, Michael Lutz, Nedda Mehdizadeh, T. J. Moretti, Lucy Munro, Vin Nardizzi, Harry Newman, Vimala Pasupathi, Tripthi Pillai, Richard Preiss, Christopher Pye, Kathryn Vomero Santos, Jonathan Shelley, Emily Shortslef, Joel Slotkin, John Staines, Alan Stewart, Jacob Tootalian, Evelyn Tribble, Scott Trudell, Henry Turner, Christine Varnado, Sarah Werner, William West, Katherine Schaap Williams, Seth Williams, Michael Witmore, Matthew Zarnowiecki, and Adam Zucker.

Fellowship grants from the Folger Shakespeare Library and the Huntington Library made the research informing this book possible. A grant to participate in Heather Wolfe's paleography seminar at the Folger helped me both conceive and complete the fourth chapter.

My colleagues at Bard have welcomed me into a warm, thriving community where I have learned much about teaching. Thank you for your collegiality and your conversation: Franco Baldasso, Alex Benson, Krista Caballero, Rob Cioffi, Ben Coonley, Lauren Curtis, Jay Elliott, Miriam Felton-Dansky, Liz Frank, Simon Gilhooley, Beth Holt, Laura Kunreuther, Marisa Libbon, Pete L'Official, Patricia Lopez-Gay, Joe Luzzi, Allison McKim, Dinaw Mengestu, Susan Merriam, Alys Moody, Keith O'Hara, Gabriel Perron, Karen Raizen, Ivonne Santoyo-Orozco, Nate Shockey, Katherine Tabb, Dominique Townsend, Marina van Zuylen, Thomas Wild, and Daniel Williams. Lory Gray gets a special shout-out for helping me through countless administrative hurdles. I also want to vociferously thank Dierdre D'Albertis, Éric Trudel, Nicole Caso, Cole Heinowitz, and Matthew Mutter for their advocacy on behalf of junior faculty members.

ACKNOWLEDGMENTS

Over the years, hundreds of students at Bard have challenged me to see the work of writing through eyes other than my own. They have been subject to my own pedagogical maturation. I want to single out Enzo Cnop, Jonathan Repetti, Oona Cullen, Sam Kiley, and Zoe Stone for trusting me with their work and for their candor.

This book obviously would not have been published without Cornell University Press taking a chance on it, and I will be forever grateful to Mahinder Kingra for his receptivity, editorial advice, and care. Karen Hwa helped keep everything organized as my production editor, and Eric Levy was an exceptionally scrupulous and thoughtful copyeditor. Many thanks, moreover, to the two anonymous reviewers, whose commentary improved the book immeasurably in both form and substance. Any errors or failings that remain are mine alone, but if there are any triumphs, they have been nurtured by several waves of readers, editors, and advisers.

There are many people who have gamely kept up with my progress on this book even while I struggled to articulate what it was about. Thanks to the (regrettably named) "Bidet Talk" chat group— Lex, Matt, Jono, Tamar, Peter, Cody, Rob, Keith, Dan, Brian, and Raffi—for two decades of friendship. Nicholas Friedman still puts up with my questions about poetry, and Dee Bowers, Dan Shanks, and Bern Funk periodically helped me stop thinking about poetry when the need arose.

No one has struggled with me through the process of writing a book during a global pandemic more than Nicole Ida Fossi. Thank you for taking care of me, for reading and listening to my ramblings, for goofy bits and silly songs, and for preparing innumerable cups of tea. I could not have finished this without you. Thanks, as well, to the whole Fossi family for their enthusiasm and support, and to Loki and Sicily, who were adamantly uninterested in helping me focus on my work but did wag their tails every time I came out of my office.

I would not have become the person who wrote this book without the support of my family. I am so grateful to the Desais, the Karwals, the Soods, and the Dodejas of all generations for everything that I am and have. My parents, Ninad and Mala Desai, taught me two important lessons that inform the chapters that follow: that the most meaningful work comes from doing service for others, and that being serious about what you're doing does not mean taking yourself too seriously. This book is dedicated to them.

Introduction

"His mind and his hand went together," wrote John Heminges and Henry Condell about the author of *Mr. William Shakspeares Comedies, Histories, & Tragedies* (1623). "And what he thought, he uttered with that easinesse, that wee have scarce received from him a blot in his papers."[1] With these words, Heminges and Condell placed William Shakespeare at the center of a literary tradition stretching from classical conceptions of the *furor poeticus* to the Romantic construction of innate literary "genius."[2] The unblotted lines have become evidence either of someone struck by divine inspiration or, as Virginia Woolf saw it, of someone with a uniquely "incandescent" mind. Either way, they figure their author as free from the clutches of a clumsy material world and as having evaded a social and political life characterized by commitments, responsibilities, and obligations. Woolf suggests that because we know so little about his personal life in comparison to poets like "Donne or Ben Jonson or Milton," Shakespeare's works appear as if free from "all desire to protest, to preach, to proclaim an injury, to pay off a score, to make the world the witness to some hardship or grievance," and he

---

1. Heminges and Condell, "Great Variety of Readers."
2. See how Jonathan Bate puts it in *The Genius of Shakespeare*, esp. 157–86; also see Burwick, "Shakespeare and the Romantics."

appears as the only human who "got his work expressed completely."³ His work continues to strike readers as sacred because, as Jonathan Bate explains, "*'genius' was a category invented to account for what was peculiar about Shakespeare.*"⁴ The blotless papers foretell this greatness and also teach each generation of new writers that anyone not born with or visited by the same transcendent genius who presumes a similar "easinesse" will be criticized for laziness and narcissism.

Ironically, Ben Jonson, cited by Woolf above as one of Shakespeare's more resolutely worldly contemporaries, famously criticized his friend and erstwhile rival for laziness and narcissism. He treated the praise by Heminges and Condell as the setup to a punchline: "I remember, the players have often mentioned it as an honour to Shakespeare, that in his writing (whatsoever he penned) he never blotted out line. My answer hath been, would he had blotted a thousand."⁵ Though laced with the "desire to protest" that Woolf found characteristic of all writers with minds tethered to worldly concerns—and featuring an envy characteristically peculiar to Jonson—his quip also marks the beginning of an ultimately failed project to decouple authorial effortlessness from popular understandings of literary achievement. Jonson's critique was not just of how, in never doubting himself, Shakespeare sometimes "fell into those things, could not escape laughter."⁶ The problem, as he saw it, was that applauding mere "easinesse" betrayed a perspective toward literary production that prioritized superficial rubrics for judgment, on the part of both writers and readers, over the effortful labor of self-reflection. Jonson felt that preemptively approving of the man because of the cleanliness of his papers meant overlooking not just the work that went into his writing but also the work that remained to be done.

The unblotted papers are a myth. Most scholars now agree with Grace Ioppolo that the obvious traces of reworking that appear throughout Shakespeare's plays reveal him to be a "deliberate, consistent, and persistent reviser who worked in an infinite variety of ways," and decades of study have confirmed that several of his plays were the result of collaboration both with other playwrights and with the actors in his company

---

3. Woolf, *Room of One's Own*, 63.
4. Bate, *Genius of Shakespeare*, 163.
5. Jonson, *Discoveries*, lines 802–5. All references to Ben Jonson's poetic and prose writings will be to Jonson, *Complete Poems*.
6. Jonson, *Discoveries*, lines 820–22.

who translated his words into performances.[7] The only surviving example of his hand at work, pages from *Sir Thomas More*, is itself a messy thicket that contains blots, corrections, and insertions made by a variety of authors. Valorizing Shakespeare for effortless, solitary writing may consequently be understood as a symptom of how modern—that is, post-Romantic—conceptions of authorship have corrupted understandings of literary production throughout history. As Linda Brodkey observes, modern readers often imagine the "scene of writing" as one in which the author is seen "not as a participant in the act of writing but as a recipient of written language."[8] Despite knowing that writing is "woven into the very fabric of her social life" as a writer and writing teacher, she confesses that even she remains "fatally attracted" to a romanticized image of "a solitary writer alone in a cold garret working into the small hours of the morning by the thin light of a candle."[9] This view of composition, centered on the act of setting words to paper, makes it seem as though writing primarily occurs as solitary flashes of insight. Anyone who has ever written a sentence, though, knows that the error-free transcription of one's thoughts requires more than simply warding off distraction, habit, and accident. Each sentence culminates time spent not just internalizing the mechanics of transcription but slowly coming to claim a language that no one, not even Shakespeare, innately possesses.

Elizabethan writers acquired the language of poetry by transcribing and imitating many passages from admired authors, studying a variety of forms and styles, reading widely across culturally significant source materials, and even collaborating with other authors.[10] Not only did they borrow heavily from classical and contemporary models, but they also treated one another's texts as invitations to appropriation, repurposing, parody, and response. Their minds and hands, even when working in frictionless tandem, both took a lot of direction from others' books. As Constance Furey points out, in contrast to views of authorship

---

7. Ioppolo, *Revising Shakespeare*, 5. See Jones, *Shakespeare at Work*; Taylor and Jowett, *Shakespeare Reshaped*; van Es, *Shakespeare in Company*.

8. Brodkey, *Writing Permitted*, 62.

9. Brodkey, *Writing Permitted*, 59.

10. William Sherman explains how Renaissance readers were taught, in the humanist schoolroom, to "mark" whatever they read with annotations and marginalia, and to record important claims, pithy phrasings, or moral maxims in commonplace books—like Jonson does throughout his *Discoveries*. Sherman, *Used Books*, 25–52. Also see Jardine and Grafton, "'Studied for Action'"; Acheson, *Early Modern English Marginalia*.

linked to "assertions of originality and proprietary self-expression," premodern models "were more often explicit about the importance of collaborative production and social influences."[11] A courtly culture prioritizing *sprezzatura* may well have incentivized these writers to conceal the painstaking work that went into their verses and boast about their blotlessness, but the ink-stained paper trail was as much of an open secret as the hours a courtier may have put into learning a new dance.[12]

Even if Shakespeare possessed a "natural" fluency for poetic composition, to assume that the texts we read today have never had their words rewritten overlooks the interventions of generations of editors, directors, actors, conservators, abridgers, and teachers. What happened after he shared his lines with Heminges and Condell is as important as what happened before, at least from our perspective as readers. Shakespeare became "Shakespeare," Jack Lynch explains, through a process by which his work "continues to be improved" by editors and directors, "continues to be co-opted" by political factions of all stripes, "continues to be domesticated" by bowdlerized volumes and school curricula, and "continues to be worshipped."[13] In reconstructing him in our own image and for our own purposes, it is "we, and our varied engagement," Emma Smith insists, "that make Shakespeare."[14] Pointing this out does not mean that Shakespeare himself contributed nothing, that he lacked talent, or even that "our holy relics are in reality pigs' bones."[15] It is merely to reaffirm that the indisputable genius attributed to him owes less to whether or not his works emerged from him already perfect

---

11. Furey, *Poetic Relations*, 23. See especially Marotti, *Manuscript*. For recent studies corroborating and expanding on Marotti's account, see Stamatakis, *Sir Thomas Wyatt*; and two essays by Dianne Mitchell: " 'Or Rather a Wyldernesse' " and "Shakespeare's Several Begetters." Even as literary texts increasingly made their way into print, poets and playwrights treated these media as participatory, collaborative, and fundamentally social. For two illuminating studies, see Fallon, *Paper Monsters*; and Pangallo, *Playwriting Playgoers*.

12. Stephen Greenblatt suggests that Shakespeare "evidently had a stake in hiding all of the hard work that went into his apparent fluency" because early modern culture, inspired by Baldassare Castiglione's writings, prized *sprezzatura*. It was also broadly "understood that the only way to achieve this nonchalance—in writing as in dancing or riding or telling jokes—was through fantastically painstaking revisions that all had to be carefully concealed." Stephen Greenblatt, "Did Shakespeare Ever Think Twice?," *Wall Street Journal*, February 5, 2011, Life and Style, https://www.wsj.com/articles/SB10001424052748703960804576120180958916212.

13. Lynch, *Becoming Shakespeare*, 275–76. Also see Taylor, *Reinventing Shakespeare*.

14. Smith, *This Is Shakespeare*, 3. Sarah Olive makes a similar point, contending that the "value" currently placed on Shakespeare has been sustained by "editors, directors, conservators, teachers, and the institutions to which they belong." Olive, *Shakespeare Valued*, 111.

15. Greenblatt, "What Is the History?," 469.

than to how we keep blotting his pages for him so that they might stay perfect.

We do this for him because Shakespeare's singular status atop the literary canon does not simply reflect the movements of his mind and hand; it also reflects the deft management of those with a stake in his reputation. The folio's reference to his scarcely blotted pages may have been part of a project of "monumentalizing" his oeuvre; in promoting the risky venture of printing the first folio, Heminges and Condell were also publicists.[16] The Romantics' valorization of Shakespeare's "native woodnotes wild" may be understood as part of the broader eighteenth-century cultural promotion of the exceptionality of Englishness in general.[17] Pride in their homegrown icon corroborated a nationalistic program that emboldened the British against other imperial powers and enabled them to justify their domination over colonized people.[18] As Gauri Viswanathan recounts, the use of English literature in educational curricula began during England's colonial occupation of India at the start of the nineteenth century. As English became the language of British colonial administration, the study of English literature (which had recently installed Shakespeare as its major icon) became a prerequisite for the administrative integration of colonized Indians.[19] At the vanguard of imperial hegemony as a "mask of conquest," Shakespeare's works became the standard of literary value across the British Empire. This literary curriculum then spread to educational institutions across the Anglophone world.[20] In the United States, the evaluation of English composition began with the Harvard entrance exam of 1874, and the first announcement formalizing expectations of "correct" English

---

16. Chartier, *Author's Hand*, 167.

17. Bate explains that "Shakespeare's rural origins proved invaluable to this process whereby he was reconstituted as the national poet. In the eighteenth century the Bard was seen as a country boy, a genius of the English earth, not a city man." Bate, *Genius of Shakespeare*, 161.

18. See Dobson, *National Poet*. Kate Flaherty points out that Samuel Johnson's elevation of Shakespeare in the mid-eighteenth century reflected the "priorities of Johnson's own political and cultural project: establishing ideological supremacy of England through that of the English language." See Flaherty, "Shakespeare and Education," 364.

19. According to Viswanathan, exposure to texts like Shakespeare's promoted, at least in spirit, a program of ideological indoctrination. His plays were a "source of moral values for correct behavior and action" that served as "a convenient replacement for the direct religious instruction that was forbidden." Viswanathan, *Masks of Conquest*, 93.

20. Kate Flaherty points out that a "recent survey by the Royal Shakespeare Company (RSC, 2010) found that 65 per cent of countries have Shakespeare as a named author on their curriculum and that a staggering 50 per cent of the world's schoolchildren study Shakespeare." Flaherty, "Shakespeare and Education," 361.

prose featured Shakespeare atop the examiners' list of those considered "standard authors."[21] Such ubiquity made Shakespeare "the keystone which guarantees the ultimate stability and rightness of the category 'Literature,'" as Alan Sinfield put it in 1985. Yet if Shakespeare is "representative of a category, of a theory, of which he is the only undoubted instance," Sinfield argued, this "absurd" status makes him an "instrument within the whole apparatus of filtering whereby schools adjust young people to an unjust social order."[22] A consequence of this hegemonic influence propping up only one indisputably great author is that the signifiers of literary greatness have become difficult to distinguish from the traits of that author. Noting this, Wendy Beth Hyman and Hillary Eklund lament that "Shakespeare, perhaps more than any other literary figure, has been trotted out as a symbol of white cultural supremacy."[23] The "natural" ease with which this early modern poet supposedly wrote has unfortunately implicated him in a centuries-long narrative about supposedly "natural" hierarchies of race, sex, gender, class, and ability.

None of this is Shakespeare's fault, nor does it necessarily determine whether the texts are, in themselves, rewarding to read. Yet it has become difficult to teach Shakespeare as *literature* without tacitly corroborating ideological assumptions about aesthetic distinction. Partly in response to a growing ambivalence about canonicity, scholars have for the past half century situated early modern literary texts amid the circulation of social energies and the organization of political and ideological power, most notably under the methodological frameworks of New Historicism and cultural materialism.[24] These methods, part of what Joseph North has termed the "historicist/contextualist" paradigm,

---

21. Quoted in Elliot, *On a Scale*, 10.
22. Sinfield, "Give an Account," 159-60.
23. Hyman and Eklund, "Introduction," 2.
24. I join Robert Matz in seeing Horace's injunction that poetry provide "profit and delight" as a central problem for both Elizabethan literary culture and New Historicist approaches to it. The absence of an aesthetic discourse justifying a universalized sense of "delight" meant that the work of writing could at best be equivocally linked to social and economic questions of "profit." Arguing that a Horatian poetics as the aesthetic principle governing Renaissance literature "compellingly accommodates the wish that literature be both connected *and* resistant to larger historical structures," Matz encourages literary scholars to "consider the costs of giving up claims to an aesthetic discourse." For Matz, "the very historical nature of the aesthetic also means that the category has no absolute set of meanings or effects" and is instead "a site of conflict and contradiction." Matz, *Defending Literature*, 15, 23-24. For more context on how the methodological traditions of New Historicism and cultural materialism relate to the literary canon, see Brannigan, *New Historicism*, esp. 9-13, 19-23.

have meant that the professional study of Shakespeare has involved cultivating skills in research, explanation, and evidence within increasingly specialized domains of cultural and political life.[25] While this crucial scholarship has restored early modern literary texts to the social and material world of their origin, what has been left unaddressed is how the precondition of this scholarship is the room and board provided by a prevailing presumption of Shakespeare's genius. Perhaps nowhere is this dynamic clearer than in the undergraduate classroom, where students approach early modern texts accompanied by contextualizing introductions, explanatory apparatuses, and primary documents curated as textual interlocutors. These encounters take for granted that the greatness of the text warrants not only the time scholars have spent compiling these materials, but the time students must spend poring over them. Doug Eskew puts it plainly: "Students recognize that we tend to ask them to dig deeply into Shakespeare's life and times for no other reason than to wrap their minds around the Shakespearean text. What is unclear to many students is why the Shakespeare text is worth all of that effort."[26] Compelling students to learn about Shakespeare and his world comes, as do all undergraduate courses, with an opportunity cost whereby students lose the chance to learn about other authors and other worlds. Thus, his privileged place in the category of "literature" reproduces itself.

Valued by proponents across the political spectrum, Shakespeare is perhaps the most unassailable element of what it means to be educated in literary history that our culture still acknowledges. Recognizing that one of the outcomes, intentional or not, of courses bearing his name is the maintenance of this status should give the professors of those courses some pause. The Shakespearean fits Bruce Robbins's definition of "the beneficiary": "the relatively privileged person in the metropolitan center who contemplates his or her unequal relations with persons at the less-prosperous periphery and feels or fears that in some way their fates are linked."[27] If the value projected on Shakespeare is for many synecdoche for the value of literary study in general, linking our fates to those of our colleagues, Shakespeare scholars might take it upon themselves to present a more clear-eyed vision of what educational encounters with literary texts can accomplish. We may begin

---

25. North, *Literary Criticism*, 1.
26. Eskew, "Shakespeare, Alienation," 40.
27. Robbins, *Beneficiary*, 5.

by recognizing that there are pedagogical consequences to affiliating literary merit with inspired genius rather than with the collaborative efforts of individuals, institutions, and ideologies engaging in ongoing work—consequences like the tacit ideological approbation, such as through the elevation of one author over all others, of individualism, hierarchy, and competition. As Kathleen Fitzpatrick argues, these values undermine the academy's capacity to promote generosity, openness, and genuinely critical thought.[28]

When pressed to articulate the role of literature in education, most teachers and defenders argue that literary study cultivates "critical thinking," which Fitzpatrick defines as "the contemplation of ideas from multiple points of view, the weighing of evidence for and against, the selection among carefully considered alternatives," arguing that these capacities are weakened by an emphasis on competition.[29] John Dewey offers a more fundamental definition, describing critical thinking as "suspended judgment," the essence of which is "inquiry to determine the nature of the problem before proceeding to attempts at its solution."[30] In practice, critical thinking operates via a "double movement" involving both induction and deduction, discovery and testing.[31] Shakespeare's plays have doubtless afforded generations of students the opportunity to think critically by challenging them to suspend their prior assumptions about concepts like justice, honor, masculinity, or race. How often, however, has Shakespeare's greatness (a greatness potentially reconfirmed by his seemingly robust ability to promote critical thought) itself been subjected to suspended judgment? Students enroll in our classes to learn about "Shakespeare," after all—not necessarily about the topics his texts make available—and one topic they are often interested in is his singular fame. This means that many of them arrive having been subjected to the mythology of his genius and in possession of an assumption ready to be tested. As teachers we consequently wield a unique ability to lay bare how the most singular of literary authors did not, in fact, reach the crest of the literary canon without some help. We might elucidate "literature," then, as cultural process constituted by individuals and institutions working together, and thereby help our students reconceptualize the scene of writing as one in which they have

---

28. Fitzpatrick, *Generous Thinking*, 33.
29. Fitzpatrick, *Generous Thinking*, xi.
30. Dewey, *How We Think*, 74.
31. Dewey, *How We Think*, 79–80.

a stake and a future. Doing so means offering students a conception of authorship rooted not in effortless production but in a process of continual critical reexamination, a process characterized by blotted lines, hesitations, and revisions.

This book argues that early modern poets like Shakespeare understood their own scenes of writing as animated by *discomposition*. Linking composition, "the action of putting together or combining," with discompose, "to destroy or disturb the composure of (a person, the mind, emotions, etc.)," discomposition describes something previously presumed whole or complete in a state of disarray. Its associated definitions link affective poise ("to perturb, agitate, unsettle"), formal logic ("to disturb the order or arrangement of; to throw into confusion or disarray"), and political practice ("to dismiss, cast out from a position or office").[32] Alongside claiming that experiences of discomposition were fundamental to how early modern writers understood the practice of poesy, in reflective interludes following each chapter I explore how experiences of discomposition might become integral to the pedagogy of early modern English literature. A commitment to unsettling routinized habits thus informs the structure and style of this book, witnessed not just in how it considers the ramifications of historicist scholarship even as it engages in such scholarship, but also in its attempt to translate for modern classrooms how both the practices of early modern poesy and the academic study of literature are both ideally undertaken in a bustling, busy, noncompetitive space in which a variety of writers and thinkers collaborate. By setting aside the alluring image of writing as solitary, blotless transcription, this book examines discomposition at work, such as within the relationship between reading and writing, the generative irreconcilability between guided instruction and free expression, the doubtfulness and thrill of invention, the labor-intensive nature of revision, the relationship between authors and editors, and the necessity of failure.

Discomposition

John Florio's English-Italian Dictionary, *A Worlde of Wordes* (1598), translates the Italian *discomposto* as "uncomposed, shap[e]less, formeless."[33]

---

32. *Oxford English Dictionary*, s.v. "Discompose, v. Defs. 1, 2a, 3a," accessed July 27, 2021, http://www.oed.com/view/Entry/53849.

33. Florio, *Worlde of Wordes*, 105.

In 1624, John Donne would deploy the anglicized form of this word (the earliest citation in the *OED*) in his *Devotions upon Emergent Occasions* to describe humanity's self-destructive tendencies: "Is this the honour which Man hath by being a litle *world*, That he hath these *earthquakes* in him selfe, sodaine shakings; these *lightnings*, sodaine flashes; these *thunders*, sodaine noises; these *Eclypses*, sodain offuscations, and darknings of his senses; these *Blazing stars*, sodaine fiery exhalations; these *Rivers of blood*, sodaine red waters? Is he a world to himselfe onely therefore, that he hath inough in himself, not only to destroy, and execute himselfe, but to presage that execution upon himselfe; . . . O perplex'd discomposition, O ridling distemper, O miserable condition of Man!"[34] As Donne's use implies, discomposition conjures not a brick-by-brick reversal of composition's steady process, but a "sodaine" affliction: "[I]n a minute a Canon batters all, overthrowes all, demolishes all." Something that had been put together with intention—a bodily comportment, an artwork, a state—finds itself jolted into disarray.

Yet despite Donne's hyperbole, discomposition does not always or necessarily imply wholesale destruction. George Crabb, in *Crabb's English Synonymes*, first published in 1816, affiliates "discompose" with "derange" and "disconcert," distinguishing these terms as lending specificity to the more generalizable "disorder": "To *derange* is to *disorder* that which has been systematically arranged or put in a certain range; and to *disconcert* is to *disorder* that which has been put together by concert or contrivance. . . . To *discompose* is a species of *derangement* in regard to trivial matters: thus a tucker, a frill, or a cap may be *discomposed*." Crabb elaborates that "those who are particular as to their appearance are careful not to have any part of their dress *discomposed*."[35] As an unsettling of abiding protocols, be they of dress, decorum, valuation, ethics, or law, discomposition lays bare the vulnerabilities, flimsiness, or limitations of those protocols.

Seemingly trivial derangements of form were the lifeblood of early modern poetics. "A sweet disorder in the dress, / Kindles in clothes a wantonness," intoned Robert Herrick in a lyric emblematic of the period's aesthetic commitments. Herrick's "Delight in Disorder" dismisses "art" that is "too precise in every part" and (as students thrill to point out) rustles its iambic meter with trochees and trips up readers with slant rhymes. The poem thus indirectly reflects a broader poetic

---

34. Donne, *Complete Poetry*, 415–16.
35. Crabb, *Crabb's English Synonymes*, 273–74.

program that Colleen Ruth Rosenfeld has described as "indecorous thinking": "Early modern poetic theory . . . treated *decorum* as the guarantee of plausibility: *decorum* was the abstraction of reigning ideological commitments into a principle of design. *Indecorum*, by contrast, provided poetry with a means of distinguishing itself from the world and its dominant ideologies: rather than mediation, *indecorum* performed the work of disarticulation." Rosenfeld locates poetic indecorousness not in "simple inversion or undoing of *decorum*'s regulation" but in the cultivation of "an alternative method" rooted in the imaginative potential of excessive figuration.[36] The conspicuous use of supposedly ornamental figures violated a principle of classical rhetoric—the subordination of *elocutio* to *inventio*—thereby threatening to subvert expectations of reason and replace logic with eloquence.

Rosenfeld's rich claim elaborates on a strain of criticism accentuating how authors in the period recognized chance, error, and disobedience as fundamental to literary epistemology. Michael Witmore's *Culture of Accidents* (2001) traces the way that "accidents," described by Francis Bacon as "intellectual monstrosities," existed for early modern writers as "halfway between the realms of fact and fiction" and as such linked "with artistic creation."[37] Confrontation with the accidental and previously unthinkable, Witmore suggests, was a catalyst for a shared project of making sense anew, a project linking imagination and intellectual accommodation. In *The Inarticulate Renaissance* (2009), Carla Mazzio focuses on instances of verbal accidents to elucidate how "departures from rhetorical competence could be seen as enabling new forms of thinking, feeling, and acting." Events such as a misdelivered phrase, an incoherent muttering, or an *aposiopesis*, Mazzio argues, "could generate a halting effect in the process of reception as well as transmission, a halting that could make space for alternative temporalities and directions of thought otherwise eclipsed by the flow of verbal fluency."[38] It was precisely at moments when the received or inherited forms of knowledge making were discomposed, when "competence" faded, that imaginative thinking and scientific knowledge making could proceed.

Hit with a sudden shock, confronted by an intellectual monstrosity or by the unexpected allure of an erring lace, how did a person come

---

36. Rosenfeld, *Indecorous Thinking*, 7. For more on early modern and classical rhetoric's relationship with indecorousness, see Rebhorn, "Outlandish Fears."
37. Witmore, *Culture of Accidents*, 5–6.
38. Mazzio, *Inarticulate Renaissance*, 56.

to carry it off, fashion it into new knowledge, or react gracefully? One response may be to forge ahead without engaging or even changing course, overpowering contingencies through the sheer force of custom and habit. Another may be to crumble and surrender, amazed or astonished into inarticulacy. Another response still, accommodation, may be driven by a variety of creative strategies. Katherine Eggert suggests that early modern thinkers, increasingly aware of the limitations of humanism as an intellectual framework, cultivated "disknowledge," which she defines as "a deliberate means by which a culture can manage epistemological risk."[39] At the heart of disknowledge is a "conscious act of choosing one system, body, or mode of knowledge over another, even if the one chosen is manifestly retrograde, ill informed, poorly supported, sloppily organized, or even simply wrong."[40] For Eggert, this conscious choice—the choice to extend the lifespan of humanism, or to accredit alchemy alongside emerging empirical sciences—resembles the claims made by early modern poetic thinking. Citing references to alchemy in Sidney's *The Defence of Poesy* (first published in 1595), Eggert sees this foundational text in early modern poetic theory as "turning away from fact-based modes and tenets of learning to modes and tenets that are not responsible for the truth in the same way."[41] Sidney's poet—as I will also argue at length in chapter 2—willingly confronted, even provoked, discomposition because it heralded intellectual and imaginative liberation. Feeling oneself break free of binding commitments, disrupting the presumed stability of the order of things, was for Sidney a prerequisite for poetic insight and artful making.

Most studies of early modern poetic education, including this one, owe an enormous debt to T. W. Baldwin's *William Shakspere's Small Latine and Less Greeke* (1944), but such studies must reckon with Baldwin's inability to depict the ways that grammar school students came to claim the title of creative *poets* rather than that of merely emulative *versifiers*. While literary scholars have tended to attribute the flourishing of literature in the early modern period in part to Elizabethan grammar schools, historians such as Anthony Grafton and Lisa Jardine have generally characterized the educational regime as stifling, stultifying, and opposed to creativity.[42] Neil Rhodes, finding a way through the

---

39. Eggert, *Disknowledge*, 8.
40. Eggert, *Disknowledge*, 40.
41. Eggert, *Disknowledge*, 208.
42. Grafton and Jardine, *Humanism to the Humanities*.

impasse, has argued that it is perhaps more accurate to say that early modern literature appeared in the form of students' "creative abuse" of the humanist pedagogical system rather than because of it.[43] Jeff Dolven's *Scenes of Instruction* (2007) similarly excavates a "counterimpulse" that manifests in humanist pedagogical writings as a "skepticism or despair about the very possibility of teaching." This skepticism influenced the students who would become poets to "turn against instruction itself as a literary project."[44] Lynne Enterline's *Shakespeare's Schoolroom* (2012) also shows how "Shakespeare's affectively charged returns to early school training in Latin grammar and rhetoric are so emotionally powerful precisely because these personifications reenact, or reengage, earlier institutional events, scenes, and forms of discipline that were not fully understood or integrated when they occurred."[45] For Enterline, the schoolroom encounter left the poets it produced perpetually at odds with themselves, torn between a desire to satisfy the stern discipline of their schoolmasters and the urge to thwart it. Indebted to these studies, this book explores how poets shaped the dissonance at the heart of poetry's relationship to education into an *ars poetica* that may help modern teachers of critical writing creatively abuse the logic of undergraduate education.

Poetic discomposition—generative confusion—arises only through encounters with friction. While Ben Jonson distinguished poetry from other kinds of writerly endeavor in terms of its freedom, in keeping with his Horatian sensibilities, he did not relinquish the poet from experiences of frustration and self-doubt. Imagining a poet struggling at his writing desk, he advises,

> If his wit will not arrive suddenly at the dignity of the ancients, let him not yet fall out with it, quarrel, or be over-hastily angry; offer, to turn it away from study, in a humour; but come to it again upon better cogitation; try another time, with labour. If then it succeed not, cast not away the quills, yet; nor scratch the wainscot, beat not the poor desk; but bring all to the forge, and file, again; turn it anew.

---

43. Rhodes, *Origins of English*, 84. Helen Hackett concurs, concluding that while the "sheer number of Elizabethan authors who attended grammar schools points to a connection between grammar school-education and later literary achievement," this connection should not be understood as "a smooth transition from skills and training enthusiastically imbibed at school to later literary success." Hackett, "'Better Scholar.'"

44. Dolven, *Scenes of Instruction*, 3.

45. Enterline, *Shakespeare's Schoolroom*, 2.

> There is no statute of the kingdom bids you be a poet, against your will; or the first quarter. If it come, in a year, or two, it is well.[46]

Part of what it took to write a poem was understanding that no one was expected to write poems at all. Bound neither by external laws nor by internal impulses, poetic composition was for Jonson a practice of freedom, which included a freedom from one's own impulses. He understood "poesy"—the "doing," rather than the "doer" or the "thing done"—as offering "a certain rule, and pattern of living well, and happily; disposing us to all civil offices of society."[47] In practice, this did not mean that poets could write whatever they liked, but it also did not mean they had to write only what they believed others would like. It meant that aspiring poets put in work for its own sake, trusting the process. "Whither a man's genius is best able to reach," Jonson argued, "thither it should more and more contend, lift and dilate itself."[48] Invoking techniques from his grammar school education—debate, elaboration, dilation—but orienting those techniques toward an unknown target, he acknowledged strain as fundamental to poetic craft: "As men of low stature, raise themselves on their toes" and "so ofttimes get even, if not eminent," poets might attempt to surpass, rather than merely emulate, writers they found admirable.[49] Anathema to poesy was complacency; even after much exercise, Jonson cautioned, poets needed to remain wary: "When we think we have got the faculty, it is even then good to resist it."[50] The heart of poesy—and the lesson of discomposition—is that writers recognize the necessity of steering into the skids of difficulty, rather than allowing either external criteria or unreflective impulse to govern their pen. Feeling momentary discomfort about not matching an implicit standard or about making a potentially dangerous new discovery, going backward to move forward, willingly pitting one's judgment against another's, cultivating humility: these are the maneuvers of poetic discomposition.

Jonson's advice that poets return their work "to the forge, and file, again" reverberates in his commentary about Shakespeare's supposedly unblotted lines. In Jonson's own contribution to the first folio,

---

46. Jonson, *Discoveries*, lines 3019–31.
47. Jonson, *Discoveries*, lines 2948–60. For the origins of Jonson's account of "poesy," see Clark, "Requirements of a Poet"; and Spingarn, "Sources of Jonson's 'Discoveries.'"
48. Jonson, *Discoveries*, lines 2148–51.
49. Jonson, *Discoveries*, lines 2151–53.
50. Jonson, *Discoveries*, lines 2144–45.

moreover, he offers another counterbalance to the idea that Shakespeare's scene of writing was notable for his effortlessness:

> And, that he,
> Who casts to write a living line, must sweat,
> (Such as thine are) and strike the second heat,
> Upon the muses' anvil: turn the same,
> (And himself with it) that he thinks to frame;
> Or for the laurel, he may gain a scorn,
> For a good poet's made, as well as born.
> And such wert thou.[51]

Great poets like Shakespeare may be born with natural talent, but they are "made," Jonson suggests, through the continual exercise of art.[52] Their successes were the product not of the victory of nature over art, but of the sparks between them. Accordingly, anyone who wants to compose a "living line" may be inspired to similar exercise by observing the careful craftsmanship of Shakespeare's "well-turnèd, and true-filèd" examples.[53] The blacksmithing metaphors reflect Jonson's broader view that good writing required continual labor: "For a man to write well, there are required three necessaries. To read the best authors, observe the best speakers: and much exercise of his own style." In his elegy, then, we see him advising aspiring poets to emulate the sweaty labors of a writer who had to "consider, what ought to be written; and after what manner"; "think, and excogitate his matter"; then "choose his words, and examine the weight of either"; and finally to "take care in placing, and ranking both matter, and words."[54]

Less concerned with either specific poets or specific poems than with the work of writing itself, this book places Shakespeare alongside an array of writers and teachers of writing from both early modernity and the modern academy. Though each chapter observes a different poet at work—George Gascoigne, Philip Sidney, John Davies of Hereford, Lady Anne Southwell, and William Shakespeare—because each of these poets was in some way preoccupied with the dynamics of teaching and learning, their writings collectively enable a broader examination of the

---

51. Jonson, "To the Memory of My Beloved," lines 58–65.
52. For a reading of Jonson's metaphor of the "muse's anvil," see Miller, "Ben Jonson,".
53. Jonson, "To the Memory of My Beloved," line 68.
54. Jonson, *Discoveries*, lines 2101–9.

relationship between literature and writing instruction. Across the reflections that follow each chapter, I draw on these writers' experiences to reframe issues relating to writing instruction that still have purchase in the contemporary university classroom. Teachers like John Warner and Susan D. Blum have foregrounded these issues in books like Warner's *Why They Can't Write* (2018) and Blum's *"I Love Learning, I Hate School"* (2017), and the field of composition studies routinely reflects on its own methods in ways that literary studies might take more seriously. Geoffrey Sirc's *English Composition as a Happening* (2002) challenges compositionists to restore aesthetic sensibilities—as well as risk and chance—to students' encounters with writing. David Smit's *The End of Composition Studies* (2004) argues for further integration between the work of writing and different discursive and disciplinary domains. Hannah J. Rule's *Situating Writing Processes* (2019) peers closely at the writing process as physically situated within lived material circumstances, a point Asao B. Inoue, in *Labor-Based Grading Contracts* (2019), takes to heart in arguing for a writing pedagogy focused on effort rather than outcomes.[55] Ideas from scholars in rhetoric and composition studies such as these don't just inform and shape how this book contextualizes the writing processes of early modern poets; they also, I suggest, provide teachers of early modern literature pathways for rethinking the role of writing in our pedagogy.

In chapter 1, the first published teacher of vernacular English poetics, George Gascoigne, offers a bedrock insight into how the acquisition and development authorial style relies on the free exercise of choice—a point made both by his humanist antecedent Desiderius Erasmus and by modern critics of writing instruction such as Warner and Blum. In chapter 2, Philip Sidney defends poetry by situating experiences of hesitation at the intersection of poetic thinking and rhetorical argument, demonstrating—as the writing teachers Laura Wilder and Wendy Bishop also demonstrate—that like critical thinking, poetic invention stems from the moments when technical knowledge yields to uncertainty. In chapter 3, the self-consciously mediocre John Davies of Hereford, who was also a teacher of ornate handwriting, considers the material conditions that preclude undertaking serious revisions of one's work. Davies anticipates how compositionists like Inoue critique standards of evaluation that overlook how the time and resources needed to meet them are often unavailable to underprivileged and working-class

---

55. Warner, *Why They Can't Write*; Blum, *"I Love Learning"*; Sirc, *English Composition*; Smit, *End of Composition Studies*; Rule, *Situating Writing Processes*; Inoue, *Labor-Based Grading Contracts*.

writers. Chapter 4 studies how Lady Anne Southwell's poetry, as well as the textual artifacts on which it was inscribed, reveals poetic writing to be an opportunity to exchange ideas and learn from interlocutors, demonstrating how the process of editing might serve as a model for critical engagement aligned with Kathleen Fitzpatrick's call for "generous thinking." The final chapter studies William Shakespeare not as a writer who never blotted his lines but as one who, especially in *Love's Labor's Lost*, was preoccupied with the contradictions of "perfection" as they applied to literary composition. Presenting him as someone who understood that the difference between literary and technical "performance" lay in the former's commitment to failure, the book ends with an appeal to dismantle the ways in which professionalism provokes performance anxiety and stifles critical thought.

Varied in terms of their backgrounds, chosen genres, and imagined audiences, the authors studied in this book's chapters collectively help us imagine how an early modern literature classroom, even one focused on Shakespeare, might resist a one-size-fits-all account of writerly process. When early modern poets sat down to compose, their experiences were not alike because their social and economic backgrounds were not alike. In their shared commitment to poesy, however, they all understood, as we might help our students understand, that experiences of discomposition were essential to their practice. To further establish the connections between these poets' experiences and the way we might help our students undertake the written work of literary criticism, the remainder of this introduction reconsiders the relationship between literary epistemology and writing instruction in the modern academy.

Poesy as Critical Pedagogy

To teach Shakespearean literature, professors must also be writers—of syllabuses, assignment prompts, essay comments, and student evaluations, but also of reviews, book chapters, peer-reviewed articles, and monographs like this one. We know that much of our writing requires us to draw on others' words as prompts, share drafts, ask trusted peers for advice, and imagine our words reaching specific audiences. What Shakespeare professors do as *writers*, however, often appears quite distinct from what they have historically been asked to do as *teachers*. This need not be the case.

The disciplinary field of Shakespeare studies now sustains scholars of history, material culture, aesthetics, adaptation, sexuality, politics, race, gender, ecology, science, law, and education; among them are theorists, formalists, philologists, book historians, theatrical practitioners, activists, archivists, poets, artists, and teachers. One thing that brings all of us together is a collection of texts that have accrued around the name "Shakespeare." These texts include his plays and poems but also, crucially, the works of dozens of writers both major and minor. We study Marlowe and Donne and Milton, but also poets who may never become household names and texts that few others would willingly want to read. Another thing we share is our awareness that when we produce scholarship, we produce it for one another. At our annual conferences, a text may be critiqued for its complicity in settler-colonialist hegemony and may also be studied (sometimes by the same scholar) for the way it discloses relationships between rhetorical figuration and scientific experimentation. Shakespeare studies, as a discipline, thus accommodates both a love for and detachment from its literary objects, in part because its commitments are no longer simply to literary authors but to the world they inhabited and to the world within which their texts still exert influence. Like all humanistic work, ours is driven by scholars making free choices about what to study and what kinds of attention to expend. It also requires that we justify those choices, usually in writing, for other disciplinary stakeholders through processes like peer review. This twinned commitment to freedom and responsibility sometimes generates tension, debate, and even discomfort among members of our discipline, but without risking these outcomes, the field would become barren. The vibrancy of Shakespeare studies as a field of academic inquiry is rooted, ultimately, in the field never being fully comfortable with itself.

An undergraduate course on Shakespearean literature might allow students to similarly access an invigorating interplay between freedom and responsibility. Empowering students lies at the heart of Ayanna Thompson and Laura Turchi's intervention in *Teaching Shakespeare with Purpose* (2016), which argues that "Shakespeare needs to be the vehicle instead of the destination for advanced learners."[56] Treating Shakespeare as a destination, Thompson and Turchi observe, precipitates a pervasive educational problem: students end up submitting what they think the professor wants rather than thinking for themselves. Reverberating Paolo Freire's critique of the "banking model" of education, they observe

---

56. Thompson and Turchi, *Teaching Shakespeare with Purpose*, 122.

that teachers who become "dispensers of received Shakespeare" risk restricting their students to "prescribed and closed interpretations."⁵⁷ This dynamic is particularly apparent in Shakespeare classrooms because his "cultural capital functions as a structural constraint," and a symptom of treating literature as cultural capital is that students try to make good on their investment.⁵⁸ They sense that they must be able to persuasively convey to other wielders of that capital that they "get it," that they know what the texts are "about" or even what they are "*really* about," and this emphasis on acquisition breeds a teacher-centric learning environment. To mitigate this, Thompson and Turchi promote classwork such as translating or imitating Shakespeare's work, writing about film trailers, doing creative assignments that "finish the scene," or engaging in student-driven research projects. These exercises, not incidentally, echo early modern writing practices: Shakespeare, too, would have translated and "modernized" older texts, adapted across media, and finished others' scenes. Yet Thompson and Turchi also recognize that movement from creativity to independent critical thought requires more than creative freedom. It also demands the cultivation of intellectual responsibility. Activities like "write-to-learn assignments," free-writes, and workshop discussions, they note, "are insufficient as demonstrations of independent facility with complex texts." One of the markers of independent facility, they suggest, is the student's ability to "generate a complex text in response."⁵⁹

If we want to position Shakespeare as a "vehicle" that enables student writing in our courses, we might consider how a "complex" response to Shakespeare's texts could begin by asking students to reevaluate why these are the texts under study in the first place. Laying out the history of the ideological domination undertaken under the banner of English literature, however, would be insufficient as pedagogy, because sharing only such critiques would offer students "prescribed and closed interpretations" in a new vein. Regardless of the political content of course materials, the political underpinnings of how the classroom environment has been structured may still undermine critical thinking. According to bell hooks, the "bourgeois values" that "overdetermine social behavior in the classroom [and] undermine the democratic exchange of ideas" reinforce a status quo that silences and marginalizes

---

57. Thompson and Turchi, *Teaching Shakespeare with Purpose*, 16.
58. Thompson and Turchi, *Teaching Shakespeare with Purpose*, 16.
59. Thompson and Turchi, *Teaching Shakespeare with Purpose*, 122.

students who are "unwilling to accept without question the assumptions and values held by privileged classes."[60] Even when professors "embrace the tenets of critical pedagogy," or even when the "subject matter taught in such classes might reflect professorial awareness of intellectual perspectives that critique domination," hooks notes that it is often the case that in such classes, the "classroom dynamics remain conventional, business as usual."[61] This business, the business of social reproduction through an institutional logic equating schooling with obedience, means that critiquing a canon to make it more inclusive and representative falls short of revising the terms under which "literature" as a concept can be interrogated and redefined. "It is much easier to make the canon representative [of a pluralist society] than a university," John Guillory argues. Political reform demands more than revising the contents of the literary canon; it requires addressing how access to "the means of literary production" remains unequally distributed.[62]

What students read is often less meaningful than how they are taught to write in response to it, as J. Hillis Miller explains: "The danger is that teachers of composition may assume that the reading chosen for the course can be liberating while the formal instruction in the rules of correct composition remains the same. This does not work. It does not work because the formal aspect of composition is even more powerful in imposing an ideology than is the thematic content of what is read."[63] Figures like "Shakespeare, Faulkner, Joyce, Woolf (or, for that matter, Derrida)," Miller suggests, "needed to defy standards of correctness in order to say what they wanted to say."[64] While it doubtless is of crucial importance for students to encounter Shakespeare as situated alongside other writers—those from his period and those from radically different contexts and backgrounds—it is also of crucial importance that students apprehend continuities between the writers on the syllabus and the writing they will be asked to undertake.

Joseph Harris observes that while writing classes may enlist critical readings and critical theory, even when such texts demystify "the workings of literary texts and then the codes of power," the "workings of this criticism itself have often remained mysterious."[65] To combat this,

---

60. hooks, *Teaching to Transgress*, 179.
61. hooks, *Teaching to Transgress*, 180.
62. Guillory, *Cultural Capital*, 7.
63. Miller, "Nietzsche in Basel," 315.
64. Miller, "Nietzsche in Basel," 313.
65. Harris, "Revision as a Critical Practice," 581-82.

he suggests that professors and students collectively engage questions such as, "How did Barthes actually go about writing his mythologies? How did Foucault construct his genealogies? What features did they look for in the texts they read? How did they move as writers from sentence to sentence, paragraph to paragraph?"[66] Why not ask—and attempt to answer—such questions of early modern literary texts in order to demystify the labor of literary production? Why not ask and attempt to answer such questions of ourselves, as writers authorized to teach students how to read and write about early modern literature? "Unless we share with students how we approach the activities of reading and writing," Harris warns, "we run the risk of once again casting them simply as the spectators of criticism, who are shown the results of our work but are not engaged in doing it, who are asked to ventriloquize our positions and interpretations but not to form their own."[67]

Foregrounding the fact that writing poetry well requires a degree of discomfort will allow us to place literary craft in closer proximity to the method at the heart of critical engagements with literary texts: close reading. Students *do* close readings so that they might *produce* close readings—it is a practice as well as a thing, a reading that is also a writing. "The ability to perform close readings," Thompson and Turchi suggest, "distinguishes between those who think they know what a complex text says (or have previously been told what the text says), and those who can independently grapple, wrestle and tease out subtle details that matter."[68] At the core of close reading is a willingness to read tactically, to make conscious choices, and to go against the grain—and then to test one's conclusions. Close readers must "grapple" or "wrestle" because they must do *more* with a text than simply understand it. Annette Federico capaciously defines the practice as "the cultivation of self-consciousness about the reading experience, a desire for more awareness of what's going on—the kind of reading that opens the door to a deeper, more critical understanding of the *particular* work being read, and of the *experience* of reading as a whole."[69] The reader starts with something small and local, and casts lines outward—to other parts of the text, to recollections drawn from personal experience—and fashions a claim that, the reader hopes, will be persuasive to others.

---

66. Harris, "Revision as a Critical Practice," 582.
67. Harris, "Revision as a Critical Practice," 582.
68. Thompson and Turchi, *Teaching Shakespeare with Purpose*, 15.
69. Federico, *Engagements with Close Reading*, 9.

This experimental practice accords with Dewey's account of the school's essential function as a "social institution." For Dewey, school ideally presents social reality in its "embryonic form" so that its overwhelming complexities do not lead children either to lose their "power of orderly reaction" or to become so stimulated as to become "either unduly specialized or else disintegrated."[70] As part of this socializing process, schools utilize literature and language study—but they must not do so merely as "the expression of thought." They must be "social instruments" whereby the "individual comes to share the ideas and feelings of others."[71] Just as poesy, according to Jonson, disposes its practitioners to "all civil offices of society," Dewey imagines a practice of education that would prepare students to think on their feet as they engage with the world. Education, as he envisions it, requires discomposition; it "must be conceived as a continuing reconstruction of experience" wherein the "process and the goal of education are one and the same thing."[72] Close reading satisfies this dimension of education because, when done well, it invites readers not just to deconstruct their assumptions, but to *restructure* their discovered knowledge into something that can be shared.

One way to think about the transition from close reading to critical writing is as paying a great deal of attention to a text before paying a great deal of attention to textual production, but in practice these moves are interlinked and reciprocal. When one is choosing what to quote, what to paraphrase and summarize, or what questions to apply to a text, writing becomes an instrument for reading, and reading becomes integral to writing. Selecting a passage to block quote pushes its features to the foreground of the writer's attention; pointing out a specific detail amid one's prose makes that detail part of the latent logic of *both* the text that is written about and the text that is being written. Substitute "writing" for "reading" in Federico's definition, and we arrive at something that has many affinities with Warner's account of a key component of the writer's practice: "Writers must learn from their experiences. A fancy term for this is 'metacognition,' or thinking about thinking."[73] Warner's writer, moreover, also sounds a lot like Jonson's account of the poet pounding his desk: "A significant part of the writer's practice . . .

---

70. Dewey, "My Pedagogic Creed (1887)," 231.
71. Dewey, "My Pedagogic Creed (1887)," 232.
72. Dewey, "My Pedagogic Creed (1887)," 233.
73. Warner, *Writer's Practice*, 19.

is recognizing that writing is difficult, that it takes many drafts to realize a finished product, and that you're never going to be as good as you wish."[74] The writer and the poet thus resemble Federico's close reader, who confronts a continual "desire for more awareness of what's going on" and assumes that there are always more questions to ask.

Composing literary criticism constitutes a writing *with* more than a writing *about*, a form of writing prompted and provoked by engaging another's writing in one's own. Jonathan Kramnick notes that literary criticism is "unique among interpretative practices" in that it "shares a medium with its object." The consequence of this unique relationship is that "the interpretative act of criticism is inescapably creative." Writing a critical reading is a practice of making, as Kramnick calls them, "novel artifacts" that register the entanglement of one's imaginative and creative perspective with those prompted and prodded by the language of the text being studied.[75] Criticism is a form of writing that blurs the distinction between reading and writing, and the practice of undertaking it constitutes a set of skills that are not easily acquired or easily explained—even at the level, as Kramnick elegantly demonstrates, of introducing quotations from a text into one's own prose. The knowledge-making of literary criticism thus often depends on what Ben Knights calls "forms of bewilderment."[76] When a literary critic offers a "reading" of a text, by navigating alongside and against prior readings their reading steers into the skids of a disputable moment. As Knights suggests, "The object of knowledge (whatever the critic, or group, or student essay writer may in fact make out of the text or texts in front of them) is inherently unstable."[77] This instability is often undermined, however, by the way in which literature classrooms are premised on professors' posture of knowingness, leaving the ways in which literary scholars arrive at their own critical insights mystically beyond the grasp of students.

One thing that professors know that their students may not automatically intuit is that professors are not unveiling what a text means; they are constructing it. The way that professors construct this meaning, Knights explains, involves a lot of trial and error:

> Inasmuch as students find themselves longing for the dogmatic, they are perpetually teased with shape-changing complexities,

---

74. Warner, *Writer's Practice*, 23.
75. Kramnick, "Criticism and Truth," 234.
76. Knights, *Pedagogic Criticism*, 11.
77. Knights, *Pedagogic Criticism*, 11.

theoretical cross-dressing, one conceptual overlay succeeding another. The whole thing can come to seem to students arbitrary, the safest recourse to lie low. Yet the instability of the object of knowledge (what it is that you might *know* or be able to do as a result of this lecture, this seminar, this morning in the library) is common to all "high" versions of the English discipline. It resides within a tension between linear, propositional knowledge (which favors accumulation and authority, and is reinforced by the recent explosion of research specialization) and conversation. And it lends itself only very obliquely to calibration against the behaviorist scheme of the "intended learning outcome."[78]

Criticism's objects of knowledge do not carry with them instruction manuals or recipes. When we challenge students to invent their own readings of literary texts, then, how, exactly, are we teaching them to do so? A "curriculum conceptualised in terms of 'delivery' drives towards summary interpretation, and safe closure," Knights argues. Unsettling the logic of delivery leads to the question, "What might be the pedagogic implication of taking incoherence seriously?"[79] Scholars and teachers who write know from experience that producing critical writing often involves a dialectic of scrupulous study and imaginative daring. We also know that making the leap from reading to writing is rarely final; we do not just come up with something to say while we read and then produce prose suited to it. It is more likely that we oscillate between our writing and the texts we are working with, read more to write more, delete writing to produce better readings, and reframe our thinking as we check it against that of others.

What if we, professors who are also writers, laid bare for our students that among the hardest and most rewarding challenges of literary study is the relinquishing of readings we already possess? By this I do not mean to suggest that we give away our earned authority or withhold our experience and knowledge from our students, or that we treat students as if they have nothing to learn from us. I only mean that we acknowledge that the seat of critical invention depends on experiences of discomposition, and that these experiences manifest most visibly when we experience surprise. Such surprises are the lifeblood of classroom conversations: what may seem like trivial hiccups, such as

---

78. Knights, *Pedagogic Criticism*, 11–12.
79. Knights, *Pedagogic Criticism*, 158.

when a student proclaims a reluctance to share an observation but proceeds to share it anyway, often throw the whole class into a moment of thoughtful uncertainty.[80] Learning to apprehend that there are different systems of interpretation that may be applied at any given moment means learning that what Knights calls the friction of "one conceptual overlay succeeding another" is necessary for constructing an interpretation. Balancing one's ethical commitments against the logic of the text, or comparing one's subjective responses to those of others, or sustaining two different paradigmatic frames through which meaning may be constructed—the conflicts between such frames make it possible to constitute a problem that provokes complex writing.

Teaching "process" rather than "product" in courses on early modern literature is easier said than done, however. Literature courses, especially courses organized around historical periods, are often constrained by tacit or explicit imperatives to cover content. In these courses, professors are pressed to treat course design in terms of giving students exciting things to write about, but when and how students learn how to write criticism is often a secondary consideration. While scholars in composition studies have frequently pointed to the mystifying unattainability of canonicity as an occasion to debate the uses of literature in writing classes, literature professors consider the reverse—the role of writing in a literature class—much less frequently.[81] If anything, literary studies has quietly assented to the marginalization, in terms of status, visibility, and funding, of rhetoric and composition in the academy. In *Textual Carnivals* (first published in 1991), a landmark critique of "the politics of composition," Susan Miller observes that composition is the "low" counterpart to literary study's "high"; it is a place for

---

80. These experiences are akin to what Joseph Vogl calls "tarrying," which requires the competition of several forces of "different principles and systems of valuation—different encodings of the social and moral world." Vogl, *On Tarrying*, 31.

81. Compositionists routinely allude to Shakespeare as an emblem of writing as a noun and as an example of the limitations of the encounter between writing instruction and literary studies: he is there to "furnish an excellent training for the student's taste," he is there as a "brand name" who advertises "not writing but canonical texts," he is the prompt to an "asymmetrical" conversation that he does not participate in. See Crowley, *Composition in the University*, 81; Brodkey, *Writing Permitted*, 66; Harris, *Rewriting*, 36. For examples of compositionists engaging with literary texts in their pedagogy, see Harris, "Undisciplined Writing"; Isaacs, "Teaching General Education Writing"; Morrow, "Role of Reading"; Fenstermaker, "Literature in the Composition Class"; Hart, Slack, and Woodruff, "Literature in the Composition Course." For commentary on the role of writing in literature classes, see Jackson, "Connecting Reading and Writing"; Knights and Thurgar-Dawson, *Active Reading*; Sullivan, "Writing in the Graduate Curriculum."

"fissures, hesitations, conflicting purposes, and the multiple origins of ideas" set against a "mythologically cool, organized space of univocal 'statement.'"[82] As such, composition offers academic institutions "an alternative to reading, and only reading, texts that constitute the quasi-religious ideal of a textual canon."[83] Wendy Bishop similarly argues that the institutional rift between textual "producers" and "consumers" in the academy is made manifest by first-year composition courses being taught primarily by graduate teaching assistants and contingent faculty. In this institutional structure, "the literary enterprise is steeped in self-preservation—the attempt to create a beneficial work environment for its members rather than to offer students, as is often espoused, free access to life-transforming literary texts."[84] Reflecting on this situation, Shakespeare scholars might start thinking more seriously about how undergraduates are taught the craft of critical writing—and how the people teaching them are compensated and enabled to engage in this time-consuming work. With what little institutional authority we have, we might also do more to acknowledge and promote the importance of writing instruction for the future of a more inclusive literary studies.

If we want to make critical writing a part of our pedagogy—if we expect critical writing from our students—the thematic content of what students read in an early modern literature classroom all but demands a shift in our classroom's formal treatment of the study of writing. This shift may mean embracing a role of departmental service to emphasize that the work of writing *with* literature is one of the ways that conceptions of the "literary" are constituted. It may mean making part of the course content students' own writing, because the texts we study are already overrepresented in discussions of what does and does not count as literature. To be clear, when I talk about the early modern literature classroom, I am concerned primarily with undergraduate education in introductory literature courses, and specifically with the paradigmatic Shakespeare or early English literature survey courses taken by prospective majors and students there to satisfy distribution requirements. Shakespeare still attracts students to literary study because he represents literary legitimacy, and we should see this as an opportunity and as an obligation. In my focus on undergraduate education, I am

---

82. Miller, *Textual Carnivals*, 27.
83. Miller, *Textual Carnivals*, 6.
84. Bishop, "Literary Text," 449.

not directly concerned with method wars, graduate students, or even upper-level courses for specialized English majors. Nevertheless, I hope my emphasis on the pedagogy of literary criticism at this foundational stage of literary education can bring about changes in how we think as a field about our critical methodologies, how we train future teachers of early modern texts, and, hopefully, how we arm students to advocate for and defend the educational importance of literary study.

While I offer some concrete practical suggestions along the way, my aim throughout is not to insist on specifics. My suggestions, I know, will be unworkable in many academic contexts. Not all professors will be able to hold individual conferences with each of their students; not all professors will be allowed to trim their reading lists. The circumstances in which we teach Shakespeare are far too varied for a single pedagogical program, and so I instead offer a series of provocations that I hope more knowledge about the practices of early modern writing can help us reflect on more pointedly. Why do we assign students the reading and writing that we do? How might we present ourselves as writers, rather than as experts, when we ask our students to write for us? What goals are served by affixing grades onto student essays? How might we treat our students as we, as writers, would like to be treated? Why do we restrict class time to talking about the course readings rather than about what students might choose to do with them? Finally: how might we grant our students' writing the advantages that Shakespeare's papers have been given for centuries, graced not just by admiring and protective readers, but by the belief that they represent a practice—the social practice the early moderns called poesy, but which we might simply call literature—worth protecting?

Chapter 1

Style

George Gascoigne's "Patched Cote"

Elizabethan children's encounters with written vernacular poetry likely began near the start of their formalized education (if they were fortunate enough to receive one).[1] Petty schools, roughly equivalent to modern kindergarten or nursery school, often used verse and song to help five-to-seven-year-olds learn basic English literacy, memorize prayers and the catechism, and develop social skills. For example, *All the Letters of the A. B. C*, a 1575 ballad, is an acrostic that introduces both the letters of the alphabet and assorted biblical passages, which are cited in the margin:

> A.
> Attend yee Youngones / and learne Understandinge
> B.
> Beare-fauor to the Loue / that she in you may have plantinge.
> C.
> Com to the meekmynded Beeing of Bounteousness.
> D.
> Directlye the right humilitie, to you it doth expresse.[2]

---

1. On the rates of education of Elizabethan children, see Stone, "Educational Revolution in England"; Cressy, *Literacy and the Social Order*, esp. 19–41; and Hackett, "'Better Scholar."
2. Hendrik Niclaes, *All the Letters*. For more on Niclaes, see Moss, "'Godded with God,'" 34.

Written by the founder of the religious sect the Family of Love, Niclaes Hendrik, it employs the mnemonic affordances of meter, rhyme, and alliteration to connect the acquisition of reading with an incipient theological "understanding."³ Following along with the broadsheet during school, children learned how to "attend" not just to the ballad's examples and instructions, but also to the congregation of voices reciting a shared text in unison. In this way, early ballads such as Hendrik's participated in a pervasive educational program linking poetry and communal piety. This linkage was most evident in how the biblical psalms were used throughout both childhood and maturity for cultivating piety; they were sung by church congregations and daily at some schools.⁴ *The Whole Booke of Psalmes Collected into Englysh Metre* (1562), widely known as "Sternhold and Hopkins," was among the best-selling books in early modern England and was used in churches to "ameliorate tedium" as a "multimedia guide to devotional practice."⁵ The psalms, and the common meter they would propagate throughout England, were the pinnacle of what Hendrik's ballad aspires toward: reverberating doctrinal decrees, introducing an archive of shared cultural media, and setting the behavioral rhythms of social life.⁶

After learning how to read (and, to a lesser extent, write) English in petty school, Tudor schoolboys with means would have entered grammar school, where poetry took on a new role.⁷ By 1530, the humanist program that Desiderius Erasmus and John Colet introduced at St. Paul's in 1512—which prioritized the acquisition of rhetorical eloquence in Latin—had become the framework that English grammar schools would adopt throughout early modernity.⁸ Grammar school

---

3. On the uses of music and song in grammar schools, see Willis, "'By These Means,'" esp. 302-3. For other (often quite endearing) examples of educational songs for children, see Clement, *Petie Schoole*, sig. A5r; S[egar], *Schoole of Vertue*, sig. Av; Beau Chesne and Baildon, *Divers Sortes of Hands*; Newberry, *Booke in English Metre*. Newberry's book may be considered alongside other "language helps" for apprentices from the period; see Wright, "Language Helps."

4. Willis points out that "Kirkby Stephen grammar school required the metrical psalms to be sung on a daily basis" as a part of early childhood musical education. Willis, "'By These Means,'" 300. T. W. Baldwin notes that at Rivington school, boys carried "the Psalms in prose and meter, besides those books he shall occupy at the School"; see Baldwin, *Small Latine & Lesse Greeke*, 1:345-46.

5. Willis, "'By These Means,'" 304-5.

6. On "Sternhold and Hopkins," see Valdivia, "Mere Meter."

7. Cressy explains that while reading and writing went hand in hand in many educational settings, writing was "a subordinate part of the elementary curriculum." Cressy, *Literacy and the Social Order*, 23.

8. Baldwin titled two chapters in *William Shakspere's Small Latine & Less Greeke* "Erasmus Laid the Egg," and Emrys Jones memorably concluded that "without humanism, in short,

students advanced through seven "forms" wherein they would encounter increasingly complex exercises in Latin prose and verse composition that tested their verbal resourcefulness and attention to tone, pacing, structure, and rhythm.[9] While some schoolmasters prohibited the use of English, others integrated scraps of vernacular verse into their techniques, usually to facilitate translation.[10] Being able to translate Latin and Greek verses into English was necessary for the foundational pedagogical technique of double translation, whereby students rendered sample texts into English and then, after some time, translated their English translations back into the original language to compare their work with that of the source. An illustration of how versification was involved in this linguistic intermingling may be seen in the seventeenth-century grammar school notebook of Robert Pendarves (Folger MS V.a.629).[11] After a series of Latin compositions on sententious themes, the notebook records a collection of "an hundred emblemes" drawn from Thomas Combe's English translation of Guillaume de la Perriere's *Theater of Fine Devices* (1614). On one page appears a drafty attempt at rendering one of the verse emblems, number 35, into Latin (figure 1.1). The student apparently began by translating "The way to pleasure is soe plaine, / To tread the paths few can refraine" word for word: "via ad voluptatem est sic plana." Underneath this effort, he reconsiders the end of the line, writing, "Sic plana est" as an alternate option—perhaps recognizing the differences between English and Latin syntax, perhaps preferring the sound, or perhaps anticipating the second half of the couplet with an opportunity for a different rhyme.

---

there could have been no Elizabethan literature," and "without Erasmus, no Shakespeare." Jones, *Origins of Shakespeare*, 13. Also see Grafton and Jardine, *Humanism to the Humanities*.

9. See Hackett, "'Better Scholar.'"

10. William Nelson traces how instruction in English composition was a necessary and desirable outcome for grammar schools long presumed to be preoccupied with classical tongues. Nelson, "Teaching of English."

11. Pendarves and Weale, "His Booke Amen." Pendarves (1633–?) appears to have shared the notebook with his brother Richard as well as someone named Job Weale over a few years the 1640s. As students in the seventeenth century, Pendarves et al. were given more access to English composition in their classrooms than students would have received a century earlier, but we can see the operations of double translation, composition, and versification at play throughout. An "index verborum," or table of Latin words with their English translations, constitutes the first twenty or so pages of the manuscript, followed by several pages of transcriptions of Latin instructions on composition ("Exordium est prima orationis pars . . ." [fol. 22r]). On fols. 31r–35r appears a practice "theme" composed on the sentence "Damnare neminem facile debemus," taken from one of the favored grammar school sourcebooks, Leonhard Cullman's *Sententiae Pueriles* (1543). The end of the book contains a few pages with rules for composing and construing Latin, presumably placed there for ease of reference.

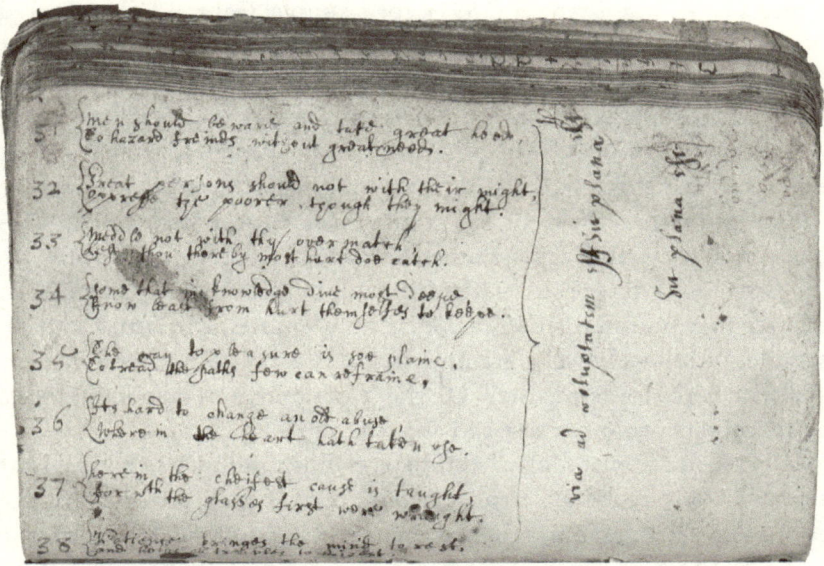

FIGURE 1.1. A from Robert Pendarves's notebook featuring an attempt at translation. *Robert Pendarves His Booke Amen* (1645–52), folio 40v. Call # V.a.629. Used by permission of the Folger Shakespeare Library.

While instructional ballads index what children were supposed to learn, exercises such as the one in Pendarves's notebook reveal how poetry could introduce even assiduous students to the possibility of outcomes different from those anticipated by their teachers. Once a student is given permission to experiment with language such as through the task of translation, distraction, inclination, or even simple misunderstanding will make new options available. By availing itself of the stuff of words, such as sounds and textures and affinities with other words, poetry could insinuate lessons into children's brains—but it could also expose children to linguistic effects such as polysemy, homophony, and punning. Poetry was useful in educating children because it mixed instruction with delight, but if it was the spoonful of sugar that accompanied doctrinal medicine, in private moments children could satisfy themselves with the sugar alone. Babbling nursery rhymes, doggerel folk songs, and folk ballads would have been part of the everyday soundscape of early modern life.[12] On a blank page in a copy of King

---

12. See Fox, *Oral and Literate Culture*, 26–27.

James VI's *Poetical Exercises* (1591), for example, Gabriel Harvey jotted down some nursery rhymes before dashing them out in an apparent fit of self-consciousness.[13] One of these rhymes goes, "When pucketts away, when shall we go play? / When the puckett is a sleap, then may wee go sow owr wheat." The other runs, "My Dame hath in a hutch at home / A little Dog / With a Clog; / Hey dogs hey." Meant to exercise the tongue more than the brain as training in elocution, such gleeful gobbledygook inevitably accompanied vernacular poetry into adulthood. Its pleasures—which Harvey himself would performatively dismiss, in a letter to Edmund Spenser, as noise that "hunt[s] the letter" and resembles "friulous boyishe grammer schole trickes"—could not be fully shaken even by its detractors.[14] On the versos of their self-serious labors, even scholars could not resist toying with trifles.

A lapse in attention or an ebullient elaboration may produce what seems at first to be an error. Yet such moves may prove charming enough, or striking enough, or potent enough to be defended in the name of "poetic license"—or what may more broadly be called style. Susan Sontag defines style as a "deviation from the most direct, useful, insensible mode of expression or being in the world" that manages to be "both autonomous and exemplary," and Theodor W. Adorno as "the inclusive moment whereby art becomes language."[15] Jeff Dolven's variation on this theme identifies in style a host of "ironies"—"part and whole, art and nature, individual and group, description and judgment"—that constitute "a life-enabling double consciousness, a way of living with contradiction, carrying on in the face of a problem that cannot, on its own terms, be solved."[16] Despite formally belonging, in the context of classical rhetoric, to the domain of *elocutio*, it may be understood as emblematic of rhetoric itself.[17] As Dolven points out, "Any new style must somehow convince us that it is

---

13. Eleanor Relle attributes Harvey's obliteration of these verses to a fear that "they were unworthy of a place in a book of serious poetry" and also points out that these verses are close to another nonsense line, "My dame hath a lame tame crane," which may have been "used as an exercise in elocution." Relle, "Some New Marginalia," 404.

14. Harvey, "Letters on Reformed Versifying," esp. 126. Also see Lerer, *Children's Literature*, 70–71.

15. Sontag, "On Style," 155; Adorno, *Aesthetic Theory*, 293.

16. Dolven, *Senses of Style*, 122–23.

17. Jeanne Fahnestock argues that among the canons of rhetoric—invention, arrangement, ornament, memory, and pronunciation—"style is arguably the most implicated in the others, since linguistic choice is the point of realization for the rhetorical precepts and theories belonging to the other canons." Fahnestock, *Rhetorical Style*, 7.

not a botched attempt at something more familiar"; it must persuade onlookers that "its difference is a matter of skill, not incompetence; that we might just want to try it ourselves, or that someone might."[18] A student suspended between not just two options but within half of a rhyming couplet, such as the author of the exercise in Pendarves's book, experiences the thrill and peril of style. Witnessing the possibility of unexpected, surprising, pleasing, or frustrating deviations, the author left the final decisions permanently unmade.[19] Style names a manner and technique of using language that invites imitation; it also names a lapse in imitation, a distracted phrasing that nevertheless ends up managing to rhyme.

This chapter focuses on the problem of style, presenting it as a problem because it names a fundamental contradiction in poetry's relationship to education in early modern England. In Erasmus's approach to rhetorical education, style was an essential component of the cultivation of eloquence. Developing a sense of style allowed students to distinguish themselves as orators while nevertheless demonstrating that they had, as Richard Halpern observes, "achieved a certain continuity and regularity" and had "learned to obey certain *decora*."[20] Poetry's role in the cultivation of rhetorical style was to present students with curated models to imitate and absorb as demonstrations of acceptable deviation. Writing verses enabled stylistic practice because it gave students a little bit of clearance to differentiate themselves; it allowed the fun of distraction to become fodder for composition. Once exposed to this clearance, however, they were also exposed to the possibility of breaching decorum and committing errors. "At the moment of its emergence," as Dolven notes, "perhaps a style can only distinguish itself by failing, failing at least to be what was expected of it."[21] In theory, humanist students would learn to fail correctly; they would, over time, have their eccentric impulses checked. As they were conditioned to put away childish things by the schoolmaster's corrections, they would eventually

---

18. Dolven, *Senses of Style*, 17.
19. Seth Lerer documents another example, pointing to a copy of Paul Bush's *The Extripation of Ignorancy* (1526) that is "full of scribbles, pictures, announcements of ownership, cryptic pen trials, and occasionally quotations from other works." Among these writings is a child's attempt at verses following the metrical patterns of Sternhold and Hopkins; these lines, Lerer observes, are "a form of metrical psalmistry in the style of the age—the fragment of a poem, an imaginative response to a printed text in a child's hand." Lerer, *Children's Literature*, 79–80.
20. Halpern, *Poetics of Primitive Accumulation*, 56.
21. Dolven, *Senses of Style*, 17.

internalize the requisite sense of restraint. It is no surprise, given the centrality of error to this educational process, that Tudor teachers adopting Erasmus's curriculum feared poetry's volatility. The failure to acquire decorous restraint could undermine the socializing project of education in general. Because poetry allowed children to "scramble and recombine received materials" and to experience the pleasure and delight of such maneuvers, Halpern pinpoints it as a site whereupon "textual decoding [broke] free from instrumental finalities and hence from social control."[22] If on the one hand poems were instruments of normalization, as witnesses to the excesses of style, they were on the other hand demonstrations of how rules could be relaxed, bent, or even broken.

The contradictions that attend the problem of style, I propose, challenge us to reconsider what it means to teach early modern poetry in the context of the modern classroom. Focusing on the writings of George Gascoigne (ca. 1535–77), the first professional teacher of vernacular English poetic style, this chapter identifies in Gascoigne's influential poetics a commitment to discomposition—that is, a commitment to resisting prescriptive protocols of compositional decorum. Gascoigne began his career frustrated by how poetry was being taught, written, and read in Elizabethan England, and in witnessing his frustrations, we might perceive some of our own.

Despite initially falling under a cloud for his own personal and literary indiscretions, Gascoigne published the first printed guide to vernacular English poetics: *Certayne Notes of Instruction concerning the Making of Verse* (1575). This document, read in the context of his career, presents the problem of style as a framework for teaching writing by teaching poetry. In what follows, I read *Certayne Notes* alongside what was probably the first literary work Gascoigne wrote in its wake: *The Glasse of Governement* (1575), a closet drama preoccupied with humanist educational practices. This understudied (for understandable reasons, as we will see) play depicts the divergent paths of pious and prodigal sons through the Tudor humanist educational system. Unlike most prodigal son narratives, however, it does not find its protagonists restored to their fathers' embraces after having learned their lessons. Instead, the prodigal sons end up disgraced and dead, and the play implies that this ignominious fate is the result of the boys *not* being transformed, or

---

22. Halpern, *Poetics of Primitive Accumulation*, 57.

even improved, by their pious teacher.[23] Showcasing what Julian Lamb describes as the closed loop of humanist instruction, which expected its students to already possess judgment in order to acquire the judgment that instruction was designed to produce, *The Glasse of Governement* invites audiences to wring their hands at the failure of the play's schoolmaster to reach his students.[24] Leaving readers confused as to whether the moral fable warrants applause or condemnation, Gascoigne connects the problem of compositional style to the challenge of teaching people to engage in critical thinking without stifling their individual intellectual propensities.

The first section below contextualizes Gascoigne's relationship to style within Tudor humanism by focusing on the resonances between his complaints about poetic education and Erasmus's attention to a particular form of student error: "patchwork" writing. Erasmus advised that in cultivating *copia*, or an "abundant style," student writers would inevitably appropriate scraps and shreds of canonical authors' discourse. To accommodate such educationally necessary appropriation, he made poetry the curricular home for reckless pilfering and verbal play. As Erasmus and Colet's program was implemented in English classrooms in the Tudor era, though, patchwork writing became the more maligned category of "botching" or "bodging." These terms for clumsy craftsmanship appeared in sixteenth-century dictionaries and meant both "repayre, or to mende" and more specifically the "patch[ing] of olde garments."[25] For English teachers like John Brinsley, the awkward appropriations of bodgery evinced inattentive work that was not near enough to its model rather than either idiosyncrasy or ambition. This transition, from an approbation of poetic license toward a pedagogy that attempted to abolish it, serves as the backdrop for Gascoigne's poetic career.

The subsequent two sections of the chapter study how Gascoigne developed his poetics at the intersection of patchy ambition and botched

---

23. For more on the contradictions of Tudor and humanist pedagogy, see Grafton and Jardine, *Humanism to the Humanities*; Bushnell, *Culture of Teaching*, esp. 18–19; Dolven, *Scenes of Instruction*, esp. 3, 57; and Lamb, *Rules of Use*.

24. Lamb, *Rules of Use*, 49.

25. "Bodges" also appears as a gloss for the Italian *sbozzi* and linked to "bunger-like workes." See Huloet and Higgins, *Huloets Dictionarie*, STC 13941, sig. Eiiiv; Florio, *Worlde of Wordes*, STC 11098, p. 346. Patricia Parker identifies "botching" as a limit case in the discourses of joinery that characterized much early modern commentary on "right writing"; see Parker, *Shakespeare from the Margins*, esp. 88–108.

discretion, with the first examining *The Glasse of Governement*. As a story about homework, the play affiliates the pedagogical machinery of poetic insipidity with the products of tragic rigidity. While the text was overtly designed to demonstrate Gascoigne's reformation, its self-conscious tedium also appears to serve as a warning. The play's disastrous conclusion suggests that affording too narrow a warrant for clumsy audacity will do more than stifle the promise of English poetic style. It warns that the eradication of stylistic experimentation among educated officials precipitates a reduction in the capacity of government to address rapid social change. Gascoigne saw "patching" and "botching" as evidence of the faltering of an author's will. In his earlier writings, and latently in *Certayne Notes*, the focus of this chapter's third section, he orients poetic composition around a principle of poetic invention he calls "quick capacity." Writers, he realized, could be lured by temptation, thwarted by distraction, or compelled by external authorities—all of which might discompose their judgment. Quick capacity, which names the stylist's ability to make free choices, was the poet's safeguard against both patchwork and bodgery.

In the reflection following this chapter, I consider what the promotion of "quick capacity" might look like in the context of the modern literature classroom. Turning to discussions among compositionists about the relationship between composition and correction, and to a specific form of compositional error that Rebecca Moore Howard calls "patchwriting," I trace continuities between the contradictions of humanist composition pedagogy and problems facing critical writing pedagogy in literary studies. When we invite students to write literary criticism, we are also, we must realize, challenging them to adjust their styles of expression into closer conformity with the norms of our discipline. Taking heed of Gascoigne's defense of the virtues of deviation for the cultivation of critical attention, I join writing teachers who argue that the teacher's role does not have to be one that passes judgment, but instead can be one that may help students become more attentive to their own choices.

The Fabric of Poetry

At the start of 1575, George Gascoigne was mending a tattered reputation. A whirlwind early career—which included participation at Elizabeth I's coronation, service as a member of Parliament, study at the Inns of Court, imprisonment for debt, and an unsuccessful stint in the military—had preceded his first publication, *A Hundreth Sundrie Flowres*, in 1572/73.[26] This book was a diverse collection of raucous poetical, dramatic, and narrative works facetiously presented as authored by several gentlemen. It apparently aroused so much scandal for licentiousness and potential libel that within two years, Gascoigne was compelled to revise and reissue the collection as *The Posies* (1575), this time claiming sole authorship of its entirety and prefacing it with a series of apologetic letters.[27] He also added to this volume an entirely new work, *Certayne Notes of Instruction concerning the Making of Verse*. While presenting its author as a poetic authority now in control of his powers by cautioning readers against indiscretion and offering concrete advice about accentual meter and stanzaic forms, *Certayne Notes* also reflects traces of the irrepressible spirit that originally motivated Gascoigne to produce *Flowres*.[28]

Certayne Notes suggests that writing poetry is an energetic balancing act more than it is an exercise in following instructions. For example, during some remarks on proper word choice, Gascoigne offers the following advice: "Frame your stile to *perspicuity* and to be sensible: for the haughty obscure verse doth not much delight, and the verse that is to[o] easie is like a tale of a rosted horse: but let your Poeme be such as may both delight and draw attentive readyng, and therewithal may deliver such matter as be worth the marking" (459.3-8). Unwilling to simply conform to disciplined and unadventurous versifying, Gascoigne makes the poet's remit acceptable eccentricity, or felicitous indecorousness.[29] Style should earn the attention of readers, he insists, without earning their scorn. Gascoigne's understanding thus reflects how poetic style in Elizabethan England accrued around the generation of *exempla* that

---

26. On Gascoigne's biography, I have relied on Austen, *George Gascoigne*.

27. On the controversy over *A Hundreth Sundrie Flowres*, see Austen, *George Gascoigne*, 84–105; Hughes, "Gascoigne's Poses"; and Pigman, "Textual Introduction," l-li. For a different perspective rooting the controversy in libel rather than licentiousness, see Clegg, *Press Censorship*, 110.

28. For example, Gascoigne admonishes the poet to avoid clichés and overworn analogies because they will prove distractingly "trita & obvia" (455.14), and to resist unfamiliar polysyllabic words because they will "cloye a verse and make it unpleasant" (458.2-6). George Gascoigne, "Additions from *The Posies*," in Gascoigne, *Hundreth Sundrie Flowres*, 359-462; all references to material from *The Posies*, including prefatory letters and *Certayne Notes*, are to this volume and are indicated by page and line number.

29. For more on the relationship between eccentricity and eloquence, see Nicholson, *Uncommon Tongues*; Rosenfeld, *Indecorous Thinking*; Jacobson, *Barbarous Antiquity*, esp. 29-53; and Mann, *Outlaw Rhetoric*.

others might quote in their own compositions.[30] In the shadow of classical authors such as Virgil or Cicero, whose *sententiae* early modern writers deployed in their own writings, poets like Gascoigne tried to distinguish themselves enough to warrant quotation, but not so much as to appear outlandish. His famously "botched attempt" with *A Hundreth Sundrie Flowres* must have made the dangers of literary risk taking abundantly clear to him, and in response to the scandal he had caused, in the second of *The Posies*' apologetic prefatory epistles he repents the "barbarousnesse of the stile" of the earlier volume. As compensation, he presents himself as a different sort of example: "Make me your myrrour," he suggests, so that you might "eschue betymes the whirlepoole of misgovernment" (368.30–36).

Though he overcame his youthful missteps and rose to become the most prominent poet of his era, Gascoigne's career traces the path of an unlucky generation that Richard Helgerson influentially termed the "Elizabethan Prodigals."[31] A product of a humanist curriculum centered on cultivating eloquence in part via poetic composition, his education in grammar school, Cambridge, and Gray's Inn resulted only in the disappointing revelation that the skills cultivated by his schooling would not automatically lead to employment.[32] Needing to market himself, he used his lively verses to seduce the attention of those who held the keys to civic offices, since compositional acumen and wittiness were believed to demonstrate both reverent governmentality and bold political savvy.[33] According to Roger Ascham's increasingly influential pedagogical guide, *The Scholemaster* (1570), the fundamental technique of humanist pedagogy, double translation, developed "a true choice and placing of words, a right ordering of sentences, an easy understanding of the tongue, a readiness to speak, a facility to write, [and] a true judgment both of his own and other men's doings."[34] *Flowres* revealed Gascoigne to have lapsed in his sense of his own and other men's doings, and to rehabilitate his career, he had to defend his own decision-making. He seems to have bristled at this. In *Certayne Notes* he acknowledges that some kinds of deviation can cajole readers into "marking" their

---

30. See Lesser and Stallybrass, "First Literary Hamlet."
31. Helgerson, *Elizabethan Prodigals*.
32. Rhodes, *Origins of English*, 46.
33. On Elizabethan literary patronage, see Van Dorsten, "Literary Patronage." Also see Sheavyn, *Literary Profession*, 22.
34. Ascham, *Scholemaster*, STC 832, sig. 1v. On Gascoigne's indebtedness to Ascham, see Salamon, "Face in 'The Glasse.'"

text—for example, catching the reader off guard with a few "straunge wordes" (455.19) or some "straunge discourse of intollerable passion" (458.39–40)—before tempering such suggestions by cautioning, "Yet I woulde have you therein to use discretion" (459.1–2). As we will see, his advice attempted to both demonstrate disciplined authority and also retain the poetic sensibility and appetite for strangeness that he cultivated in *Flowres*. Knowing that he had a knack for winning attention, he felt that his "great diversitie both in stile and sense" was being overlooked and undervalued (368.23–24).

As noted above, Gascoigne's *Posies* begins with a collection of letters apologizing for the apparent indiscretions of *A Hundreth Sundrie Flowres*. The first of these is addressed to "the reverend Divines"—that is, to the Court of High Commission—and it sees the poet trying to defend himself while also performing his own reformation. Torn between these somewhat mismatched impulses, his account of how he thought his first volume would fare glimpses the rift between the urgent aims of aspiring poets and the rigid expectations of Elizabethan authorities:

> For although I have bin heretofore contented to suffer the publication thereof, only to the ende men might see my Methode and maner of writing: yet am I nowe thus desirous to set it forth eftsoones, to the ende all men might see the reformation of my minde: And that all suspitions may be suppressed and throughly satisfied, by this mine unfeined protestation which I make unto you in that behalfe. Finally, were it not that the same is alreadie extant in such sort as hath moved offence, I should rather be content to cancel it utterly to oblivion, than thus to returne it in a new patched cote. (363.15–24)

Had *A Hundreth Sundrie Flowres* not "moved offence," Gascoigne admits, he would have been content to have the book serve as a demonstration of his personal style—that is, of his "Methode and maner." Michael Hetherington notes how in such invocations of "method," Gascoigne endeavors to "have his cake and eat it" by appearing "to avow and disavow statements and attitudes about his own artfulness in almost the same breath." He thus "manages to occupy a shifting yet fertile middle ground, laying claim to just enough method to win him authority and to just enough daring opportunism to elicit admiration."[35] When his

---

35. Hetherington, "Gascoigne's Accidents," 38–39.

efforts at seeking acclaim were poorly received, however, Gascoigne felt compelled to show evidence of "reformation" by rereleasing his work in a "new patched cote." This most directly refers to how the most controversial work in *The Posies*, "The Adventures of Master F.J.," had been "so clensed from all unclenly wordes, and so purged from the humor of inhumanitie, as percase you woulde not judge that it was the same tale" (363.13–15).

Gascoigne's immature perspective toward poesy, as reflected by an idea pervasive throughout *A Hundreth Sundrie Flowres*, was that a poet's style may excuse or even justify certain indiscretions.[36] In his apologies, he retracts that perspective by conceding that some issues cannot be excused by that "shrewde fellow," poetic license, who, as he suggests in *Certayne Notes*, otherwise "covereth many faults in a verse" (459.29–30). Or at least, he *seems* to concede this. As Felicity Hughes notes, despite all of his posturing, "the 'revised' and supposedly expurgated volume of 1575 is not really any 'cleaner' than the first." He could not fully bring himself to conceal the fruits of his labor, and so, as Hughes puts it, he sought to "brazen it out with the censors."[37] This maneuver, however, was evidently transparent enough that *The Posies* was itself recalled by the Court of High Commission in 1576.[38]

At least initially, Gascoigne had a hard time figuring out how to write poetry he found pleasurable while also avoiding the sorts of things that invited rebuke. The safest solution, his letter to the divines suggests, was to hyperbolically cede his agency before the censors' corrections. But he also could not help drawing attention to this gesture; if his opening letters are an apology, they also advertise the presence of illicit materials in ways that may have enticed young gentlemen readers. Being ideologically right, Gascoigne knew, was not the same as being widely read, and in the parsimonious Elizabethan court, being read was a pathway to employment. In April of 1575, just three months after the publication of *The Posies*, he published the closet drama *The Glasse of Governement*. I read this play as an extreme version of his "patched cote": parts of it are so self-consciously cobbled together that they read

---

36. Throughout *A Hundrie Sundrie Flowres*, Gascoigne suggests that a poet's style may be excused through the lens of the poet's original occasion for writing—and if not through that, then through its demonstration of "Aliquid salis" or through the affordances of "licentia poetica" (145.1; 282.46.11–12).

37. Hughes, "Gascoigne's Poses," 1.

38. See Austen, *George Gascoigne*, 85–86; and Pigman, "Textual Introduction," liii (esp. n19).

as if the playwright is thrusting others' words into readers' faces, challenging them to reapprove that which has already been deemed acceptable. By having an opening half burdened with such passages, the play actively risks *not* being read—and challenges those who stick with it to revise their own demands about what sort of literary material they truly desire. In the following section of this chapter, I read the play as a rallying cry against the sort of pedagogy that created a demand for poetry prioritizing obedience and piety above all else. In order to construct this reading, however, in this section I recount the origins and principles of that pedagogy.

As has been well documented, thanks largely to the monumental scholarship of T. W. Baldwin, the Elizabethan grammar school curriculum was inspired by the reforms put in place by Erasmus and Colet at St. Paul's School.[39] These reforms instituted a composition pedagogy that hinged on accumulation, imitation, and recombination; as Emrys Jones puts it, Tudor grammar schools produced "[b]oys who had spent the best part of six long days a week for perhaps as many as ten or eleven years reading, translating, analysing, and explicating Latin literature" and who "would have memorized hundreds, perhaps thousands, of lines or scraps of lines from [classical] poets, as well as having innumerable phrases, constructions, and rhythms from the prose writers impressed on their minds."[40] This focus on reading widely and memorizing fragments of others' writings owes to injunctions like this one from Erasmus's *De copia*: "We must keep our eyes open to observe every figure of speech that [the great authors] use, store it in our memory once observed, imitate it once remembered, and by constant employment develop an expertise by which we may call upon it instantly."[41] The pursuit of one's own style, which Erasmus regards as "to thought as clothes are to the body," was from its start a fundamentally social practice.[42] Appropriating words from others would help those who are "unable to clothe our thought in other colours or other forms" avoid being "tongue-tied" or "bor[ing their] wretched audience to death."[43] To enhance students' store of ready phrases, Erasmus advised allowing them chances at practicing audacity through poetic manipulation.

---

39. Baldwin, *Small Latine & Lesse Greeke*, 1:75–133.
40. Jones, *Origins of Shakespeare*, 12–13.
41. Erasmus, *De copia*, 303.
42. Erasmus, *De copia*, 306.
43. Erasmus, *De copia*, 302.

Taking fine-sounding phrases and injecting them into new contexts gave students opportunities to tame strange language within structure and form. When their "employment" of snatches of language went to an extreme or their words borrowed too obviously, Erasmus equated such writing to a "patchwork," or *cento*.[44]

The cento was a genre of poetry composed by stitching together lines from classical sources such as Virgil or Homer.[45] While in his youth Erasmus himself apparently composed at least one cento, in his mature writings he reveals a negative appraisal of them as insincere and shallow, because "they neither impart information, nor stir the emotions, nor rouse to action." Regarding those who restrict their compositions to such patchworks, "[t]he best you can say of them," he writes, "is that they know their Virgil, and have put a lot of effort into constructing their mosaic."[46] Writers must internalize rather than imitate, Erasmus explains in *The Ciceronian*, so that their "speech will not be a patchwork or a mosaic, but a lifelike portrait of the person you really are, a river welling out from your inmost being" (nec oratio tua cento quispiam videatur aut opus Musaicum).[47] He warns that writing means that "[a]ll that you have devoured in a long course of varied reading must be thoroughly digested and by the action of thought incorporated into your deepest mental processes, not your memory or word-list."[48] He adopts a similar warning in his treatise on epistolary composition, recommending that writers employ a "living model" for their composition before "borrowing" the "best words and sentiments" from great authors and applying necessary changes "to suit the topic at hand." If this is not done, he says, the letter will appear "like a bit of bad patching or faulty soldering" (male assuta, maleque conferruminata).[49] Sourcing one's imitations to a variety of texts was not sufficient in and of itself to produce eloquence; students had to learn how to make educated choices about how to incorporate others' words and stitch them together.

Erasmus regarded patchwork writing as an inevitable step in the cultivation of eloquence and style. It signaled engagement with a variety of authors and the infusion, at first intermittently and eventually more pointedly, of words claimed as one's own. "It will be of enormous value

---

44. Erasmus, *Dialogvs Ciceronianvs*, 626 (LB 985, line 38).
45. For more on the early modern cento, see Tucker, "From Rags to Riches."
46. Erasmus, *Ciceronian*, 368, 438. For Erasmus's cento, see "Cento from Homer," 139.
47. Erasmus, *Ciceronian*, 442; Erasmus, *Dialogvs Ciceronianvs*, 704 (LB 1022, lines 27–28).
48. Erasmus, *Ciceronian*, 402.
49. Erasmus, *Writing of Letters*, 74.

to take apart the fabric of poetry and reweave it in prose," he writes in *De copia*, "and, vice versa, to bind the freer language of prose under the rules of metre, and also to pour the same subject-matter from one form of poetic container into another."[50] Beyond advising attention to the thread-like sinews of sentences, Erasmus encourages boldness: "It will also be very helpful to emulate a passage from some author where the spring of eloquence seems to bubble up particularly richly, and endeavour in our own strength to equal or even surpass it."[51] In the effort to "surpass" great ones, students are meant to grasp for something *more* than what the sources have to offer. Trusting in their copious stores, they might eventually deviate from models on surer footing. Erasmus concedes that missteps in this process would appear as "faults in a mature writer," but that they "are inevitable in those who are learning proficiency."[52] Such errors signal a mind at work attempting to practice judgment, and consequently, things should be allowable during poetic composition that would be unacceptable or rare elsewhere.[53] In a memorable object lesson, right after his famous practical demonstration of *copia* with the sentence, "Your letter pleased me mightily," wherein he tries to show "how far we can go in transforming the basic expression into a Protean variety of shapes," he concedes that some of his excesses may strike fans of prose writing as extreme. "If anyone thinks that some of these suggestions would hardly be tolerable in prose," he writes, "he should remember that this exercise is designed for the composition of verse as well."[54]

The implementation of Erasmus's curriculum both on the Continent and in England—and consequently as witnessed in *The Glasse of Governement*—involved many compromises. One of them was an understanding of style as something with identifiable and teachable contours. Ascham mentions style when approving of how Demosthenes has "so straite, fast, & temperate a style," but he more often brings up stylistic failures of texts not worthy of imitation. In one instance, for example, he sees style as "ouer rancke and lustie" and therefore signaling a lack of temperance; in another, it is "ouer rough" and therefore

---

50. Erasmus, *De copia*, 303.
51. Erasmus, *De copia*, 303.
52. Erasmus, *Writing of Letters*, 40; Erasmus, *De conscribendis epistolis*, 317 (LB 381, line 19).
53. Erasmus, *De copia*, 327, 339. Erasmus has in mind such errors as the use of patronymics, the use of metalepsis, or certain kinds of repetition.
54. Erasmus, *De copia*, 348, 354.

unsuited to "learned judgement."[55] Nearly all grammar school teachers in Ascham's wake were influenced directly or indirectly by this sensibility. Their composition pedagogy involved roughly four interlinked phases, as outlined by William Kempe, the headmaster at Plymouth in the 1580s: "First the scholler shall learne the precepts: secondly, he shall learne to note the examples of the precepts in vnfoulding other mens workes: thirdly, to imitate the examples in some worke of his owne: fourthly and lastly, to make somewhat alone without an example."[56] Style formed one of the bridges between these phases, as it almost certainly came up when students noticed that revered authors failed to consistently demonstrate proper grammatical precepts. Whether working through sentences, epistles, themes, or verse forms, students were asked to take an example, digest it, and reproduce it according to their internalization of acceptable discursive patterns. They would invariably deviate from the "perfect" translation—or what the original writer would have done—based on their own habituated grammatical instincts, and those instincts could then be gently reformed by a teacher "unfolding" how Cicero's or Virgil's errors actually amounted to stylistic techniques. After sufficient exposure to authoritative examples, students were supposed to have a storehouse of linguistic resources and, moreover, a sense of the kinds of techniques that writers were allowed to employ in order to reanimate this storehouse as eloquence.

A century after Erasmus's and Colet's implementation of the humanist curriculum at St. Paul's, John Brinsley's *Ludus Literarius: Or, the Grammar Schoole* (1612) was first published. Brinsley, who had taught at Ashby-de-la-Zouch for over two decades, devotes an entire chapter of his guide to the problem of students' "bodging," which he does not explicitly define but which, it quickly becomes clear, is akin to what Erasmus described as patchwork writing. Here is Brinsley's advice on how to control and contain bodgery:

> To keepe them that they shall neuer bodge in their entrance, neither for phrase nor otherwise, but to enter with ease, certainty and delight; this you shall finde to be a most speedy way:
>
> Take *Flores Poetarum*, and in euery Common place make choise of Ouids verses, or if you find any other which be pleasant and easie: and making sure, that your schollars know not the verses

---

55. Ascham, *Scholemaster*, 44r, 43v, 49v.
56. Kempe, *Education of Children*, F2.

aforehand, vse to dictate vnto them as you did in prose. Cause also so many as you would haue to learne together, to set down the English as you dictate.

Secondly to giue you, and to write downe all the words in Latine *verbatim*, or Grammatically.

Thirdly, hauing iust the same words, let them trie which of them can soonest turne them into the order of a verse: which they will presently doe, being trained vp in the vse of the translations; which is the same in effect.

And then lastly, read them ouer the verse of Ouid, that they may see that themselues haue made the very same; or wherein they missed: this shall much incourage and assure them.[57]

Brinsley adapts the program of double translation, which he appropriates nearly wholesale from Ascham, to poetic composition. Students are told to sift through commonplace books or reference volumes like the *Flores poetarum* for Ovid's verses, translate these verses into English, then translate them into Latin verbatim, and then finally reattempt the translation in "the order of a verse" to compare with Ovid's original.[58] Authority explicitly lay with the source texts; there was a correct answer. While Erasmus directed writers to a plurality of authors to imitate, such that they might have a copious store of language with which to play, Brinsley's pedagogy oriented each student toward predetermined targets. As Ascham puts it, "In double translating a perfite peece of *Tullie* or *Caesar*, neyther the scholer in learning, nor ye Master in teaching can erre. A true tochstone, a sure metwand [measuring rod] lieth before both their eyes."[59] Students internalized the "style" and "phrase" of Ovid and Virgil, and after enough time would hopefully "pass" as poets, in both the sociological and academic sense.[60] "[T]hose who take a delight in Poetry, and haue sharpness & dexterity accordingly," Brinsley boasts, "will in a short time attaine to that ripenesse, as that they who know not the places which they imitate, shall hardly discerne

---

57. Brinsley, *Ludus Literarius*, 192–93.
58. Octavio Mirandula's compilation of Latin poetic commonplaces, widely known as the *Flores poetarum*, was first published in 1480 in Cologne as *Flores poetarum de virtutibus et viciis*. It saw multiple reprints over the course of the Renaissance as *Illustrium poëtarum flores*. It was printed in London in 1598 and 1611 prior to Brinsley's mentions of it. For more, see Watson, *English Grammar Schools*, 468–84.
59. Ascham, *Scholemaster*, 42; see also *Oxford English Dictionary*, s.v. "Metewand, n.," accessed July 1, 2021, http://www.oed.com/view/Entry/117525.
60. Daniel Bender cites a moment in Ascham wherein the schoolmaster castigates a boy for not imitating Cicero perfectly, as evidence of "the hidden curriculum of Latin schools" that reaffirms the "elite capacity for social control." See Bender, "Whip Hand," 67–68.

in many verses, whether the verse bee Virgils verse, or the schollars."[61] Such pedagogy, to impose on it a modern phrase, teaches to the test.

Lurking in the background of patchwork compositions is the successful forgery: the document that does not show its seams and satisfies the stylistic terms of the discursive community within which it wishes to pass. It was and continues to be important to learn this sort of compliance as part of participating in discursive communities, but there are drawbacks to treating composition as if it has a predetermined end. Tracking the gradual institutionalization of Erasmian *imitatio* in the Elizabethan grammar school, Dolven finds that because Erasmus's vision of composition "would be more difficult to judge," programs like Kempe's and Brinsley's prioritized imitation: "*Imitatio* is a method: a step-wise, rule-based project in which every stage ought to be present in the mind of the imitator, and demonstrable to his teacher."[62] Imitation thus "teaches students to see through texts to the skeleton of principles by which they were constructed," but the program's stress falls on "method" and a "rule-bound account of the mind's work in learning."[63] Schooling began with precepts that Dolven argues would ultimately "regulate and even displace the instinct that it nonetheless claims as its mainspring."[64] Anthony Grafton and Lisa Jardine similarly conclude that the "practical emphasis on procedure signals a shift in intellectual focus on the part of the pedagogic reformers, from the ideal end-product of a classical education (the perfect orator, perfectly equipped for political life), to the classroom aids (textbooks, manuals and teaching drills) which would compartmentalise the *bonae litterae* and reduce them to system."[65] The skillful student reanimated others' words to suit the present, but this reanimation also risked revivifying the corpses of ancient authorities as unstylish creatures shuffling through the world with their seams visible. One such monster is visible in a school exercise undertaken by King Edward VI as a twelve-year-old. Reprinted in Baldwin, it is described by Grafton and Jardine as an example of the "carefully competent and utterly soulless orations, crafted out of Cicero's and Erasmus' borrowed phrases."[66]

---

61. Brinsley, *Ludus Literarius*, 194.
62. Dolven, *Scenes of Instruction*, 23, 26.
63. Dolven, *Scenes of Instruction*, 21.
64. Dolven, *Scenes of Instruction*, 26.
65. Grafton and Jardine, *Humanism to the Humanities*, 124.
66. Grafton and Jardine, *Humanism to the Humanities*, 155. See Baldwin, *Small Latine & Lesse Greeke*, 1:211–12; also see Mack, *Elizabethan Rhetoric*, 26.

If, in Erasmus's program, patchwork was the product of students trying *too hard* to imitate the styles of ancient authorities and sacrificing their own liveliness, in English classrooms bodgery arose when students did not try hard *enough* to sound like their source texts. For Erasmus, patchwork signaled when students' use of others' words was too easily discerned and seemed superficial, but for later teachers like Brinsley, bodging was when students' own words crept in too obviously and marred the illusion of ventriloquism. Between these two poles, both historically and practically, was George Gascoigne. When he refers to his revised poems in *The Posies* as a "patched cote," then, one thing he means is that the revised document bears the marks of nonauthorial hands. If one's style, or individual "Methode and maner," proved acceptable only once patched, what use was there in cultivating it at all? This question might have animated the composition of *The Glasse of Governement*, as well as the resentment rippling under its fabric. Through dramatizing the wholesale rehearsal of others' words, Gascoigne shows off a well-honed ability to write *without* style, foreshadowing Theodor W. Adorno's contention that "[t]he more ambitious art works are, the more vigorously do they pursue the conflict between style and nonstyle, if need be at the expense of success." Adorno goes on to add that "an obligatory style is unthinkable except within the objective structure of a closed, repressed society."[67]

The appraisal of a text as "patchwork," "botchery," or "bodgery" was usually employed by later Elizabethan writers to condemn others' rough craft, but it was also an index of the vagaries of judgment. "Bodger" became a favorite insult of Thomas Nashe, who used it to accost the Gabriel Harveys of the world, whom he felt were inauthentic, pedantic, and too committed to abandoning vernacular English for stuffy obscurities and importations.[68] In Shakespeare's plays, references to botching sometimes signal insincerity on the part of authors or performers—*Henry V* charges bodging hypocrites with "glistering semblances of piety," and Feste in *Twelfth Night* undermines the perfection of all pretentions by observing, "Anything that's mended is but

---

67. Adorno, *Aesthetic Theory*, 294–95. As Kenneth Charlton observes, faced with "religious atomism, political danger, and economic dislocation," English monarchs and the state "saw the schools as an important instrument with which to maintain public order and achieve political and religious conformity." Charlton, *Education in Renaissance England*, 130.

68. See Nashe, *Strange Newes*, B4r–v.

patched."⁶⁹ Elsewhere, however, botching also connotes misconstrual by audiences and readers. In *Hamlet*, an anonymous gentleman suggests that "the unshaped use" of Ophelia's mad speech "doth move / The hearers to collection; they aim at it, / And botch the words up fit to their own thoughts."⁷⁰ On the writer's end, patchwork aligns with Roland Barthes's sense of a text as a "tissue of quotations," but on the reader's end, bodging emerges as akin to Michel de Certeau's account of reading as "poaching."⁷¹ Whereas the Elizabethan grammar school might have seen bodgery as a failure of execution, Erasmus anticipated English poets like Gascoigne, Nashe, and Shakespeare, who understood that the scene of writing, like the scene of reading, is always unruly, compromised, and contingent—that as authors and readers proceed in stitching an idea together, the thread itself might be called the stuff of style.

Tedious Traditions

The Glasse of Governement begins with two fathers hiring a "godly Tutor," Gnomaticus, to instruct the four sons they have between them in piety and obedience. These boys—two elder brothers who are quick-witted but easily distracted, and two younger brothers who are slower learners but dutiful—have just finished grammar school and are intent on going off to university. In order to ready the boys for the world beyond their hometown, Gnomaticus, after learning that they had become familiar with writings by Erasmus, Cicero, Terence, and Ovid in grammar school, issues a series of lectures about the importance of revering God and obeying authorities. The elder brothers find these long lectures arid, while the younger brothers ponder them attentively. Accordingly, although the elders do well in school because of their ability to regurgitate familiar moral lessons, they descend into a life of debauchery and crime. The younger brothers are slower to excel, but are ultimately rewarded with respectable jobs.

This narrative takes as one of its governing principles a maxim Ascham records as "Quicke wittes commonlie, be apte to take, vnapte to keepe."⁷² As noted above, despite this conventionality, what proves

---

69. *Henry V*, 2.2.111-15; *Twelfth Night*, 1.5.40-41. All references to Shakespeare are from Greenblatt et al., *Norton Shakespeare*.
70. *Hamlet*, 4.5.7-10.
71. Barthes, *Image-Music-Text*, 146; Certeau, *Practice of Everyday Life*, 165-76.
72. Ascham, *Scholemaster*, 4v.

surprising about *Glasse* is that the prodigal elder brothers do not ultimately reform and return to their fathers' embrace. One is executed after a trial for robbery—at which his supposedly eloquent younger brother speaks unsuccessfully on his behalf—and the other is whipped nearly to death and cast out of the city for fornication. As a result, the "straight" reading of this play, shaped by the Gascoigne biographer Charles Tyler Prouty, sees it showcasing Gascoigne putting away impious and childish things.[73] But while Richard C. McCoy observes that "[t]here is nothing playful or equivocal about [the play's] assertions of obedient piety, and no chances are taken with censors," other critics have found it difficult not to read in *Glasse* a deep ambivalence.[74] Indeed, most have found the play difficult to read at all, with Linda Bradley Salamon describing its "longueurs" as "sermonizing" and "mechanical," and Ursula Potter calling it a "a dreary and ominous picture of what happens when censorship and reformist policies control education."[75] Building on these responses, I propose that *Glasse*'s seemingly willful dramatization of tediousness is evidence, if not of Gascoigne insisting on the aesthetic costs of compositional compliance, then at least of his failure to reconcile poesy's irrepressible creativity with demands that compositions be reverent.

Gascoigne's program of compliance begins on the play's title page, which announces the play as having been "seen and allowed, according to the order appointed in the Queenes majesties Injunctions" (1).[76] That it was printed by "C. Barker," or Christopher Barker, gave it a further seal of approval, as Barker was the queen's printer and best known for producing Bibles. A few pages in, among the play's prefatory materials, Barker's guiding hand is further emphasized through the suggestion that he literally prompted Gascoigne's labor. "This worke is compiled upon these sentences following, set downe by mee C.B." appears atop a table of moral axioms, including, "Feare God, for he is just," "Obey the King, for his aucthoritie is from above," and "Studie to profite the common wealth, for it is commendable with God and man" (7).

The play's plot elaborates on Barker's sentences with Gnomaticus's lectures, which are laden with quotations affirming the theses that God, the state, and one's father should be obeyed. These lectures are

---

73. Prouty, *George Gascoigne*, 240.
74. McCoy, "Gascoigne's 'Poëmata Castrata,'" 44.
75. Salamon, "Face in 'The Glasse,'" 48; Potter, "'No Terence Phrase,'" 384.
76. Gascoigne, *Glasse of Governement*. All references appear in text and are to page numbers.

prolix and exhausting. After the nearly six-page first lecture, the two elder brothers, Phylosarchus and Phylautus, reveal their proverbial quick-wittedness by having no difficulty regurgitating the main points. "Who is ignorant," they snidely whisper after class, "that God is to be feared above all things?" (34). They later call these lectures a rehearsal of "tedious traditions" (48), tacitly affirming what must have been on the minds of at least some of Gascoigne's initial readers. After a number of such classes have passed, Gnomaticus presents the students with a writing prompt, and it is their responses to this prompt that foreshadow the students' divergent outcomes. The assignment includes a summary of Gnomaticus's lectures that is nearly identical to those paratextual sentences from Barker, and it challenges the students to convert this summary into poetry. By this we must understand that the main characters of the play are given a task fundamentally resembling the one their author was himself undertaking.

Presented a series of "sentences," the students are told they must translate them into "verse" and labor to prove the "pleasantest Poet" (48). The assignment is versification rather than poetics, evincing Gnomaticus's belief that poetry is best used as a mnemonic aid, as a "comforte or recreation," and as a demonstration of students' internalization of principles of *"decorum."* He clarifies that decorum mainly means that students avoid anything inappropriate, such as the use of "tryfling allegories" to render serious matters (47–48). While he gives instruction on how to avoid offending, however, he offers no advice on how the pupils are meant to prove the "pleasantest." The poems this prompt elicits consequently show that the ideal student within the Tudor humanist program regarded poetry as a means mainly to satisfy the teacher.[77] This sanctioned approach to composition is given the descriptor "compendious," which generally means "economical" and "succinct."[78] By applying this term to Gnomaticus's regurgitation of "tedious traditions," however, the play renders his teaching ironic. We might better sense the valence of the term by affiliating it with the one Gascoigne uses to describe his own project: the play has been "compiled" out of

---

77. As McCoy argues, Gnomaticus's use of this "grim pedagogical exercise" reveals how, in his classroom, poetry "subverts instead of enlarging freedom in two ways: first by serving as a means of subservient paraphrase of another's ideas and secondly by reconciling its practitioners to subservience through its ameliorative charms." McCoy, "Gascoigne's 'Poëmata Castrata,'" 45–46.

78. *Oxford English Dictionary*, s.v. "Compendious, adj.," accessed July 2, 2021, http://www.oed.com/view/Entry/37538.

sentences provided to him. Unlike compendiousness, compilation evokes accumulation rather than curation. If compendiousness at its best suggests synthesis—the digestion and internalization for which Erasmus hoped—for Gascoigne it tokened an artless patchwork of permissible doctrine.

When the first of the younger brothers, Phylotimus, shares his poem, he prefaces it by declaring that he followed the directions as precisely as he could: "I have no more but conveied in to verse," he explains, "the verie briefe which our Master delivered us in prose, adding neither dilatations, allegories, nor examples" (55). Gnomaticus's written summary of his lectures begins in this manner: "1 Feare God because he is mightie, / 2 Love God because he is mercifull, / 3 Trust in God because he is just . . ." (33). Here are the first four lines of Phylotimus's poem:

Feare God alwais whose might is most, & joyn thy feare with love
Since over all his worthy workes, his mercie stands above:
In him thou mayst likewise be bold, to put thy trust alwaie,
Since he is just and promyse keepes, his truth cannot decay.

(55)

The young student demonstrates a willingness to embellish a little, flashing some alliteration in "his worthy workes" and employing the figure of truth "decaying." He also takes some degree of license by contorting syntax in order to maintain the meter ("Since he is just and promyse keepes"). In reverse engineering these lines, as Tudor schoolmasters might have done with curious phrases in the writings of the ancients, we might recognize that Phylotimus's lines grab from Gnomaticus's lectures beyond the remit of the summary prompt: "*Feare him then* for he is most mightie . . . And yet with this feare you must also joyne love . . . *Love him then* since his mercy is over all his works . . . *Trust in him then* for his woords shall never fayle" (19–21). The labor involved in Phylotimus's compiling now looks fairly straightforward, and akin to what went into King Edward's "carefully competent and utterly soulless orations": take your teacher's words, tweak them enough to satisfy your meter and rhyme scheme, and use the pool of words from his lectures to patch up any gaps.

We should remember that Phylotimus's lines of regular iambic heptameter were actually written by an accomplished poet, George Gascoigne, self-consciously offering something less than remarkable. After all, for the sake of the narrative, the first poem must be outshined by the second—that of Phylomusus, whose name has "muse" in it. He prefaces his reading with the caveat that he has "some what more dilated and enlarged everie point" (56). Here are his opening stanzas:

> The man that meanes, by grace him selfe to guyde,
> And so to lyve, as God may least offende:
> These lessons learne, and let them never slide,
> from out his mynde, what ever he pretende.
>
> Since God is greate, and so omnipotent,
> as nothing can withstand his mighty powre,
> he must be fearde, least if his wrath be bent:
> we perish all, and wither lyke a flowre.
>
> (56)

Regardless of what we think about this poem as a work of art, it is clear that we are meant to see it as more accomplished than Phylotimus's, if only because it shows more *work*—that is, a greater willingness to demonstrate one's compliance by risking noncompliance. While nevertheless still mainly drawing phrases and ideas from Gnomaticus's lectures to supplement its backbone of *sententiae*, it flaunts precisely the kind of creativity demanded by a narrow view of decorum. Phylomusus reflects the ideal outcome of the puritanical grammar school, and by writing in his voice, Gascoigne reveals himself to be an accomplished graduate as well. In the margins of the play, Phylomusus's stanzas are even marked by the topics they concern, signaling to readers that Gascoigne has self-consciously constructed passages worth extracting. The students, and their creator, in this way know that they have succeeded even before being evaluated. Phylotimus gloats, upon hearing his peer's poem, "[V]erie glad I am that wee have eche of us so well accomplished our dueties, nothyng doubting but that our enstructer will also like the same accordingly" (58).

By evacuating the writers' doubts, *The Glasse of Governement* presents poesy as craft that, because it does not worry over its decisions, also does not merit the reader's attention to those decisions. It is busywork, and is meant to turn a moment of recreation into a site of compliant labor. When the quick-witted elder brothers receive Gnomaticus's homework assignment, by contrast, one of them appears to be at a loss: "Oh that I had now the vayne which *Virgill* had in writing of a delectable verse,"

Phylosarchus complains. He reveals shortly thereafter that his frustration has nothing to do with the assignment:

> [S]hall I tell you *Phylautus*, wherfore I desired the excellencie of *Virgil*, in compounding of a verse? not as they thinke God knoweth, to convert our tedious traditions there into: for a small grace in a verse wil serve for such unpleasant matter, but it was to furnish me with eloquence, for the better obteyning of this heavenly dame, whose reme[m]brance is sweet unto me, neyther yet am I able to expresse such prayses as she doth deserve. Oh how it delighteth me to behold in myne imagination the counterfeyt of her excellent face, me thinkes the glimsing of her eyes have in it a reflexion, farre more vehement than the beames of the Sunne it selfe, and the sweetnesse of her heavenly breath, surpasseth the spiceries of *Arabia*. Oh that I had skill to write some worthy matter in commendation of her rare perfections. (48–49)

Phylosarchus knows how to quickly turn sentences into verses, so the challenge of the assignment does not bother him at all. Moreover, he regards the source material provided him as "unpleasant matter," and resolves that he needs only "a small grace" to versify it (48). It would be difficult for readers to disagree with this assessment. The assignment was mainly meant, after all, to help Gnomaticus's lessons stick in the students' memories. The elder brothers, whose memories took up the ideas quickly for verbal regurgitation, found the assignment simple enough to be not worth doing at all. Phylosarchus's complaint here consequently reveals a different problem: he currently holds something in his "remembrance" quite deeply but does not know how to treat it in verse. Seeking after Virgil's "vayne," or a distinctive stylistic attitude, he has the aspiration to make something of his wit but confronts his own lack of skill. His limitations in aspiring after "worthy matter," moreover, are manifest: his descriptions of his beloved as having eyes like the sun, breath sweeter than Arabian spices, are utterly commonplace. Whatever poem he might produce would be just as bland as his homework. In order to improve, he would require precisely the faculties his education was meant to instill: *copia*, compositional acumen, and decorousness. This student *wants* to sound like Virgil—just not in the way his teacher expects.

Glasse in fact repeatedly insists that Phylosarchus and Phylautus are not really delinquents. Their plan was always simply to go to college;

they say they want to attend "lectures daily read of all the liberall sciences, of all languages, and of all morall discourses" and "have choyse company of gallant young gentlemen, with whom we might acquaint our selves, and passe some times in recreation" (35). Such ambitions were likely not too reprehensible in the eyes of the young gentlemen Gascoigne envisioned as his primary readership. Gnomaticus even recognizes that the boys are not entirely responsible for their failures, and that he is partly culpable as their guardian because they fell "into the snares which [he] least of al mistrusted." The "entisements of others," he claims, are the real culprit here, and in identifying them, he also confesses his inability to thwart them (69). The blame for the play's ending thus falls most directly on his methods:

> [T]heir misgovernment may become not onely a great grief to their parents, but also a hinderance to such commendation as I might else have gayned by the others: . . . Well I will go talke with their parentes, and if they wilbe ruled by my councell, they shall give them leave a little to see the world, and to followe any exercise that be not repugnant unto vertue, for unto some wittes neyther correction, nor frendly admonition, nor any other perswasion will serve, until their owne rodde have beaten them, and then they prove oftentymes (though late) men of excellent qualities. (80)

Recognizing that learning often happens through experiences of meaningful but not catastrophic failure, Gnomaticus resolves to give his wayward students a little more license. "Such fine wittes have such an universall desire commonly," he later explains, "that they never prove stayed untill the blacke oxe hath troden on their toes." Unfortunately his new curriculum emerges too late—instead of being gently punished by their "owne rodde" (80–81), the elder brothers have been ensnared by the state and are set to be patched out of both society and existence. This ending comes to pass despite other characters repeatedly resisting the idea of imposing harsh punishments. Gnomaticus knows that "in florishing youth every punishment may not be used, but discretion must foresee what kynde of punishment wil most prevaile and best gayne reformation in the mind of the offender" (53). This principle of leniency even extends to local authorities, such as the local margrave, appropriately named Severus, who reveals that he takes no joy in enforcement. "What pleasure redoundeth unto an honest minde," he complains, "to pronounce sentence of death upon an offendor?" The problem with the law, he reflects, is that the world changes too quickly for policy to keep up, and "constitucions are needful to be devised or renewed, for to meete with the dayly practises and inventiones of lewde persones" (67). The law is too slow, so it ends up using its bluntest instruments to compress and eradicate anything—any sort of "invention"—that might threaten the norms it is meant to uphold.

Quickness, in *The Glasse of Governement*, is the domain of "parasites, and bawdes" who repeatedly gull "yonkers" with fleet-footed lies (43). This term, slang for "youngster" or "young gentleman," is one Gascoigne also employs for those in danger of being fooled not just by deception but by the misapprehension of poetry itself.[79] Gascoigne warns the "lustie yonkers" in the second epistle of *The Posies* to realize that true understanding does not reside with those who "thinke it sufficient if (Parrot like) they can rehearse things without booke" (365.34–35). The idea that schoolroom activities and book smarts must be supplemented with experiential knowledge is dramatized onstage in real time: one of the parasites' deceptions of Gnomaticus, which he later boasts of as being wholly improvised and "upon the sodeyne," takes form in the space of a few seconds: "[W]el, we must find some device to bleare his eye for a while: let me alone, I knowe how to bring it to passe" (38–39).[80] While yonkers are working hard at regurgitating old lines, parasites use simple lies and misdirection to gull them into disorientation and ruin.

In contrast to the quick inventions of deceivers, moreover, the play presents the boys' parents, who try to work quickly but find themselves always a step behind. When they realize that they must rescue their sons from their perilous dalliances, they, too, strive for "sodaine" wit (76)—but they prove too tragically slow. If deviance is quick, the play suggests, correction needs to try and match its pace, lest its only recourse be the executioner's axe. It is with this realization that *Glasse* concludes, without even asking its audience to applaud. Offering only a garish solution to youthful folly, it makes the final word spoken by a character a barb against the main cause of the play's woes: "[T]he common saying is clap your handes, but the circumstance of this wofull tragicall comedie considered, I may say justly unto you wring your hands, nevertheless I leave it to your discretion" (88).

---

79. *Oxford English Dictionary*, s.v. "Younker, n.," accessed July 2, 2021, http://www.oed.com/view/Entry/232175.

80. Lorna Hutson's bravura reading of this scene locates *The Glasse* in a trend of increasingly realistic early modern representations of legal workings. See Hutson, *Invention of Suspicion*, 201–16.

Quick Capacity

How might things have gone differently? Near the end of *The Glasse of Governement*, Gnomaticus realizes his errors and changes his methods to allow the elder brothers "their choyce what kinde of lyfe they will followe, so that it be vertuous, and not contrary to Gods worde" (81). This transformation arrives too late, of course, but I propose that it is fundamentally the basis of Gascoigne's own approach to poetry's role in education. By successfully tempering license with gentle correction, Gnomaticus might have helped the elder brothers put their good wits to good use. The younger brothers, who begin the play pious, do not necessarily learn how to *become* pious—just how to parrot piety's inventory of quotations. Unlike their younger siblings, Phylosarchus and Phylautus never actually complete Gnomaticus's assignment. Later in the play, the schoolmaster finds that the former had "spent the time in wryting of loving sonets" while the latter "made verses in praise of Marshiall feates and pollycies" (60). The play never actually shares those poems with the reader, and even as the prodigal brothers careen toward depraved lives ending in unceremonious deaths, it cannot help but present them as tragic emblems of lost promise. The teacher they needed, it turns out, was George Gascoigne, and his manual, *Certayne Notes of Instruction concerning the Making of a Verse*. It is to this text that I now turn, to present the regrettable end of *The Glasse of Governement* as an act not of submission to the "reverend Divines," but of subtle admonition.

In *Certayne Notes*, Gascoigne adopts the posture of a reluctant instructor invited by a noble young friend for guidance in versification. His first advice is that a poem must have an "invention" savoring of "aliquid salis [a pinch of salt]," by which he means, "some good and fine devise, shewing the quicke capacitie of a writer" (454.19–20). While to modern ears, "invention" may sound like the purview of creativity, for much of European history the term—which derives from the Latin *invenire*, meaning "to come upon, discover, find out, devise, contrive"—connoted "finding out or selection of topics to be treated, or arguments to be used" in a rhetorical debate.[81] It was the first phase of oratorical composition, and the study of it, as Peter Mack explains,

---

81. *Oxford English Dictionary*, s.v. "Invent, v.," accessed July 7, 2021, http://www.oed.com/view/Entry/98960#eid184603; and *Oxford English Dictionary*, s.v. "Invention, n.," accessed July 10, 2021, http://www.oed.com/view/Entry/98969.

included learning "ways to obtain the sympathy and interest of the audience at the start of a speech; lines of argument appropriate to different types of case . . . ; topics of invention to assist in discovering arguments about any subject; forms in which to present arguments; and topics for emotional appeals."[82] Especially as taught in the humanist curriculum, rhetoric understood "invention" not as the generation of an original idea but as the outcome of a process of study rooted in logical method and the accumulation of authoritative moral arguments. It was fundamentally rooted in two interlinked approaches: (1) discovering claims by proceeding through the "topics" and commonplaces of invention, and (2) considering "both sides" of a given problem or issue (arguing *in utramque partem*).[83] Elizabethan schoolboys practiced these approaches through composition exercises such as Apthonius's *Progymnasmata* and as oratorical declamations or debates—the latter often with theatrical flair.[84]

The next chapter will examine the rhetorical practices of invention with much greater scrutiny, but this background nevertheless reveals Gascoigne's poetics both as a product of this rhetorical training and as resistant to it. By way of an example that might have proven useful to Phylosarchus, in *Certayne Notes* he treats as a case study what he himself would do if he were compelled "to wryte in prayse of a gentlewoman." He immediately cautions against simple regurgitation in the form of cliché: "I would neither praise hir christal eye, nor hir cherrie lippe, etc" (455.11–13). In the absence of canned phrases and poetic commonplaces, he offers some suggestions. The first one, "find some supernaturall cause wherby my penne might walke in the superlatiue degree," is not particularly practical, but he follows the appeal to the muses with some other options: "[O]r els I would vndertake to aunswere for any imperfection that shee hath, and therevpon rayse the prayse of hir commendacion. Likewise, if I should disclose my pretence in loue, I would eyther make a strange discourse of some intollerable passion, or finde occasion to pleade by the example of some historie, or discouer my disquiet in shadowes *per Allegoriam*, or vse the couertest meane that I could to auoyde the vncomely customes of common writers" (455.14–22).

---

82. Mack, *Elizabethan Rhetoric*, 9. The other phases are by *dispositio* ("placing that material in an appropriate structure"); *elocutio* ("clothing the ideas of the speech in the most effective words"); *memoria* ("memorising the speech"); and *accentio* ("the use of voice and gesture").

83. Sloane, *On the Contrary*, 38-39.

84. See Mack, *Elizabethan Rhetoric*, 27-28; also see Peltonen, *Rhetoric, Politics and Popularity*, 68-70.

As advice for a grammar school student emerging from years of emulative composition, this is not a bad place to start. The instructions are somehow both constraining and liberating. On the one hand, Gascoigne tells poets to use the techniques provided them by their rhetorical education—debating, comparison, and circumlocution—and insists on compositional discipline. On the other hand, he allows poets to source their inventions from practically anywhere: "To deliver unto you generall examples it were almoste unpossible, sithence the occasions of Inventions are (as it were) infinite" (455.8–10). Echoing Aristotle's recognition that metaphor "has clarity and sweetness and strangeness" that "cannot be learned from someone else," Gascoigne encourages the poet to test out novel conceits.[85] By licensing discourse that is cautiously "strange," he injects poetic composition with the "quicke capacitie" absent from Gnomaticus's compendious world. Among the instructions, after all, is to "avoyde prolixitie and tediousness," qualities that *The Glasse of Governement*, or at least the first half of it, obviously evinces (461.22).

Quickness is tethered to the shifting sands of occasion, and while the occasion selected may be frivolous, scandalous, or even libelous, the poet's art will be regarded as successful if the occasion is handled well. By this, Gascoigne means a style that can capably sustain invention without lapsing into either tired tropes or impulsive irrationalities. In Gascoigne's conception of poetic composition, invention extends throughout the whole process and is animated by quick capacity. One's challenge as a poet becomes that of the plate spinner—exercising continual attention and engaging steady reflexes to ensure that one's mind will not go astray into patches of corruption or compromise. Invention's entanglement with style cannot be overstated: each twist and turn of the writing process must be checked against an original principle. The main problem faced by the elder brothers in *Glasse*, in this light, is focus; they are not stimulated by the task at hand, and so, seeking other means of engaging themselves, they fall prey to the quicker "inventiones of lewd persons."

Gascoigne explains that one of the reasons one's own invention may go awry is the allure of simple solutions, and here we can infer the advice he might have given students like Phylosarchus:

> I would exhorte you also to beware of rime without reason: my meaning is hereby that your rime leade you not from your firste

---

85. Aristotle, *On Rhetoric*, 200 (1405a).

Invention, for many wryters when they have layed the platforme of their invention, are yet drawen sometimes (by ryme) to forget it or at least to alter it, as when they cannot readily finde out a worde whiche maye rime to the first (and yet continue their determinate Invention) they do then eyther botche it up with a worde that will ryme (howe small reason soever it carie with it) or els they alter their first worde and so percase decline or trouble their former Invention: But do you always hold your first determined Invention, and do rather search the bottome of your braynes for apte wordes, than chaunge good reason for rumbling rime. (458.7–18)

The invention is a "platforme" that dictates the shape of the poetic edifice that will be constructed on it. Recognizing that an unskilled writer can "botche" a poem by being lured by a facile rhyme, Gascoigne shows his personal awareness of how the writing process is invariably subject to the vicissitudes of inattention or laxity. The poet attracted to flourishes or derailed by lexical shortcomings might drift toward a rhyme that sounds good at the time but threatens to sideline one's wit and will. He thus envisions poetic composition as a continual struggle between one's "quick capacity" and the contingencies, both alluring and coercive, that influence the turning of thoughts into things. Caught between constructivist resignation and a fantasy of pure expression, Gascoigne's poet confronts the problem that every word constitutes an active choice. He wants aspiring poets to catch themselves—whether it is to sustain a central conceit or make it to university without being derailed by rogues. Contingency, as Hetherington observes, preoccupies Gascoigne's own poetry, as "accident and occasion" are for him "always inescapable elements of the creative process."[86]

In the space between one word and the next, writers are subject both to the comfort of thought easing into habituated patterns and to the danger of thought veering off into distraction. Barthes, for one, observes how even something as simple as adjectives can "imprison" writers and threaten the "purity" of language, due to the "pleasure of the lure."[87] The challenge of cultivating style, then, is the challenge of maintaining attention. In *The Ignorant Schoolmaster* (1991), Jacques Rancière defines attention as "the act that makes an intelligence proceed

---

86. Hetherington, "Gascoigne's Accidents," 57.
87. Barthes, *Neutral*, 60–61.

under the absolute constraint of a will."[88] Recounting the program for "universal teaching" practiced by Joseph Jacotot in France and Belgium at the turn of the nineteenth century, Rancière argues that a pedagogy of explanation presumes the incapacity of learners. Jacotot's method evacuated explanation by prioritizing attention: his Flemish students taught themselves French despite Jacotot knowing no Flemish himself. The students simply studied a dual-language book at length while their teacher verified that attention had been paid by asking them questions. In time, they became fluent readers of French. This led Jacotot to posit that one could teach something one did not know, only by finding strategies to verify that the students had paid attention.

The methods employed by Brinsley and Gnomaticus may be seen as stultifying schoolchildren by convincing them of their inadequacy before the intelligences of Virgil, Cicero, and the schoolmaster. Allowing intelligence to believe itself complete is not just a recipe for reaffirming knowledge as a matter of institutional accreditation, however—it is a recipe for error. Rancière describes the "logic of explanation" as "a time-machine producing at the same rhythm an imaginary concordance and an actual discordance of times"; this rhythm reaffirms a social hierarchy while sensing in its offbeats that hierarchy as not fixed or self-evident.[89] In Gascoigne's *Glasse*, which ends with teachers, parents, and siblings alike racing to rescue the prodigal brothers, even the margrave Severus feels this drumbeat bearing down on the crimes of the young prodigals. He bemoans it even as he must continue playing it. One way to derail the rhythm, Rancière observes, is via a pedagogy that "unties the stitches of the veil that the explanatory system has spread on everything." This pedagogy of unstitching restores things to their "opacity" and builds a "community of equal speaking beings" who may debate and argue about what it is that they see.[90] "Stumbling is nothing" when one attempts to articulate perception; "the wrong is in diverging from, leaving one's path, no longer paying attention to what one says, forgetting what one is."[91] If the stultification of explanation robs students of their own will, so does temptation. A pedagogy of intellectual liberation would strive to help the student proceed in thought by choice rather than via manipulation.

How does poetry fit into this pedagogy? As we saw, in Erasmus's ideal system, poetry would afford students opportunities to experiment.

---

88. Rancière, *Ignorant Schoolmaster*, 25.
89. Rancière, "Un-What?," 33.
90. Rancière, "Un-What?," 35.
91. Rancière, *Ignorant Schoolmaster*, 57.

Given license to imitate and to overgo, the student writer might tear apart language and, in so doing, find new ways of expressing thoughts. They would do this alongside their other more strictly emulative exercises that subordinated that play to compliance. Poesy was where writers could let their intelligence run rampant, so that they could learn to constrain it via the exertion of will. Bodgery was not necessarily evidence of a failure of attention; it might just as likely index a student experimenting with license. The next step in their education would be to discover the limitations of that license. Gascoigne's warnings about rhyme demanded just this sort of cognizance. He required that poets' own inventions guide their hands while selecting each new word—to help them resist both the distractions of alluring temptation *and* the coercions of rote method. His poetics were founded on the exercise of attention and the conscious awareness of one's own choices.

In *A Hundreth Sundrie Flowres*, the work he was forced to retract, Gascoigne labored to show off his ability to pay close and sustained attention to the world around him. Throughout the collection, he performs his nimble quick-wittedness by framing his poems with accounts of the occasions that supposedly prompted them. In many instances, this meant providing a paratextual gloss recounting the poem's rhetorical situation. A section of verses commending "Gascoignes memorie," for example, is presented as having been solicited by members of Gray's Inn prior to his admission into their coterie. It reveals that Gascoigne was presented with five "themes" on which he was to compose verses (274.0.8).[92] In his poem responding to Alexander Nevile's prompt, "Sat cit, si sat bene" (quick enough, if good enough), he adapts the theme to reflect on his catastrophic earlier attempts to be a courtier:

I moughte have kepte a chaire of quiet state,
But hastie heades can not bee settled so,
Till crooked Fortune give a crabbed mate:
As busye braynes muste beate on tickle toyes,
As rashe invention breedes a rawe devise,
So sodaine falles doe hinder hastie joyes.
                (289.76–81)

---

92. Many poetic exercises at the Inns of Court, Jessica Winston explains, were "similar to the verse on set themes that the authors were required to write in school, verses that affirmed the importance of work, friendship, duty, humility, and other social and moral virtues." Winston, *Lawyers at Play*, 77.

Even here, prior to his public chastening, Gascoigne recognizes that "rashe invention" can lead to failed poetic conclusions. Rambunctious wits' "busye braynes" only end up producing flashes in the pan; their "rawe devise[s]" are just as suddenly dismissed as they are begot. His sonnet sequence's conclusion offers the same advice with which he began his instructions about poetic invention: "I fynde this proverbe true, / That Haste makes waste, and therefore still I saye, / No haste but good, where wysedome makes the waye" (281.96–98). How one becomes "wise" enough to become a poet, in a context wherein even the supposedly learned could not agree on what makes a good poem, posed a challenge that humanist pedagogy did not really have the tools to address. Nevertheless, in these early poems reflecting on his own early rashness, Gascoigne actively cultivated an image of himself as "quick"—after the last of the five "themes," he boasts that they amounted to "the number of. CCLVIII. verses" and were devised "riding by the way, writing none of them untill he came at the end of his Journey, the which was no longer than one day in riding, one day in tarying with his friend, and the third in returning to Greys Inne" (282.6–9). His theme argues that rash inventions breed raw devices, but he also clearly expects readers to be a little impressed with how quickly he produced it.

"Gascoigne's Woodmanship" is perhaps the most notorious example of this quickness. It invites the reader to witness how the poet's alert attention used experience to provoke his imagination, and his imagination to produce poetry excusing other kinds of failure. The poem is set during a day of hunting, and this occasion finds Gascoigne's speaker first justifying his refusal to shoot at passing deer by talking about his lifelong habit of shooting "awry." He then shifts gears and contrives a new argument on the spot:

> But since my Muse can to my Lorde reherse
> What makes me misse, and why I doe not shoote,
> Let me imagine in this woorthlesse verse:
> If right before mee, at my standings foote
> There stoode a Doe, and I shoulde strike hir deade,
> And then shee prove a carrion carkas too,
> What figure might I fynde within my head,
> To scuse the rage whiche rulde mee so to doo?
>
> (316.125–32)

A poem, Gascoigne suggests, can be an exculpatory instrument that can imagine alternative answers to familiar questions. His own verses could thereby be a means by which a mistake or personal failing might be translated into something others might find tolerable, or even pleasurable. While poesy might have presented an opportunity to showcase his own nimble powers of attention, however, the reception of *A Hundreth Sundrie Flowres* revealed a readership incapable of mirroring those powers. By performatively patching his audacious work, he attempted to publicly acknowledge his deviations from social norms and show that he was capable of taking instruction. At the end of his letter to the reverend divines, he points to his poetic labors as training for more serious duties because of their explicit demonstration of continuous attention: "Surely you shall finde me no lesse readie to undertake a whole yeares travaile in anie worke which you shall thinke me able to overcome," he advertises, "than I have beene willing heretofore to spende three houres in penning of an amorous Sonnet" (363.28–31). We might read *The Glasse of Governement*, then, as Gascoigne's dutiful completion of an acceptable compilation. It dramatizes, in painstaking (and painsgiving) fashion, what it took to get a courtly appointment in Elizabethan England. Even as it buys into the fiction of ready opportunities, however, the world that *Glasse* reflects in its mirror is a cold, slow, and strict one.

Reflection: The Academic Death Penalty

In a foundational essay in composition studies, David Bartholomae confesses, "I don't expect my students to *be* literary critics when they write about *Bleak House*." Bartholomae defines the literary critic as "a person who wins publication in a professional journal," a goal beyond the grasp of nearly all undergraduate writers. Instead of aiming for this standard, Bartholomae argues, "what our beginning students need to learn is to extend themselves, by successive approximations, into the commonplaces, the set phrases, rituals and gestures, habits of mind, tricks of persuasion, obligatory conclusions and necessary connections that determine 'what might be said' and constitute knowledge within the various branches of our academic community."[93] There are many resonances between Bartholomae's account of what it means to become an academic writer and the assumptions of humanist grammar schools discussed in the preceding chapter. Like the grammar school teacher who fears that his or her students' indecorousness will leave them ill equipped for public service, Bartholomae reminds his students, "The language is not yours.... You did not invent it; it is not yours and yet, ironically, it is one of the most crucial ways you have of being present—of being present in the world, in the workplace, in the academy."[94] While students doubtless have much to learn about academia's discursive conventions, a pedagogy of approximation reaffirms the idea that, as new initiates, their primary task is to ventriloquize those who already seem authoritative.

It is partly for this reason that Geoffrey Sirc, in a response to Bartholomae, argues that composition studies is often guilty of institutional practices that actively diminish writing's capacity to surprise, shock, and offer new ideas. "Can we allow a composition that is definitively unfinished," Sirc asks, "deferring this need for writing as a revision toward a *certain* style, toward a *certain* end?"[95] Teachers of literature concerned with cultivating their students' critical writing skills—skills that would see them reconcile the invention of a novel argument with the observance of formal protocols—might follow Sirc's lead and attend more closely to the ironies of style. When students are asked to write about written works that openly chafe and bristle against formal

---

93. Bartholomae, "Inventing the University," 69.
94. Bartholomae, "Living in Style," 15.
95. Sirc, *English Composition*, 49.

prescriptions, to what extent are the classroom's formal prescriptions undermining their capacity to critically engage with those texts? Can we try to reconcile the stylistic exuberance of the texts in our syllabuses with the sorts of assignments we challenge our students to write—assignments that, we tell them, must look and sound a certain way?

It is unsurprising that, in response to tacit or explicit cues to practice formal obedience, many students produce bodgeries—cribbed-together writing assignments with their component patches apparent. "This is how we teach students to write," John Warner laments. "Don't be a writer, we tell them, just do some things that make it look like you know how to write. And when in doubt, at least sound smart by using words like *ubiquitous* and *plethora*."[96] Warner observes that when students are assigned an essay in an undergraduate course, the assignment is "treated not as an occasion to discover something previously unknown—to the author, above all—but as a performance for an audience of one, the teacher, one hoop among many to be jumped through as part of the college grind."[97] Confronted with this grind—a frantic "busy-ness" that Susan D. Blum describes as bred from a "focus on evaluation as the goal of education"—many students strive to sound exactly like their teachers, as the younger brothers in *The Glasse of Governement* do, while also working at the quick pace of their prodigal elder siblings.[98] These contradictory pressures lead many to "dash off a paper, seeking mainly to satisfy requirements regarding number of pages, references, quotations."[99] When such techniques prove inadequate, the students may avail themselves of more insidious techniques in order to sound "correct," and end up committing plagiarism. Blum observes that while some students plagiarize intentionally with the explicit goal to deceive, others "don't know how to avoid it, because the rules are terribly subtle and take many years to master," and others still "deliberately do so to get the job done."[100] The fact that many students end up poorly navigating the terrain between clumsy academic style and outright plagiarism should make us reflect on our own pedagogy, because, as Blum suggests, students' acts of plagiarism are in part a response to "all the supporting messages from the educational and social contexts in

---

96. Warner, *Why They Can't Write*, 7.
97. Warner, *Why They Can't Write*, 155.
98. Blum, *My Word!*, 4.
99. Blum, *My Word!*, 4.
100. Blum, *My Word!*, 6.

which they find themselves."[101] If our goals are different from those of humanist pedagogy, how different are our methods?

Rebecca Moore Howard emphasizes that there is a difference between accidental and intentional plagiarism, a distinction that I align with the one described above between Erasmian "patchwork writing" and Elizabethan "bodgery." When student errors relating to imitation and appropriation are not inherently deceitful, Howard argues, the perpetrators do not deserve the "academic death penalty"—failure or expulsion. Instead, such instances present "pedagogical opportunity, not a juridical problem."[102] Inadvertent slips may be a form of academic writing Howard calls "patchwriting," a compositional phenomenon of "copying from a source text and then deleting some words, altering grammatical structures, or plugging in one-for-one synonym substitutes."[103] Patchwriting, like patchwork poetry, reveals students attempting to wield a discourse that does not yet belong to them. Errors of this kind may be associated with what Bartholomae sees as "evidence of choice or strategy among a range of possible choices or strategies" and "evidence of an individual style of using language and making it work." In this light, patchwriting may not be "a simple record of what a writer failed to do because of incompetence or indifference," but rather a record of "stylistic features, information about *this* writer and *this* language."[104] When students try to sound like their professors or like formal literary criticism and come up short, the difference may be a mistake. It may also be their own latent style bursting the seams of the text. What would it take, considering this awareness, to take "sounding like their professors" out of the classroom equation—to make the standard for students' writing something other than their professor's gnomic speech? How might literature classes avoid enforcing students' words by constraining their wills and implement the pedagogy Gnomaticus decides on too late: allowing them license "to followe any exercise that be not repugnant unto vertue"?

Just as Gascoigne recommends that poets manage their style so as not to either blandly proceed on autopilot or veer into indecorous muck, Warner champions writing for how its demands on an author's attention also enable intellectual liberation. Central to the writer's practice is

---

101. Blum, *My Word!*, 6.
102. Howard, "Plagiarisms," 788.
103. Howard, "Plagiarism Pentimento," 233. Also see Hull and Rose, "Rethinking Remediation."
104. Bartholomae, "Study of Error," 258.

choice, which Warner identifies as "the writing equivalent of balance when it comes to writing on a bicycle." The absence of choice lies at the center of Warner's diagnosis: "[T]he way our nation's schoolchildren are taught—and, more importantly, the way their learning is assessed—gives them little experience with making choices in the context of writing. These distortions of what it means to write offer students even less opportunity to write about things that matter to them or to engage with their own passions."[105] Allowing students latitude to practice making choices first requires acknowledging the constraints they are under when presented with writing assignments: the threat of evaluation, the absence of a variety of models, feelings of alienation from the readings.

Faced with such circumstances, professors might acknowledge and warn students against the ethical impropriety of plagiarism, but they might also try to promote approaches to writing wherein the advantages and appeal of plagiarism are nullified. One way to diminish the threat of evaluation is to adopt "ungrading" or labor-based assessment for all assignments—both creative and critical—in our classrooms, indicating to students that their effort and attention will be assessed rather than the quality of their writing.[106] One way to diversify the number of models that students have available is to ask them to find genres, forms, and styles to imitate of their own choosing, and help them appraise the successfulness of their emulation. One way to address feelings of alienation might be to engage with the "relevance" of early modern literary texts as a concept rooted in political positionality and in relation to community service.[107] If we are interested in soliciting the risky work required of actual thought, we must help students recognize that imitation and deviation are both choices available to them. Sometimes we must require students to demonstrate facility with certain textual forms, and in doing so we might make clear that the lesson at hand is how to assert their will over their own impulses and to practice imitation. The primary consequence of failing to hit a target, when practicing imitation, should be more knowledge about the target. Sometimes we might want students to venture out on their own, to show us what they can do—in doing so, we might make clear that the lesson at hand is how to assert their wills over cliché, convention, and banality. This latter challenge is a much more difficult one, and one explored in depth by the subsequent chapters of this book.

---

105. Warner, *Why They Can't Write*, 5.
106. Blum, *Ungrading*; Inoue, *Labor-Based Grading Contracts*.
107. See Bender, "Whip Hand"; and Eklund, "Embattled Humanities."

The Glasse of Governement, a parable for the uses of literature in education, encourages us to cultivate a more student-centered approach to the role of writing in the early modern literature classroom. What writers like Gascoigne—including the other writers studied in this book—possessed, and what we today are quickly conceding to the pressures of professionalization, is a sense that writing is an opportunity to exercise agency and to reckon with how agency may be taken away. While we retain the privilege of teaching their texts, we might follow the poets' lead and advance an argument for the social benefits of the writing process as a site of contestation—not only with institutional norms and protocols, but also with oneself and one's ingrained and acquired habits.

Chapter 2

Invention
Philip Sidney's "Fear of Maybe"

The most influential sonnet sequence of the Elizabethan era begins with a scene of writing:

> Loving in truth, and fain in verse my love to show,
> That she (dear she) might take some pleasure of my pain:
> Pleasure might cause her read, reading might make her know;
> Knowledge might pity win, and pity grace obtain;
>   I sought fit words to paint the blackest face of woe,
> Studying inventions fine, her wits to entertain:
> Oft turning others' leaves, to see if thence would flow
> Some fresh and fruitful showers upon my sunburnt brain.
>   But words came halting forth, wanting invention's stay;
> Invention, nature's child, fled step-dame study's blows;
> And others' feet still seemed but strangers in my way.
> Thus great with child to speak, and helpless in my throes,
> Biting my truant pen, beating myself for spite,
> "Fool," said my muse to me, "look in thy heart and write."
>
> (*A&S*, 153, 1.1–14)[1]

---

1. All references to Sidney's work, unless otherwise noted, will be to Sidney, *Sir Philip Sidney*, and indicated in-text by page number and, in the case of sonnets, sonnet number and line numbers. *Astrophil and Stella* is abbreviated *A&S*, and *Certain Sonnets* is abbreviated *CS*.

Sir Philip Sidney's alter ego, like the elder brothers in Gascoigne's *The Glasse of Governement*, is an aspiring poet, and he imagines himself as a schoolboy with an itch to turn truant. Inspired by his love for Stella to write a poem, Astrophil resorts to a skill presumably acquired in a humanist schoolroom: emulating other authors.[2] When he sifts through the books on his shelf, the barren terrain of his "sunburnt brain" manages to sprout new life.[3] Reading catalyzes his imagination, and sometimes a seemingly potent phrase stamps and rears in his mind like an untamed horse. Finding no discipline or guidance, no "stay," to manage this surprise, though, these words find that they have nowhere to go. Three times over the course of the sonnet, Sidney uses the same word—invention—to name three seemingly distinct aspects of Astrophil's writing process. It appears as something a poet might seek in others' work ("inventions fine"), something that might discipline racing thoughts ("invention's stay"), and something that shirks both study and discipline to pursue its own inclinations ("Invention, nature's child"). As Astrophil is pulled both toward the schoolroom and its books and away from it, Sidney's poem characterizes invention—the beginning of composition—as akin to the "throes" of a protracted pregnancy. This condition persists until his muse speaks up and instructs him to let his own heart be his example.

Astrophil and Stella (ca. 1581, first printed in 1591) presents poetic invention as a confused and "halting" enterprise—a depiction that, I argue, we may join with Gascoigne's "quick capacity" to advance a view of poesy as a mode of critical reflection and philosophical reexamination. As discussed in the previous chapter, invention was the first phase of rhetorical composition, and in the humanist schoolroom it primarily consisted of discovering arguments for use in a debate. By the late sixteenth century, invention was taught in the manner depicted in Gascoigne's *Glasse*: as an exercise in compilation and emulation following the model of textual authorities. This approach was symptomatic of an increased emphasis on treating rhetoric as a means of conflating decorous obedience with eloquence. While early humanists who adapted the five "offices" of Ciceronian classical rhetoric (*inventio, dispositio, elocutio,*

---

2. As William Ringler puts it in his notes on the poem, by beginning with *elocutio* rather than *inventio*, Astrophil undertakes his composition "in the wrong order with an inadequate method." Ringler, *Poems*, 458–59.

3. For more context on this line, situating it among humanist debates over Ciceronianism, see Armstrong, *Ciceronian Sunburn*, 8–9.

memoria, pronuntiatio/actio) into neo-Latin treatises emphasized the interrelations between rhetoric and dialectic, thereby presenting rhetoric as both a technical and philosophical practice, the outsize emphasis these treatises placed on *elocutio* precipitated a severing of style from substance. Erasmus's *De copia,* with its plenitude of stylistic precepts and examples, became the core text of Renaissance rhetorical practice, and ultimately charted a trajectory that would see Peter Ramus influentially allocating *inventio* and *dispositio* to dialectic and leaving just *elocutio* and *pronuntiatio* to the domain of rhetoric.[4] When Sidney was writing *Astrophil and Stella* in the early 1580s, read against this context, the connotations of "invention" had begun to shift, unsettled by a deepening affiliation between rhetoric and imitation. As more poets began questioning how to translate inspiration into verses worthy of attention, the question of how to begin was left unresolved even by treatises like Gascoigne's *Certayne Notes*, which admitted that it could offer only examples rather than concrete guidelines for invention.

The previous chapter concluded by heeding Gascoigne's warning and emphasizing how choice and lenience were necessary components of early modern poetic endeavor. In the reflection that followed, I proposed that these principles might inform the writing pedagogy of the modern literature classroom. With Sidney's help, in this chapter I complicate these lessons by exploring early modern poetry's preoccupation with how lenience decoupled from experiences of difficulty proves just as pedagogically irresponsible as overly rigid rules.

Posing the problem of how to proceed with invention—how to start writing a poem—the opening sonnet of *Astrophil and Stella* arrives at what seems like a solution: looking in one's heart. One way to read this solution is as documenting a shift in approaches to writing from careful emulation to free expression, foreshadowing a rupture between imitative rhetorical composition and "original" poesy. To modern writing teachers, Astrophil's decision sounds like it promotes what compositionists call the "expressivist" paradigm of writing instruction, a paradigm that manifests most concretely in the form of free-writing exercises. Yet this rift between rhetoric and poetics, or between emulation and expression—ramified in the modern academy as the disciplinary separation of composition, literary criticism, and creative writing—would have been perplexing to Elizabethan humanists like

---

4. Plett, "Rhetoric and Humanism," 379–80.

Astrophil and his author. The humanist schoolboy might have grown frustrated by rhetoric's rigorous protocols, but he could not help but be influenced by them. Recognizing this interplay between freedom and responsibility, Ben Jonson argued that poets must not be afraid of "steering out of [their] sail" if "a fair gale of wind" favors them: "For all that we invent doth please us in the conception, or birth, or else we would never set it down." He quickly hastens to add, however, that a poet out at sea must nevertheless practice a caution armed with the judgment acquired through rigorous rhetorical training: "[T]he safest is to return to our judgement, and handle over again those things, the easiness of which might make them justly suspected."[5]

Locating poetic composition within a scene populated both by respect for "others' books" and by the recklessness of a "truant pen," Sidney renders poetic invention as being in perpetual conflict with regulation and instruction. If the opening sonnet of *Astrophil and Stella* appears to prize invention as "nature's child," ungoverned and ungovernable by external pressures, the second sonnet might be read as a tacit rebuttal of this view. In it, Astrophil concludes that his craft is fundamentally delusional: "I call it praise to suffer tyranny; / And now employ the remnant of my wit / To make myself believe that all is well, / While with a feeling skill I paint my hell" (*A&S*, 153, 2.11-14). The third sonnet veers back toward a defense of Astrophil's project, rejecting the poetics of "Pindar's apes" (*A&S*, 153-54, 3.3) to assert that instead of copying familiar figures, he will read only "Stella's face" and copy "what in her nature writes" (*A&S*, 153-54, 3.12-14). Rather than suggesting that he can invent a poem simply by "looking in his heart," Astrophil in this way grants Stella's face the authority he would otherwise have sought in "others' leaves." The fourth sonnet again recognizes that this approach may leave the poet vulnerable to sin and confusion; finding himself prioritizing Stella's face over moral authorities, Astrophil opens by asking "Virtue" to let him "take some rest" and to return to "Churches or schools" so as not to intervene even if "vain love have [his] simple soul oppressed" (*A&S*, 154, 4.1-6). As he swings back and forth between shame and pride throughout the remainder of the sequence, Astrophil acknowledges that he risks sabotaging his reputation by constructing a false deity while also acknowledging that he cannot help himself in his idolatry. This experience resembles one that Sidney

---

5. Jonson, "Discoveries," *Complete Poems*, 425-26.

himself confessed to having: in a letter to his sister Mary regarding his first poetic masterpiece, the *Arcadia*, he described the work as a "child, which I am loath to father" and ventriloquized his own father figures by renouncing his "young head" as "not so well stayed as I would it were (and shall be when God will)." Yet even as he confessed his shame, he admitted that if the "fancies" in his head had not "been in some way delivered," they "would have grown a monster" and he would have been "more sorie . . . that they came in, than that they gat out."[6]

True poetic invention, as Sidney came to depict it, was a necessarily difficult process characterized by doubt, hesitation, and reflection. While sonnet 1 of *Astrophil and Stella* opens with a poet resolved to trust his own instincts, the remainder of the sequence and his landmark *The Defence of Poesy* (1581) reveal Sidney to be a member of what Georgia Brown has called the "generation of shame." An offshoot of Helgerson's Elizabethan prodigals, the generation of shame was a group of writers who exploited their own feelings of affective ambivalence about poetry to "redefine literary activity as an alternative epistemological process, one that is no longer justified by reference to privileged modes of thought and the privileged modes of rationality."[7] By recognizing the inherent shamefulness and triviality of their poetic endeavors, these poets—with Sidney as their most prominent example—foregrounded the ways in which the shameful and trivial may be understood not as hindrances to thought but as enablers of it. Sidney eventually became "a Daedalus to his countrymen," William Ringler suggests, of the very sort Sidney himself cites in his *Defence of Poesy*: a guide who could "teach [others] rules of right writing, and to provide them with models to follow."[8] I propose that the model Sidney offered paradoxically challenged a pedagogy rooted in obedience to models.

The first section of this chapter locates experiences of doubt at the heart of Sidney's dissatisfied appraisal of the paradigm of invention afforded to Elizabethan schoolboys: forensic rhetoric, the sort of rhetorical argument practiced in courts of law to resolve disputes. Perceiving limitations in *stasis* theory, the bedrock method of this paradigm—a systematic and rule-bound method of resolving disputes by deciding on a specific question up for debate—Sidney sought to place poetic invention beyond the complete grasp of method. While he entertained modes

---

6. Sidney, *Countess of Pembroke's Arcadia*, A3r-v.
7. Brown, *Redefining Elizabethan Literature*, 18-19.
8. Ringler, *Poems*, lii.

of invention rooted in *kairos*—which licensed open-ended attentiveness to occasion and audience—the poetics he envisioned were nevertheless committed to the cautious exercise of judgment. His ambivalence about whether poets should be bound or free placed invention at an apex of rhetorical perplexity: *aporia*, at which orators "hesitate on both sides of a question."[9] Connecting aporia to the more mundane experience we today call "writer's block," the first section sees Sidney dramatizing the conditions that may lead a poet to self-silencing. In the chapter's second section, I find Sidney depicting Astrophil resolving his blockage via an illusion of presumed mastery. As Astrophil seems to arrive at a solution to his self-doubts in poems such as Sonnet 50 and Sonnet 74, however, I interrogate this solution by resituating it within a broader trajectory extending from Sidney's earliest poems to the end of *Astrophil and Stella*. This broader trajectory reveals Astrophil's fantasy of expressivity to be just as impotent as the frustrated method with which he begins the sequence. The absence of easy solutions, I argue, was foundational to Sidney's conception of poetic invention throughout his career.

Reflecting on Sidney's example, following this chapter's conclusion I sketch a pedagogy of literary criticism that embraces as a goal the cultivation of doubt and hesitation. While students in literature classes are not challenged to become poets, they are asked to invent arguments rooted in their careful study of texts. Confronted by teachers with seemingly authoritative insight into textual meaning, they are often shielded from the discomfiting reality that making critical meaning out of literary encounters often involves a lot of trial and error. The poetics of discomposition envisioned by Sidney, I propose, can lead us to pedagogical practices that communicate the differences between choices, obligations, and impulses. I propose that as teachers we must develop strategies for laying bare how experiences of hesitation betoken an exposure to genuine choices and how frustration signals an encounter with a problem worth slowing down to solve. Drawing on studies of the invention strategies of literary critics as well as cautionary examples from writing teachers, I envision ways that the early modern literature classroom may help students grow comfortable with experiences of self-doubt by acknowledging, in theory and in practice, how inventing an argument is often quite difficult, risky, and perhaps even fruitlessly confusing work.

---

9. Mann, "Aporia."

With Wit My Wit Is Marred

While invention took a subordinate role to style in the Tudor grammar school, the meaning of "invention" itself also gradually shifted from "discovery" to "conception" over the course of the sixteenth century. By the seventeenth century, it took on its more modern connotation of "an original contrivance or production of a new method or means of doing something."[10] The former meaning of invention, "discovery," aligned it primarily with the juridical posture of forensic rhetoric and the compositional methods rooted in appeals to authoritative arguments. Roland Greene explains that these methods posit "a more or less inert object, a concessionary (if not a superstitious) approach to textual authority, and a temporal project that brings matter out of the past into the present." The bedrock of legal argumentation, invention as discovery studied the facts on the ground and considered them in light of revered precedents. By contrast, Greene suggests, the emerging view of invention as conception aligned the term more closely with "a lively, sometimes ineffable object, a greater degree of independence from past authorities, and a project that creates fictions in the present destined to be encountered in the future."[11]

Rather than constraining itself to the facts on the ground or the books on the shelf, invention as conception turned a poet's present experience into a platform for imagining what might be instead. This liveliness arose, in part, through invention's affiliation with dialectical reasoning. After the seventeenth century, an invention was a *new* thing rather than something constructed largely via a process of studying others' texts. Philip Sidney preceded this transformation; in effect, he witnessed it happening. Caught Janus-faced in a movement where invention was affiliated with both past and future, he came to apprehend it both as a practice overseen by "step-dame study" and as something for which it was originally conceived by classical rhetoricians: a philosophical practice oriented toward new questions and new ideas. Witnessing rhetorical practice abandoning the latter mode of invention

---

10. *Oxford English Dictionary*, s.v. "Invention, n., Def. 3a.," accessed July 12, 2021, http://www.oed.com/view/Entry/98969.

11. Greene, *Five Words*, 20. Hannah Crawforth similarly observes that in the sixteenth century, it became an "etymological crux" that captured twinned commitments to both the recovery of already extant arguments and the creation of novel ideas. Crawforth, *Etymology*, 2–3. Also see Sumillera, "Poetic Invention and Translation."

as central to its method, Sidney found in poetry a means of critiquing this dereliction of duty.

How did the rhetorical training of Elizabethan humanism prepare—or fail to prepare—poets for practicing invention? I approach this question by unpacking how Sidney's *The Defence of Poesy* and *Astrophil and Stella* together respond to an occasion for rhetorical argumentation that arose in 1579, in the form of Stephen Gosson's antipoetical treatise, *The Schoole of Abuse*. For reasons that remain unclear, Gosson, a reformed poet and playwright, dedicated the treatise to Sidney, perhaps unaware that the young nobleman had been experimenting with vernacular poetry as an outlet for his otherwise sidelined courtly talents.[12] Having already authored a masque for Queen Elizabeth I, Sidney had also begun composing the *Arcadia* to entertain his sister Mary while on leave from court.[13] It is as a result unsurprising that, as Edmund Spenser reported, Gosson was "for hys labor scorned" by the young courtier.[14] What *is* surprising, however, is that in *Defence*, Sidney would concede many arguments made by antipoetical writers like Gosson. He admits that poetry could be and often is a "nurse of abuse" (234) that "abuseth men's wit, training it to wanton sinfulness and lustful love" (236), and also that much of the poetry written by his countrymen was frivolously undertaken by "base men with servile wits" (241). Such concessions are representative of a pattern that readers have frequently noticed, wherein *Defence* struggles to develop a firm ground from which to cogently counterpoint antipoetical claims.[15] Catherine Bates characterizes it as "a text terminally in conflict with itself" because an "unofficial voice" continually undermines Sidney's "official" arguments for poetry's profitability, many of which are themselves derivative and drawn from classical and continental writers.[16] Through the "hesitancies and qualifications" it injects into the prose, this unofficial voice exposes the speaker of *Defence* as a

---

12. For more on Gosson and Sidney, see Duncan-Jones, *Sir Philip Sidney*, 221.

13. For Sidney's biography, I have relied on Duncan-Jones, *Sir Philip Sidney*; Osborn, *Young Philip Sidney*; Rudenstine, *Sidney's Poetic Development*; and Berry, *Making of Sir Philip Sidney*.

14. Spenser also commented, to confirm his own apprehensions about patronage and publication, "Such follie is it not to regarde aforehande the inclination and qualitie of him to whome we dedicate oure Bookes." Spenser's letter to Harvey can be found in Smith, *Elizabethan Critical Essays*, 1:87–92; quote on 89.

15. See below for more discussion of Levao, "Sidney's Feigned Apology." Also see Helgerson, *Elizabethan Prodigals*, 128.

16. Bates, *On Not Defending Poetry*, 141.

"self-doubting, self-contradicting, and self-divided creature."[17] Gosson may have impudently brought a debate to Sidney's doorstep, but it seems as if Sidney dismissed Gosson and staged the debate entirely with himself.

Recognizing his situation as a moment of conflict between competing disputants—those who would condemn poetry for its sins and those who might defend it for its virtues—Sidney would have regarded the occasion as an incitement to invention. In disputes involving an accuser and a defender (known to rhetoricians as forensic or judicial arguments), invention proceeded by the disputants first deciding on the exact point of contention, a point known to rhetoricians as *stasis*: the "standstill" or "halt" between conflicting accounts.[18] Variously rendered as *status*, *basis*, or *constitutio*, stasis named the place from which each disputant would construct his argument. Stasis theory was first outlined in ancient Greece by Hermagoras of Temnos and formalized as a procession of questions: "Is there a problem? What is the essence of the problem? How serious is the problem from the standpoint of its non-essential attributes and attendant circumstances? Should there be any formal action on the problem (and, if so, should it be undertaken by this particular agency)?"[19]

Once the disputants identified the specific question about which they disagreed, they would have a warrant for a specific line of questioning. These lines were housed under the "topics" of invention: for example, if the accusation is that a theft has occurred and the disputants disagree on whether or not the actions constituted theft (a stasis rooted in definition), the topics direct them to inquire into the legal definition of theft before comparing the specific circumstances of the crime to that definition.[20] Derived from the Greek *topoi* limned by Aristotle—the "turns" or "places" from which an argument might proceed—the topics of invention corresponded, Corbett suggests, to "how the human mind thinks" by abstracting, generalizing, and classifying the supposedly

---

17. Bates, *On Not Defending Poetry*, 9–10.
18. On the meaning and etymology of "stasis," see Dieter, "Stasis." As Peter Mack notes, none of the textbooks used in Tudor grammar schools addressed stasis at length, despite it being a major concern of classical rhetoricians. See Mack, *Elizabethan Rhetoric*, 40.
19. See Nadeau, "Classical Systems," 53. As Laura Wilder summarizes, modern rhetoricians have added one question to this system and affiliated the questions with five stasis "issues": existence (Did it happen?), definition (What is it?), evaluation (Is it good?), cause (What caused it?), and proposal (What should be done about it?). Wilder, *Rhetorical Strategies*, 17.
20. For Thomas Wilson's account of stasis, or "state," see Wilson, *Arte of Rhetorique*, 48v.

natural "tendencies" of cognition.²¹ As rhetorical pedagogy became increasingly formalized over centuries, the *topoi* became the content-based Latin *loci*, which later became "the inspiration for the so-called commonplace books that Renaissance schoolboys were later required to keep."²² Janice Lauer explains that once the "topics" became textually "bound" in Latin textbooks like the widely used *Rhetorica ad Herennium*, they began "losing their power as a set of investigative heuristics for the process of knowledge creation or inquiry" and "became a search for material to develop parts of the text."²³ The kind of composition we saw Gnomaticus and the pious younger brothers practice in the previous chapter, which consisted of compiling and reciting authoritative platitudes, can be traced to this method of invention via textual accretion.

When accosted with the assertion that poetry was guilty of crimes and should be banished, then, Sidney's first problem was that the forensic arguments against it were formidable. Poetry did, he had to concede, contribute to idleness, lasciviousness, and indecorousness. Moreover, authorities as revered as Plato had "banished [poets] out of his commonwealth," and such a contention would ostensibly leave any defender of poetry without much recourse for proving its fundamental honorableness. His response to this latter argument points out that "of all philosophers" Plato was "the most poetical," and that philosophy picks its "true points of knowledge" out of the "sweet mysteries of poetry" (238). The primary difference, he suggests, between poetry and philosophy is that the philosophers put knowledge "in method" and make of it "a school-art" whereas poets have opted to "teach by a divine delightfulness" (238) rather than any set method. What might seem like a "truant," Sidney figures as a prophet.

This move of distinguishing poetry via its resistance to "school-arts" reverberates throughout *Defence*, and is anticipated by the very first

---

21. Corbett, *Classical Rhetoric*, 95.

22. As Corbett puts it, "The Latin *loci communes* . . . were set pieces, stored away for future incorporation into a speech when the need for such arguments presented itself." Corbett, "The *Topoi* Revisited," 48.

23. Lauer, *Invention*, 23. As Wilder observes (citing Carolyn Miller), for Aristotle it was the special topics (*idioi topoi*), as opposed to the common topics (*koinoi topoi*), that enabled rhetoric to serve as a "compromise between the promise of rhetoric as a broadly applicable and teachable subject, for which complexity must be reducible to useful precepts, and rhetoric as a field of research, where careful observation of discourse practices reveals the messiness of specificity and diversity." See Wilder, *Rhetorical Strategies*, 17–18; and Miller, "Aristotle's 'Special Topics.'"

move Sidney makes in his argument. Called to defend poetry against rhetorical charges of abuse by rhetoricians, he veers into a parody of rhetorical argumentation itself: his speaker describes the florid expostulations about horsemanship by one "John Pietro Pugliano" as threatening to persuade the poet to have "wished [himself] a horse" (212). In this jocular mood, Sidney offers the context that he had been "provoked to say something unto you in the defense of that my unelected vocation" and modestly offers to make a "pitiful defense of poor poetry" by compiling "some more available proofs" (212). Poetry would need someone to make a rhetorical defense of it, he observes, because a rhetorician "is by no man barred of his deserved credit" while a poet "has had even the names of philosophers used to the defacing of it" (212). He makes clear that he is assuming the role of defense attorney despite knowing that taking up this case means beginning at a disadvantage. As a result, part of the defense Sidney ends up making is an argument against the methods of rhetorical argumentation.

Like philosophers, Sidney suggests, rhetoricians argue by "considering what in nature will soonest prove and persuade" and so "thereon give artificial rules, which still are compassed within the circle of a question, according to the proposed matter" (216). The "circle of a question" binds the disputants to contend only through established protocols of proof and evidence; thus, Sidney invokes stasis theory, which was designed specifically to light on a single question around which disputants might frame their arguments. Proceeding from this question, debaters may point to concrete evidence or, worse, to commonplace answers, which, Sidney suggests, restricts their ability to imagine new answers or even new questions. Poets need not limit their compositions to disputes, evidence, or "artificial rules"; they are not circumscribed, it seems, by anything. They are the prophets, and the tricksters, who may challenge evidence's claims to compel a reconsideration of opinion. Thus, Sidney sets his poet loose, "lifted up with the vigor of his own invention" to a place from whence he might "grow in effect another nature: in making things either better then nature bringeth fort, or, quite anew, forms such as never were in nature" (216). This poet "nothing affirms, and therefore never lies," and so "never makes any circles about your imagination, to conjure you to believe for true what he writes" (235). Concomitantly, this poet does not cite "authorities of other histories" and does not labor "to tell you what is or is not, but what should or should not be" (235). This critique of resorting to commonplaces or precedents in practicing invention is corroborated by

Sidney's critique of many of his poetic contemporaries: he complains that many of them, writing "under the banner of unresistable love," were formulaically issuing verses: "[S]o coldly they apply fiery speeches, as men that had rather read lovers' writings [and] caught up certain swelling phrases" (246). The worst kind of poetry clumsily compiles stale figures; it is the license to fabricate new inventions out of whole cloth, Sidney stresses, that makes poets uniquely capable of persuading otherwise unwilling minds to noble aspirations.

Despite granting the "divine gift" of poetry only to an elect few, Sidney recognizes that "as the fertilest ground must be manured, so must the highest-flying wit have a Daedalus to guide him."[24] He knew that too many English poets believed themselves to be divinely inspired and that, left unchecked, these "paper-blurrers" (241) would reduce Elizabethan literary culture to an artless heap. Even those with innate talent might make a mess of their gifts, and so would need a teacher to set them straight:

> That Daedalus, they say, both in this and in other, hath three wings to bear itself up into the air of due commendation: that is, art, imitation, and exercise. But these, neither artificial rules nor imitative patterns, we much cumber ourselves withal. Exercise indeed we do, but that very fore-backwardly: for where we should exercise to know, we exercise as having known; and so is our brain delivered of much matter which never was begotten by knowledge. For there being two principal parts, matter to be expressed by words and words to express the matter, in neither we use art or imitation rightly. (242)

Lacking any other pedagogical framework, what Sidney proposes as a model for proceeding "rightly" looks almost exactly like the study of rhetorical composition he elsewhere appears to satirize. He alludes here to the widely used grammar school textbook *Rhetorica ad Herennium*, which recommends that students engage in "Theory, Imitation, and Practice" (arte, imitatione, exercitatione).[25] By reaffirming these foun-

---

24. This position, like many in the treatise, derives from Horace: "I do not see of what avail is either study, when not enriched by Nature's vein, or native wit, if untrained." Horace, *Satires. Epistles. The Art of Poetry*, 485 (lines 409–10).

25. "By theory is meant a set of rules that provide a definite method and system of speaking. Imitation stimulates us to attain, in accordance with a studied method, the effectiveness of certain models in speaking. Practice is assiduous exercise and experience in speaking." [Cicero], *Rhetorica ad Herennium*, 6–9 (1.ii.3).

dational rhetorical principles, Sidney implies that English poets have been engaging in "exercise" without concern for either art or imitation. Even when imitation is undertaken, they do it without "poetical sinews" (243), so that if someone put their verses "in prose, and then ask the meaning," it would appear only as a "confused mass of words" (243) instead of coherent ideas marshaled into an "assured rank" (242).[26] Observing that all poets need something to write *about* ("matter to be expressed by words") and a way to go about writing it ("words to express the matter"), with the advice above Sidney appears to emphasize only the words and to sidestep the matter.

Where does Sidney think poets get the matter they might choose to write about? He resists offering a concrete answer, locating the poet's practice within "the zodiac of his own wits" and therefore "not enclosed within the narrow warrant of [nature's] gifts" (216). His conviction in poets' freedom to practice their own inventions leads him to set aside "divine poets" like the biblical David as well as "philosophical" poets, who are "wrapped within the fold of the proposed subject" and so do not consider "the course of [their] own invention" (218).[27] These poets do not have to come up with what to write about, because either divine inspiration or a proposed theme supplies it to them. Sidney's primary concern for the majority of *Defence*, he explains, is the third sort of poet, the "right poets" who invent on their own and have "no law but wit" (218). Such poets may "borrow nothing of what is, hath bin, or shall be," he says, "but range, only reined with learned discretion, into the divine consideration of what may be and should be" (218). Wherever poets get their ideas, he insists, it is not rooted in the past, or the factual, or even the plausible. Poetic imagination, and its capacity for constructing alternate futures and novel possibilities, emerges as essential to the aspect of rhetorical invention that could not be systematized, reduced to a method, and taught.

Decoupling poesy from the constraints of method exposes Sidney's argument for radical license to charges that poetry is uncontrolled and dangerous.[28] How does one practice a "divine consideration of what

---

26. Sidney's poets come to resemble exemplary rhetoricians such as those envisioned by Crassus at the start of Cicero's *De oratore*, who possess "a knowledge of very many matters" because without this, "oratory is but an empty and ridiculous swirl of verbiage." Cicero, *On the Orator*, 13–15 (1.v.17).

27. Sidney appears to derive this from Scaliger; see Scaliger, *Select Translations*, 2.

28. Gosson, for example, characterizes the poets as akin to the "wanton whelpe" that "leaveth the game to runne riot." Gosson, *School of Abuse*, 9.

may be and should be" without falling into presumptions that, if left unchecked, could lead poets to blasphemous, dangerous, frivolous, vain, or simply wrong ideas? To account for this, Sidney's framing introduces a crucial caveat—"reined with learned discretion"—that yokes dreaming up "what may be" to the moral, rational, and ideological consideration of what "should be." What "may" be is an unfettered imaginative exercise, but what "should" be entails persuasion, calculation, and ethical responsibility. The right use of poesy enlists both of these because it depends on propagation of a virtuous idea among those who may not already be receptive to it. When Sidney attributes the poetic skill to "that *idea*, or fore conceit of the work, and not in the work itself," he makes clear that this idea cannot remain in the realm of the "wholly imaginative" (216). It is fully achieved by the "excellency" of its articulation, an excellency that hinges on readers seeing what the poet sees, and what the poet sees must necessarily be *better* than what already exists in nature—a "golden world" to nature's "brazen" one (216). The poetic "idea" must in turn inspire readers to embrace that better version of reality as a prompt to future action. A poet thus works "not only to make a Cyrus, which had been but a particular excellency as nature might have done, but to bestow a Cyrus upon the world to make many Cyruses, if they will learn aright, why and how that maker made him" (216-17). The right poet's excellency rests on a convergence of workmanship and readerly attentiveness; poetic invention, as Sidney describes it, can be perfected only if the world of readers "learn aright" why the poem was made in the way that it was.[29]

This tacit emphasis on the audience's response clarifies that for Sidney, poetic invention is exactly as Karen Burke Lefevre describes it: a "social act."[30] As noted above, rhetorical invention via stasis emerged as a manner of resolving disputes, and to proceed it required the disputants to first agree about the question under dispute. The accuser might be trying to argue that poetry is a "nurse of abuse" while the defendant might be arguing that poetry's social benefits outweigh its costs. These disputants would end up talking past one another, because

---

29. According to Brady Wagoner, Sidney anticipates accounts of creativity in social psychology as "present in both the internalization or subjectification phase, where different objects and meanings freely coalesce and combine, as well as the externalization and objectification phase, where subjective imagery must be given order and structure to be communicated to others." See Wagoner, "Creativity as Symbolic Transformation," 26. Also see Runco, "'Big C, Little c' Creativity."

30. LeFevre, *Invention as a Social Act*.

they would be arguing from different premises and conjuring arguments in support of their positions without really acknowledging the other side. If invention is conceived not as an argument made in isolation, in preparation for a confrontation, but rather as the product *of* the confrontation, it comes closer to Lefevre's "dynamic view of invention as the creation of something new—new for the individuals or groups who have not previously thought of it, or new in that it has not previously been conceived of by anyone at all."[31]

As Thomas O. Sloane observes, the teaching of "topical" invention has long been prioritized over the crucial "controversial" dimension of stasis, in which "debate is the process that defines rhetorical thought" and "pro and con reasoning is the context within which the topics are to be used."[32] By forcing orators to imagine themselves as nimbly responsive to the best arguments that might be wielded against them, invention via stasis was meant to be an "analytical process."[33] The most practical manifestation of this analytical process was arguing *in utramque partem*, or what in Greek was known as the use of *dissoi logoi*. While arguing on both sides was fundamental to the stasis-theory-inspired humanist classroom, the use of *dissoi logoi* began prior to the advent of stasis.[34] While stasis theory afforded both disputants instructions for preparing their arguments according to logical topics and commonplaces, *dissoi logoi* compelled orators to respond in real time to one another's claims. As stasis became more formalized and embedded in textual study, the role of interlocutors was not to dynamically develop a new understanding, but to serve as opponents who might be defeated.

The *dissoi logoi* emerged because, according to Phillip Sipiora, the sophists held that "things exist in an uncertain, ultimately unknowable way" and so "we are compelled to maintain contrary perceptions, interpretations, and arguments."[35] In response to this relativism, they championed a sort of thinking that demanded "a multiple awareness, an awareness at once cognizant of its own position *and* those positions opposing it," as John Poulakos explains.[36] As part of this awareness, Poulakos continues, the sophists privileged the ability to "capitalize on opportune rhetorical moments," or *kairoi*. From this sense of "the right time" emerged

---

31. LeFevre, *Invention as a Social Act*, 7.
32. Sloane, *On the Contrary*, 38.
33. Sloane, *On the Contrary*, 40.
34. Carter, "Stasis and Kairos," 103. See also Stephenson, *Forecasting Opportunity*, 6.
35. Sipiora, "Introduction," 4.
36. Poulakos, "Logic of Greek Sophistry," 17.

the concept of *kairos*, which names "one's sense of timing and the will to invent"—a mode of invention rooted not in precedent but in anticipation.[37] Over time, Sipiora notes, kairos has become affiliated with a host of other concepts, such as "'symmetry,' 'propriety,' 'occasion,' 'due measure,' 'fitness,' 'tact,' 'decorum,' 'convenience,' 'proportion,' 'fruit,' 'profit,' and 'wise moderation.'"[38] Kairos assumes that being attuned to the possibility of antithesis at all times promotes adaptation, improvisation, and a consciousness of one's ethical commitments.[39] It was kairos that led rhetoricians to insist on *exercitatio* as a component of rhetorical training, to account for the fact that, as Sipiora puts it, "rhetorical theory cannot cast its net over the unforeseen, unpredictable, and uncontrollable moments."[40] If, on the one hand, kairos names principles of appropriateness and proportion and helps orators "fit" their words to the present moment, on the other hand, according to Carolyn R. Miller, it also names "not the expected but its opposite: the uniquely timely, the spontaneous, the radically particular" and so "resists method, making rhetoric unteachable."[41] Rather than being attributable to forces beyond cognition, however, kairos emphasizes the rhetor's capacities for observation, speculation, and attunement; rather than being inspired by the gods, moreover, kairos is animated by discursive exchange.[42]

---

37. Poulakos, "Logic of Greek Sophistry," 18.
38. Sipiora, "Introduction," 1. For more on kairos, see Kinneavy, "Kairos." The essays in Sipiora and James S. Baumlin's edited volume, *Rhetoric and Kairos: Essays in History, Theory, and Praxis*, also offer a broad and crucial introduction to the concept. Reconsiderations of the concept for Renaissance studies, and especially Shakespeare studies, have been emerging; see Paul, "Use of Kairos"; Beehler, "'Confederate Season'"; Baker, "Hamlet and the Kairos"; Hunt, "Ripeness of Time"; and Witmore, *Culture of Accidents*, 79.
39. As Paul Tillich observes, kairos connects the timeless ideality of customs and laws, or *logos*, with the immediacy of present circumstances. Tillich, *Interpretation of History*, 129-51.
40. Sipiora, "Introduction," 6. Debra Hawhee explains that "*kairos* emerges often in Greek literature and philosophy in the context of athletic and rhetorical encounters—in short, *kairos* is the time of the *agōn*, the immediacy that calls for quick, cunning response." In its quick, deftly tuned responsiveness to live circumstance, kairos recalls its original affiliations with athletics and embodiment, pointing to the "opening" at which the skillful archer might place a well-timed and aimed shot—"the *kair-* root is used adjectivally (*kairios*) to indicate a critical, fatal spot on the body." Hawhee, *Bodily Arts*, 12, 71.
41. Miller, foreword, xii-xiii.
42. Responding to Dale Sullivan's account of a "kairos of inspiration" as a kind of nonrational "flow" state connected with "romantic concepts of genius or vitalism or with divine madness," Hawhee sees "kairotic inspiration" as more materially grounded and embodied. It is akin, she says, to "the act of breathing in, or a commingling of momentary elements" wherein "the rhetor opens him or herself up to the immediate situation." See Sullivan, "Rhetoric of Belief," 319; Hawhee, *Bodily Arts*, 71. For Lisbeth Lipari, Hawhee's account of kairos links it fundamentally to a posture of *listening*. Lipari, "Ethics, Kairos, and Akroasis," 89.

Together, stasis and kairos account for how, when speakers compose utterances, they inhabit a particular circumstance and regard the specific audience before them while also drawing on learned techniques to isolate and decide on what to say. Kairos leaves speakers open to the contingency and density of the present; stasis arms them with the linguistic resources and logical habits of mind they already possess. The collaboration of kairos and stasis describes the operations of an attention that resists lapsing into either preprogrammed routines or irrelevant trivialities—an invention that ranges while also remaining reined by learned discretion. Their collaboration also recognizes that the resources of the past may not be adequate for the future, that the practice of invention must proceed dialectically, probing after new knowledge by oscillating between different vantages. Thus, while the humanist schoolroom prioritized modes of composition relying on argument via stasis, the kairotic dimensions of invention, which could not be taught, found little explicit pedagogical representation. Schoolboys might have waged disputes, but, bound as they were to commonplaces and to the authority of the adjudicating schoolmaster, they were not necessarily taught how to consider their rivals' arguments as prompts to improve upon their own.

In making the responsibility of "right poets" a capacity not only to "deliver forth" ideas excellently but to have those ideas propagate in the minds of readers, Sidney charges them with anticipating and counteracting readers' resistance to their words. Poetry differs from other human sciences, he explains, because the poet "doth not only show the way, but giveth so sweet a prospect into the way, as will entice any man to enter it" (226). This high bar challenges poetry with being rhetorically successful, persuasive, and tempting—and makes a keen attentiveness to one's audience and occasion part of the challenge. In this light, poetic invention becomes a practice of continual self-consciousness, and Sidney's *Defence* ultimately suggests that the cultivation of such self-consciousness requires a reversal of the traditional functions of audience and author. Rather than criticizing and condemning, the readership he imagines for poetry becomes more generous, more receptive, more permissive—he imagines a readership that will "learn aright" why and how the poet had made the poem. At the same time, the right poets he imagines set aside their narcissism and instead become more rigorous and more critical of themselves. To promote this vision, he appeals to his countrymen to be less harsh toward their peers' poetic offspring: he wants England to cease being "so hard a stepmother to poets" (240) and to stop offering only "a hard welcome" (241) to poetic endeavor. He also simultaneously cautions that "they that delight in poesy itself"—that is, aspiring poets—"should seek to know what they do and how they do" (242). Poets, Sidney advises, must become severe critics of their own work and must "look themselves in the unflattering glass of reason" (242) before assuming any value in their verses.

In *Astrophil and Stella*, the scene of writing becomes a perpetual struggle between the poet's need to express and a fear of what others will think. Sidney knew that poetry had a dangerous edge, but he also felt that poesy's virtues derived from the poet's ability to set virtue and reason aside, at least temporarily. Though he cautioned, "[W]ith a sword thou may'st kill thy father," he also conceded, "and with a sword thou may'st defend thy prince and country" (237). A newly conceived invention may become a benefit to society, but it may also threaten the very foundations of society. Analogizing poetry to such "martial sports" (*A&S*, 173-74, 53.1), *Astrophil and Stella*'s scenes of writing are preoccupied with poets at once presuming a powerful capacity to "conceive" and internalizing how this presumption exposes them to dangerous error. Sometimes Astrophil feels as if he has been struck by a flash of inspiration: "Stella behold, and then begin to endite" (*A&S*, 158-59, 15.14). Other times, he feels constrained, bottled up, and bound by fears of public humiliation: "My youth doth waste, my knowledge brings forth toys" (*A&S*, 159-60, 18.9). Other times still, he feels simultaneously confident and impotent: "My words, I know, do well set forth my mind; / My mind bemoans his sense of inward smart; / Such smart may pity claim of any heart; / Her heart (sweet heart) is of no tiger's kind: / And yet she hears, yet I no pity find, / But more I cry, less grace she doth impart" (*A&S*, 170, 44.1-6). Taken as a whole, the sequence does not allow Astrophil to settle on a poetic method.[43] Sonnet 34 addresses these concerns directly, throwing Astrophil into the conflict between an appeal for grace and the disgracefulness of poetry itself:

> Come let me write, "And to what end?" To ease
>   A burdened heart. "How can words ease, which are
>   The glasses of thy daily vexing care?"
> Oft cruel fights well pictured forth do please.

---

43. "Having opened on a poem that focuses on failure," as Heather Dubrow puts it, Sidney "proceeds later in the sequence to present his own verse as a source and symbol of both his power ... and his powerlessness." Dubrow, *Echoes of Desire*, 107.

"Art not ashamed to publish thy disease?"
   Nay, that may breed my fame, it is so rare.
"But will not wise men think thy words fond ware?"
Then be they close, and so none shall displease.
"What idler thing, then speak and not be hard?"
What harder thing then smart, and not to speak?
Peace, foolish wit, with wit my wit is marred.
Thus write I while I doubt to write, and wreak
   My harms on ink's poor loss; perhaps some find
   Stella's great powers, that so confuse my mind.
                              (A&S, 166, 34.1–14)

The cautionary admonitions of mentors and teachers—Sidney's father, his mentor Hubert Languet, even critics like Gosson—reverberate in Astrophil's mind and leave him discomposed. Poetry, they warn, is useless, idle, profitless.[44] He first replies to this inquisition by repeating the image of an irrepressible internal urge. To this, the voice in his head rejoins that his words are simply the "glasses of thy daily vexing care." This both ventriloquizes the disdain of those who saw love poetry as narcissistic and affirms the idea that language is an impersonal system of articulation. To these contentions, Astrophil has another answer ready, remarking that drama, tension, and conflict—in this case, of the lover wrestling with passions—might still please audiences. This retort, one akin to the one in Sidney's *Defence* that "those things which in themselves are horrible, as cruel battles, unnatural monsters, are made in poetical imitation delightful" (227), recasts Astrophil's writing as a public rather than a private affair.[45] Splitting the poet between self-therapy and the services he might render to the world, these lines redouble Astrophil's conflicted energies. Expression may be profitable to him but profitless to the world. If his audience is the public, his censorious and rational conscience shifts its assault to argue that "wise men" will criticize it. When Astrophil replies that he will not publish

---

44. Edward Berry recounts how Languet inculcated in young Sidney the ideal values of the humanist program: "duty to parents, service to state, a thrifty use of time, a preference for moral philosophy and history over poetry, truth to one's self." Berry, *Making of Sir Philip Sidney*, 31.

45. This poem sees Astrophil "born to self-division, to alienation from himself," writes Gavin Alexander. "[T]he comfort of self-expression . . . has slipped into the pleasure of reading," raising the question of to whom the "end" of writing poetry is ultimately directed. Alexander, *Writing after Sidney*, 18.

them, his interlocutor again refutes him with the pointlessness of writing for no one.

The shame involved in writing, Elspeth Probyn suggests, makes writing *about* shame—as Sidney does throughout much of *Astrophil and Stella*—an inevitably self-reflexive process.[46] Shame arises "from a collision of bodies, ideas, history, and place," and because of this, writing about shame while feeling shame about writing means documenting the collision from amid the wreckage. *Astrophil and Stella* begins with a poet "loving in truth" and hoping to equal this love in words, but by the fifth line, when he begins to seek "fit words," it becomes clear that the subject of the sonnet is not the poet's love but his own tormented writing process.[47] Probyn suggests that writing about shame makes the writer's body a "battleground where ideas and experiences collide," but that such collisions "sometimes . . . produce new visions of life"; Sidney, throughout *Astrophil and Stella*, makes these collisions the domain of poetic invention.[48] "The blush of having failed to connect with readers," Probyn argues, "should compel any writer to return to the page with renewed desire to do better—to get better—at this task of communicating that some of us take on."[49] Sidney's defense of poesy, we might say, places a lot of trust in that "should." "[P]oesy must not be drawn by the ears," he cautions, "it must be gently led, or rather it must lead" (242). Doing the work of poesy will improve one's poetic labors; the resistance offered during invention, like the friction of an argument, will make one's own invention stronger.

Promoting self-consciousness while also offering specific instructions about what and what not to do leads Sidney to contradict himself throughout *Defence*. The qualifications and hesitations that infuse this text—evident even in the final quotation of the previous paragraph—partly reflect the limitations of invention through writing—that is, when one may argue only with oneself. Sidney debates with himself as to whether poets are divinely inspired or in need of concrete pedagogical guidance, but on the page, he can only ever offer his own voice. How can one make a case for poetry, *Defence* ultimately seems to suggest, without availing oneself of what poetry itself solicits from readers: their willingness to "learn aright" why this case was made and how? In an

---

46. Probyn, *Blush*, 149.
47. Probyn, *Blush*, 147.
48. Probyn, *Blush*, 162.
49. Probyn, *Blush*, 162.

important reading, Ronald Levao sees its author playing "not only the rhetorician but the poet as well" in order to demonstrate rather than decide on the dilemmas that characterize defending poetry. Noting how Sidney's discussion of poetic inspiration appears "deliberately tangled and ambivalent," for example, Levao argues that Sidney "presents us with 'something for everyone,' aiming different claims at different readers, hoping that all will find something to serve as 'an imaginative ground-plot of a profitable invention.'"[50] *Defence* thus performs its own poetic commitment to neither affirming nor denying anything; it presents readers with conflicting points that serve only to remind them of the dilemma of making a formal argument to defend something that evades formalization.

Picking up on the same strain of polyvocality, Catherine Bates identifies in the texture of Sidney's prose "a resistance or irresolution of some kind" and through them discerns Sidney "groping towards a newer, more radical conception of poetry that is, for all that, very far from fully formed."[51] As Bates puts it, "The real argument of the *Defence*—what Sidney wants to say but dare not, or dare not openly, or has not yet found a means to say—is, in this text, still inhibited, still held back. The plea for a non-idealist, non-profitable, non-bankable model of poetry is still unsayable, and remains the unspoken, unofficial argument that has to be deduced, inferred, from the traces it leaves symptomatically on the page."[52] Readers must learn to read what Sidney cannot say, Bates suggests. They must invent their own argument for poetry based not on what he has already said, but on what he appears to have tried, and even failed, to say.

Without anyone with whom to converse, solitary writers must rely on their own inventive resources. The density of potential arguments against the inscription of another word—the nagging echo, "and to what end?"—is often enough to make such writers outwit themselves into not writing. As Mike Rose points out, many student writers experience such blockage because "(1) the rules by which they guide their composing processes are rigid, inappropriately invoked, or incorrect;

---

50. Levao, "Sidney's Feigned Apology," 230. Citing claims like the "Platonic-Augustinian argument" that locates poets' access to divine ideality within notions of inspired genius as being made by affected voices, Levao argues that Sidney's actual position is that "inspiration is not the *cause* of the poet's conceit but the *effect* that the conceit has on the reader." Levao, "Sidney's Feigned Apology," 224.
51. Bates, *On Not Defending Poetry*, 9–10.
52. Bates, *On Not Defending Poetry*, 141.

(2) their assumptions about composing are misleading; (3) they edit too early in the composing process; (4) they lack appropriate planning and discourse strategies or rely on inflexible or inappropriate strategies; (5) they invoke conflicting rules, assumptions, plans, and strategies; and (6) they evaluate their writing with inappropriate criteria or criteria that are inadequately understood."[53] Writer's block manifests as a form of self-contradiction—literally, speaking against oneself to the point of total silencing.[54] In a psychological study, Jerome L. Singer and Michael V. Barrios observe that blocked writers "present themselves as worried, self-doubting, and highly constrained by rigid rules and standards for their work." They "are less likely than nonblocked writers to report an attachment to their current professional roles and relationships," "report lower levels of ambition," and "also report more active disdain and dissatisfaction with colleagues and available role models." Moreover, they "present an impression of holding on tightly to the uncomfortable status quo while simultaneously complaining about it."[55]

Compare these accounts of writer's block with Edward Berry's description of the conflicts that determined Philip Sidney's upbringing: "[B]etween the humanistic idealization of public service and the actuality of life at court; between the Spartan study of Xenophon at Shrewsbury School and attendance on the queen in full regalia at Oxford; between the moral earnestness of Henry Sidney and the moral ambiguity of the earl of Leicester; between an educational system that valued poetry in the teaching, as a source of moral education, but dispraised it in the making, as a mere recreation for ladies."[56] If he was ever *actually* blocked, Sidney endured and came to write about it. Seeing him in this light illuminates how even writing that seems inspired or produced by innate talent may be traced to experiences of dissatisfaction and hesitation. Throughout the sequence, but especially in Sonnet 34, Sidney depicts

---

53. Rose, *Writer's Block*, 19.
54. Zachary Leader suggests that these contradictions far exceed the cognitive discipline encouraged by teachers: "[B]locked writers fail to negotiate rival or opposing claims, variously associated with pairings such as inner and outer, primary and secondary processes, emergence and embeddedness, independence and incorporation, inspiration and elaboration, defusion and merger, subject and object, written and oral, 'male' and 'female.'" Leader, *Writer's Block*, 251.
55. Singer and Barrios, "Writer's Block," 225, 229. Also see Birk, "Sounds of Silence," 14; and, for an account closer to home for academic writers, Crosby, "Writer's Block."
56. Berry, *Making of Sir Philip Sidney*, 24–25. Also see Rudenstine, *Sidney's Poetic Development*, 273.

the poet writing while he doubts to write, hoping that perhaps readers might at least see something of his doubtfulness.

Kissing Fire

As the primary concern of Sonnet 34 is what Astrophil should do rather than what he has done, the argument it provokes requires deliberative—rather than forensic—invention. Like forensic oratory, deliberative rhetoric weighs questions on two sides; as Quentin Skinner explains, it aims to "persuade someone to act or refrain from acting in some particular way."[57] According to Aristotle, deliberative oratory is "nobler" than forensic oratory because it is "worthier of a statesman" who has to address a general assembly about plans for the future. Though he remarks that "the method of public [deliberative] and forensic rhetoric is the same," neither he nor any other classical rhetorician appears to have systematized deliberative rhetoric in the way Hermagoras and his followers developed stasis theory for forensic arguments.[58] *Rhetorica ad Herennium* enlists deliberative rhetoric for when "the question concerns a choice between two courses of action, or of the kind in which a choice among several is considered." For one example, it entertains the question, "Does it seem better to destroy Carthage, or to leave her standing?"[59] To make such a case, the orator might take his advantage by appealing to either possibility, expediency or benefit, or honor.[60] In Sonnet 34, as Astrophil rebuffs the claims made by his conscience and as his conscience shifts the grounds of its own assault, it becomes clear that the polity that resides within him never reaches any kind of deliberative stasis. Whether the ends to which Astrophil hopes to write poetry are possible to achieve, whether they are expedient or beneficial, and

---

57. Skinner, *Forensic Shakespeare*, 20.
58. Aristotle, *Art of Rhetoric*, 7 (1.1.10). Such an oversight led Yameng Liu to point out that stasis was in itself not all that important to Aristotle's theory of rhetoric because "deliberative speech does not necessarily contain 'a conflict of opinion.'" Liu, "Aristotle," 57.
59. [Cicero], *Rhetorica ad Herennium*, 159 (III.ii,2).
60. Building on examples like this, Robert Shenk suggests that there was a "rough consensus upon a deliberative counterpart to traditional stasis" among classical rhetoricians, a consensus that coalesced around what Shenk calls a "forestasis." The forestasis would essentially consist of three questions: "Is it possible?" "Is it expedient, or beneficial?" and "Is it honorable, or just?" Shenk, "Deliberative Stasis," 195. For Aristotle and other ancient rhetoricians, however, any generalized systematization for deliberation would threaten to restrict the truly expansive reach of deliberative rhetoric, because in Aristotle's framing, the rhetoric's purpose "is not so much to persuade, as to find out in each case the existing means of persuasion." Aristotle, *Art of Rhetoric*, 13 (1.1.14).

whether they are honorable all remain frustratingly open questions. As a result, he casts a hope out to a future audience that may learn to read him aright: "perhaps some find / Stella's great powers, that so confuse my mind." The best his deliberation can offer is a rendering of his complexity and confusion—a rendering encapsulated in Astrophil's "perhaps."

When participants in a dispute do not listen to one another's arguments, all involved may become irritated with themselves, with one another, with the topic of conversation. Words either recede into silence or rise to the level of drowning one another out, as neither party gives up any ground. When this happens—"when interlocutors can find no mutually acceptable solution to the problem they have engaged"—the result, Stephen Yarbrough explains, betokens a disagreement about the problem itself and, with it, a disagreement about the merits of any further debate. Resolving this irritation and changing someone's mind requires that the participants maintain a baseline position of charity toward one another and reserve the ability to shift their own prevailing assumptions.[61] To decide what should be done in response to a problem, the concerned parties need to at least agree about the problem itself; otherwise the result will inevitably be an impasse. Jacques Derrida affiliates this impasse with *aporia*—a state of "nonpassage" that "appears to block our way or to separate us in the very place where *it would no longer be possible to constitute a problem*, a project, or a projection" (emphasis in the original).[62] Broadly speaking, aporia may be described as a systemic inconsistency; it is a site at which the commitments that inform thought or practice undermine themselves. For Aristotle, aporia names a logical knot that entangles "the divergent views which are held about the first principles" of an inquiry. These knots, because they arise from irreconcilable differences in the fundamental premises of an inquiry, provoke a "perplexity of the mind" like that of "people who do not know where they are going."[63]

Aporias are often the cruxes of Socratic dialogues, and in addition to indexing the real stakes of a discussion, they also precipitate experiences of frustration and aggravation in Socrates's interlocutors.[64] As

---

61. Yarbrough, "Deliberate Invention," 92.
62. Derrida, *Aporias*, 12.
63. Aristotle, *Metaphysics*, 97 (III.2).
64. In Plato's *Meno*, for example, Socrates drives Meno to "utter perplexity" when Meno perceives an aporia and feels his "soul and [his] tongue quite benumbed" and himself "at a loss." Plato, *Laches. Protagoras. Meno. Euthydemus*, 297.

an instigator of and a response to apparent contradictions, over time aporia also began to function as a *figure* of confusion, in addition to a condition of it, and was deployed as the performance of humility. In early modernity, George Puttenham would define it as "the Doubtful, [so] called . . . because often we will seem to caste perils, and make doubts of things when by a Plaine manner of speech we might affirm or deny them."[65] Upon encountering an aporia, or to make it seem as if an aporia existed, one might enlist the rhetorical figure of aporia to perform doubt.

The muddled relationship between rhetorical and philosophical irresolution, according to Jenny C. Mann, led deconstructionists like Derrida to identify aporia as "the site at which a text undermines its own philosophical structure by revealing the rhetorical nature of that structure."[66] Evoking the terminology of stasis by describing aporia as a failure to "constitute a problem," Derrida locates it in an instructive distinction, between justice and law: "Law (*droit*) is not justice. Law is the element of calculation, and it is just that there be law, but justice is incalculable, it requires us to calculate with the incalculable; and aporetic experiences are the experiences, as improbable as they are necessary, of justice, that is to say of moments in which the decision between just and unjust is never insured by a rule."[67] Laws, Derrida observes, "suppose the generality of a rule, a norm or a universal imperative," and therefore cannot directly engage with the radical particularity of justice, which "must always concern singularity, individuals, irreplaceable groups and lives, the other or myself *as* other, in a unique situation."[68] Echoing Sidney's advocacy for a poesy unconstrained by all manner of law and rule, Derrida locates the project of deconstruction as reckoning with the simultaneous impossibility and necessity of "calculat[ing] with the incalculable." Beyond naming a moment of knotted discourse, however, for Derrida aporia becomes a call to action—and, in a sense, the root of all ethical action. Its "undecidable" nature extends to the "experience of that which, though heterogenous, foreign to the order of the calculable and the rule, is still obliged . . . to give itself up to the impossible decision, while taking account of law and rules."[69] The crucial

---

65. Puttenham, *Art of English Poesy*, 311.
66. Mann, "Aporia."
67. Derrida, "Force of Law," 16.
68. Derrida, "Force of Law," 17.
69. Derrida, "Force of Law," 24.

contention here is that any "decision that didn't go through the ordeal of the undecidable would not be a free decision, it would only be the programmable application or unfolding of a calculable process."[70]

Sidney anticipates Derrida's account of ethical practice by distinguishing between the lawyer's enforcement of obedience and the poet's appeal to ideal virtues. The lawyer, he notes, "doth not endeavor to make men good, but that their evil hurt not others"; the poet, by contrast, seeks to "plant goodness even in the secretest cabinet of our souls" (221). By compelling readers to "learn aright," through the mysterious force of an imaginative idea's persuasiveness, the poet promotes a "purifying of wit" that may "lead and draw us to as high a perfection as our degenerate souls, made worse by their clayey lodgings, can be capable of" (219). Poetic knowledge is not one of the "serving sciences" that "have each a private end in themselves," Sidney insists; it stands "in the knowledge of man's self, in the ethic and politic consideration, with the end of well-doing and not well-knowing only" (219). The work of justice, Derrida implies, entails the work of poetic invention: "If I were content to apply a just rule, without a spirit of justice and without in some way inventing the rule and the example for each case, I might be protected by law (*droit*), my action corresponding to objective law, but I would not be just."[71] Sidney might add that he would not be a poet, either.

Confronting an aporia is easier said than done, and for poets such confrontations might most immediately resemble, as described above, experiences of writer's block. Deborah P. Britzman identifies writer's block as a "constellation of libidinal conflicts that bring to the fore matters of loyalty, affiliation, ideality, separation, and finding one's own way."[72] The writing process threatens to disperse the writer's sense of competence amid a sea of competing conflicts, making an aporia out of what first seemed like a self-willed opportunity. This discomfort, however, may itself become the platform from which the writer issues a new complaint: "Whether anxiety opts for the paragraph, sentence, or word, a story is being unwritten, and the writer can become interested in his or her aesthetic conflicts and, in writing, transform phantasy into a commentary on problems in the wider world."[73] Most commentaries

---

70. Derrida, "Force of Law," 24.
71. Derrida, "Force of Law," 17.
72. Britzman, *Psychoanalyst in the Classroom*, 112.
73. Britzman, *Psychoanalyst in the Classroom*, 109.

on modern writer's block conclude in this way, recognizing, as Zachary Leader does, that "blockage and breakthrough often go together."[74] Such a conclusion, however, leaves the hard work up to the struggling writer without any real guidance on how to proceed. One might become "interested" in one's "aesthetic conflicts," but where to go from there?

Sonnet 34, which ends with Astrophil writing while he doubts to write, appears to be a representation of such conflicts, but as the sequence develops, his relationship to aporia fluctuates. Nicholas Rescher suggests that aporias are exigencies that "constitute situations of *forced choice* among the alternative contentions" (emphasis in the original), and these choices may be understood as "a venture in cognitive damage control."[75] The resigned "perhaps" of Sonnet 34 reflects one strategy, but as Sonnet 50 demonstrates, this is not the only method of "cognitive damage control" Astrophil deploys:

> Stella, the fullness of my thoughts of thee
> Cannot be stayed within my panting breast,
> But they do swell and struggle forth of me,
> Till that in words thy figure be expressed.
>   And yet, as soon as they so formed be,
> According to my lord love's own behest,
> With sad eyes I their weak proportion see,
> To portrait that which in this world is best;
>   So that I cannot choose but write my mind,
> And cannot choose but put out what I write,
> While those poor babes their death in birth do find:
> And now my pen these lines had dashed quite,
>   But that they stopped his fury from the same,
>   Because their forefront bare sweet Stella's name.
>   (*A&S*, 172, 1–14)

Astrophil's thoughts of love "swell and struggle forth" to find expression and emerge as failures burdened with "weak proportion." A central category of Elizabethan aesthetic appraisal, "proportion" was prized by writers adapting classical training to vernacular poetics for both its relationship to social decorum and its technical delimitations of quantity

---

74. Leader, *Writer's Block*, 252.
75. Rescher, *Aporetics*, 4, 8.

and measure.⁷⁶ Sidney himself says that things "disproportioned to ourselves in nature" (245) provoke corrective laughter, and also distinguishes poetry from "words as they chanceably fall from the mouth" because true poetry involves "peising each syllable of each word by just proportion according to the dignity of the subject" (219). The weakness of Astrophil's lines thus marks his effort as laughable; in striving to "express" Stella's figure, he instead issues something radically unworthy both of her and of his own investments. Dramatizing a discordance between his desire to write and his execution—"I cannot choose but write my mind," he laments, before acknowledging that he "cannot choose but put out what I write"—he reanimates the tension with which the sonnet sequence opened. Whereas Sonnet 1 found Astrophil helpless in a pregnant pause until the intervention of his muse, however, Sonnet 34 ultimately threatens "death in birth," a dashing out of words via the expenditure of the same ink that constituted them. At the "now" of the twelfth line, Astrophil's quill abruptly hesitates—not to write, but to obliterate what he has written.

Sonnet 50 threatens the same self-silencing and confusion that threatened Sonnet 34, portraying an internal dispute worn lightly as a series of cascading conjunctions: five of its lines begin with "but," "and," or "so." Over the course of the sequence leading up to this point, Astrophil's internal conflicts, and his willingness to resolve them in pursuit of his own desire, had already begun to manifest. Sonnet 47 charts the transformation of similar self-addressed questions—"What, have I thus betrayed my liberty?" (*A&S*, 171, 47.1)—into a performance of self-admonishment in real time. "Virtue awake," Astrophil rouses himself, "I may, I must, I can, I will, I do / Leave following that, which it is gain to miss." He resolves to relinquish Stella, but immediately draws back his declaration: "Let her go. Soft, but here she comes" (*A&S*, 171, 47.9-12). At the end of Sonnet 50, however, such hesitations evaporate. Regarding his ability to write the poem's forefront word—*Stella*—as legitimizing the poem itself, Astrophil sees the almost stillborn "babes" rouse to defend themselves. Sonnet 19's assertion that his "very ink turns straight to Stella's name" here becomes literal, but in this case Astrophil does not see his labors as "vainly spent" (*A&S*, 160, 19.6-8). We might say that by founding its legitimacy in its "forefront" word, Sonnet 50 champions the virtues of *impulse*. Astrophil is

---

76. For more on the aesthetics of proportion, see Wiseman, "Poetics of the Natural."

not blocked—"stopped"—because he does not have ideas or doubts his skill; he tarries because his ideas do not look as he at first believed they ought to look, traced over as he had been by the stylistic imperatives of propriety and proportion. Taking a cue from Victoria Nelson's self-help guide to writer's block, we might understand the word "Stella" that Astrophil finds himself thoughtlessly inscribing in Sonnet 50 as an inner child escaping the repressions of "step-dame study." As Nelson puts it, "The bravest act a writer can perform is to take that tiny step forward, put down the wretched little word that pricks the balloon of inflated fantasies with its very mundanity, and then put down another word directly after it. This act marks the decision to be a *writer*."[77] Stella's name, and the poem it initiates, might be read as a breakthrough.

Whereas in the opening sonnet, Astrophil struggles to figure out how to show his love in verse before being told by his muse to look in his heart, in Sonnet 50 he finds himself nearly dismissing what his heart is telling him. His final decision is to let his heart's cry echo out. By Sonnet 74, he has not only embraced what his heart has to say, but now believes himself truly inspired:

> I never drank of Aganippe well,
> Nor ever did in shade of Tempe sit;
> And muses scorn with vulgar brains to dwell;
> Poor layman I, for sacred rites unfit.
> Some do I hear of poet's fury tell,
> But (God wot) wot not what they mean by it;
> And this I swear, by blackest brook of hell,
> I am no pick-purse of another's wit.
>   How falls it then, that with so smooth an ease
> My thoughts I speak, and what I speak doth flow
> In verse, and that my verse best wits doth please?
> Guess we the cause: "What, is it thus?" Fie, no;
>   "Or so?" Much less: "How then?" Sure, thus it is:
>   My lips are sweet, inspired with Stella's kiss.
>   (A&S, 184, 74.1–14)

On the other side of doubt, Astrophil no longer concerns himself with the springs of Parnassus, divine inspiration, or the use of others' words.

---

77. Nelson, *Writer's Block*, 15.

He reflects on how easy his writing process has been—"My thoughts I speak, and what I speak doth flow." As these verses surge, moreover, Astrophil finds them warmly received by the so-called "best wits." Rather than staging his own confusion and uncertainty—and never coming near any encounters with aporia—he finds them reflected in the responses of others: "How then?"

The reason for Astrophil's poetic virtuosity, he explains, is Stella's kiss—a kiss that Astrophil stole from Stella as she slept. It is explicitly narrated in the Second Song of the sequence as a violation: "Yet those lips so sweetly swelling / Do invite a stealing kiss: / Now will I but venture this; / Who will read, must first learn spelling" (*A&S*, 182–83, Song 2.21-24). Sonnet 74, which is the second sonnet after the inclusion of this song, reveals the kiss as a solution to Astrophil's poetic problem. The fact that the opening eight lines of the sonnet borrow a heap of tropes renders this story of triumph ironic, however. The first four lines imitate, as confessed by a pun on "pick-purse" in line 8, the prologue to Persius's *Satires*.[78] Moreover, that Stella's kiss is a Platonic ideal situated at the crest of knowledge is itself a conventional device. Imitators of the Petrarchan sonnet tradition, for example, pointed to the "epiphanic moment" usually provoked by an encounter with a beautiful woman as a *salute*, a greeting operating as salvation from a divine beloved. Such greetings often provoked a breakdown in communicative faculties. Astrophil, however, does not succumb to inexpressibility.[79] Having literally "stolen" his epiphany through sexual assault, he proceeds to "pick-purse" the images he uses write about it.

While Astrophil no longer hesitates, then, perhaps we should. Even he seems to acknowledge that the kiss he stole from Stella was an unequivocal violation. He has seen his love functioning like a poison eating away at his moral and civic duties, but even so, he justifies his theft as warranted. Yet the Second Song reports that when Stella woke up from the kiss, he fled because her "[l]ouring beauty chastens me" (*A&S*, 182–83, Song 2.26). In the subsequent poem, he reflects on his tawdry conquest as a dalliance attributable to Cupid, a boy "[s]chooled only by his mother's tender eye" (*A&S*, 183–84, 73.2). This overly permissive homeschooling

---

78. "Nec fonte labra prolui caballino, / nec in bicipti somniasse Parnaso / memini, ut repente sic poeta prodirem" (I never got my lips well drenched in the hack's spring / Nor do I recollect having had a dream on the two-forked Parnassus / so as to burst upon the world at once a full-blown poet). Flaccus, *Satires*, 3-6.

79. See Spiller, *Development of the Sonnet*, 23.

supposedly excuses his behavior by affiliating it with the force of love—but this tinges the sweetness his lips proclaim to possess with some bitter gall. Sonnet 79 echoes the first line of Sonnet 1, with the poet again wishing to set his thoughts in verse—"Sweet kiss, thy sweets I fain would sweetly endite"—but the metaphorical associations Astrophil conjures for the kiss are revealing: it is branded "schoolmaster of delight" for "[t]eaching the mean at once to take and give" (A&S, 186, 79.1, 8-9). These images perversely emphasize mutuality and cooperation, despite the reader's knowledge that the kiss was taken rather than granted. Sonnet 80 refers to Stella's lips as "[t]he new Parnassus, where the muses bide" and as "wisdom's beautifier" (A&S, 186, 80.5-6), but the poet's goals are no longer to express his desires or even win love, but to earn further sensual rewards. These worldly goals are emphasized by a poet earlier incapable of self-restraint now more than willing to "stay" his mouth in "spite of [his] heart" (A&S, 186, 80.10) if it means further kisses. It takes until Sonnet 82 for Astrophil to even hint at regret when he explains that he was "full of desire, empty of wit" and requests that Stella "[p]ardon that fault" by promising that he "never more will bite" (A&S, 187, 82.9, 14). Her kiss made Astrophil capable of writing without obstruction, but it also reduced him to a braggart proud of his sexual impropriety.

Humanist rhetoric armed its students with a host of tools with which to set about writing, but Tudor England's ideological resistance to novelty blunted the efficacy of these instruments.[80] An overemphasis on liberation from disciplinary measures, however, might have proven just as dangerous—and just as conducive to bad art. Francis Bacon would point to poetry as "extremely licensed" discourse rooted in "the Imagination; which, being not tied to the laws of matter, may at pleasure join that which nature hath severed, and sever that which nature hath joined, and so make unlawful matches and divorces of things."[81] These characterizations reverberate claims in *Defence* about poetry's freedom to recombine and reconfigure nature into "Heroes, Demigods, Cyclops, Chimeras, Furies, and such like" (216). Astrophil's conduct, however, makes Bacon's imputation of poetry's "unlawful" qualities ring out more ominously. Sidney contends that the "right" poet's inventions would reconcile the proponent of what *should* be with the irresponsible dreamer of what *may* be. A testament to deliberating about the risky, reckless, violent thing, the first two-thirds of *Astrophil and Stella* have no

---

80. On the resistance to novelty, see Brown, "New Poet."
81. Bacon, *Works of Francis Bacon*, 202.

advice about how to resolve writer's block while still holding oneself up to the external standards of validation. By Sonnet 74, however, Astrophil has veered, biased by desire, and has broken the leash meant to rein in his impulses. The "unofficial voice" whom Bates reads as sabotaging Sidney's *Defence* has become Astrophil's silenced conscience. Though it cautions Astrophil against his own desires early in the sequence, it is ignored by the end of Sonnet 50 and utterly muted in Sonnet 74 as Astrophil's explosive libido takes the reins in the scene of writing.

In his youth, Sidney felt that playing by the rules limited his ability to think, to communicate, and to share his dissatisfactions. His earliest work provides a sort of thesis for his poetic ambitions, a thesis that he would ambivalently reflect on throughout *Defence* and *Astrophil and Stella*. A collection of that early work, *Certain Sonnets*, was first published in 1598 but was largely composed shortly after Sidney's travels in Europe in the 1570s. Reading it in retrospect reveals ideas he would more fully develop later. For example, Neil Rudenstine suggests that the collection "probably represents Sidney's first half-random thoughts on the possibility of attempting a lyric sequence" because he "group[ed] the poems according to form and theme in an effort to suggest the growth and final decay of a courtly love affair."[82] The bulk of *Certain Sonnets* busies itself with exercises in formal imitation: many are written expressly to the "tune" of extant pieces of music such as "the Spanish song, *Se tu señora no dueles de mi*" (*CS*, 17–18, 7) or "*a* Neapolitan *song, which beginneth*: No, no, no, no" (*CS*, 32–33, 26). Two of the poems are translations, *CS* 12 out of Horace and *CS* 28 out of "the Diana of Montemayor in Spanish."

Perhaps most remarkable of all are the poems in which Sidney experiments with quantitative metrical signatures. For these, he even provided scansion marks so that readers would have the prosodic equipment to recognize his efforts—perhaps no one would be able to "see" their proportion otherwise. If Astrophil worries about "weak proportion" in Sonnet 50, people like Sidney, Edward Dyer, Edmund Spenser, Gabriel Harvey, George Puttenham, Thomas Campion, and Samuel Daniel were worried about what "proportion" even signified when it came to vernacular English verse.[83] Sidney abandoned quantitative efforts in his later poetry, but in these experiments he self-consciously wrestled with the requirements of form. Elsewhere in *Certain Sonnets*,

---

82. Rudenstine, *Sidney's Poetic Development*, 117.

83. The authoritative account of these debates about meter is Attridge, *Well-Weighed Syllables*.

however, he wrestles not with the apparel his fancies might wear, but with the matter a poet might see fit to apparel in meter.

Certain Sonnets 16a–b are two poems, the first by Dyer and the second a response by Sidney, presenting competing fables. Dyer's poem tells the story of a satyr who sees the fire that Prometheus brought down to earth from the heavens. Driven by desire, the satyr gives the fire a kiss. Burning his lips, the satyr then runs into the woods "with shouts and shrieking still." The poem's speaker then analogizes himself with the satyr, because upon beholding "an angel from above," he now finds that he must "run and rest as pleaseth love" (*CS*, 23, 16a.6–12). Whereas the satyr burned his lips through his foolishness and fond desire, however, the speaker carries his pain in his heart, and pines from afar. The Second Song of *Astrophil and Stella* might be read as Sidney's burlesque of this poem. In it, Astrophil comes across his "heavenly jewel" while she is asleep and resolves, unnervingly, to "invade the fort" (*A&S*, 182–83, Song 2.15). Like Dyer's satyr, Astrophil kisses the perceived miracle, but he places responsibility for his actions on "those lips so sweetly swelling" (*A&S*, 182–83, Song 2.21). Whereas in Dyer's poem the satyr is the one who engages in the kiss while the poet's speaker merely gazes and admires his beloved from a distance, however, Sidney's poem has the lover directly participate in blasphemy.

We can trace this impudence back to Sidney's initial response to Dyer, *Certain Sonnets* 16b. In it, Sidney reframes the motives of the impulsive satyr:

> A satyr once did run away for dread
> With sound of horn, which he himself did blow;
> Fearing and feared, thus from himself he fled,
>   Deeming strange evil in that he did not know.
> Such causeless fears when coward minds do take
>   It makes them fly that which they fain would have:
> As this poor beast, who did his rest forsake,
>   Thinking not why, but how, himself to save.
> Even thus might I, for doubts which I conceive
>   Of mine own words, my own good hap betray,
> And thus might I for fear of maybe, leave
>   The sweet pursuit of my desired prey.
>   Better I like thy satyr, dearest Dyer,
>   Who burnt his lips to kiss faire shining fire.
>   (*CS*, 24, 16b.1–14)

Sidney's fable is about a timorous satyr who scares himself with his own horn. In the poem's final stanza, Sidney associates himself with the satyr in a mysterious allusion to the "doubts" that he "conceive[s]." These doubts understand that what "may be" is not necessarily what "should be"; we might associate them with the unwelcome love that Astrophil and Sidney nurture in their hearts for unavailable women, with an unquenchable desire that is at best indiscreet and at worst toxic. The young Sidney, in this friendly poetic contest, recognizes himself as too timid to keep up the pursuit, but he nevertheless sides with impudent transgression. As he matured, he would grow into a reputable—if tetchy and disagreeable—statesman, and as a reformed prodigal he would show that he could play it safe. This early poem, however, glints with fiery irresponsibility. "Better I like thy satyr," Sidney writes; better to transgress in the belief that you might have been struck by inspiration than to be a coward. He saw that one way around or through writer's block was with a truant pen, but it is important to emphasize that in the fullness of *Astrophil and Stella*, he would not suggest that reckless expression become the final seat of poesy.[84] While Astrophil blows past his dilemma in Sonnet 74, in ceasing to doubt himself he becomes like one of those amorous poets Sidney criticizes in *Defence*, who coldly apply fiery speeches borrowed from others' pages.

Throughout the sequence, Astrophil presents the tensions inherent to public utterance in the form of silence hesitantly taking the shape of sound: "But when their tongues could not speak," Sidney writes in the Eighth Song, "Love itself did silence break; / Love did set his lips asunder, / Thus to speak in love and wonder" (*A&S*, 195–98, Song 8.25–28). At times, Astrophil finds his writing to be divinely inspired, flawless, and met with wide applause; other times, he is forced to wonder why it is met with indifference and not having the effects he had anticipated. This culminates with the poet disappointed during a clandestine meeting, at which Stella confesses her love for Astrophil but ultimately refuses him. There are simply too many competing and conflicting pressures, she reasons, that obstruct them. Finding his love unrequited, his reputation withering, and his poems impotent, he concludes the sequence resigned to frustrated hopes:

When sorrow, using mine own fire's might
Melts down his lead into my boiling breast,

---

84. On rebellious schoolboys, see Lamb, *Reading Children*, 131.

> Through that dark furnace to my heart oppressed
> There shines a joy from thee, my only light:
> But soon as thought of thee breeds my delight,
> And my young soul flutters to thee, his nest;
> Most rude despair, my daily unbidden guest,
> Clips straight my wings, straight wraps me in his night,
> And makes me then bow down my head, and say:
> "Ah, what doth Phoebus' gold that wretch avail
> Whom iron doors do keep from use of day?"
> So strangely, alas, thy works in me prevail,
> That in my woes for thee thou art my joy,
> And in my joys for thee my only annoy.
>
> (*A&S*, 211, 108.1–14)

Astrophil's final bind encapsulates the entire sequence's relationship to writing. Oscillating between affective poles—sorrow and joy, delight and despair—the poem reveals its poet as remaining torn between a need to write and the impossibility or impotence of writing. This conflict manifests in the competing forces of Astrophil's "young soul" about to take flight and the pinioning it experiences—a "halting" creature violently stayed. The raw material of poetic inspiration, "Phoebus' gold," proves too pliant when battered against "iron doors" impeding its reception, and so the poet is left feeling strange, perplexed, uncomfortable. Though Astrophil is finished setting pen to paper, rather than about to begin, *Astrophil and Stella* ends just as it began, with a fluttering fire in the poet's fingertips. A perpetual contest between disciplined decisiveness and restive desire, poesy shudders on both sides of writing.

Reflection: Released into Language

By what means do literary critics invent their claims? In "The Rhetoric of Literary Criticism" (1991), Jeanne Fahnestock and Marie Secor surveyed a collection of articles published between 1978 and 1982 in journals of "established reputation" and categorized the forms of argumentation they witnessed therein against the classical stases (existence, definition, evaluation, cause, proposal).[85] They observed that while literary scholars rarely adhered to the expected causal linkages predicated by these stasis issues, the scholars nevertheless tended to rely on several "special topoi," which Fahnestock and Secor describe as "warrants that Aristotle and later rhetoricians identified, to supplement the common topoi, as most useful in particular persuasive situations."[86] The most prevalent special topic provoked by the "particular persuasive situation" of academic literary studies at the end of the 1970s was "appearance/reality," or the idea that there is "something underneath" the superficial surface of a text. Other common topoi were "ubiquity" (the critic finding "many examples of the same thing" or "one thing in many forms"); "paradox" (the critic locates "the prized unification of apparently irreconcilable opposites in a single startling dualism"); "*contemptus mundi*" (the critic finds through the reading "an assumption of despair over the condition and course of modern society"); and "paradigm" (the critic locates a "recognizable set of relationships drawn from the world outside the literary text, and then detects its avatars in a particular genre or work," thereby allowing the critic to "bring many apparently diverse works under a single definition").[87] Even if literary critics are not explicitly taught to emulate these topoi, enough experience with reading and citing others' arguments encourages aspiring writers toward them.

Laura Wilder's *Rhetorical Strategies and Genre Conventions in Literary Studies* (2012) revisits Fahnestock and Secor's analysis, surveying articles published between 1999 and 2001 to observe that many of the special topics Fahnestock and Secor identified still hold. I would wager that, a decade after Wilder's study, they still would. This chapter comprises a constellation of them—but primarily makes a case for the ubiquity of hesitation in Sidney's conception of poesy.[88] Seeing these patterns of ar-

---

85. Fahnestock and Secor, "Rhetoric of Literary Criticism," 77.
86. Fahnestock and Secor, "Rhetoric of Literary Criticism," 84.
87. Fahnestock and Secor, "Rhetoric of Literary Criticism," 87–89.
88. In addition to tracking this consistency, however, Wilder observes that in the more recent articles the topoi showed that they had "evolved with the discipline and prompted new

gumentation as "the almost imperceptible and generally taken-for-granted fibers that hold together this disparate and diverse discourse community," Wilder then surveyed teachers about their responses to student writing, finding that their "understandings of persuasiveness, originality, and complexity appear to have been so thoroughly shaped by their disciplinary training that student essays are found more persuasive, original, and complex the more they follow the conventions of the professional genre of the literary-analysis journal article."[89] This makes sense: the way professors are taught to invent becomes the way they eventually evaluate their students' inventions.

In response to these findings, Wilder proposes making these special topoi explicit to undergraduate students. Wilder, along with Joanna Wolfe, designed a set of experimental classes in which the "special topoi" would be introduced to students as structuring elements in the way writing and reading would be discussed:[90]

> Instructors wove explicit references to the special topoi into peer-review guidelines and grading criteria. They asked students to read examples of student writing and published criticism and analyze them for their use of the topoi. They assigned critical theory and modeled for students how to use this theory in service of the paradigm topos. They referred explicitly to the topoi in their written comments on student work and in student conferences. Perhaps most important of all, they demonstrated how to use the special topoi as tools for invention in class brainstorming sessions and in nearly all discussions of literary texts.[91]

When papers by students presented with this experimental pedagogy were evaluated alongside papers by students from classes in which the special topoi were mentioned only tacitly (or left unmentioned), their writing was found to be more persuasive, more complex, and more "original."[92] At the same time, Wilder and Wolfe found that the method had its drawbacks. Some students, they observed, imposed the special topics on the texts, applying conventions rather than attending to the texts themselves. "One student" writing about a novel, Wilder notes, "made

---

topoi"—the "mistaken-critic topos, the context topos, and a topos that subverts contemptus mundi, the social justice topos." Wilder, *Rhetorical Strategies*, 34.
    89. Wilder, *Rhetorical Strategies*, 54, 97.
    90. Details of their study can be found in Wilder and Wolfe, "Tacit Rhetorical Knowledge."
    91. Wilder, *Rhetorical Strategies*, 121.
    92. Wilder, *Rhetorical Strategies*, 117.

glaringly inappropriate use of these conventions" by "explicitly naming the topoi and claiming that they exist in the novel (rather than using them to analyze the novel)," consequently producing "phrasings that would never appear in the kind of professional discourse that was the target for this course."[93] To recall a key term from chapter 1, what this student produced was a bit of bodgery. Students who see any topics of invention as prescriptions, rather than resources—students who practice invention as a formal process without any kairotic engagement with the text and its immediate details—may fall into this trap. Wilder and Wolfe also received some pushback from the colleagues who taught these experimental classes, regarding giving the students such explicit instructions; some teachers, they found, felt that introducing these strategies stifled creativity and encouraged students to professionalize too quickly.[94]

The special topoi, like the five-paragraph essay, can be useful only when students treat them as an invitation to stage a debate between their thoughts and the structures of argumentation expected by their readers. While these conventions and templates risk becoming prescriptive, that does not make them useless. As teachers who expect certain formal standards to be met, we must demonstrate what it means to claim these standards as instruments for thought, as paths that students might choose to walk while nevertheless armed with tactical agency.

Throughout her career as a writer and teacher, Wendy Bishop recommended moving away from prescriptive writing pedagogy, proposing instead that adopting a workshop model, as in creative writing classes, would allow students to learn "what it feels like to be a writer, someone who generates, drafts, revises, shares, and publishes writing, someone who experiences blocks, anxiety, elation, and success."[95] In *Released into Language* (1990), Bishop offers strategies for leading students to the *feeling* of making or struggling to make a discovery, of recognizing the difficult and potentially dangerous passage between free private play and regulated public life. Even as she noted and embraced challenges to "current-traditional rhetoric" by expressivist compositionists advancing "subjective

---

93. Wilder, *Rhetorical Strategies*, 119.
94. Wilder, *Rhetorical Strategies*, 54. For Wilder's response to these critiques, see 174–201.
95. Bishop, *Released into Language*, 2–3. Also see Bishop, "Crossing the Lines"; and Hawkins, "Irrational Element." As Patrick Bizzaro suggests in a retrospective essay, Wendy Bishop's most enduring contributions to the pedagogy of writing were her emphasis on the "interconnectedness of creative writing and composition studies" and her insistence that the teaching of writing be informed by ethnographic study of what experienced writers do when they go about their work. Bizzaro, "Writers Wanted," 258.

theories of instruction that were not dissimilar to those promulgated in graduate creative writing workshops," however, Bishop sympathized with constructivists who labeled these challenges guilty of romanticized views of authorship. In response, Bishop proposed an approach centered on neither texts nor authors but on the transactions between them. Its goal was to expose "the way in which individual writers borrow, adapt, steal from, acknowledge, and are consciously or unconsciously influenced by other texts they have encountered."[96] As part of this pedagogy, she appropriated invention exercises from rhetorical compositionists—activities such as having students use clichés intentionally, or deploy a variety of different metaphors about a character, or reverse perceived truths or stereotypes—because, as Bishop explains, invention lies "on a continuum from writer's apprentice work and, often experimental, self-assignments to more conventional, commissioned work."[97]

Protocols of invention, models, and exercises, in this light, are meant to give novice writers "insights into professional writers' self-challenges."[98] These exercises, Bishop explains, can be used "to help writers get started, to help writers continue writing and avoid writing blocks, and to help explore writers' activities and rituals."[99] Like Wilder, Bishop feels that professors should endeavor to lay bare as much as they can what the discursive habits of the discipline are, but she also feels that they should recognize that every example threatens to become a rule, and that rules can stifle reflection. Models, templates, and heuristics will always have a role to play in writing instruction, but the degree of authority with which they are invested need not be static or unquestioned.

In "Places to Stand," Bishop laments how "we tend to do to our students what is done to us" because "if we feel pushed toward writing a certain type of professional text, we will probably expect the same of our students."[100] This corroborates points made by Lindsay Parker and James Gifford, who find within the operations of a university a host of lumbering contradictions between thinking, doing, and making. The university, they note, will often "extol rational thought and the necessity for self-determination in decision-making" but also simultaneously "establish relations and institutional conformity of a constraining, directive sort that

---

96. Bishop, *Released into Language*, 14, 41.
97. Bishop, *Released into Language*, 69–70; the exercises mentioned appear at 85, 101, and 111.
98. Bishop, *Released into Language*, 71.
99. Bishop, *Released into Language*, 48–49.
100. Bishop, "Places to Stand," 21.

seek to subordinate the exercise of reason to structure, form, and tradition." Such an institutional setup creates and promotes a "risk-averse environment" that renders "competition petty and ambitions pedestrian."[101] In order to teach critical inquiry as a process of deliberation whereby budding writers develop confidence in their ability to ask new questions, literature professors might create spaces in which students can actually experience what it feels like to inquire, to think out loud and on the page, without a fear of stepping beyond the velvet ropes of structure, form, and tradition. One way to do this, Parker and Gifford suggest, is "low-stakes learning," which "permits high-risk intellectual engagement via low competition and by temporarily suspending the false adversarial binary of winners and losers in risk taking and evaluation."[102] Can we reimagine the literature classroom so that it does not evaluate products and, instead, focuses on process—where students may be corrected and challenged without feeling as if they have failed? The next chapter explores this question in greater detail. Yet even if we choose to assess process over product and set evaluation aside, the fact remains that we still need to teach some sort of process, and that this process will involve the production of wrong answers, incoherence, and bad writing.

I have adopted a classroom practice that terrified me when I initiated it years ago, after I first encountered Bishop's writings.[103] When I assign students a critical essay, in the subsequent class I connect my laptop to a classroom projector, open a blank document, and begin undertaking the assignment myself. I treat it as an improvisational game: I solicit specific topics and moments that students remember from the reading (Astrophil's horse! Cavendish's outfits! The monkey in *Utopia*! Donne's obsession with eyeballs!), or we simply flip to a random page and work from there. After we collectively decide on a topic by discussing what might be interesting about each option, I challenge the class to hunt down and help me transcribe a passage related to it. I then do my best to make sure that we read the passage very slowly by imposing strict guidelines on how we are to pay attention to it. We are not allowed, I insist, to talk about things not present in the passage itself. To start, we document what we see—everything from punctuation marks to metaphors to less-than-common words. Then we elaborate on specific features within the passage that strike us

---

101. Parker and Gifford, "Rethinking How Humanities Think," 110.
102. Parker and Gifford, "Rethinking How Humanities Think," 110.
103. This practice felicitously resembles one suggested by Wilder, involving "think-aloud" recordings of professors. Wilder, *Rhetorical Strategies*, 122.

as significant for any reason at all—how the metaphor evokes other parts of the text, how the punctuation creates a kind of rhythm, and so on. Third, we try to connect whatever we found significant in the passage to our prior sense of why the topic or question we decided on was worth pursuing. As we talk things over, I messily transcribe students' comments on the document. (This part took a little practice, but it also forced me to keep my own mouth shut.) After we amass a wealth of observations, I pick over them, forming clusters of ideas that relate to one another, explaining what I perceive the relationships to be. I then start typing a paragraph, introducing the quotation with a few sentences before pasting it in. After the block quote, I pull from the discussion notes to craft sentences of analysis. I make it a point to emphasize that most of what we talked about is *not* making its way into my analysis—that our notes were important to our thinking but would only be distracting for the reader.

We generally do not get very deep into composing the essay after an hour of class. Usually we end up with (what I would call) a drafty paragraph offering an attempt at close reading. Really, the only difference between this lesson plan and a standard practice of engaging in classroom close reading is the open document and the imperative to turn the conversation into writing, but the open document and its white space are crucial to disambiguating process. I force myself, in doing this, to explain both the mundane and the vital aspects of composing criticism. The multiple points of radical incoherence involved in this approach are liberating, even thrilling. We start with nothing and slowly build, unsure of what we are building. Rather than offering students a template, this exercise puts the template to work as a tool we can choose to use—and a tool that cannot do the thinking for us. Sometimes our collective analysis of the passage is somewhat flimsy. Even in these instances, the process lets students see how they might get started on their own essays by clarifying how the process will and should be challenging. By steering into the skids of critical invention imagined neither as a flash of inspiration nor as an airing out of familiar arguments, it imagines criticism as akin to poetry in a commitment to collaboratively reimagining what may be.

Chapter 3

Revision
John Davies of Hereford's "Rough Hewings"

John Davies of Hereford's "Of My Selfe," which appears as prefatory material to his sonnet sequence *Wittes Pilgrimage* (1605), begins with the poet questioning his motives for writing poetry at all: "What meane I miscreant my Braines to beate, / To forge these Fancies light as *Leuity*?" ("Of My Selfe," *WP*, 2:5).[1] As he muses while disappointedly surveying his own works, personified Reason intervenes and advises him to "vndoe" what he had written and start over. Davies did not heed this advice—a fact to which the mere existence of the volume preemptively attests—and he explains this decision in the final lines of "Of My Selfe":

> Then *Reason* I acquite thee from disgrace,
> Sith thus thou promptst me what I ought to write:
> Let *Tyrant* shame with bloud stil fil my face.
> For so abusing thy right ruling might.
> My frinds (though fraile as I am) pres me stil

---

1. Davies of Hereford, *Complete Works*. All references to Davies's literary works will be to these volumes and indicated in-text by the title of the text and that of the work in which it appears, the volume number, and the page number. *Wittes Pilgrimage* is abbreviated as *WP*, *The Scourge of Folly* as *SF*, *To Worthy Persons* as *TWP*, and *Paper's Complaint* as *PC*.

> To presse these lines (more fraile) to publike view:
> If I should saie it is againste my will
> I shoulde speake truly, and yet most vntrue:
>> For my wills fixt my fast friends stil to please:
>> But yet still wauers thus, to publish these,
>>> Yet sith, in wauering wise, thus fixt, it stands
>>> *Fames* wind, *Wits* weather-cocke, my will, commands.
>>> ("Of My Selfe," *WP*, 2:5)

In the previous chapter, we saw Astrophil claim Stella's divine name as justification for refusing to dash out his lines; by contrast, Davies here claims only the flimsy epiphany of friendly encouragement. Though he deploys the common trope of blaming anonymous peers for goading him to publish his work, however, he also immediately confesses that he did not need much compelling. Whereas Sidney's *The Defence of Poesy* advised poets to consult the "unflattering glass of reason" before believing themselves worthy of adulation, here we find Davies glancing in the mirror to acknowledge his own blemishes and nevertheless hurrying out the door.[2] Potential fame, it seems, could dispel rational concerns about potential shame.

The other prefatory materials of *Wittes Pilgrimage* corroborate this attitude: the collection opens with two poems appealing for patronage to Philip Herbert (Sidney's nephew) and James Hay, prominent favorites of King James I. Appealing to wealthy courtiers—either through dedicatory verses or encomiastic epigrams—was a tactic of nearly all socially ambitious poets of the era, and John Davies of Hereford was an uncommonly prolific practitioner. But despite Davies's willingness to grasp at fame, his career never reached any kind of prominence, either in his own lifetime or in the centuries since. One problem was that his poems were just not very good: as Philip J. Finkelpearl notes, Davies "condensed, simplified, and omitted much from his sources, and the product was an incoherent and clumsy patchwork of philosophical fragments, often in unreadable technical language." While he "may have been one of the most voluminous didactic poets of the age," Finkelpearl concludes, Davies was "also one of the most tedious"—a point echoed in Brian Vickers's appraisal of him as "busy but mediocre."[3] Perhaps he should have listened to Reason when it told him to revise his lines.

---

2. Sidney, *Defence of Poesy*, in *Sir Philip Sidney*, 242.
3. Finkelpearl, "Davies, John (1564/5–1618)"; Vickers, *Shakespeare*, 16. Finkelpearl points out that Davies "never gained any recognition or financial profit from his poetry" and that

What compelled poets to revise their work in early modernity, and what prevented them from doing so? While the previous chapter presented invention as a debate undertaken with oneself, this chapter examines how the work of revision continues that debate amid the material and temporal circumstances of professional life. If poesy, as Sidney presents it, must be approached as difficult work vulnerable to experiences of doubt and hesitation, it must also be understood as work that will likely take more time to undertake than the poet can anticipate. At the threshold of revision, already-written words argue through their obstinate physicality for their own persistence; blotting a page, in this light, means canceling the time and effort that went into setting words down in the first place. Quintilian points out that revision requires "a double effort, because we have both to condemn things which we once liked and discover things which had escaped us."[4] The willingness to condemn one's own words means choosing to do more work, and if this decision is extrinsically enforced, the work risks becoming onerous and cumbersome.

The approachably mediocre John Davies of Hereford, a poet who knew his limitations but also recognized his own potential, may become a new sort of hero for the work of writing in the literature classroom. What distinguishes him from nearly all other poets of his era—and the reason his writings, so undervalued by his contemporaries, are invaluable to the project of this book—is that Davies also happened to be, in a very specific sense, a teacher of writing. He was for a time one of England's most famous writing masters, a profession that rose to prominence in the sixteenth century, Richard S. Christen notes, "as increasing numbers from all ranks and walks of life coveted proficiency or even mastery of one or more of the several 'hands' practiced during the era." Due to this demand, the writing master, according to Christen, ended up being "a prominent figure on the early modern professional landscape."[5] Writing masters shared some responsibilities with grammar school instructors like John Brinsley (whose *Ludus literarius*

"only one of his works [*Microcosmos*, 1603] ever reached a second edition." For more on Davies's social aspirations, and for his biography more broadly, see Vickers, *Shakespeare*, 30–33. In a review of Vickers's book, David Bevington voiced his uncertainty about Davies's authorship of Shakespeare's *A Lover's Complaint* based on the same premise of his mediocrity; pointing to a "splendidly vivid" line, he concludes, "I find nothing of comparable genius in the writings of John Davies." Bevington, review of *Shakespeare*, 1465-66.

4. Quintilian, *Orator's Education*, 353 (10.4.1).
5. Christen, "Boundaries," 32-33.

also contains instruction on orthography) but focused primarily on the acquisition of ornate styles and orthographic correctness.

Davies's day job thus entailed a professional preoccupation with the way ink sat on paper, and so when he wrote poems he could not help but hold a consistently bifocal view of the effort as a confluence of the manual techniques of "fair writing" (inscribing stylish letterforms in neat rows) and as the uncertain exercise of "inditing" ("giving a literary or rhetorical form").[6] His poetry bears the residue of his professional life, and is as a result perpetually torn between the different responsibilities that attended setting pen to page. He worries about penmanship, in other words, as much as about prosody. This attention to the material conditions of writing extended beyond the management of his hand, however, and led him to ruminations about the broader forces that make poesy a difficult undertaking. His work consequently demonstrates how making the decision to embrace discomposition—to undertake revision for its own sake—is largely a problem of *labor*. More vividly than most of his contemporaries, Davies voices the complaint that he simply was not given enough time, or paid well enough, to undertake revision in earnest.

Born in Wales in 1565, Davies was a direct contemporary of Marlowe (son of a shoemaker), Nashe (son of a parson), Shakespeare (son of a glovemaker), Jonson (son of a bricklayer), and Drayton (son of a butcher-tanner). When Sir Philip Sidney's poetry was printed in the 1590s, the "unemployably eloquent" members of Davies's generation witnessed increasing legitimacy for poetry but also quickly confronted the fact that opportunities for patronage and courtly appointment were scarce.[7] Though his own will suggests that Davies died "a respectable distance above poverty," for much of his professional life he worried about money.[8] He was self-consciously one of an emerging class of what Laurie Ellinghausen terms "laboring writers," who understood their work in relation to social conditions rather than to divine inspiration, and who reflected on their "self-professed marginality" in order

---

6. *Oxford English Dictionary*, s.v. "Indite, v. Def. 3a," accessed July 11, 2021, http://www.oed.com/view/Entry/94620.

7. Rhodes, *Origins of English*, 46.

8. In some epigrams responding to unfair taxes assessed on him for lands he saw as worthless, he complains, "Is my portion in this world but rime?" Alexander Grosart, the only modern editor of his collected works, observes that even "if well married, from the start his was a struggle with narrow circumstances and irregular supplies." See Grosart, "Memorial-Introduction," xiv.

to construct "an alternative kind of authority to that of the socially privileged."[9] Davies aspired to make a name for himself by affiliating with the "socially privileged," but he was also very aware that he was not even the best poet in London *named* John Davies—that would have been the nobly born Sir John Davies, who had become a favorite of both Queen Elizabeth and King James I. Finding it difficult to attract the same kind of attention, our Davies churned out writing with yeoman-like labor and published nearly every kind of verse—theological treatises, epigrams, sonnets, satires, lyrics, histories, translations—without ever really breaking through.

What did it take to become a working poet in early modern England? David Cressy estimates that by 1600, as few as 25–30 percent of men and 5–10 percent of women in England showed evidence of being able to sign their own names.[10] Several scholars have disputed these figures as an index of general literacy—particularly on the grounds that reading was taught prior to writing, and so it is likely that many more people had basic reading skills than had basic writing skills—but what remains clear is that the acquisition of writing skills posed both individual and social challenges that were not overcome by many members of the English citizenry.[11] Beyond mere literacy, writers who may have been lucky enough to receive grammar schooling but did not attend university or proceed into legal careers were competing for literary renown with those who had. Higher education at institutions like Oxford, Cambridge, and the Inns of Court not only was increasingly becoming an emblem of privilege, but also enabled those who attended to form political alliances and cultural coteries.[12] As a result, for early modern writers, "breaking through" was determined by their sociocultural background both directly, in the sense of the degree of education they could claim, and indirectly, in the sense of their marginalization from elite cultural communities. Those whose technical skills might

---

9. Ellinghausen, *Labor and Writing*, 4.
10. Cressy, *Literacy*, 176–77.
11. See Cressy, *Literacy*, 34. For critiques of and elaborations on Cressy's accounting, see Spufford, *Small Books*, 19–44; Dolan, "Reading, Writing, and Other Crimes," 143; Hackel, *Reading Material*, 56–68; Brink, "Literacy and Education."
12. While the number of commoners attending university had increased during the sixteenth century, Kenneth Charlton suggests that an "influx of nobility and gentry" into the universities over this time led to them claiming an increased proportion of places. Charlton, *Education in Renaissance England*, 136. For how the social dynamics of these institutions informed literary sensibilities, see Ellinghausen, "University of Vice"; O'Callaghan, *English Wits*; Winston, *Lawyers at Play*.

have rivaled those of university-affiliated poets rarely had access to the spaces and networks, such as the royal court, private coteries, or educational institutions, within which elite aesthetic tastes were developed and consolidated.[13]

By the end of the sixteenth century, many poets like Davies found themselves torn between effort and expediency in their quest for fame—and with fame, a chance at patronage or courtly employment. Writing poetry was not really a viable professional pathway, but the allure of financial gain and social mobility nevertheless influenced poetic craft both directly and indirectly. As Richard McCabe points out, "[T]he lack of anything resembling a professional career structure (even within the emergent book-trade where stationers were guildsmen but authors were not), or any formal mode of public recognition or legal copyright, forced writers to employ a variety of idealized paradigms and sociocultural templates in an attempt to flatter, cajole, or shame prospective patrons into a sense of 'obligation' variously expressed in ethical, personal, intellectual, or nationalist terms."[14] While print circulation afforded poets an alternative pathway toward financial reward, McCabe notes that participation in this economy "threatened, at its worst, to downgrade the author to the level of hired penman, the mere employee of some printer or publisher" rather than a legitimate creative artist. In the poem preceding "Of My Selfe," Davies even hints at the ways his authorial will had been corrupted, and he worries that he had become a mere "people-pleaser" ("The Author to his Muse," *WP*, 2:5).[15]

Reflecting on these circumstances in his own poetry, Davies offers a more concrete defense of poesy than the one we saw Sidney make in the previous chapter. The courtier-poet requested that readers be more generous to poets' attempts and that poets themselves aspire to take their own work far more seriously. Davies would insist that taking one's own work seriously requires more than just generous readers—it requires access to material resources such as time and financial security. Reading *The Writing School-master* (ca. 1620), his manual for "fair writing," alongside his epigrams, the first section below locates Davies's defense of poetry within the way he navigated the blurry distinction

---

13. On early modern aesthetic elitism, see Schmidgall, *Shakespeare*, 107–17.
14. McCabe, *"Ungainefull Arte,"* 4.
15. This view of literary history, as Trevor Ross puts it, corresponds to a shift toward aligning "canon-formation with the judgment of the market and the popular voice." See Ross, *English Literary Canon*, 121–22. For accounts of the changing marketplace of early modern poetry, also see McCabe, *"Ungainefull Arte"*; and McCarthy, *Doubtful Readers*.

between "writing" and "inditing." As a creature of ink and paper who aspired for perfect, blotless regularity, he struggled to reconcile himself to poesy's rough workmanship of risk.[16] A sensitivity to how marred pages could blemish his professional reputation led him to perceive the inky blot itself as a figure for the aesthetic contradictions inherent to poesy. A formless form indexing both the ink that makes writing possible and the obliterations that make it distinct from speech, the blot emblematized for Davies the dissonance produced by restless Fantasy's discomposing encounter with calm Reason.

Affiliating the stuff of imperfection with the stuff of poetry in this way allowed Davies to recognize poetic composition as a marring as well as a making, as an art of illegibility as well as an art of writing. This realization, as we will see in the chapter's second section, was coupled with a heightened awareness that poesy's conditions of possibility were often available only to the idle elite. Self-conscious enough to anticipate appraisals of his hard work as "mediocre," Davies was openly frustrated by the fact that he never rose to the stature of his more famous contemporaries. He compared himself on the one hand to elite poets like Jonson, Donne, and (of course) Sir John Davies, and on the other to working-class and aesthetically disdained "pot-poets" like John Taylor, the Water Poet. From the middle (*medio-*) of the mountain (*-ocris*), Davies not only could discern what lay above and below himself but could also vividly chart the rocky terrain on which he stood. This perspective appears both in his early theological rumination, *Microcosmos* (1603), and in his satirical tirade, *Paper's Complaint* (1611). In the latter, personified paper pleads with writers, including Davies himself, to commit to the attentiveness and patience required of poesy rather than smearing it with excremental outpourings. In doing so, however, it also articulates that one of the reasons writers fail to revise their work is less a personal failing than a matter of time and resources. Paper's appeal on behalf of meaningful revision—positioned in opposition to impudent overproduction or timid correction—hinges on a plea for reforming social conditions in ways that might afford writers time for unproductive labor.

At the end of the chapter, I adopt Davies's pleas for social reform as the starting point for a defense of poetry enacted through the practices of the modern literature classroom. As teachers of literature who are also teachers of writing, we must explore how work produced in

---

16. For more on the "workmanship of risk" and the "workmanship of certainty," see Pye, *Workmanship*. For more context on writing and inditing, see Goldberg, *Writing Matter*, 126–27.

idleness, in time left unburdened by obligation, may become central to our pedagogy. We must develop ways, as John Bean suggests, to "create an academic environment that encourages revision."[17] Given the elitist, white supremacist, and colonialist history that prefigures any class in early modern English literature, teachers of these classes might recognize that to truly encourage revision in our students we must revise our own ways of doing business. If doing the hard work of poetic and critical writing is accessible only to those who can already financially support undertaking it, the study of the literature of the past will grow increasingly irrelevant to political life and become, even more than it already is, a pastime for the idle elite. Our classrooms might work to counteract this by extending to students the sorts of advantages that poets such as John Davies of Hereford knew they lacked. By creating time and space for the hard work of literary idleness, we might make a small stand in defense of our students' right to engage in labor that is purposefully unproductive, or even gleefully subversive. The early modern literature classroom might, in this way, aspire to revise the way students think about writing and what they might do with it.

Thoughts in Blots

A page of writing in early modernity was appraised visually as well as literarily; this is partly the reason the profession of "writing master" existed at all.[18] Wendy Wall notes how the fact that "readers had set expectations when they approached books that did not disappear when print technology was founded or when it became more popular" led to printed books embracing stylistic conventions of manuscript texts. Yet the coexistence of manuscript and print in the seventeenth century sees Wall's "pseudomorphic" relation as more of a two-way street: manuscript writing also responded to the expectations catalyzed by print.[19] Rosemary Huisman observes that "printing [led] to a more fixed sense

---

17. Bean, *Engaging Ideas*, 35.
18. This section builds on work by many scholars who have studied how bibliographic materiality can augment or complicate writing's meaning: Fleming, *Graffiti*; Smyth, *Material Texts*; Calhoun, *Nature of the Page*.
19. Wall, *Imprint of Gender*, 230. Books proliferated at the turn of the seventeenth century to address topics such as the care required in preparing one's pen, the manner of holding the pen, how to sit, how to prepare a desk, the importance of maintaining a steady hand, and the differences between roman, secretary, and italic hands. For more on the increased demand for handwriting instruction, see Schulz, "Teaching of Handwriting."

of visual layout for printed or handwritten poems," but that while the effect of print "up until, say, 1640, was . . . to 'privatize' handwriting" and allow manuscripts to retain the effects of subjectivity, "in the century after the introduction of printing," poets' writing "indicates a stronger consciousness of the literate sense of the poem, that its lines and stanza shape together are 'seen' as a clearly differentiated visual object, interdependent with the rhythm and heard patterns of the speaking of those words."[20] Written poems were apprehended from at least two imbricated vantage points: typographic appearance corresponding to shape, line regularity, and "fairness," and appraisals of literary merit.

Building on Jonathan Goldberg's study of early modern handwriting in *Writing Matter* (1990), this section studies the relationship between writing and inditing as they played out in how "the hand moves in language" and how "its movement retraces the 'being' of the individual inscribed within the simulative social practices that are lived as ordinary experience."[21] Goldberg deconstructs the ways in which "habits of behavior begin with the control of the hand" to consider how a writer's management of a pen reflects the management of the social order.[22] I argue, to extend this analysis, that foregrounding experiences of discomposition reclaims some ground for poesy from the "regime of copying."[23] In Davies's writings, we can perceive one of this regime's senior officials openly doubting himself, thereby illuminating for modern readers a poetic process driven neither by inspired fury nor by careful imitation, but by the dissonance between the different sorts of labor poetry demanded of poets.

Revision was what one *did* with poems in early modern England; in its purest form it is effectively synonymous with Jonson's account of the "doing" of poesy.[24] Looking at an early modern manuscript, or

---

20. Huisman, *Written Poem*, 129, 127.
21. Goldberg, *Writing Matter*, 161.
22. Goldberg, *Writing Matter*, 55.
23. Goldberg, *Writing Matter*, 113: "The ideology of script does not come from the hands of the nobility but is given to them within the pedagogical apparatus that re-marks them. Nobility is the legibility taught in the regime of copying."
24. Chris Stamatakis argues that by subordinating or ignoring "variant witnesses, strikethroughs, the import of hand-type, multiple pennings, relocation by compilers, and interventions by readers" when considering a given "text," modern editions of Thomas Wyatt's poems "have overlooked the traces of an ongoing manuscript discourse." Stamatakis, *Sir Thomas Wyatt*, 38. Discussing the work of a poet working a century after Wyatt, Dianne Mitchell's account of the various writings of Dudley, Third Baron North, similarly suggests a theory of literary production in which "no single text . . . could embody a version of North's writings that was truly perfected or finished." Mitchell, "'Or Rather a Wyldernesse,'" 369–70. Both Mitchell

even revised printed versions of it, we are only ever looking at pieces of poesy's puzzle. Here we might reflect on the distinction between early modern literature's "foul papers" (rough drafts) and "fair copies" (versions intended for transmission and presentation). This distinction, the terms of which largely derive from concern for the transmission of Shakespeare's plays, has a complicated history.[25] Early modern writers knew that the first impression their work gave to readers was often independent from its content, and at some point, they certainly decided to train their pens toward legibility. We might consequently presume that making something "fair" in both hand and function—fair writing for a fair copy—was the ultimate goal of a poet's endeavor. Matthew Zarnowiecki resists this presumption. A "fair copy," he explains, is neither "the best copy out of many (as in copy-text) nor the single copy in the author's hand presented to all eternity (the presentation copy)." A fair copy instead reflects early modern poesy's investment in "creative copying," wherein "mutation" could always occur "at the moment of reproduction."[26] To account for this instability, Zarnowiecki proposes "medium close-reading"—a style of analysis that tracks a poem through its different publication contexts and that "requires attention not only to how poems change across these media, but how poets adjust their formal and generic choices to both canonical and emergent lyric forms."[27]

Yet even in attending to the movements of a text and its changing meanings in different contexts, we can still, at best, glimpse the activity that precipitated them. As Lisa Gitelman argues, once any object is "framed as or entered into evidence—once it is mobilized—it becomes a document," and as such becomes an instrument for "knowing-showing."[28] Seeing a draft may offer further knowledge about how a

---

and Stamatakis corroborate Arthur Marotti's contention that the "manuscript system was far less author-centered than print culture and not at all interested in correcting, perfecting, or fixing texts in authorially sanctioned forms." Marotti, *Manuscript*, 135.

25. Used most often to describe the phases of production of early modern plays, the distinction between "fair" and "foul," as Paul Werstine has observed, stems both from a commitment to the bibliographic ideal of a stable copy text and from a literary New Critical emphasis on textual unity. The idea that there is one final version that coordinates an author's intentions overlooks not only the contingencies—death, deadlines, persons from Porlock—that influence an author's ability to sustain ongoing attention, but also the reviewers, censors, compositors, and editors that intervene between the author's final inscription and the text as it arrives before a reader. Werstine, "Printed Shakespeare Texts."

26. Zarnowiecki, *Fair Copies*, 12.

27. Zarnowiecki, *Fair Copies*, 8.

28. Gitelman, *Paper Knowledge*, 3, 2.

thing was made, but it also reveals the limits of our knowledge about what we can definitively know. Reflecting on our own experiences as writers, we may acknowledge that the "mutations" Zarnowiecki attributes to the transmission of texts could occur even at the moment of those texts' initial *production*. The slip of a pen, the look of a line, the inattentive autopilot of a facile rhyme could have provoked new creative energy that modified poetic invention.

Revision takes place *between* document states, witnesses, variants. John Bryant uses the term "fluid texts" to describe literary documents under revision, because their "apparent instabilities and indeterminacies ... give us a vivid material impression of the *flow* of creativity ... that constitutes the cultural phenomenon of writing."[29] Accounting for this flow, Bryant adopts "energy" as a metaphor for naming "the power of a people and culture to create a text."[30] That last phrase is crucial: the energy that powers the creation of a text circulates between people and culture but is wholly attributable to neither. Bryant revises the Romantic conception of authorial intention and origination by positing that although the "design of a textual revision may not be consciously crafted, ... the designs are there, and with them the impress of writers interacting with cultures."[31] When we write, our words attach themselves to the discursive communities within which we are ourselves embedded—but these attachments are neither permanent nor perfectly solid. Revision senses that underneath the architecture of discourse throbs a restless volatility, the potential energy of doing things in a different way.

The poetics of revision may be understood as akin to what Andrew Pickering calls the "mangle of practice" inherent to scientific experimentation.[32] Lab technicians, in Pickering's account, wrestle with their equipment in a "dance of agency," which "takes the form of a *dialectic of resistance and accommodation*, where resistance denotes the failure to achieve an intended capture of agency in practice, and accommodation an active human strategy of response to resistance, which can include revisions to goals and intentions as well as to the material form of the machine in question and to the human frame of gestures and social

---

29. Bryant, *Fluid Text*, 6.
30. Bryant, *Fluid Text*, 61.
31. Bryant, *Fluid Text*, 63. Reading "fluid texts" thus requires acknowledging that *"the fact of the shifting* of words (not just the shifted words themselves) has meaning." Bryant, *Fluid Text*, 97.
32. Pickering, *Mangle of Practice*.

relations that surround it."³³ Pickering's adumbrated account of this process may be applied, if with some limitations, to the development of a new poem. "As active, intentional beings, scientists [poets] construct some new machine [poem]," Pickering posits. "They then adopt a passive role, monitoring the performance of the machine," at which point they cede agency to the machine, which likely does not perform flawlessly. This moment of resistance prompts "another reversal of roles" as the human agents are "once more active in a revision of modelling vectors," which is followed by "another bout of human passivity and material performance, and so on."³⁴ The scientists' orientation can change and may even change as a function of the resistance offered by the machine, just as the poet may find, upon lighting on a specific configuration of words or dazzling metaphor, new inspiration for the work as a whole. Creative invention, in this way, originates not in fixed intention, but in the interaction between author and text, or experimenter and equipment, tuning themselves to each other. Once words are written, the poem-machine poses a challenge to the writer's intentions by compelling the poet to tune subsequent words to an emergent occasion—one in which there are already words on the page.

Perhaps no one in early modern England reflected on writing's mangle of practice as acutely as John Davies of Hereford. At the end of the 1590s, he was selected by Mary, Countess of Pembroke, to transcribe a presentation copy of the Sidney Psalter, and his manual on "fair writing," *The Writing School-master* (ca. 1620), would eventually go into multiple reprints—unlike all but one (*Microcosmos*) of his twelve volumes of poetry. Thomas Fuller's *Worthies of England* (1662) cites him as "the greatest master of the pen that England in his age beheld" (and, like much of literary history, nods at his "pretty excursions into poetry" only as an afterthought).³⁵ In his own estimation, Davies was distinguished from other writing masters by his punctiliousness. As he insists in *The Writing School-Master*, fair writing demands a considerable investment of time and attention, even though "many Imposters . . . undertake to teach perfectly in two and twenty hours, or a moneth at most" despite being

---

33. Pickering, *Mangle of Practice*, 22.
34. Pickering, *Mangle of Practice*, 22.
35. Fuller, *Worthies of England*, 224–25. Davies's neatness is evident in a holograph letter expressing gratitude for patronage to Thomas, Lord Ellesmere, in a presentation copy of *The Holy Roode* (1609) at the Huntington Library. A transcript can be found in Collier, *Rarest Books*, 1:185. It can also be seen in his annotations to a copy of *Coryats Crudities*, images of which appear in Palmer, "'Progress of Thy Glorious Book.'"

"not able to judge of, much lesse perform perfect writing." For Davies, writing's singular difficulty was a direct consequence of its vulnerability to even momentary slips: in vocations like "Limming, Painting, Clocking, Graving," he argued, practitioners might "mend and correct their errors," but scribes did not have such leeway.[36] A "perfect" page was the result of conformity, compliance, and consistency, and other manuals on "fair writing" corroborate this by presenting blots and blemishes as insidious threats.[37] Blotted leaves betrayed a lack of discipline and inattention, as Jean de Beau Chesne and John Baildon's manual proclaims: "Who that his Paper dooth blurre or elles blott, / Yealdes me a sloven it falles hym by lotte."[38] In another of their mnemonic aids, they explicitly link the visuality of the written page to rational, mathematical protocols: "To writing belonges good things two or three, / As drawing, Painting, and eke geometree."[39] Fair writing, despite there being some debates about it in the seventeenth century, was a mechanical art that could be, with time and patience, perfected.[40]

From the perspective of a writing master, unconventional or unregulated scribal hands would signal either inattention or eccentricity. In a passage discussing the virtue of "running hands"—like cursive, in which the letter forms are joined—Davies recounts the development of such eccentricity in a noteworthy pupil. Explaining that the "old ordinary slow Romane hand," which required that the pen be "taken up at every letter," proved an encumbrance to many students, he recalls that Prince Henry, the son of King James I, grew to resent it. This "dull slow hand" prompted the "apt, ingenious and docible" prince to "devise a hand of his own, wherein the letters were linked for his use" because the Roman hand had "made writing but odious to him, as it is to all them that can write non other hand."[41] Davies knew how boredom, frustration, and confusion could arise if students disdained the mere management of

---

36. Davies of Hereford, *Writing Schoolemaster*, sig. A4r. The first edition appears to have been out by 1620; the 1631 edition announces itself on its title page as the "sixt edition enlarged."
37. For example, among other cautions, David Browne advises writers to "wette the point" of their quills, discard ink that is too thick, and reject inkhorns that are too "high or long" in order to avoid inadvertent blots. Browne, *New Invention*, 12, 16, 19.
38. Beau Chesne and Baildon, *Divers Sortes of Hands*, n.p.
39. Beau Chesne and Baildon, *Divers Sortes of Hands*, n.p.
40. For these debates, see Christen, "Boundaries." Simran Thadani explains how copy books like William Panke's *Breefe Receite* (1591) "assume[d] no skills at all" by breaking down each letter into "an orderly *progression* of strokes, rather than merely attempting to recreate a static *collection* of strokes." Thadani, "'Faire Writing,'" 427.
41. Davies, *Writing Schoolemaster*, sig. B2r.

their quills. Even the spaces between written characters could prove too strong a resistance. Yet however ingenious, the prince's invented hand would have likely proved socially embarrassing, so Davies presumably substituted it with instruction in a more established running hand, such as cursive or secretary.[42]

Davies's account of "running hands" turns to glance briefly at poetic composition, and as he does so he acknowledges the disadvantages of rigidly aligning oneself with external standards of correctness. Observing how the Roman hand was imposed on women, he complains about what he perceived as arbitrary and ignorant rules:

> Of which number women (for the most part) are, who out of the ignorance of their teachers (for very view or no English teachers write this hand kindely) are perswaded that the dull set Romane is the womans right hand, but nothing lesse; for women naturally have as much facility in joyning, and are as nimble handed in all manuall qualities (to their praise be it spoken) as men. Many of them are Poets, and indite in verse as well as prose with rare commendation: then in their composition, should they use to take up the pen at every letter, they had need to have good memories, lest their invention should be lost ere they could record it with their pen.[43]

Several women were included among Davies's pupils—notable among them, the playwright and historian Elizabeth Carey—and his admiration for poets and patrons like the Countess of Pembroke and Lucy, Countess of Bedford, made it abundantly clear to him that such arbitrary regulations could be stifling.[44] A hand that mandated lifting the pen, and, indeed, anything that posed resistance to the poet's ability to wrangle thoughts into words, threatened her attentiveness to invention. Since the hand that inscribes is also the hand that endites, these twinned functions vie for dominance in a dance of agency.

Davies confesses this outright when he subsequently offers the reader an intimate glimpse into his own writer's garret: "[F]or when I am about any such businesse my self, I am fain to neglect the fairenesse of my hand, for the freenesse of it to help my memory: so that should some see my first rough hewings in this kinde, (though it be

---

42. On James's advice to Prince Henry, see Goldberg, *Writing Matter*, 126–30.
43. Davies, *Writing Schoolemaster*, sig. B2r-v.
44. H. R. Woudhuysen offers an account of Davies's pupils in *Sir Philip Sidney*, 37–38.

better perhaps then every one can do) yet little would they think it to be my hand, especially writing (as often I do) in my bed: for as our divine Sir *Philip* well said, ease is the nurse of *Poesie*, which makes many Poets so idle-busie."[45] When setting out to compose poems, he set aside his identity as a writing master to free up his poetic attention. The work of poesy, he acknowledges, is partly one of refining clumsy bodgeries and uncorked spewings, or what Anne Lamott candidly terms "shitty first drafts."[46] Davies even invites the reader to imagine what his "first rough hewings" looked like, parenthetically suggesting that they would probably still be inscribed with better penmanship than "every one [else] can do." This confession reveals that even when he tried to break his hand's musculature loose from the social forces that had conditioned it, he could not help flexing. Letting oneself grow discomposed is easier said than done. Positioning the idle business of poetry against his actual occupation in this way, Davies confesses that the former compels him to neglect, but not necessarily abandon, the latter. A perceptive reader of Sidney, he also recognized that poetic idleness did not mean unreflective leisure.

Inefficiency is an important aspect of how creativity proceeds. Drawing on Pickering's account of the mangle of practice to discuss musical composition, Tasos Zembylas and Martin Niederauer invoke his concept of the "disciplinary agency" of different discursive domains to explain that expectations exert pressure that can derail the flow of invention and also promote creative resourcefulness. Disciplinary agency may emerge in music as "notation systems," in essay composition as the five-paragraph structure or prohibitions against passive voice, in early modern poetry as meter and rhyme. Reckoning with these discursive criteria—oscillating between laboring to adhere to patterns and laboring to depart from them—can be cognitively and physically draining: "During most composition processes, there are days of few ideas and very meagre work results. Such work days are just as important as days with clearly measurable outputs: composers eliminate specific options by heading into impasses, as it were—by trying out things and then discarding them. These acts mean that the 'unproductive' days are simply productive in a different way. Making cannot be reduced to efficient and effective action."[47]

---

45. Davies, *Writing Schoolemaster*, sig. B2r-v.
46. Lamott, *Bird by Bird*, 21.
47. Zembylas and Niederauer, *Composing Processes*, 62.

If human intentionality arrives at creativity by accommodating resistance, as Pickering's account of the mangle of practice suggests, this implies that *incapacity* and *failure* are fundamental to creative production. The creative process labors, in part, after *differently productive* labor—inherent to revision is the gesture of "trying out things and then discarding them." In this way, revision is not merely an authorial practice, but paradigmatic of "how we pay attention to the world," according to Richard Lanham: "We alternatively participate in the world and step back and reflect on how we attend to it. We first write, absorbed in what we have to say, and then revise, look at how we have written it."[48] By oscillating between conception and completion, resistance and accommodation, revision subsists on potential energy. Thoughts become things that may still, in turn, be rethought. Negotiating between creative fantasies, rational calculations, disciplinary agents, affective impulses, formalized grammars, and coercive imperatives, revisers exercise restless judgment without committing to binding verdicts. Revision, as such, is the epicenter of discomposition; it is when a text wavers; it is what makes labor discontinuous with productivity.

In contrast to the calm, even-handed attentiveness of fair writing, poesy is animated by revision's restlessness. As Davies recounts in his first book of poetry, *Mirum in Modum* (1601), the mind grapples with the world by way of *"Fantacie,"* which, as a "through-fare" to the *"Intelligence,"* activates when the senses "cannot discerne" something. In these moments, Fantasy "resteth not" and "doth so forme reforme, and it deforms" the perceiver's conception of what faces him or her. Fantasy is the *"Ape of Nature"* but also, importantly, adds her own "Patterns" via "[a] thousand toyes which in hir Bowells breede."[49] Recalling Spenser's allegorical depiction of *Errour* in Book 1 of *The Faerie Queene*, Fantasy appears monstrous, feminine, and excessively reproductive. Davies quickly clarifies, however, that even though she births *"Chimeraes,"* Fantasy also creates *"Beauties"* that "do the *Mynde* beheau'n with matchless blisse." Neither good nor evil, Fantasy but "makes and marrs as she disposèd is"; her "double diligence" involves taking impressions from the world and remaking them into "imprintes" on the mind, sometimes with the aid of forms that she had devised herself. An engine of discomposition, Fantasy leads images in the mind through turbulent encounters

---

48. Lanham, *Economics of Attention*, xiii.
49. Suparna Roychoudhury underscores Fancy's "purposeless self-indulgence" as a function of its idle playing with "toys." See Roychoudhury, *Phantasmatic Shakespeare*, 57–58.

with the world. At this juncture, Davies's poetic speaker reemerges to describe how the restless Muse of Fantasy eventually arrives at Reason:

> Halla, my *Muse*; heere rest a breathing while,
>   Sith thou art now arriu'd at *Reasons* seate;
>   To whom, as to thy *Sou'raigne* reconcile
>   Thy straying thoughts, and humbly hir entreate,
>   With hir iust measure all thy lines to meate,
>   Lest that like many *Rimers* of our time
>   Thou blotst much Paper, without meane or measure,
>   In Verse, whose reason runneth al to Rime:
>   Yet of the *Lawrell* wreathe they make a seasure,
>   And doth *Minerua* so, a shrewde displeasure.
>   (*Mirum in Modum*, 1:8)

The "many *Rimers*" of Davies's age are said to blot paper because of their haste and inattention; their very words, Davies suggests, are errors. Such metaphorical blots are distinct from the blots the Muse will inevitably produce as a function of her "straying thoughts" being brought into order in compliance with Reason's "iust measure." The Muse is made to align with correctness by pausing, resting, and bracing itself for Reason's judgment, which will require a different sort of blot. As both the spilling of ink and the obliteration of it, the blot becomes emblematic of revision's mangle of practice. It is the offspring of Fantasy and Reason, of ebullience and assiduousness, produced when writers choose to sacrifice and readjust what they have already written.

In the early modern period, blots were metonymic for the materiality of writing, making its primary metaphorical connotations contingency, embodiment, sin, and waste.[50] Yet any blot could tell two stories: of error or of amendment. Writers blotted the page to literally materialize the word out of ink's primordial chaos; they also blotted the page to

---

50. Wendy Wall notes how the word "blot" meant "either the ink mark on the page, or the incoherent stain that disfigures writing itself" during a period in which writing itself was considered "deviant" because of its associations with obscurity, pollution, and damnation. Wall, "Reading for the Blot," 132-33. Laura Estill, in *"Richard II* and the Book of Life," discusses how blotting was invoked as a mode of expunging both kings and commoners from the divine "book of life." Christopher Pye observes that in Elizabethan culture, "the most unspeakable of crimes is always marked in that unmarked form" but adds that "to erase a blot is of course to renew it once again," since "the mark of the king's undoing has always underwritten his absolute power." Pye, "Betrayal of the Gaze," 580-81.

cover a mistake. Making blots required that pages be rewritten, thereby risking more errors that would delay once more the final blotting. Being thus overruled, or rather overrun, was apparently the fate of Davies's commissioned copy of the Sidney Psalter: according to William Ringler, Davies was given the task of rendering the Sidneys' work "in a single beautiful Italian hand with the capitals, and loops of the other letters, in gold" for presentation to the queen, but the copy was apparently never presented "because the many corrections made in the process of copying marred its appearance."[51] Writers avoided sharing blotted leaves for fear of impropriety, and we might read confessions that their work was too blemished for publication as a performance of modesty.[52] As evidence both of error and of care, however, such confessions also narrated energetic expenditure. Rather than presenting oneself as someone pressed to speak without a say in the matter, an announcement of spilled ink redefined authority as the ability to revise. Sir John Harington does this explicitly in the preface to his translation of *Orlando Furioso* (1607), when he rebuffs criticisms of his feminine rhymes. He first appeals to conventional authorities by arguing that French poets and Philip Sidney also use feminine rhymes, before ultimately pointing to his "many blotted papers," because this paper trail "might affoord me authoritie to giue a rule of it."[53] The "authoritie to giue a rule" derived from a willingness to countenance one's own unruliness.

Though Davies wielded great authority in rules about *inscribing* words in clean lines, he openly foundered when he could not do the same for *inditing*. In another of his many epigrams about himself, he reflects on this schism:

A drie friend, lately, thus did write of mee;
But whether well or ill, the World shall see:
   There's none were fitter then thou to endite,
   If thou couldst pen as well as thou canst write.
This praise is Capitall: ah, so wer't scand,
Then should my *Head* bee prais'd before my *Hand*.
But this doth lightly lift my Hand so hie

---

51. Quoted in Vickers, *Shakespeare*, 18.
52. For important reframings of the *modesty topos* and its relationship to authorship, see Dunn, *Pretexts of Authority*; Pender, *Early Modern Women's Writing*; and Wolosky, "Modest Claims."
53. Harington, "Answer to Critics," 221.

> To fall on mine owne *Heade* more heauily.
> If I deserue it, still so let it fall;
> So shall my shame not fame bee Capitall.
> If not; that *Heath-bredde Muse* is but a Drabb,
> That (*Ioab*-like) embraceth with a Stabb.
> ("Of Myselfe [Epig. 251]," *SF*, 2:36)

Davies's "drie friend," as the penultimate line indicates, was John Heath, a fellow at New College, Oxford.[54] Even in his defensive retort to this acquaintance, he showcases a career-long insecurity: entertaining doubts about what Heath could have meant, Davies leaves the decision to however "the World" will choose to interpret it. Deferrals to external validation appear throughout his work. In *Wittes Pilgrimage*, for example, the speaker explains that he "maketh happlesse Blotts in eu'ry *Line* / To simbolize his *Loue* vnfortunate" and proceeds to underscore that the page's discomposition is a function of the writer's: "Pen, Ynke, and Paper, then, are quite vndone, / (As is their Master) with Sad *Sorrowes* smart" ("Sonnet 67," *WP*, 2:15). This conceit reflects Davies's habit of noting that the mark he made on culture was interrelated with the marks he made on paper. Another poem echoing this theme advises his brother Richard Davies, also a writing master, by cautioning, "Conforme thine head and heart vnto thine hand, / Then staidly they thine actions will command" ("To My Brother Mr. Richard Dauies," *TWP*, 2:58). The hand's effects were inextricable from the head's endeavors; the act of poetic composition was supposed to bring intelligence and manual technique into alignment.

In an irony for a writing master whose primary role was to train students away from blotting, then, Davies felt at times as if poetry was diminished once blots were excised. A prefatory poem to his *Microcosmos* (1603) celebrates the recently coronated King James I by depicting poets having a difficult time expressing their joy:

> Some bend their *browes*, and wroth with their *conceite*
> Doe scratch their *Cogitation's* hardest *Hold*
> For having no *Worths* in their rude *Receipt*
> Worth the bestowing, though the worst be *gold*;

---

54. Heath concocted the witticism in an epigram titled "Ad. I. D., Scribam, eundemq; scriptorem," and for his addressee, that "eundemque," the phrase "If thou couldst" and the ambiguous difference between "endite" and "write" struck sour notes. See Heath, *Two Centuries of Epigrammes*, sig. D1v (epigram 89).

> Which is but *Drosse*, compar'd with what they would:
> Some other write and blot, and blotting write,
> So *thoughts* in Blots infolded, *thoughts* vnfold;
> Bewraying so the *Worlds* of their *delight*,
> Is more then *Worlds* of *thoughts* can well recite.
>
> (*Microcosmos*, "A Preface," 1:13)

While some poets arrive at "gold" despite believing their work to be "*Drosse*" compared to what their ambitions had promised, in the circularity of cogitation other poets "write and blot, and blotting write." By this, Davies suggests that the blots best depict their authors' actual inventions by disclosing the "*Worlds* of their *delight*." Just as a blot can depict deformity—such as when Ben Jonson asks the painter William Burlase to make "one great blot" in order to render his own bulky frame[55]—they can also conjure obstreperous joy as rhetorical conjurations of the sublime. Joshua Calhoun notes that a blot, unlike other forms of revision that enabled deletion, "can function as paralipsis, as an explicit gesture toward a thing that is emphasized even as it is overtly ignored."[56] Here, Davies presents them as an earnest *aposiopesis*: a breaking off of speech in the middle of conversation as if overcome with emotion. Within the blot lives poesy's endeavor; it materializes both self-censure and irrepressible utterance. Writing doubts about his own words, or even about words' capacities for representation, Davies equates cancellation with composition.

In another poem about himself, this one an epigram responding to a poem by Thomas Bastard, he documents in detail the roughness of his hewings:

> BASTARD, thine Epigrams to sport inclines;
> Yet I protest that one delights me best
> Which saith the Reader soone deuoures thy lines,
> Which thou in many houres couldst scarce digest.
> So fares it twixt the Reader and my Muse;
> For that which she compiles with paine (God wot):
> This word she chooseth, that she doth refuse;
> This line she enterlines, that she doth blot;
> Heere's too much ornament, and there it lackes;

---

55. Jonson, *Complete Poems*, 199.
56. Calhoun, *Nature of the Page*, 79.

This figure's farre-fetcht, out with it againe;
That phrase of affectation too much smackes;
This reason, rime doth racke and too much straine;
That simil's improper, mend the same;
This application's harsh, harmonious make it;
Fye, out vpon't, this verses foote is lame,
Let it goe vpright, or a mischiefe take it;
Yet it runnes ill, the cadence crabbèd is,
Away with it, for shame, it marres the rest;
Giue it sweet accent; Fy, fy yet I misse;
Store makes me scarce I know not which is best.
Heere is a bodge, bots on't; farwell my pen,
My Muse is dull'd, another time shall serue;
To-morrow she (perhaps) shall too't agen;
And yet to-morrow she (perhaps) may swerue. . . .
    ("To Mr. Tho. Bastard, and the Reader," *SF*, 2:20)

Davies has caught hold of a writing prompt after perusing Bastard's *Chrestoleros* (1598), in which the poem "Ad lectorem" explains that the poet's verses are "easie of digestion" because of his concerted effort: "How many verses haue I cancelled? / How many lompes of meaning seasoned[?]" While epigrams "sprowte forth," Bastard explains, "I vse mine arte, and prune them with my pen."[57] Like a well-trained humanist, Davies copiously elaborates on Bastard's example. He describes the physical ramifications of his muse's endeavors, and as he documents these traces, he also points to a host of formal and aesthetic decisions. In a cascade of verses divided by medial caesuras, the poem directly reckons with the disciplinary agents of early modern poetry: figurative language, meter, rhyme, cadence, tone, affectation.[58] Any or all of these things place pressure on the poet's hand, and any of them can mar the work. Each decision being made with respect to one element complicates the standing of others. "Store," says Davies, alluding to the options available to him at every turn, "makes me scarce I know not which is best." Looking down at his work midstream, he cries out,

---

57. Bastard, *Chrestoleros Seuen Bookes*, 179–80.
58. The collection of vectors recalls Quintilian: "[P]rune the turgid, raise the mean, control exuberance, organize the disorderly, give rhythm to the unrhythmical, and restrain the exaggerated." Quintilian, *Orator's Education*, 353 (X.4.1).

"Heere is a bodge, bots on't" and relents, awaiting his muse's return on another night.

At the end of his pen's fantastic voyage, after his muse has returned and at the point when he feels ready to pass his restless energy forward, Davies finds the journey rendered irrelevant by greedy, superficial readers:

> Well yet at last the poem being pend
> The Printer it presents to Readers view;
> Some foule-mouth'd Readers then (which God amend)
> So slop them vp that it would make one spew,
> To see how rudely they deuoure at once
> More with then ere their head-peece held perchance;
> As if my wit were mincèd for the nonce,
> For them with ease to swallow with a vengeance.
> Yet preethee Reader be not so vnkinde,
> (Though I am bold with thee) to eate me too;
> I beg (being thy poore cooke) but thy best winde;
> If thou wilt not do this thou'lt little doo;
> But f[y], I shall not be beholden to thee
> A rough ryme choake thee; eate and much good do thee.
> ("To Mr. Tho. Bastard, and the Reader," *SF*, 2:20)

Proud of his labors, he despairs about how easy it is for readers to ignore them. Even here, however, he is self-deprecating, and the last six lines vacillate like the wavering indentation that closes "Of My Selfe." At first they implore ("Yet preethee Reader . . ."), then they judge ("If thou wilt not do this . . ."), and then they dismiss ("I shall not be beholden to thee"). The poem's final line then again deploys a medial caesura, first blurting out how the poet *really* feels—"A rough ryme choake thee"—before suggesting either that his poor cooking will stick in readers' throats or that the food may be nourishing despite their shallow tastes. As with his poem responding to Heath, the judgment is left out of Davies's overtaxed hands, and the final verdict of praise or blame remains an open question. The poem thus aligns a collection of "choke" points across writers' and readers' encounters with the poem itself: Davies's muse stopping up his pen and pressing him down a surer path, him pausing in his efforts night after night until finally issuing something, readers rushing headlong into his verses and risking indigestion, and the author angrily critiquing those readers, dismissing them, and then finally resigning himself to the situation. If only God would "amend" the readers, the poem parenthetically prays, with as much attention as a poet reworking his creations.

Fantasy never rests, but the muse, poets, and readers alike may grow tired and inattentive—as Horace noted, even Homer might sometimes be caught nodding off.[59] In another epigram addressing himself, Davies complains about how writing drains him: "Lord! my poore braines now busily I beate, / My temples toile with chafing of my hand; / My sleepes disturb, my meales cutt short at meate; / My time consume" ("Of Myselfe," *TWP*, 2:64). In his concern with material want, Davies echoes comments made by other writers interested in the tenuous alignment between labor and recognition.[60] Participating in this trope, he ventriloquizes the carping criticisms of a shallow reader who pays little attention to an actual composition. Pointing to "some gull" who might declare about his poem, "[I]ts pritty, pretty," he hears such a reader then question why someone would spend "so much witt" to "so small purpose." Some other reader, he then expects, might concede some value in the work, but then find cause for remarking on trivial errors—"And then (perhapps) he cauills with a T / That was misplaced, or at the most missuted" ("Of Myselfe," *TWP*, 2:64). As we have seen, Davies distinguished between "writing" and "inditing," between what the page looked like and the poesy that produced it. When turning his attention to the reader's experience rather than the writer's, he imagines this distinction collapsing. Any ungenerous reader could choose to brood on a typo. In such a context, no writer could be certain of the conditions or standards by which his or her work might be appraised.

A successful poetic business depended in no insubstantial part, Davies came to realize, not just on privileged access to idleness but also on poets' capacity to market themselves and to win the benefit of readers' doubt. Because he lacked the ability to adjust his readers' expectations and make them endeavor to read him "aright," he ended up unwillingly documenting the trajectory of a poet correcting himself in accordance with norms and expectations. The problem with revision, after all, is

---

59. Horace, *Satires. Epistles. The Art of Poetry*, 481 (lines 358–60).
60. For example, Thomas Nashe grumbles, "But all in vain I sat up late and rose early, contended with the cold, and conversed with scarcity, for all my labours turned to loss, my vulgar Muse was despised and neglected, my pains not regarded, or slightly rewarded, and I myself, in prime of my best wit, laid open to poverty." Nashe, "Pierce Penniless," 52. Pender explains that such accounts of travail were a rhetorical trope; a writer's allusion to working by candlelight was "a strategy which ostensibly places emphasis on the author's diligence rather than on his natural gifts." Pender, *Early Modern Women's Writing*, 23.

that if it is not sustained with the same alacrity as invention—if the poet is disallowed the straying frenzy of Fantasy—it may lapse either into impulsive necessity, exhausted compromise, or rationalized correction. Undertaking revision requires having enough energy, time, ink, and paper, and Davies, watching the movements of his own hand as he lay awake in his bed, understood that his idleness was not the same as that of the idle rich. Aware of the conscious and unconscious compromises he made by trading the blotted circumlocutions of poesy for the linear logic of productivity, he witnessed himself becoming busier only to become more mediocre.

Wealth and Wit

"Mere *bric-a-brac* by dull conceited fool!"
    So dry-as-dusts, snatch-and-run readers, prate
    O' Davies of Hereford; and then elate
Ween they have damn'd him. Men not of their school,
With brains, and heart, and judgment true, to rule
    Their verdicts—both of late and early date:
    Men who far up transfigured heights had sate—
Differ. Granted, the books are over-full;
Granted they are unsifted, hurried, mixt
    Of tares and grain; fair flowers with weeds entwined:
    Yet there *is* genius; and, my friend, you'll find
Thought, feeling, fancy, wit, rounded and fixt
    As stars; with happy memories and traits
    Of Shakespeare and "The Mighties" of those days.[61]

This poem prefaces the only modern printed edition of John Davies of Hereford's collected works. Composed in the late nineteenth century by Alexander B. Grosart, who edited over forty volumes of writings by Tudor and Stuart "worthies," it foreshadows how the volume's critical introduction intends to refute the "un-golden asses" who have dismissed the poet despite being "in utter ignorance of his books."[62]

---

61. Grosart, "Dedicatory Sonnet."
62. It bears mentioning that Grosart's two volumes are part of a series of works by early modern "Worthies"—the "Chertsey Worthies Library." The hundred subscribers of the Chertsey list consisted of university libraries, rich men, church fathers, and the queen of England. While these volumes have been digitized and are now available for perusal at the Internet Archive (https://archive.org/details/completeworksjo00grosgoog and https://archive.org/

Even as he makes his strenuous case in Davies's favor, however, Grosart concedes that the poet's works are often "unsifted, hurried, mixt" and that his poems—riddled with "superfluities of commonplace"—"render any lofty claim for Davies as a Poet impossible." Nevertheless, his justifications for producing the volume anyway are aesthetic: "If there be not in this poem the sign-manual of POWER of a very noticeable type," he writes to introduce his favorite excerpt, "I confess I am incapable of discerning what is and what is not powerful."[63] As careful a reader of Davies as anyone—his sonnet itself closely echoes Davies by borrowing some of his phrases—even Grosart quails at fully affiliating his reputation with this lowercase-*p* poet. Both the poet and his eventual editor surveyed the poetic landscape of early modern England to declare what they saw as worthwhile, or at least not worthless—but Grosart, unlike Davies, presumes a learned authority that Davies himself would never access. Over time, as we will see, Davies consciously distanced himself from the practice of adjudicating on poetic work; he resolved to be an admirer rather than an evaluator of writing, because judgment proved to be an unreliable standard for appointing value. Grosart's own posture, one more typical of literary history, is less accommodating: those who damn Davies outright, without even acknowledging those few traces of "power," he suggests, are of a different "school" than those with "brains, and heart, and judgment true, to rule / Their verdicts." This defense relies on confidence in his own schooling, which has determined Davies to have passed—just barely—an implicit test (to which the correct answer was and remains Shakespeare).

Unlike his future editor, Davies understood that his restless wit and educational background were not the only engines driving his hand across the page.[64] In his verses, poesy appears as a concrete practice involving actual physical expenditure. It names a struggle to exceed the things within one's grasp and a struggle to resist grasping only that which was within reach. This conflict between ambitious impulse and

---

embed/completeworksjo03grosgoog), I was able to comfortably read them as physical copies (and consequently devote this chapter to Davies) at the Folger Shakespeare Library, whose copy was donated by the Earl of Derby. I was able to do research at the Folger only after receiving a generous fellowship, which I mention to underscore that the scenes in which we encounter poetic texts and produce scholarship about them are as wrapped up with the material conditions of work, access, and privilege as the scenes in which those writings were first created.

63. Grosart, "Memorial-Introduction," xxi.

64. As Hans Magnus Enzensberger puts it, the social imperatives of compliance enable mediocrity to "[take] revenge on its opponents"; these imperatives are a means whereby "monsters are made to order." Enzensberger, *Mediocrity and Delusion*, 184.

decorous self-restraint required that poets orchestrate their time, deplete their materials, and exhaust their mental faculties. Tabulating these costs, Davies could not help but comment on the fact that his work was typically unrewarded and unremunerated.

Earlier in "Of My Selfe," Davies plays on the resonances of the word "vain"—frivolous, worthless, narcissistic—to interrogate his own labors:

> And who doth loue this vaine of fancy vaine
> But vainest men? then, ô how vaine am I
> That thus the powers of my wit doe strayne,
> To please vaine Skums with skumme of vanity?
> ("Of My Selfe," *WP*, 2:5)

Unable to distinguish between his approach as a writer and the attitudes and habits of his readers, Davies deplores the vanity of writing for vain men. As we know, however, "Of My Selfe" ends with him deciding to publish anyway. When he points to his "vaine of fancy vaine"—the worthless ore he has excavated with the help of Fantasy—he nods at the "strayne" of this fruitless effort. This straining also appears in a poetical essay in a phrase adapted from Terence's *Eunuchus*: "Nihil tam bene dictum, quod no fuit dictum prius" (Nothing is well said, that was not said already). Riffing, as "Of My Selfe" also does, on Ecclesiastes, Davies claims that "Our Actions, and Inuentions are fast fixt / Vnto the Spheare of Vniformity" ("Nihil tam bene dictum," *WP*, 2:53). Even though some writers may mix in some variations and changes to their source materials, these hodgepodge creations inevitably still "hold conformity" with the disciplinary agency of poetic traditions. Davies's contemporaries could only ever remain schoolchildren trailing after the ancients, he supposed, while the ancient poets "strained their Braines / Beyond our reache, though we in vaine, haue sought / To straine our Wits beyond their Wisedoms Straines." It was only "Self-conceit" (another form of vanity) that had led poets to imagine that they had lighted on "some Inuention, past the modern Straine" ("Nihil tam bene dictum," *WP*, 2:53). Only if a poet recovered every trace of his cultural literacy by reading every extant book and still found that "some, or all" of his poetry was *not* determined by preceding works, this would make him "a Spirit and no Man Naturall" ("Nihil tam bene dictum," *WP*, 2:53). Davies, however, keenly sensed that he was *not* a "Spirit," to the extent that he sometimes felt he did not deserve to make a claim over his own work. While he rubbed elbows with many of the most prominent poets of his age, he was never bold enough to imagine himself truly great. He was not one of the "self-crowned laureates" who could affix his name to a recognizable vein.[65]

Given the "authorless" transmission patterns of epigrams, wherein lines were written with the understanding that they would be reproduced without ascription, a poet's "vein" rather than his or her actual words became a calling card.[66] Prior to the advent of copyright, the idea that one could steal from other writers was complicated by the traditions of "compilation" and "emulation" that informed humanist writing practices.[67] Achieving literary fame in the early modern period may consequently be better understood, Max W. Thomas suggests, as an author negotiating "his or her own *name*" (emphasis in the original) within the limitation of recognizing poetic works as "common property."[68] A kind of compositional fingerprint in an atmosphere where poetic achievement could precipitate patronage and official posts, a poet's vein, metonymic for the poet's name, was social capital.[69]

Davies appears so consistently self-effacing across his epigrams that he counterproductively tries to make a name for himself by diminishing his own stature, warping the modesty *topos* into a self-fulfilling prophecy. In a poem to Jonson, he confesses feelings of envy by invoking those of his addressee: "[W]ould thou couldst enuy mee: / But (ah!) I feare my vertues are too darke / For enuies shadow, from so bright a Sparke" ("To My Well-Accomplish'd Friend Mr. Ben Iohnson," *SF*, 2:26). Praising John Donne, he appraises himself as among "some poets

---

65. See Helgerson, *Self-Crowned Laureates*. We might approach his sense of a "vein" as a subset of what Samuel Fallon describes in *Paper Monsters: Persona and Literary Culture in Elizabethan England* as authorial "personae" in early modern England.

66. See Doelman, "Circulation," 65. In one epigram in *Chrestoleros*, for example, Bastard declares that "if *Heywood* liued now againe / . . . If he would write, I could expresse his vaine, / Thus he would write, or else I am deceiued." Bastard, *Chrestoleros Seuen Bookes*, 59–60. In another, he makes a tentative charge of theft against Samuel Daniel—"Me thinkes thou steal'st my Epigrams away / . . . For reading thee me thinks thus would I say. / This hits my vaine, this had been my conceipt"—before confessing that were he to try and "doe the like," he would be at a loss. Bastard, *Chrestoleros Seuen Bookes*, 140.

67. For the politics of authorship and ownership, see Simonova, *Early Modern Authorship*.

68. Thomas, "Eschewing Credit," 290.

69. We can see a similar discussion of the commercial value of poetic veins in Macray, *Pilgrimage to Parnassus*. These academic dramas begin with two recent graduates from Cambridge finding that they lack the funds to continue residing at university. As they journey through the world outside the academy, they encounter a wealthy and foolish city gallant, Gullio, who requests that one of the graduates produce verses for him to share with his beloved: "Make mee them in two or three divers vayns, in Chaucer's, Gower's and Spencer's and Mr. Shakespeare's" (58).

of our times / That spoile good paper with their byting pen" ("To the No Lesse Ingenious Than Ingenuous Mr. Iohn Dun," *SF*, 2:18). Comparing his muse to that of Sir John Harington's, which is "plum'd on woodcockes, wrens, and ostridges," he laments that his "pownces not so strong, / Hauing some geese to pull" ("To the Worthy, Ingenious and Learned Knight Sr Iohn Harrington," *SF*, 2:22–23). To the rival epigrammatist John Owen, he even seems willing to relinquish his own claims to authorship. "Lend me thine hand; thine head I would haue said," he writes, correcting himself when he realizes that all he truly has to offer is his manual labor—"(For my hand's firmer though thy head's more staid)." If Owen would "add some merry measures" to Davies's own verses, he suggests, "Then shall my booke be prais'd (at least) for thine" ("To Myne Ingenious and Learnedly Gamesome Friend Mr Iohn Owen," *TWP*, 2:58).[70]

Such subordination of his own name becomes most obvious in Davies's reflections on his emergence under the intimidating shadow of another poet with whom he was and remains sometimes confused—Sir John Davies.[71] Hereford was a writing master who taught students advanced orthography at Oxford and near the Inns of Court; Sir John had matriculated at Oxford, studied law at the Middle Temple, and was often reprimanded for bad behavior before seeing his poetry win approbation from both Queen Elizabeth and King James I. Sir John lacked discipline but had social connections and wealth; he would eventually become attorney general of Ireland. Hereford cultivated a reputation for discipline but lived at best an effectively middle-class life. In a poem

---

70. In his request that Owen add measures to his book, Davies may be reflecting on his own practices of engagement with others' epigrams. In a copy of Thomas Coryate's *Coryats Crudities* (1611) now held at the Pierpont Library, Davies himself wrote a poem in response to a mock-panegyric poem by Nicholas Smith, which was itself mocking both Coryate and the poets who were engaging in the game of mock-panegyrics: "Lo here a Smith, / That firiest Witts doth knock, / With his Witts Hammer giues him self a strok: / For, here hee iudgeth Tom, and not misdeemes, / Then hee's his Peere as hee him self esteemes." In adding this finely inscribed mockery of Smith, who had mocked Coryate and by extension poets like Jonson and Donne who were playing Coryate's game, Davies recognizes the relativism of aesthetic judgments in general, and tacitly perceives how aesthetic power relies on social affiliation. Davies's marginal poem can be seen and read in transcription in Palmer, "'Progress of Thy Glorious Book,'" 349; see Palmer's extended discussion of Davies's annotations for a rich picture of his practices as a reader.

71. As R. J. Schoeck puts it, "Sir John Davies was unquestionably the greater poet, and he had already published his *Nosce teipsum* in 1599 when the lesser John Davies [of Hereford] published his *Microcosmos* four years later." Schoeck, "'Nosce Teipsum,'" 307. He also might have had to brand himself as "of Hereford" because of yet another John Davies, a well-known mathematician at Oxford implicated in the Essex rebellion.

addressed to his noble namesake, he writes, "Good Sir, your nature so affects my Name, / That both your Name and Nature are mine owne / And in their loue to both, affect your fame, / Yet hauing not like fortunes, liue vnknowne" ("To My Right Worthily-Beloued Sr Iohn Dauies Knight," *TWP*, 2:53).

Davies knew that his life and work were generally appraised as mediocre; his "fortunes" confirmed as much.[72] While there are no records of him attending university, throughout his professional life he situated himself near centers of higher learning—likely because they produced a steady stream of pupils seeking to present themselves at court in elaborate hands. In London, he lived near the Inns at Court, and he associated himself with Oxford—namely, with Magdalen College and with several Oxford students who had been his pupils. As a poet, however, he initially made a distinction between living "in the middle" of the social order and writing mediocre verses, arguing that middling men could still be great poets.[73] In a poetical essay developing a theme from Publilius Syrus, "Fortuna vitrea est, que cum splendet, frangitur" (Fortune is fragile, after it glitters, it shatters), he writes that it is better to live unseen in order to better observe the ebb and flow of greatness and baseness. The poet may be "like a looker on a Tragedie, / Within the Middle Room, among the Meane." Not participating in the travails of a great life protects the poet from the calamities that breed true poverty; *observing* the rise and fall of the reckless greats could instead offer inspiration to compose "matter far aboue the reache of Words" ("Fortuna vitrea est," *WP*, 2:48). Those who do not experience great risk, he felt, may still find means to write about it.

He repeats this conceit in another poem, a sonnet possibly referencing the work of a more blatantly ambitious poet, Christopher Marlowe's *Tamburlaine*: "When, with my Minds right Eye, I do behold / (From nought, made nothing lesse) great Tamburlaine." Davies the theatergoer notes how figures in tragedies may be raised high in order to be brought low, and he concludes that it is wiser to stay "among indiffrent Things" ("Other Sonnets vpon Other Subiects," *WP*, 2:22). This poem, too, places poetry outside the karmic calculus of acquisition and debt: "And so I liue, in Case, to take or giue, / For Loue, or

---

72. Vickers suggests that "Davies looked up to more gifted writers, expressing admiration from below, but he did so in neither an envious nor a sycophantic manner." Vickers, *Shakespeare*, 37.

73. Fleming, *Exemplarity and Mediocrity*, 27–28.

Meed, no Scepter but a Crowne: / Yet Flowres of Crownes, for Poesies expence,/Poets might take, and giue no recompence" ("Other Sonnets vpon Other Subiects," *WP*, 2:22). Poets may exceed the mean because poetry can break the economy of taking and giving, of economic advantage and individual agency. Through poetry, pangs of desire bubble upward, past the realm of worldly things—somehow, Davies imagines, it may become the vehicle by which one might raise one's spiritual, if not socioeconomic, stature.

It is one thing to watch Tamburlaine's rise and fall, or even to be a spectator at Marlowe's self-consciously audacious *Tamburlaine*, and another thing entirely to try and emulate greatness while exercising caution. For much of European history, terms like "mediocre" and "mean" invoked the "middle style" of rhetorical discourse, which *Rhetorica ad Herennium* defines as "words of a lower, yet not of the lowest and most colloquial, class of words."[74] Accordingly, mediocrity also named a social and behavioral status valued for common civility. Attaching to concepts like the "golden mean," the *via media*, and the "mean between extremes," it named a standard worth inhabiting— but also one that was a notoriously difficult one to describe or define. Like "common," as Neil Rhodes explains, the "mean" eventually came to denote both an "average" and something "low or base."[75] This proved especially true as it became a term employed in aesthetic appraisal. Developing Ernst Robert Curtius's view of European literary history as a "tradition of mediocrity," Paul Fleming adjusts the phrase to "the tradition of exemplarity" because, in the Horatian lineage that inspired much of European poetics until the eighteenth

---

74. [Cicero], *Rhetorica ad Herennium*, 253 (4.8.11). In classical rhetoric, mediocrity denoted a specific stylistic category, between the *gravis* (a "smooth and ornate arrangement of impressive words") and the *extenuata/adtenuata* ("brought down even to the most current idiom of standard speech"). Describing words of a "lower, yet not of the lowest and most colloquial, class," the middle style, in *Rhetorica ad Herennium*, tempered the grand style so as to prevent it from becoming "swollen." As Joshua Scodel points out, the influence of Aristotle's *Nicomachean Ethics* and Cicero's *De officiis* on grammar school curricula also linked mediocrity to a desirable sense of measure, proportion, and moderation. Scodel, *Excess and the Mean*, 2-4.

75. Neil Rhodes relates *mediocritas* to the term "meane" and the ethical ideal of the *via media*, and apprehends in it a formal no-man's-land. This ambiguity, Rhodes suggests, parallels the socioeconomic distinction between "elite and common." Rhodes, *Common*, 164. In *The English Secretary* (1586), Angel Day calls rhetoric's "high" style "sublime," which for Patrick Cheney affiliates this conception of rhetorical style with the Latin *sublimitas* and thereby the notion of the "sublime" that undergirds much of modern aesthetic thought. This adjacency corroborates the transformation of "mediocre" from a category of rhetorical style to an aesthetic appraisal. See Cheney, "'Forms of Things Unknown,'" 138.

century, unimpressive artfulness was associated primarily with "the inability to observe rules and thus to maintain tradition."[76] Fleming observes that it was only after the rise of "the eighteenth-century genius," and the revival of interest in Longinus's writings on sublimity, that greatness became associated with originality, and mediocrity with hacky derivativeness. What Horace meant by "mediocre" (i.e., evoking but not quite capturing the greatness of Homer) is quite different from what Pierre Bourdieu calls the products of "middlebrow" culture (i.e., "accessible" versions of the avant-garde).[77] Yet as Fleming also reminds us, if in one sense mediocrity means that something "fails to achieve completion or perfection," in another it means "the art of the politician: made to please" and to appeal to the common, the popular.[78]

Davies's marginal position relative to poetic greatness allowed him to perceive how mediocrity, popularity, and socioeconomic insecurity were intertwined. In this way, he anticipated the rebirth of Longinus's views of the aesthetic sublime, because for Longinus, mediocrity implied a safeguard against risk: "Perfect precision runs the risk of triviality, whereas in great writing as in great wealth there must needs be something overlooked. Perhaps it is inevitable that the humble, mediocre natures, because they never run any risks, never aim at the heights, should remain to a large extent safe from error, while in great natures their very greatness spells danger."[79] This account of mediocrity traces "great writing" and "great wealth" to the same origin—the capacity to engage in risk. To say that Davies was mediocre from a Horatian perspective suggests that his was a failure of artful craftsmanship; to say that he was mediocre from a Longinian perspective is to assert derivativeness. Retracing the slow reemergence of Longinus's *On the Sublime* over the course of the European sixteenth century (the first known edition was printed in Italy in 1554, the first Latin edition in 1566), Patrick Cheney argues that these printings and the "sixteenth-century use of the new word 'sublime' suggest that something was in the water much earlier" than the first English translation, which appeared in 1636. According to Cheney, "[T]wo historical phenomena emerging during the late sixteenth century—the modern author and the classical

---

76. Fleming, *Exemplarity and Mediocrity*, 26.
77. Bourdieu, *Distinction*, 321.
78. Fleming, *Exemplarity and Mediocrity*, 23.
79. Longinus, *On the Sublime*, 265–67.

sublime—are interconnected." Both authorship and sublimity share a "commitment to the project of *literary greatness*"; both are "produced through imitation of preceding authors; they are written primarily in the grand style (occasionally in the plain style); they proceed through elevated figuration; they represent our most serious cultural ideas; and they aim for artistic immortality."[80] We might place Davies's career squarely within the literary transformation Cheney describes, noting in his poesy the competing imperatives of Horace and Longinus, of an impulse to perfection and the self-contradictory art of leaving "something overlooked."

To declare something mediocre is to say very little concrete about it—mediocrity can only be relatively determined—thereby inviting a conversation about the manner and terms by which judgment itself is being exercised.[81] Heinrich von Kleist observes that people "only argue and squabble about artworks that are not entirely excellent."[82] Fleming presses this insight toward an appreciation for mediocrity as a testing ground for social practice: "[T]he necessarily argumentative nature of dissecting mediocrity as well as the conflict of opinion it implies" means that "average art offers a truer model of the *sensus communis*—a community discussing and perhaps agreeing on what is mediocre and why—that aesthetic judgment presupposes."[83] Declarations of mediocrity are invitations to reflect on the habits of judgment being applied to a given work at a given time, and Davies, as we have seen, openly declared himself mediocre. Because mediocre poetry *invites* and even *provokes* social critique, it is in the bland light of mediocrity that we may view him not as a model poet, but as an engaged critic of the literary economy of early modern London.

While he had courtly ambitions, Davies also recognized himself as part of a developing hierarchy of literary quality. Near the bottom of

---

80. Cheney, "'Forms of Things Unknown,'" 141.
81. Sianne Ngai points out that aesthetic declarations are always wedded to how "other judges, abstract figures standing in for our relations to others in general, are already 'inside' our most spontaneous, affectively immediate experiences of form." Consequently, issuing a judgment of something as beautiful is also a demand for agreement that "binds the way in which we face or address others to appearances we can only perceive for ourselves." Ngai, *Theory of the Gimmick*, 22. Judging something as middling, however, may also be an invitation for further specificity. As with Ngai's accounts of the "gimmick" and the "interesting" as aesthetic categories, the appraisal that something is mediocre gradually reveals an equivocality that puts "*aesthetic misgiving as such* at the heart of our encounter with compromised form" (24).
82. Quoted in Fleming, *Exemplarity and Mediocrity*, 39.
83. Fleming, *Exemplarity and Mediocrity*, 41.

this unstable literary hierarchy was a class of writers who explicitly used their work to comment on public affairs, and their favored genre was the epigram. These writers were known as the "pot-companion poets" or "pot poets," and as Thomas Cogswell explains, they took advantage of their "rough and ready adult education" to anonymously disseminate scurrilous doggerel. A shade above balladeers and far below courtiers in their technical polish, pot poets exploited anonymity to libel and critique prominent figures. Their name gestures toward a metonymic web that also describes their cultural haunts: the "pot" may refer to their close affiliation with the alehouse, with the cheap "pot paper" on which they wrote, with pots circulated for coins in exchange for verses, and with the privies in which one might read and relish their rubbish. A sort of open-air literary underground that tacitly licensed sharp criticisms of public affairs, pot poetry drew the ire of more respectable sorts—among whom Davies imagined himself.[84] Yet even though pot poets were maligned by cultural elites for "social roughness and aesthetic worthlessness," they represented a form of writerly endeavor that could still achieve fame and financial compensation. Davies was familiar with their work—and with their critiques of the literary system of elite London.

Among the most prominent of the pot poets was John Taylor. Because of Taylor's and Davies's inverted positions at the margins of early modern literary culture, reviewing Taylor's unique professional career alongside that of Davies sheds light on the increasing inscrutability of literary value. Davies and Taylor seemed to know each other, and both were, in different ways, "middling" writers who perceived a frayed relationship between the effort a poet might invest in his work and the degree to which he might be compensated. If the ragged Taylor was less educated and less well-connected than the comparatively smooth Davies, however, he was also arguably more famous as a poet. He was known as "the Water Poet" because his day job was as a waterman, or ferry driver on the Thames, garnered him a wide following in early modern London.[85] He made this poetic career for himself in part by enter-

---

84. Poets such as Thomas Bastard and Everard Guilpin were prominent representatives of this group, though, as Andrew McRae notes, the advantages of anonymity mean that "'pot poet' is a category that could include either all men writing poetry at the time or only a tiny and shifting number." McRae, "Early Stuart Libeling," 372.

85. Katharine Craik explains that his unregulated avenue of authorship afforded a "vocabulary to describe, and enact, new strategies of professionalism in print." Craik, "John

taining his ferry fares with extemporaneous wit and poetry, and in part by developing "subscription" modes of remuneration and advertising wherein he would accept payment for putting landmarks and taverns into his works.[86]

In *The Praise of Hemp-Seed*, Taylor critiques conceptions of value decoupled from ability and social utility: the often overlooked and devalued hemp seed, he contends, is the hardworking source of both fine clothing and tattered rags. Within that poem, he ruminates on paper (a hemp-seed product) as representative of England's broken value system. He remarks that paper may be a democratizing medium: "For who can tell from whence these tatters springs? / May not the torne shirt of a Lords or Kings / Be pasht and beaten in the Paper mill / And made Pot-paper by the workemans skill?"[87] Defending the potential of even the lowest born, Taylor concedes that his work is less refined than that of other poets. He brandishes his lack of education as an asset, though, and facetiously reviews how "[s]ome Authors doe the name of Paper gather, / To be deriv'd from *Papa*, or a Father," while others, because "it's made of rags and pouerty, / In stead of Paper name it *Pauperis*."[88] In this framing, paper becomes both the foundation of textual authority and the material evidence of ephemerality. As a ubiquitous good, it allows Taylor to develop a conception of poetic value whereby hard but potentially imperfect work is worth as much as, if not more than, lazy, smooth compilations. Riffing on his own last name, he concedes that he has compiled his verses out of others' books and stolen phrases and patches, defending himself by arguing, as we saw Erasmus argue in chapter 1, that it was better to show the seams of one's effort than to pass off wholly borrowed robes as one's own.

Taylor's Pot-Poetry," 187. For important studies of Taylor, see Fall, "Popular Nonsense"; Aune, "Thomas Coryate."

86. As Craik argues, Taylor overcame his self-conscious mediocrity by explicitly resisting a literary philosophy centered on *ingenium* and *imitatio*, or innate genius and emulation, instead favoring one that emphasized *exercitatio*, wherein "literary value depended on the intellectual and physical labor involved in writing." Craik, "John Taylor's Pot-Poetry," 185. In glorifying his own effort, Laurie Ellinghausen observes, Taylor occupied a position of sociopolitical indeterminacy: he challenged social hierarchies by elevating his own humble labors, but did so with an "authorial persona that is distinctly self-promoting, individualist, and entrepreneurial." Ellinghausen, *Labor and Writing*, 94.

87. Taylor, *Praise of Hemp-Seed*, sig. D4v.
88. Taylor, *Praise of Hemp-Seed*, sig. E2r.

We have seen Davies's self-deprecations when he positions himself against the literati; here, by contrast, is his commendatory verse to Taylor's *Urania* (1615):

> In every Art, save Poetry, the meane
> Is praisd: but therein meanely-well to do
> Is base, too base: then Iudgment cannot leane
> On whats too base, but base it must be too.
> Then each man that his Reputation huggs
> For Judgment, praise no lines of but meane Reach:
> And laude but what drawes dry Minervaes duggs,
> Lest they their Iudgments might thereby impeach.
> Then is my Iudgment Iack, perplext in thee;
> For thou dost write so well with meanes so ill
> That thine Admirer I confesse to be,
> Much rather then the Iudger of thy skill:
> > Art makes not Poetry, thou dost plainly prove,
> > But supernaturall bountie from aboue.
>
> ("John Taylor, the Water Poet,"
> *Commendatory Poems*, 2:9)

The poem spells out some dimensions of Davies's career-long ambivalence about literary value. It opens by invoking Horace's declaration—one quoted in Sidney's *Defence*—that even though a "lawyer and pleader of middling rank" still has value, "that poets be of middling rank, neither men nor gods nor booksellers ever brooked."[89] A consequence of such disdain for middling poets, Davies observes, is that readers are typically ungenerous to any work that appears "of but meane Reach." No reader would want to "impeach" his or her own judgment in public by praising what others may deem merely mediocre. Carping criticism has always been easier to venture than approving alignment. Diagnosing this social force, Davies acknowledges the difference between a poet at the "mean" and a poet who is able to "write so well with meanes so ill." Instead of judging Taylor's "skill," he resolves instead to simply be an "admirer," though he couches his admiration not in Taylor's work ethic but in "supernaturall bountie." By this logic, the fact that an uneducated person from a lower-class background could achieve "meanely-well to do" poetry was something of a miracle in itself, and

---

89. Horace, *Satires*, 481, quoted in Sidney, *Sir Philip Sidney*, 223.

it was unfair to "judge" that poet's work by the same standards as the work of elites.

Davies's second published collection of poems, *Microcosmos* (1603), describes a society in which the vagaries of fortune restrict writers, and literary arts in general, from reaching their full potential:

> *Artes* perish wanting *praise* and due *support*;
> And when *want* swaies the *Senses Common-weale*,
> *Witts* vitall *faculties* was al amort:
> The *Minde*, constrain'd the *Bodies want* to feele,
> Makes *Salves* of *Earth* the *Bodies hurt* to heale,
> Which doe the *Mind* bemire with *thoughts* vnfitt;
> He[n]ce come those dull *Conceipts* sharp *witts* reveale,
> Which nice *Eares* deeme to come from want of *witt*,
> When want of *wealth* (indeede) is cause of it.
> How many *Poets*, like *Anatomies*,
> (As leane as *Death* for lacke of *sustenance*)
> Complaine (poore *Staruelings*) in sadd *Elegies*
> Of those whom *Learning* onely did advaunce,
> That of their *wants* haue no considerance.
> What *Guift* to *Greatnesse* can lesse welcome be
> Then *Poems*, though by *Homer* pend perchaunce?
> It *lookes* on them as if it could not see,
> Or from them, as from *Snakes*, away wil flee.
> (*Microcosmos*, 1:49)

Affirming that the mind's labors cannot be disentangled from the body's, Davies attributes some of poets' "dull *Conceipts*" to a lack of "*praise* and due *support*." He makes clear that money is not the only thing that produces good art by acknowledging in his running marginal commentary that "if some mens wittes were measured by their wealth, they would be accounted Salomons that are nothing else but money-baggs, in whõ[m] there is nothing but money" (*Microcosmos*, 1:49). In the poem itself, however, he raises the salient counterpoint that deprivation has consequences for the liveliness of wit. If Sidney suggests that poetry advances the "purification of wit" and that its "final end is to lead and draw us to as high a perfection as our degenerate souls, made worse by their clay lodgings, can be capable of,"[90] Davies argues that those

---

90. Sidney, *Sir Philip Sidney*, 219.

clay lodgings, when put under strain and want, make for themselves "*Salves* of *Earth*" and consequently drag down any chance the wit has of purifying itself. It is no surprise, *Microcosmos* implies, that the nation's poets have issued so much dreck—their poverty consumed the care they might have granted to writing.[91]

When the mind is bound by a body vulnerable to distraction, compromise, and lethargy—and the body is confined to impoverishment, want, and hunger—the work, poesy, will suffer. Early in his career, Davies appeals to poetry's transcendent qualities to ignore such material concerns. Diagnosing a disparity between the labors of poesy and the transcendent heights of capital-*P* Poets, he argues that while poets may be poor, the work remains worth doing: "So make them pure (at least most pure in sight) / Which to *Posterity* may be a *light*." Poetry's value lies in attaching the earthly present to eternity, so what matter if a poet is not appreciated in the poet's own time?[92]

By the time of *Paper's Complaint* (1611), however, Davies's perspective appears to have changed. Posing as paper itself to satirize the sluicing filth that "becackes" (*PC*, 2:75) its breast, he presses poets to feel as if even their pages can see their laziness. After first railing against the pot poets, ballet mongers, and others who array it with their "*Offals* of wit," Paper also turns its yellowed eye on the immorality that had preoccupied antipoetical writings. It takes *Venus and Adonis* to task for its "bawdy Geare" and rails against Nashe's "Choice of Valentines" for making it wear the word "dildo" (*PC*, 2:75). The main thrust of Paper's argument links the wasting of material components of writing to the mismanagement of social expenditure. Bad poetry is a symptom of the unthinking profligacy of London in general, the denizens of which were coming to prioritize rapid consumption. Commercialization coupled with poor editorial standards had created a class of "infant Rimers" like pot poets and eager mediocrities who "ply their Pens as Plow-men do their Plow / And pester Postes with Titles of new bookes" (*PC*, 2:76). Paper does not even spare its own author: "And thou (O Poet) that dost pen my Plaint, / Thou art not scot-free from my iust complaint, / For, thou

---

91. For connections between Davies's *Microcosmos* and Shakespeare's Sonnet 111, see Jackson, "Shakespeare's Sonnet CXI."
92. This sentiment also appears in an epigram addressed to George Chapman that ranks the translator of Homer with "the rarest men" while also complaining, "[I]n thy hand too little coyne doth lye." He affiliates himself with Chapman—"[T]hou wert accurst, and so was I"—but still counts them both as "blessed" by poetry even if unrewarded by the public. Davies, "To My Highly Vallued Mr George Chapman," 2:59-60.

hast plaid thy part, with thy rude Pen, / To make vs both ridiculous to men" (*PC*, 2:75). Yet even as Paper chastises those who have mistreated it with their crude ink, it concedes that transcendent poetry will endure. It generally approves of poetry, since poetry makes Paper wear its "rich and gaudiest Geare." Its favorites, it confesses, remain those who "in too earnest Game / (Or little spleene) did me no little shame," because despite these lapses, "They oft haue me araid with royall *Rimes*, / That rauish *Readers*" (*PC*, 2:76).

As Paper recognizes the virtues of poetry, it also laments the art's vulnerability to forces outside of poets' control:

> O *Poetry*! that now (as stands thy case)
> Art the head *game*; and yet art out an *Ace*:
> An *Ace*? nay two: (for on thee *Fortune* frownes)
> That's out of Credit quite, and out of Crownes.
> Thou art a worke of darknesse, that doest damne
> Thy *Soule* (all *Satire*) in an *Epigram*.
> Thou art, in this worlds reckoning, such a Botch
> As kills the *English quite*, how er'e the *Scotch*
> Escape the mortall mischiefe: but, indeed,
> Their *Stars* are better; so, they better speed.
> Yet *Poetry* be blith, hold vp thy head,
> And liue by *Aire* till Earthly *Lumpes* be dead.
> But, if *Aire* fat not, as through thee it passes,
> Liue vpon *Sentences* gainst golden *Asses*.
>   (*PC*, 2:76)

Gone unheralded, unapproved, and underfinanced, poetry that has fallen "out of Credit" and "out of Crownes" has only one recourse: the benighted work of satirical epigrams. If denied access to transcendence because of material want, poets are encouraged to become more caustic, more venomous, and more critical. The first half of "idle-business" is as important as the second; being forced to work by external pressures is as destructive to poetic endeavor as periods of thoughtlessness. Writers, Paper concludes, should embrace idleness as an opportunity to think, learn, and wait: "[L]et your reason idle bee the while; / Let Reason worke, and spare your Writings toile" (*PC*, 2:79). Moreover, Paper warns those who presume to possess wisdom that any such apprehension divorced from the restless energies of fantasy and desire—of a perpetual and impulsive grasping—is a delusion. Idleness, in this light, is not *rest*;

it is "differently productive" labor that knows that not everything it may produce is worth sharing with the world. Making this case, Paper ultimately bemoans how poets do not all have opportunities to escape, even if fleetingly, the heavy burdens of the *other* pressures driving hands across pages. "Although your *Minde* be clog'd with Bodyes weight," the piece of paper tells the writing master working on it, if you come to write after allowing yourself some idleness, "ye grace me with eternall *lines*, / That compasse can, and gage the deep'st Designes" (*PC*, 2:79). Throughout history, far from everyone has been afforded the opportunity to undertake this time-consuming labor. Until all might have this chance, Paper suggests that it is poets' job to launch critiques, to sustain themselves by feeding on the "golden *Asses*" who value false idols and equate wealth with wit.

Reflection: Teaching without Judging

Nancy Sommers's influential study of revision reveals that in experienced writers, a willingness to labor further is sparked by their understanding of the critical importance of "dissonance."[93] Characterized by their ability to discover meaning by confronting "incongruities between intention and execution," these writers know that writing thoughtfully, or using writing to think, is a practice of reflection and reconsideration.[94] Inexperienced and learning writers, by contrast, are often guided by instructions, "struggle to bring their essays into congruence with a predefined meaning," and orient their labors "toward a teacher-reader who expects compliance with rules."[95] As bell hooks points out, beyond stifling genuine revision, institutionally enforced "correctness" also perpetuates the silencing of writers from marginalized social classes, or writers who have not already been initiated into the academy's discursive community.[96] Getting a good grade, like achieving fame, demands that the work be submitted in accordance with whatever clues the writer might have picked up about what the teacher wants. Experiences of discomposition only derail the timeline of productivity, and students know from experience that dissonance is rarely a people pleaser.

To introduce students to the virtues of revision, Peter Elbow suggests separating the writing process into two stages: free writing and revision. This separation would engage the "two opposing muscles" of creativity and critical thinking.[97] To depict the struggle that occurs when these muscles are simultaneously taxed, Elbow imagines two writers: one who is "blocked and incoherent" and another who "can always write just what he wants." Their different approaches manifest not just in terms of the quality of their prose but, via an analogy that John Davies of Hereford might have appreciated, in their management of their pens: "Picture the two of them: one has uneven, scrunched handwriting with pointy angles, the other has

---

93. Sommers, "Revision Strategies."
94. Sommers, "Revision Strategies," 104–5. As Susan Sontag bluntly puts it, "What I write about is other than me. And what I write is smarter than I am. Because I can rewrite it. My books know what I once knew—fitfully, intermittently." Sontag, *Where the Stress Falls*, 267.
95. Sommers, "Revision Strategies," 104–5. Also see Murray, *Craft of Revision*, 4.
96. bell hooks describes this process: "Individual white male students who were seen as 'exceptional,' were often allowed to chart their intellectual journeys, but the rest of us (and particularly those from marginal groups) were always expected to conform. Nonconformity on our part was viewed with suspicion, as empty gestures of defiance aimed at masking inferiority or substandard work." hooks, *Teaching to Transgress*, 5.
97. Elbow, *Writing with Power*, 9.

round, soft, even handwriting. When I make these two people freewrite, the incoherent scrunched one is often catapulted immediately into vivid, forceful language. The soft handwriting, on the other hand, just continues to yield what it has always yielded: language that is clear and perfectly obedient to the intentions of the writer, but lifeless. It will take this obedient writer much longer to get power. It will take the scrunched writer longer to get control."[98] For Elbow, handwriting metonymically captures the cleaving of a writer's attention between the riotous impulsive urges constitutive of "power" and the externally disciplined technique that bolsters "control." The shapeliness of smooth letterforms analogizes conventionality, formality, and obedience; the scrunched pointiness, vibrant life. Writing *should* be a struggle, Elbow suggests: "[Y]ou are trying to wrestle a steer to the ground, to wrestle a snake into a bottle, to overcome a demon that sits in your head," and you "must overpower that steer or snake or demon," but "not kill it."[99]

Both the "soft" and the "scrunched" hands exhibit lack—one of power, the other of control—and so both are part of a class of writers whom Elbow characterizes as "in the middle." These writers are defined as "those who manage to write but don't write especially well," because the muscles that drive creativity are at odds with those that animate critical reflection. "Either creativity has won out and produced writers who are rich but undisciplined," he observes, or "critical thinking has won out and produced writers who are careful but cramped." Separating freewriting from revision can alleviate this drive toward mediocrity, Elbow suggests: the clay may "fight you a bit in your hands as you try to work it into a bowl, but that bowl will end up more alive and powerful."[100] In dissociating power from control, however, Elbow's analogies arrive at the same problem that Davies arrived at when he attempted to subordinate "Fantasy" to "Reason." If Reason and control get final say, how much of a say do Fantasy and power ever really get?

Davies had to explicitly send Reason out of the room and excuse it from disgrace, because otherwise Davies would have been compelled to "vndoe" his own lines. If we affiliate "revision" with control, in the end both the "soft" and the "scrunched" students will have simply made the bowl they were asked to make. The problem with linear conceptions of process—drafting then revising, or prewrite/write/rewrite—is that

---

98. Elbow, *Writing with Power*, 18.
99. Elbow, *Writing with Power*, 18.
100. Elbow, *Writing with Power*, 19.

despite the intention to break down the mechanics of composition, they nevertheless obscure the degree to which invention and revision function reciprocally. If students are asked to proceed into revision as something done to meet a specific end—such as the teacher's evaluation—then revision loses its centrality to the writing process and becomes supplemental to it. Of course, the student's writing must be shared at some point. Semesters come to an end, and clear deadlines are as necessary for cultivating good writerly habits as clear prompts. If we want to present revision as something a writer will do in response to the gift of time, as volitional "idle-business," however, we might consider the ways the classroom and its coursework could be structured to introduce revision not as an obligation but as an opportunity.

Crucial to reframing revision, I propose, is recognizing the pernicious effects of imposing conclusive external judgments on student writing. In a 1973 essay, Barrett John Mandell declares, "I cannot teach and judge as the same person."[101] The problem, he explains, is that when students sense "that they have not truly been heard (that is to say, understood), they—like their teachers or any other people—either harden into a strident dogmatism or shrink insecurely away from the fire." In order to be in a position to "hear" a student, the teacher must resist applying "fixed judgments" and instead create space for students to experiment with their own thoughts. "It does not make me ... less of a professor of literature," Mandel observes, "if I free a student to grapple with Donne by saying, in one way or another, 'Sure you're lazy! Who isn't lazy? I'm lazy. Donne was lazy too! Now let's talk about what else we are—energetic, creative, and educable.'"[102] Finding continuities between the embodied experiences of students and the history of poetic and critical thought exposes literary practice as requiring labor, energy, and encounters with resistance met by strategies of accommodation. To suggest that even John Donne was sometimes lazy, that even Homer sometimes snored, is to acknowledge that what looks like laziness is a part of the writing process too—and that lapses in attention or motivation do not diminish someone's authorial potential. Donne need not only appear to students as a difficult text that they must write correct compositions about; he may also and just as easily appear as a working writer who, at times, needed to take breaks, or needed more time to finish what he set out to do.

---

101. Mandel, "Teaching without Judging," 623.
102. Mandel, "Teaching without Judging," 628.

If revising requires paying attention to multiple factors at once—structure, audience, style, syntax, formatting—then revisers will be inevitably inattentive to some things in order to focus on others, only to repeat this process on the next pass through.[103] Mandel's solution to teaching without judging, taking stock of the fact that there is simply a lot of work involved, was to grade "entirely, though flexibly, on a quantitative basis, rather than a qualitative one." Anticipating and inspiring the labor-based grading system developed by Asao B. Inoue, this method allowed him to openly affirm that what he was asking of students would be difficult, and that their only responsibility was to try and rise to the challenge. Creating a system whereby the student would get a grade "the moment he or she hands in the project, regardless of its quality," Mandel invested in a belief in students' willingness to learn and recognized that there were some who could not "avail themselves of the opportunities to learn."[104] Inoue makes explicit that the essential problem with grading student writing is the way grading amplifies the potential discrepancies between different students' opportunities to learn: "[A]ll grading and assessment exist within systems that uphold singular, dominant standards that are racist, and White supremacist when used uniformly." Teachers, Inoue argues, must decide whether writing, in their classrooms, is enlisted as a form of thinking or as a consolidation of dominant power structures. Simply recapitulating the standards of assessment that determined the teacher's own legitimacy, a legitimacy founded on an institutionalization of a specific image of what "standard" writing is, risks reproducing writing as a matter of rule-following compliance.[105]

Beyond serving as a more receptive audience for student work, teachers of writing might work more consciously to adhere to Davies's warning that being generous readers means little if writers are not given the opportunity to take themselves and their own work seriously. When we grade student work, what about their work are we evaluating? We may want to be appraising students' critical engagement with early modern literary texts, but how much time do we spend revealing to students what it takes to engage these texts critically? If we lecture, walking students through the relationship between specific passages in a text and its formal and thematic architecture, or the relationship between a text and its historical context, what tools are we giving them to attempt to undertake

---

103. On the multiple dimensions of revision, see Bean, *Engaging Ideas*, 33-35.
104. Mandel, "Teaching without Judging," 629-30.
105. Inoue, *Labor-Based Grading Contracts*, 3.

this feat on their own? Do we explain what we are doing when we single out a textual crux and explain its pertinence to the meaning of a text as a whole? If we do explain what we are doing, do we also explain how long it took us to discover this crux, to process it, to develop a reading around it?

In the previous chapter, I cited Laura Wilder's study of how making explicit some of the common "special topics" of invention improved students' ability to formulate their own critical arguments. Even if we make these moves visible, however, all we have done is set our students on a course of analytical practice that will require careful and slow study. If they wish to make an argument about the ubiquity of a textual phenomenon, they will need time to take an inventory. If they wish to make an argument about a feature of the text that they feel is latent but nevertheless crucial, they will need time to review not just how the text gives glimpses of this latent feature, but whether other readers regard this feature as latent, as well. Some students may pick up on the conceptual moves their professors are making during class and come to a baseline sense about what their professors want, but what happens in class happens very quickly, managed by an authoritative professor who appears to generate readings without much effort at all. At home, when these students face their own words, it more than likely seems easier to take canned observations and package them into canned arguments. With salves of Google-fed Earth, they patch up whatever ideas they might have had just to meet the deadline.

What if a literature class simply gave its students *time*, too much time, time they would not otherwise have? What if our classes, citing figures like Davies and Taylor complaining about their lack of access to idleness, made the temporality of creative work part of how they "teach" early modern literature? What if, to match this course content with pedagogical form, our classes then allowed students to start writing their essays in class, granting their writing, their words, some footing on the course schedule alongside the writing of early modern poets? What if, as will be discussed in the next chapter, we devoted class time to conferences wherein we serve as sounding boards and editors? A classroom that embraces poesy, rather than poets and poems, is a classroom that concedes that nothing might be achieved other than the expenditure of thoughtful labor, experiences of idle uncertainty, and the production of discarded drafts. Such a classroom regards time as a gift and a privilege, presenting poesy in its purest form: as a threat to the economy of efficiency and debt.

"When I am about any such businesse my self," Davies reflected, "I am fain to neglect the fairenesse of my hand." When he set about to the doing of poesy at home in his bed, he consciously tried to neglect the obligations of his day job. He stayed up late, claimed some idle hours for poetry, at least partly because he derived some pleasure from it. We might theorize the nature of such idle business of poetry in our classrooms, but we might also remember that our students often have literal jobs and often treat their schoolwork as a pathway toward future employment. Is poetry, are critical thinking and reflection, is revision only for the writers on the syllabus? By reducing the demands we place on our students' time—requiring less reading, issuing fewer assignments—and by giving them clear expectations about what we want them to do and what we have to offer them in return, we may give all of them the opportunity to choose to make the most of their time with us. If we revise our classroom to focus on the *doing* of literature, we may make a more robust case for why literature remains something worth doing.

Chapter 4

Editing
Anne Southwell's "Extent of Paper"

Copied into the volume now known as the Southwell-Sibthorpe Commonplace Book (Folger V.b.198) is a letter that Lady Anne Southwell (1573-1633) sent to her friend, Cicely Mackwilliams, Lady Ridgeway.[1] Prompted by Ridgeway's posture as "a sworne enemye to Poetrie," Southwell conjures three metaphors in poetry's defense: she calls it the "meere Herald of all Ideas," "The worldes true vocall Harmonye, of wch all other artes are but parte," and—most evocatively—"the silke thredd that stringes your chayne of pearle; wch being broken, your iewells fall into the rushes; & the more you seeke for it, the more it falles into the dust of obliuion" (4). Taken together, the metaphors suggest that poetry promotes invention (herald), represents the orderliness requisite of artfulness (harmony), and maintains a canon of virtuous examples for pious emulation (thread). Southwell's letter then demonstrates poetry's ability to forge links by extending an invitation to Ridgeway: "Therefore, (Noble & wittye Ladye) giue

---

[1]. Klene, *Southwell-Sibthorpe Commonplace Book*. All references to works by Southwell, unless otherwise noted, will be to this edition, and indicated in-text by title and line numbers, and in footnotes by page number. Klene's edition refers to folio pages in its margins; the original commonplace book may be found at Anne Southwell, Henry Sibthorpe, and John Sibthorpe, *Miscellany of Lady Anne Southwell*, Call # V.b.198, MS V.b.198, Miscellany of Lady Anne Southwell, manuscript (ca. 1587-1636), Folger Shakespeare Library.

mee your hand, and I will lead you vpp the streame of all mankind." She closes the epistle in a similar vein, proposing a longer discussion: "But noble Ladye, I will trouble you noe further now; yett when I haue your honorable word of reconciliation, I will then delineate out euery lim̃e of her, & how shee is envelloped vpp wth the rest of the artes" (4). Southwell's defense of poetry, itself borrowing arguments from Philip Sidney's, thus emphasizes poetry's ability to translate instruction and inheritance into tools for building community across time and space.

Though Southwell invokes Sidney's claims in her letter, she does not seem to have been troubled by the contradictions we saw him deal with in chapter 2. Sidney conceded that poetry could sometimes be a "nurse of abuse" but questioned, "[S]hall the abuse of a thing make the right use odious?" Southwell mirrors this move, suspecting that Ridgeway's disdain arose because she had been exposed to "[s]ome wanton Venus or Adonis" and consequently allowed a "cloude [to] disgrace the sunne" (5).[2] Retorting that "[i]t is the subiect, that com̃ends or condemnes the art," she goes on to echo Sidney's example of "divine" poets who "did imitate the inconceivable excellencies of God" in observing that poetry's best works are appointed by heaven: "Then, see the kingly Prophett, that sweete singer of Israell, explicating the glorye of our god, his power in creating, his mercye in redeeming, his wisedome in preseruing; making these three, as it were the Com̃a, Colon, & Period to euery stanzae" (5).[3] Where Southwell differs from Sidney, however, is in how his defense would go on to confound poetry's special relationship to divinity by distinguishing "divine" poets from "right" ones. Like Sidney, she was an adherent to the Calvinist doctrine of total depravity and understood that one could not rely on the assurance of divine will behind the placement of one's punctuation marks. This lack of assurance led Sidney to a poetics paradoxically driven by hesitation, blockage, and frustration; he recognized that while a poet might labor to "bestow a Cyrus upon the world to make many Cyruses," to actually create such a Cyrus the poet needed both a teacher to guide him and readers who would "learn

---

2. For more on Southwell's debts to Sidney, see Clarke, "Anne, Lady Southwell," 64; and Clarke, "Gender," 116.

3. Sidney, *Sir Philip Sidney*, 217. Danielle Clarke and Marie-Louise Coolahan argue that Southwell "prioritizes subject matter over technique and, in rejecting secular in favor of divine love, makes a claim for a different kind of aesthetics" wherein the "poet's authority is derived from the devotional subject matter rather than from its poetic treatment." Clarke and Coolahan, "Gender, Reception, and Form," 147.

aright why and how that maker made him."[4] Southwell, by contrast, saw the encounter forged between poets, their advisers, and readers as a source not of anxiety but of possibility. As none of them—poet, adviser, reader—could guarantee the divinity of their perspective, the "profitable invention" of poesy could consist only of a collective practice of discomposition, of testing out ideas and discovering their limitations.

Joining Anne Southwell's poetic congregation, this chapter considers what happens to revision when it becomes, like invention, a "social act" whereby a writer learns from a trusted interlocutor. The term we use for the rewriting that one does under advisement, as opposed to that done alone, is *editing*. Like revision, editing is often treated as a synonym for correction, but to "edit" more accurately means to "give out" or "put out" [*e* + *dare*], underscoring that while editors may polish a text, they also participate in the uncertain process of extending private labors into the public sphere.[5] Even the best editors cannot be assured that their advice will guarantee acclaim. In this way, editors appear in Karen Burke Lefevre's account of invention as "resonators," a term she adopts from Harold Lasswell and explains as follows: "Resonance comes about when an individual act—a 'vibration'—is intensified and prolonged by sympathetic vibrations."[6] Distinct from authorial collaborators who may begin a project together, resonators aid the "principal discoverer" by serving as "catalysts who make discovery possible," but they do not "usurp the writer's task of evaluation."[7] Editors serving as resonators thus multiply Quintilian's account of the reviser's "double effort" because, as Susan L. Greenberg puts it, they participate in a process "consciously drawing on the powers of imagination in two ways; a doubling up of points of view representing not only the reader, but also the author."[8] The editing process is one whereby authors' texts are brought into alignment with perspectives other than their own. So long as authors retain the ability to make final decisions, editing becomes a practice of productive and collaborative discomposition. Told where

---

4. Sidney, *Sir Philip Sidney*, 216–17.
5. *Oxford English Dictionary*, s.v. "Edit, v.," accessed July 20, 2021, http://www.oed.com/view/Entry/59546.
6. LeFevre, *Invention*, 65.
7. LeFevre, *Invention*, 68–69.
8. Quintilian, *Orator's Education*, 353 (10.4.1). Greenberg, *Poetics of Editing*, 19. An editor's contributions thus entail "asking similar questions about the text as the author" but "com[ing] to the text with a fresh human consciousness and therefore the potential distance to break habitual patterns." Greenberg, *Poetics of Editing*, 14, 19.

they may need to rethink their work, authors may choose to accept or reject correction.

The first professional editors in Europe were scribes, and in England this vocation emerged around 1200, according to Greenberg, "as demand for books exceeded the ability of monasteries to produce them in sufficient numbers." With this professionalization rose a "shift in textual authority" away from centralized ecclesiastical settings and toward the accuracy of source materials and "exemplar" texts. This remediation of a text by nonauthorial hands connects, if loosely, the behaviors of medieval scribes to those of printers who aligned manuscripts with print-shop capabilities and, eventually, to periodical editors in the nineteenth century who started to enforce house styles as well as decisions about taste.[9] In the midst of this centuries-long rise of the professional editor were the complicated interrelations between print and manuscript authorship poetry in the seventeenth century. While writers like Ben Jonson were beginning to consolidate a conception of authorship related to property and print—turning one's work into a collected *Works* sold with one's name on its cover—others, and particularly women writers, were developing different strategies for cultivating authorial influence within the social ecology of manuscript composition. Lady Anne Southwell's works afford a unique perspective on this context of manuscript authorship, then, because they expose the cultural logic of editing in seventeenth-century poetics in two ways. The first is that Southwell wrote and thought about how poetry itself was a form of social interaction that involved discomposing encounters with the perspectives of others. The second is that her texts cannot be accessed—cannot even be read—without provoking questions about what it means to read a poem that has clearly undergone a process of editing.

Southwell's poems survive in two manuscripts: the Southwell-Sibthorpe Commonplace Book, which was a private household miscellany/table book, and Lansdowne MS 740 at the British Library, a "fair copy" prepared for the king of England.[10] Taken together, they reveal her to have been both a humble poet and an ambitious one, both introspective and extroverted. Gillian Wright suggests that the writings

---

9. Greenberg, *Poetics of Editing*, 88-91. As Carlo M. Bajetta points out, "[S]ince its inception" in the authorizing practices of ancient Greek editions of Homer, "editing was a negotiation of authority." Bajetta, "Authority of Editing," 308.

10. Klene identifies Anne's hand in published writings related to the Overbury circle; see Klene, introduction, xxvii-xxix. Also see Clarke, "Pamphlet Debate."

in the Commonplace Book depict a "direction of textual travel [that] is typically inwards" because Southwell appropriated others' writings, largely from somewhat unfashionable print sources, for her own development.[11] By contrast, the Lansdowne manuscript reveals a desire to directly influence royalty (though it is unclear whether it was prepared for James I or Charles I). Although the Commonplace Book appears to be more akin to a private notebook and the Lansdowne appears to be a fair copy for external readers, even the former witnesses the social embeddedness of Southwell's poetry. Not merely a journal of her thoughts, it is a document of asynchronous conversation filled not just with letters like the one to Ridgeway but poetic epistles, imitations, and replies.[12] As Sarah C. E. Ross points out, these poems participate in forms of "lyric sociality" built on "the commonality of images, tropes, and poetic lines and forms" and "the operations of communal lyrics as literary tokens and artefacts in a context of socio-poetic exchange."[13] Beyond the allusive and appropriative web of manuscript composition, the Commonplace Book also captures how the everyday labor of verse composition was more complicated than a solitary author revising poems in bed. It contains poetry and prose inscribed in a variety of hands, with corrections and insertions appearing throughout; most of the poetic material attributed to Southwell was inscribed by scribes who were likely members of her household.[14] The volume was likely compiled, moreover, not by Southwell herself but by her husband, Captain Henry Sibthorpe, as a compendium of her "works." Her own difficult handwriting contributes some of the corrections and insertions, though not all of them; the leaves written exclusively in her own autograph drafts were apparently tipped into the book by Sibthorpe after her death.

The complicated provenance and frequent illegibility of Southwell's manuscript poems clarify, ironically, how early modern poetic composition prior to publication must be understood in terms beyond originality and ownership. As we will see, Southwell invited interventions

---

11. Wright, *Producing Women's Poetry*, 46.
12. Sarah C. E. Ross finds the tension between private and public writing even within the Commonplace Book, arguing that the way Southwell transcribed, emulated, and appropriated others' words reveals her "use of poetry simultaneously to forge networks and to assert her socio-political affiliations." Ross, *Women, Poetry, and Politics*, 80.
13. Ross, *Women, Poetry, and Politics*, 79.
14. Klene suggests that the "sometimes indecipherable lines illustrate how a woman could know little about penmanship even though she was very well read," though she acknowledges that at times Southwell "does write correctly and legibly." Klene, introduction, xxxvi.

from collaborators like her husband in ways that allowed her to construct an authorial identity in terms of the ongoing, restless, and fundamentally interactive practice of poesy itself. Joining her in the crowded scene of writing consequently means joining a collective endeavor—one that also enlists modern readers in Southwell's poetic process. Wright observes that "like other manuscript-based poets of the early modern period, [Southwell] is a corrective to the anachronistic assumption that a poet who took writing seriously must inevitably aspire to print-publication."[15] Taking writing "seriously" for early modern poets had more capacious connotations than aiming to produce something that would endure and win fame, renown, or approbation. In early modern manuscript culture, Arthur Marotti explains, "it was normal for lyrics to elicit revisions, corrections, supplements, and answers" as they proceeded through coteries of trusted peers, because poems were "part of an ongoing social discourse." The manuscript system was, as a result, "far less author-centered than print culture and not at all interested in correcting, perfecting, or fixing texts in authorially sanctioned forms."[16] While Harold Love describes the process of "scribal publication" as one tracking the "movement from a private realm of creativity to a public realm of consumption," bringing this definition into conversation with Marotti's account of the poem as "social text" suggests a writing practice that wavered between public and private, between individual author and discursive community.[17] Between private creativity and public consumption was an intermediary stage of creative collaboration that our classrooms might foreground for student writers, a stage wherein writing becomes more like a jam session, a period of open-ended collective experimentation, exploration, and inevitable discomposition.

The first section below recovers traces of the social approaches to writing in early modern manuscript culture, emphasizing how scholarship on women's writing in particular offers crucial correctives to the affiliation of authorship and legitimacy with individualism and originality. In recovering a more crowded scene of writing, I situate writers like Southwell amid the development of poetic editing as a social and professional practice. The chapter's second section unpacks how, for Southwell, poetry, like salvation, required relinquishing oneself into others' hands, and how she appears to have embraced the prospect of

---

15. Wright, *Producing Women's Poetry*, 28.
16. Marotti, *Manuscript*, 135.
17. Love, *Scribal Publication*, 36.

being edited—by her husband, her priests, her friends—as one of poesy's redeeming virtues.[18] Though a defender of poetry and a critic of misogyny, she was also sometimes ambivalent about poetry's role in a reformed Protestant society and about women's place in public life.[19] Writing to and with others allowed her to think through these ambivalences. Her forthrightness about the collaborative nature of early modern authorship in this way enabled her to use her own presumed lack of authority as a social instrument; asking for help became a pretext for developing and sharing her own ideas. Her work consequently demonstrates how the scene of editing can provoke the discomposition not only of the text being examined but also of the relationship between authors and readers.

Examining this complex relationship as it applies to the Southwell-Sibthorpe Commonplace Book itself, the chapter's third section discusses how the physical documents on which Southwell's poesy occurred afford opportunities to open pedagogical conversations about editing's affinities with critical reading and writing. The traces of several hands on Southwell's two manuscripts reveal that her work has always availed itself of interlocutors—ones she consciously enlisted, ones who amended and arranged her works after her death, and ones she could never have imagined. The materials of the Commonplace Book may be seen as a space within which Southwell's poesy remains continuous with an ongoing editing process. As such, they reveal that in the scene of editing, the practice of composition (a word that in early modernity also meant "agreement") reveals itself to be a simultaneously textual and social practice, a means by which individual expression blurs with those of communities of enthusiasm, affinity, and interpretation.

Before moving into the body of this chapter, I want to openly recognize those readers who served as my editors in the composition of this book.

---

18. Ross, *Women, Poetry, and Politics*, 65. Elizabeth Clarke identifies her as a "Calvinist conformist in the pre-war Church of England" and suggests that her "attitude to intellectual pursuits, and to poetry in particular, is one of cautious enthusiasm." Clarke, "Anne, Lady Southwell," 68.

19. The Commonplace Book shows direct engagement with poems by Walter Ralegh, Henry King, and Francis Quarles. Southwell includes an unattributed copy of Walter Ralegh's oft-copied "The Lie," and adds a few stanzas apparently of her own composition. Elsewhere, she would include copies of poems by Henry King and put them to use in a personal process of mourning. See Burke, "Medium and Meaning," 101. Despite her mainstream Calvinism, Southwell evinces some sympathies with Puritanical views, and moderates her response to James I's more licentious proclamations, such as the Declaration of Sports, which sharply divided the Arminians from the Puritans who, like Southwell, valued the sanctity of the Sabbath. See Clarke, "Anne, Lady Southwell," 59–60.

The earliest draft of this chapter was read by Dianne Mitchell. The earliest readers of chapter 1 were Debapriya Sarkar, Laura Kolb, David Hershinow, and Caralyn Bialo. The earliest reader of chapter 2 was Jenny Mann, and of chapter 3, Phil Pardi. The earliest reader of chapter 5 was Wendy Beth Hyman, who was also the first reader of the entire book (!) and a gentle influence over many pivotal decisions. Mahinder Kingra, editor extraordinaire at Cornell University Press, shepherded this book into its final form, and Eric Levy offered many thoughtful recommendations while gracefully copyediting away my most embarrassing errors. I recognize these readers—who must not be blamed if they could not always usurp my own poor judgment—here as well as in the acknowledgments to underscore that this work of critical writing was produced within a community marked by mutual aid, collaboration, generosity, and shared investment.

Academia, when it lives up to its ideals, represents a shared endeavor that not only cares about knowledge production but also strives to care—materially, psychologically, and politically—for those willing to join the fold. Do we not want our students to be, even if only for the duration of the semester they may spend with us, part of the same academy we hope to inhabit, the academy that believes that thinking closely, deeply, and slowly about things, and even disagreeing about them, is essential to whatever better world we may want to build? The way that literature scholars commune over a shared interest at academic conferences, usually in conversations predicated on and mediated through writing, is for many of us the best part of the job. What might the feedback, advice, and instruction we give our students look like if we chose to treat what they write as part of a disciplinary field that is open to them? How might this feedback make it clear to them that the field explicitly needs their perspectives and their feedback to uphold its commitments to poesy?[20] In the reflection following this chapter, I convene a discussion about what resisting competitiveness, practicing humility, and taking student writing seriously—a pedagogy of generosity, to borrow Kathleen Fitzpatrick's framework—might look like.

Marked by Thy Hand

Around the turn of the sixteenth century in Italy, vernacular books started announcing that they had been "revised," that they contained

---

20. Nancy Dejoy asks similar questions of composition studies in *Process This*.

"additional material," or that they had been "newly corrected." This signals, according to Brian Richardson, the emergence of what today we understand as editors in vernacular literary production.[21] The role of these early editors was that of the *correctore*, whose textual emendations "tended to achieve not authenticity but conformity to contemporary standards" of spelling, punctuation, grammar, and style, even despite the shifting nature of those standards.[22] Editing was a manner of constructing and conferring legitimacy; going through the editing process afforded authors authority they could not always claim on their own. As Richardson explains, "During the first century of printing, an investment in editing came to be seen as one of the keys to success both by ambitious printers and publishers and by authors."[23] These attitudes migrated across the continent during the Renaissance, and editors quickly became active participants in the construction of modern authorship. Robert Iliffe suggests that during the seventeenth century in England, "the manifestation of the 'editor' was intimately bound up with the appearance of the 'author'" because the former's role and function were "connected by virtue of their ability to make 'names' for their authors and construct public 'identities' for them."[24] Beyond helping authors encounter the reading public on better terms, moreover, a culture of editing also informed the way those readers would ultimately receive texts. For the Elizabethan author, John Kerrigan observes, the "reader has an incipient editorial function" that sometimes "becomes explicit." Editing was part of an "unfamiliar nexus of relations" that also included writing and reading, and practices such as correction and commentary were not only anticipated by authors but also generative of new authored texts.[25]

---

21. Richardson, *Print Culture*, 1.
22. Richardson, *Print Culture*, 7.
23. Richardson, *Print Culture*, 7.
24. Iliffe, "Author-Mongering," 168–69.
25. Kerrigan, "Editor as Reader," 116–17. Kerrigan observes how Thomas Lodge's *Workes of Seneca* acknowledges that readers might "Correct" but requests that they "bee considerate," and points to an example of how John Suckling supplemented an "imperfect Copy of Verses" by Shakespeare in order to compose a "Shakespearean pastiche" in the style of *The Rape of Lucrece*. "Instead of an author producing a text, inflected by publication, which 'calls out' responses to readers," Kerrigan observes, "we have materials rendered 'profitable' by the editorial reading-interventions of writers (e.g. Phineas Fletcher's notes to *The Purple Island*), their annotators (e.g. Selden's commentary on Drayton's *Poly-Olbion*), their printers (e.g. the marginal summaries added by Thomas Snodham to *The Rape of Lucrece*), and, of course, individual readers. . . . If commentary is generated by correction, rewriting follows from both." Kerrigan, "Editor as Reader," 117–18. As William Sherman documents, during the first centuries of

In the transition to print, authors' manuscripts were necessarily manipulated in order to accommodate printshop capabilities. Early modern authors were attentive to these manipulations: John Lyly explains in a letter to Thomas Watson that he resisted sending his manuscript to the printer because he was "loth the printer should see, for that my fancies being neuer so crooked he would put the[m] in streight lines, vnfit for my humor, necessarie for his art."[26] When editors—teachers, reviewers, publishers—have to make decisions about setting a line according to house conventions and standards while also taking into account the author's goals for the original text, they continue the process of poesy. A microcosm of this appears in the printer Joseph Moxon's explanation of how to manage verse indentation when setting type. First he explains the basic house style: "[W]hen Verses are *Indented*, two, three, or four m *Quadrats* [or blank spaces] are used, according to the number of the Feet of the Verses." Because verses and verse makers are fickle, however, he acknowledges that the print house must also be flexible and indent lines "according to the fancy of the Author."[27] There were "rule of thumb" procedures for setting verse, evidently, but even printers understood that those rules needed to be somewhat sensitive, but not subservient, to the restless engines of authorial fantasy.[28] Compromise between what was possible, habituated, or conventional, and the little bit of ingenuity that such compromise might provoke, was (as seen throughout this book, from Gascoigne's "patched" verses in chapter 1 to Davies's account of Prince Henry's invented scribal hand in chapter 3) a hallmark of poetic discomposition, of how poetry could discompose the world built around it.

That poetry's path from author's pen to reader's apprehension was mediated by hands invisible to both was not simply a function of print publication. Horace's *Ars Poetica*, here in Ben Jonson's translation, acknowledged the importance of working and reworking a poem in consultation with trusted advisers:

If to Quintilius you recited aught;
He'd say, "Mend this, good friend, and this; 'tis naught."

---

print, English Renaissance "readers continued to add to texts" via marginalia and other interventions. Sherman, *Used Books*, 9.

26. Lyly, "Lyly to the Authour," 8. Marotti discusses this passage alongside a similar example from Gascoigne. Marotti, *Manuscript*, 165–66.

27. Moxon, *Mechanick Exercises*, 218.

28. See Maruca, "Bodies of Type"; Jacobson, "How Should Poetry Look?"

If you denied, and had no better strain,
And twice, or thrice, had 'ssayed it, still in vain:
He'd bid blot all, and to the anvil bring
Those ill-turned verses, to new hammering.
Then: if your fault you rather had defend
Than change; no word, or work, more would he spend
In vain, but you, and yours, you should love still
Alone, without a rival, by his will.[29]

Quintilius Varus was a poet Horace memorialized in *Odes* book 1, poem 24, for his "Modesty, and incorruptible Good Faith (sister of Justice), and naked Truth," and it is worth noting that Horace recognized that even once the wise reader makes recommendations, a poet may still rather "defend / Than change" the work. The choice, however foolhardy or stubborn, remained with the original author.[30] Jonson's translation of Horace unsurprisingly aligns with the critique that we saw Jonson make of Shakespeare in this book's introduction: that poets who do not blot their lines and do not seek the advice of learned critics are in love with themselves. Jonson himself seems to have taken this advice to heart, despite his notorious condescension toward readers he regarded as unequal to his talent.[31] In an epigram addressed to John Donne, he reveals his pride in merely engaging in such peer review: "Who shall doubt, Donne, whe'er I a poet be, / When I dare send my *Epigrams* to thee?" Remarking that Donne "alone canst judge" because he "alone dost make," Jonson brandishes Donne's editorial capacities as proof of his own commitment to the ongoing work of poesy. While other readers may censure and criticize based on presumptions about what to "allow" and "disallow," Donne, Jonson trusts, will approach censure "evenly" and with "free simplicity."[32] The implication is that Donne is the sort of reader that Jonson conjures in his opening epigram: one who would, in taking Jonson's work in hand, labor "to understand."[33] "Read all I send," Jonson requests, outlining his hopes; if he "find[s]

---

29. Jonson, *Complete Poems*, 370 (lines 623–32).
30. Horace, *Odes and Epodes*, 69. As Mark Edward Clark suggests, the balance between "modesty" and "naked truthfulness" that Horace prizes in Quintilius fits "the description of a truthful friend who knew the limits of his criticism." Clark, "Quintilius' Ethos," 230.
31. For Jonson's relationship to readers, see Meskill, *Ben Jonson and Envy*, 20–22.
32. Jonson, *Complete Poems*, 67–68 (epigram 96).
33. Jonson, *Complete Poems*, 35 (epigram 1).

but one / Marked by thy hand" and "with the better stone," he promises to wear this mark as a badge of the renowned poet's approbation.[34]

Without ceding the "integrity of individuals participating in collaborative ventures," which Heather Hirschfeld cautions against, some scholars have recognized that a traditional view of collaboration as a product attributable to two (or more) names only mystifies collaboration in ways that perpetuate the mystification of authorship itself.[35] The problem is partly the allocation of works to names in general—the supposed doers, the poets, take precedence over the doing, the poesy, once more. When Jonson published *The Workes of Benjamin Jonson* in 1616, which included his epigram to Donne, the role the latter might have hypothetically played in marking up Jonson's verses became even more obscured. Margaret Ezell argues that just like "so many other nineteenth-century depictions of the act of authorship" (including "the natural spontaneous writer who never revises but instead channels inspiration directly to the page"), a "model of collaboration based on a personal affective relationship does not fit well with what is found when one examines early modern textual production."[36] For Horace and Jonson, according to Karen Burke LeFevre, Quintilius and Donne function as "resonators," as "enabling agents" in the process of invention, who could "[furnish] the writer with additional information on which to base decisions."[37] Yet mentioning this interaction in his epigram to Donne and then printing that epigram for audiences other than his collaborator also cultivates Jonson's name. By suggesting that his work had passed over Donne's table, Jonson's poem becomes a strategy by which he could shape his public identity as someone who took writing seriously. There were other ways of being legitimized as an author, he realized, than merely printing one's name on the cover of a book.

One of the most severe consequences of prioritizing names in print, then, is that it perpetuates ignorance of other kinds of authorship—and other kinds of authors. Ezell points out that the "at times hyperbolic celebration of masculine, commercial literary collaboration is one

---

34. Courting criticism and revising verses were the behaviors that constituted true poets and emboldened poems. Garth Bond explains that "Donne's discerning judgment is here imagined as embodied in the physical marking of Jonson's manuscript" and that these marks "serve as physical proof that Donne finds Jonson a legitimate poetic peer." Bond, "'Rare Poemes,'" 384–85.

35. Hirschfeld, "Early Modern Collaboration," 619.

36. Ezell, "Afterword," 246.

37. LeFevre, *Invention*, 69.

of the agents that helps to block twenty-first-century perceptions of early modern authorship, and in particular, how women participated in it."[38] There are now many studies of the ways in which early modern women turned to poetry, epistolary correspondence, translations, and pamphlets to participate in the world of letters, and these studies note that such work happened within a manuscript system driven by private circulation, which often treated individual works as "social texts."[39] As Patricia Pender and Alexandra Day suggest, however, emphasizing early modern women's authorship as often primarily social—and as such characterized by appropriation, responsivity, and enforced occasionality—may come to threaten "the hard-won legitimacy of the women writers we have already recovered." A basis of writerly legitimacy that rests on "the conventional categories of originality, autonomy, and authority" can suggest that women's work was somehow, by its collaborative nature, less legitimate.[40] The mythologization of original male geniuses—and the attendant mystification of how their works reached our tables—thus creates opportunities for bad-faith denials of women's agency, such as those trenchantly recorded by Joanna Russ: "What to do when a woman has written something? The first line of defense is to deny that she wrote it."[41]

Yet Pender and Day also observe that the role of women as participants in the social project of literary production exposes alternative means by which literary authority was cultivated. Reconsidering Mary Sidney Herbert's "role in editing, revising, and publishing her brother Philip Sidney's works," they propose, can "position her in more authorial roles than previous centuries of scholarship have been willing to imagine."[42] Studies such as Julie Crawford's *Mediatrix* furthermore show how women like Herbert and Mary Wroth managed "structures of affiliation" in the form of literary communities that became "at once heuristics of interpretation, and materially real."[43] Literary enclaves centered on women could determine interpretive communities that shaped aesthetic tastes and political affiliations. Invention and

---

38. Ezell, "Afterword," 247.
39. Some examples are Phillippy, *Early Modern Women's Literature*; van Elk, *Early Modern Women's Writing*; Pender, *Gender*. For an anthology of diverse writings by women, see Ostovich and Sauer, *Reading Early Modern Women*.
40. Pender and Day, "Introduction," 1.
41. Russ, *How to Suppress Women's Writing*, 20.
42. Pender and Day, "Introduction," 2.
43. Crawford, *Mediatrix*, 6.

composition were consequently not limited to what happened on the page; they extended to the broader sphere of literary production, in which women often played pivotal roles as curators, editors, patrons, and critics. Scholars of early modern women's writing such as Pender, Day, and Crawford have themselves cultivated a community of critical work resistant to the dominant, patriarchal strain of how authorship is conceived in the literary canon. Still, this work of resistance sometimes operates uncomfortably within the modern academy, as Kate Lilley points out: "As we have mapped the rhetorical strategies and generic interventions through which early modern women defended or regretted their entry into discourse and/or circulation, so we have been forced to defend (and, perhaps, sometimes regret) our deviation from canonical practices and justify our activities according to indices of academic value and prestige which continually fold back into the discourses of authorization we set out to critique."[44]

The work of Anne Southwell, I propose, presents an opportunity for scholars who wish to contest the "indices of academic value and prestige" while nevertheless demanding that the study of writers underrepresented in the literary canon be legitimized in the modern academy. Southwell was a defender of poetic *writing* more than she was a defender of poets and poems. Her works underscore how legitimacy rooted in poets and poems rather than in poesy not only misrepresents the active contributions of women writers but also misrepresents how *all* early modern writers undertook their work.[45] Embracing representations of authorship rooted in collaboration, resonance, and a culture of editing can in this way prompt us to revise what kinds of writing "belong" in an undergraduate course on early modern literature—both in terms of texts on the syllabus and in terms of the writing we ask our students to do.

Emphasizing the collaborative nature of early modern authorship is not meant to imply that no writers could lay claim to any of their words. It is simply to reaffirm, as Jonson's poem and Mary Sidney Herbert's role in shaping her brother's canonical fame imply, that collaboration informed textual production even for figures who have become central to the literary canon.[46] Even as we recognize the ways in which women

---

44. Lilley, "Fruits of Sodom," 177–78.
45. Dianne Mitchell makes a similar case in a discussion of the "several begetters" of sonnets like Shakespeare's and Donne's. Mitchell, "Shakespeare's Several Begetters."
46. Much work has been done on how collaboration shaped theatrical authorship, and how thinking about theatrical collaborations may provoke reconsiderations of authorship

participated in these alternative avenues of authorial practice, though, reading their poetic exchanges with men reveals them reckoning with the patriarchal premise that corrections made by men were to be prioritized over words written by women. Jonson could approach Donne with a fantasy of equal footing, but opportunities for women to do so in the same way were necessarily restricted. Against this context, Southwell's commitment to poetic discomposition found ways to turn the unfinished page into a platform for reaffirming the uses and goals of poetry itself. As Gillian Wright observes, for Southwell, "composition in manuscript created opportunities that print-publication could not feasibly afford."[47] The creation of these opportunities entangles poetics with politics in a material sense: the imaginative restlessness of poesy, the license to indulge in verbal play and self-reflection, became for Southwell a foundation for satire and ideological critique. As we will see in the next section, she extended repudiations of misogyny before readers who might otherwise have ignored them, partly by asking for their editorial help. Asking a reader to follow one's train of thought means that both readers may arrive, at least provisionally, at the same place. Enlisting them as editors in a project of reading carefully and reflecting on her words, she conceived of editing as a means of empowering herself. She reminded her editors that taking their own authority seriously meant recognizing that authority itself is contingent, constructed, and most vulnerable when most assured of itself.

Condemn, Amend, or Ratify

Anne Southwell, née Harris, was born in 1573 into a well-connected, noble, and politically important family. Her father, Sir Thomas Harris, was both an MP and a sergeant-at-law in the Middle Temple. She married Thomas Southwell in 1594, and he was knighted, along with her father, by King James I in 1603. Sarah C. E. Ross speculates that Southwell "may have served as maid of honour to Queen Elizabeth in the 1590s," and it seems likely that she sought the favor of James's queen

---

in general. See Hirschfeld, "Early Modern Collaboration"; Brooks, *Playhouse to Printing House*; Masten, *Textual Intercourse*.

   47. Wright, *Producing Women's Poetry*, 28. While Wright suggests that the focus of Southwell's manuscript is a poetic practice that looks "predominantly inward" (44) and was not for sharing with others, I join Ross and Coolahan in seeing Southwell's participation in the social dynamics of poetic exchange as reflected throughout the Commonplace Book. See Ross, *Women, Poetry, and Politics*, 80; Coolahan, "Ideal Communities," 71.

in a potentially embarrassing affair that ended in her being escorted away from court.[48] She appears to have moved with Southwell to Ireland shortly after James I's coronation, presumably because of financial difficulties, and after Thomas died in 1626, she remained in Ireland and married Captain Henry Sibthorpe, though she retained Southwell's more prestigious name. "In a status-conscious world," Wright explains, "Anne Southwell—and her less eminent second spouse—consistently ascribed to her the most impressive designation she could plausibly (if not quite accurately) claim."[49] During her time in Ireland, Southwell may have exchanged gossipy pieces of witty writing with members of the literary circle around Thomas Overbury, whose death in 1613 was the source of courtly scandal. Such exchanges with the London literati suggest, for Erica Longfellow, that Southwell "used her literary skill as a means of establishing networks of influence"—a pattern of practice that Southwell would recreate in Ireland.[50] As a transplant in Ireland, however, her situation was somewhat less than enviable. According to Longfellow, she "enjoyed some influence," but with limited reach; some addressees of her letters, such as Lady Ridgeway, "may have been important in Ireland," but others, like the Countess of Somerset, had "suffered serious political upsets."[51] We might read the social orientation of many of Southwell's poems, then, against this context of ambitious networking.

It is unclear whether Southwell ever discussed poetry with Ridgeway in the manner she proposes at the end of her letter. What is clear is that the letter was not the end of her attempts to reach her friend. A separate epistle to Ridgeway takes the form of a mock elegy, "An Elegie written by the Lady A: As: to the Countesse of London Derrye. supposeinge hir to be dead by hir longe silence," requesting a reply from her long-silent correspondent.[52] Her playful (and, as will become clear, misguided) conceit—that only Ridgeway's death and ascension to heaven could explain her silence—lets Southwell ponder the fundamental inadequacy of sinful humans left to their own devices. As she imagines Ridgeway's ascension from the "vaute circular" of Earth to a "large heaven," she asks

---

48. Ross, *Women, Poetry, and Politics*, 67; also see Longfellow, *Women and Religious Writing*, 96.
49. Wright, *Producing Women's Poetry*, 30.
50. Longfellow, *Women and Religious Writing*, 98.
51. Longfellow, *Women and Religious Writing*, 98–99. Marie-Louise Coolahan for this reason groups Anne with a cohort of "planters' wives" who settled in Ireland and confronted both "alienation and cultural incomprehension." Coolahan, "Ideal Communities," 84.
52. Klene, *Southwell-Sibthorpe Commonplace Book*, 24–27.

her friend to report back: "Yet in thy passage, fayre soule, let me know / what things thou saw'st in riseinge from below?" ("An Elegie," 10, 19–20). After she makes some imaginative queries about the cosmos, she turns to reflect on the limited knowledge attainable by fallen humanity:

> Fayne would I know from some that haue beene there?
> what state or shape caelestiall bodyes beare?
> For' Man, to heauen, hath throwne a waxen ball,
> In wch hee thinks h'hath gott, true formes of all,
> And, from the forge howse, of his fantasie,
> hee creates new, and spins out destinye.
> And thus, theise prowd wormes, wrapt in lothsome rags,
> shutt heauens Idea upp, in letherne baggs.
> ("An Elegie," 51–58)

The poem then reflects on the imaginative operations of poetry itself, equating poetic fancy with Catholic delusions: "Poets, and Popelings, are aequipolent, / both makers are, of Gods, of like descent" ("An Elegie," 77). This condemnation, albeit one specifically targeting writers of love poetry, rehearses doctrinal views of humanity's need for divine correction as well as women's particular fallibility. "In Eue's distained nature, wee are base," she writes, "And whipps perswade vs more, then loue, or grace" ("An Elegie," 89–90). This reverberates in her comment that "when a Lythargye, o^r braynes doth fetter, / the onely way, to rouse againe o^r witts, / is, when the Surgions chiefest toole, is whips" ("An Elegie, 96–98), echoing Calvin's account of how divine law "acts like a whip to the flesh, urging it on as men do a lazy, sluggish ass."[53] As her own poem comes to a close, then, Southwell jokes that she has grown wayward in her own attention:

> But stay my wandringe thoughts? <a>'las <whether>^where wade I?
> In speakeinge to a dead, a sencelesse Lady
> Yow Incke, and pap__er__, be hir passeinge bell,
> The Sexton to hir knell, be <Answer'd well, >Anne Southwell
> ("An Elegie," 117–20)[54]

---

53. Calvin, *Christian Religion*, 225. Lilley reads these lines as an "erotic sadomasochistic burlesque" exemplifying an interplay of queer desire and religious piety within early modern female sociability. Lilley, "Fruits of Sodom," 180.

54. Angle brackets are Klene's method for denoting text that, in the original, was struck through.

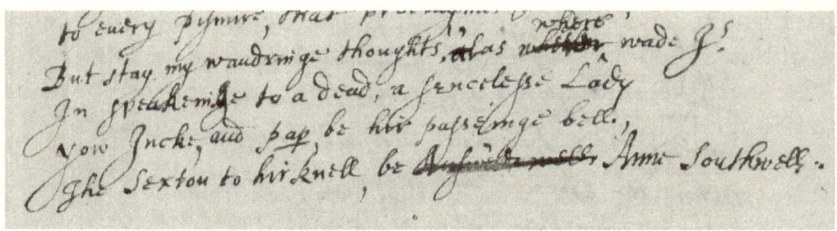

Figure 4.1. Lady Anne Southwell (1573–1636), *Miscellany of Lady Anne Southwell* (ca. 1587–1636), detail of folio 20v. Call # V.b.198. Used by permission of the Folger Shakespeare Library.

In the manuscript (figure 4.1), the revisions and insertions in these lines show Southwell's own ink and paper recording the nonlinear, "wandringe" progress of her pen. The last line, in retrospect, appears like the performance of correction: the final words synesthetically clang like a bell, first tolling a response ("Answer'd well") before substituting that "answer" with Southwell's own name. The fair copy of this manuscript draft, sent to Ridgeway, might have suppressed the blotted lines, but here we can see the poet materially, if inadvertently, emphasizing her own unheard status. In the context of a poetic conceit about not receiving answers to her correspondence, these final lines go to the extreme length of joking that the only explanation for Ridgeway's lack of response is that she had died.

Conversation is one of the only bright spots in Southwell's sustained critique of human frailty and depravity; it is the sole element of earthly experience that she imagines capable of transcendence. She mourns it by asking, indirectly, if Ridgeway will miss it when she ascends to heaven. "Good Lady, freind, or rather louely Dame," she asks, imagining Ridgeway to have transcended in imagery recalling Donne's *Anniversaries*, "if yow, be gone, from out this clayie frame, / tell what you know, whether th' Saynts adoration? / will stoope, to thinke on dusty procreation" ("An Elegie," 61–64). Though the angels may disdain to pay any attention to the earthbound business of "prowd wormes," Southwell suggests that they may nevertheless have reason to eavesdrop on the exchanges between herself and Ridgeway: "The Angells ioy in o^r conversation, / yet see vs not, but by reuerberation" ("An Elegie," 67–68). The closing lines, read as a culmination of these claims, dramatize their silenced conversation as a one-sided echo—a sexton ringing a bell over an empty grave—and equate Southwell's ruminations on the relationship between earth and heaven with the relationship between herself and her absent friend.

Southwell's doubt about poetry's limited ability to transcend the "vaute circular" of earthly existence was immediately and bracingly affirmed: while she was preparing the above mock elegy, Lady Ridgeway really did die of dropsy. Upon learning of this, Southwell wrote another poem, this time the earnest and stunned "An: Epitaph vppon Cassandra MackWilliams Wife to S[ir] Thomas Ridgway Earle of London Derry":[55]

> Now let my pen be choakt wth gall.
> since I haue writt Propheticall
> I wondred', that the world did looke,
> of late, like an vnbayted hooke
> Or as a well whose springe was dead
> I knew not, y^t her soule was fledd
> Till that the mourneinge of hir Earle
> did vindicate, this deare lost pearle.
>
> ("An: Epitaph," 1–8)

Again invoking the physical stuff of poesy by citing one of the ingredients of ink in the line, "Now let my pen be choakt [with] gall," Southwell registers the frivolousness of her "Propheticall" earlier verses. The image of Ridgeway as a "lost pearle" recalls her epistolary defense of poetry, and so connects poetry's archive of exemplars with Southwell's own community of interlocutors. As Ross observes, Southwell's inspiration for parts of this elegy appears to have come from a sonnet by Arther Gorges that is also transcribed in her Commonplace Book. She would also return to that sonnet's imagery in another epitaph for a different friend, the Countess of Somerset: "Since shee fled hence see how ye world doth look / naked, and poore, like an unbayted hoocke / Or' as a ringe, whose Diamont is lost / Or as euidence', whose lines are crost" ("An Epitpah vpon the Countess of Sommersett," 3–6).[56] Within the volume of assorted drafts, then, Ridgeway and Somerset appear as precious jewels chained together in a poetic network that also includes both Southwell and Gorges. Her "social" poems, even in their apparent metaphysical maunderings, endeavor to compose and recompose relationships not just

---

55. Klene, *Southwell-Sibthorpe Commonplace Book*, 27–28.
56. Klene, *Southwell-Sibthorpe Commonplace Book*, 34; Ross, *Women, Poetry, and Politics*, 71–74.

with earlier writers, but with potential readers who would place her with certain communities.[57]

The entanglement in Southwell's work between literary endeavor and social striving is even more explicit elsewhere in the Commonplace Book. On folio 18r, positioned just prior to her mock elegy for Ridgeway, appears a poetic epistle, "A Letter to Doctor Adam B^pp of Limerick," addressed to Bernard Adams, bishop of Limerick.[58] Ross observes how this piece "fuses religious and social discourses" by conflating the biblical Adam with her addressee and culminates in reminding Adams that "virtue consists in action."[59] If the bishop will follow the divine precepts of faith, hope, and love, Southwell suggests, he might "singe / An Halleluiah to heauens glorious Kinge / whose sweete resultance cordinge wth the spheres / may wth delight rauish o^r mortall eares" ("Letter to Doctor Adam," 120–23). In the middle of the epistle, however, Southwell modestly confesses her own diminished capacity to sound such music:

> If this extent of paper could suffice
> to show how Adam fell how hee might rise
> Good reuerend Father I will doe my best
> and where I fayle doe yow supply the rest
> A songe of eight tymes three parts I would singe
> assist my feeble Muse heauens mighty Kinge
> And grant my pen portraict true harmony
> wth out a discord in Diuinitye
>
> ("A Letter to Doctor Adam," 13–20)

This is a performance of modesty, but it is also a concession of incapacity at odds with Southwell's own exhortations to the "reuerend Father" to heed her earlier advice. Yet in pointing Adams to the divine precepts, Southwell tacitly affirms Calvin's instruction that even believers sometimes need to be reminded, perhaps by whipping, of divine laws. She also extends the image of poetry she presented to Ridgeway as "vocall Harmonye" by combining editing, expansion, and collaboration. A "songe of eight tymes three parts" is too much for one person to sing

---

57. On Southwell as a "metaphysical poet," see Wilson, "Anne Southwell, Metaphysical Poet."
58. Klene, *Southwell-Sibthorpe Commonplace Book*, 21–24.
59. Ross, *Women, Poetry, and Politics*, 88.

by herself; Adams is meant to "supply the rest," with "heauen's mighty Kinge" perhaps completing the trio.[60]

Bishop Adams was not the only theological adviser Southwell would consult for poetic assistance in this manner. She repurposes parts of the epistle to Adams in another poem copied on folio leaves 26r–v. Victoria Burke points out that this poem was likely addressed to Roger Cox, who was an assistant curate at Acton.[61] Southwell praises Cox in a separate poem in her Commonplace Book, her household owned a pamphlet written by him, and he appears to have grown familiar enough with Southwell herself to have written an elegy for her after she died. (This, too, is transcribed in the Commonplace Book.) Thanks to Jonathan Gibson's careful attention, we know that the poem to Cox was tipped into the Commonplace Book backward and begins on page 26v.[62] Read in this way, it begins with a rather bold appeal to its intended reader:[63]

> S^r. giue mee leaue to plead my Grandams cause.
>   and prooue her Charter from Iehouæs Lawes.
> Wherby I hope to drawe you ere you dye.
>   From a <peruerse> $^{resolu'd}$ and wilfull herresye.
> In thinkinge ffemales haue so little witt
>   as but to serue men they are only fitt
>   ("S^r. giue mee leaue," 1–6)

Citing the crime of Eve, her "Grandam," Southwell offers the curate a different interpretation of the events of Genesis that recalls Aemelia Lanyer's apology for Eve in *Salve Deus Rex Iudaeorum* (1611). She underscores how because Eve was made out of Adam's rib, she was actually made of purer stuff than that "read claye" (S^r. giue mee leaue," 11) from whence Adam himself was made. She also argues, pointing to the strict language of the source text, that "God made a helper meete" and that it would consequently be foolish to "think / a foole a help" ("S^r. giue mee leaue," 23–24). Shifting the ground of her defense a little, she then says

---

60. As Dianne Mitchell pointed out to me in private correspondence (on February 25, 2021), augmenting existing texts was a pretty common phenomenon in both verse miscellanies and narratives like Sidney's *Arcadia* and Marlowe's "Hero and Leander."
61. Burke, "Medium and Meaning," 100.
62. Gibson, "Synchrony and Process," 90–93.
63. Klene, *Southwell-Sibthorpe Commonplace Book*, 40–43. The poem begins on the middle of page 42, continues to the middle of 43, picks up again on 40 and runs through 41, and ends, incomplete, again at the top of 42.

that "God called them Adam both," and so the curate may "either count her wise, or him a foole" ("S^r. giue mee leaue," 25, 29). After establishing this premise, she goes on to argue that while women may want "witt for stratagems of state" or "skill to purchase Crownes and thrones," these concerns are "but guades that makes men proude and iollie" ("S^r. giue mee leaue," 35-39). As Danielle Clarke notes, this manner of "identification with the figure of Eve is daring, and only possible because of Southwell's adherence to the idea that the consequences of Eve's fall extend to all mankind, not just to women."[64] Southwell's concern thus ultimately does not appear to be blame or resentment, but rather leading her addressee to sense how human judgment—even his own—was constrained and limited.

This lament for humanity's general fallen state prefaces the material repurposed from Southwell's poem to Bishop Adams. In elaborating on the same lines, she also suggests that if such reading no longer engages Cox, he can pass it along to another potential reader:

> If this extentt of papar could suffice
>   to show how Adam fell, how he must rise
> My noble Neighbour I will doe my best
>   and wheare I faile, please you supplye the rest,
> Who hath a minde and hoards it vp in store
>   is poorer then a beggar at the doore
> Let your cleare Iudgment, and well tempered soule
>   Condemne, amend, or rattifye this scrole
> Twi'll prooue your fairest Monument and when
>   your Marble ffailes, liue with the best of men
> If you haue lost your fflowinge sweete humiddities
>   and in a dust disdaine theise quantities
> Pass it to oure beloued Docter Featlye
>   his tongue dropps honnye, and can doe it neatlye
> Meanetime a Durge of aight times three I singe
>   assist my ffeeble muse, heauens mightie Kinge
> And grante my penn portraite true harmonye
>   Without a discorde in deuinitye
>   ("S^r. giue mee leaue," 65-82)[65]

---

64. Clarke, "Animating Eve," 165.

65. These line numbers correspond to the poem read as if begun at "S^r giue mee leaue . . ."; Klene's edition treats this as a poem beginning on page 40 at the line, "Vnless

Southwell explicitly requests that Cox "Condemne, amend, or rattifye this scrole" as an act of collaborative creation, in the way Jonson asks Donne to mark up his verses. This, it is worth repeating, is immediately after she has criticized him for his "<peruerse> ^{resolu'd} and wilfull herresye" ("S^r. giue mee leaue," 4) relating to the intelligence of women. The prudent strikethrough softens her tone, and she also flatters him by suggesting that the result of their collaboration would be a monument not to her achievement, but to his own. Southwell sought feedback, but also sensed that in asking for correction, she would be appealing to his ego. The poem thus becomes both the premise and the purpose for the exchange with Cox and serves as a means by which she might have expanded her literary network. She even sensed the potential to expand this network; the "beloued Docter Featlye," Burke explains, was Daniel Featley, the rector of St. Mary's, who "was a scholar, writer, and prominent disputer, both in Europe and England." Southwell's closer correspondence with Cox perhaps emboldened her to think that he "had enough contact with Featley to enable Southwell to ask him to act as a type of literary mediator."[66] She understood that poetic labor was continuous with Calvin's recommendation that humans relinquish pretensions of knowledge and mastery, and consequently appears to have anticipated the prospect of being edited as one of poesy's redeeming virtues. Editing, in this light, was a gesture of concession and self-effacement—one that she hoped Cox, with his own claims to piety, would be able to embrace with respect to his own past statements.

That [Not So] Secret Book

Invitations to editing were not simply a performative social gesture for Southwell. Editing was, quite evidently, a part of her composition process. On folio 47v of the Commonplace Book begins one of her extrapolations on the Ten Commandments: "Thou shalt not commit Adooltery."[67] It appears, primarily, to be a condemnation of Southwell's first husband's infidelities and again reiterates a defense of Eve. It also does not suggest that Eve was without flaw. Southwell concedes that "Oure lazy grandome Eve in paradyse" had succumbed to vanity in

---

himselfe against himselfe weare bent" (line 57 read in the right order); in this edition the line numbers are 9–26.
   66. Burke, "Medium and Meaning," 100.
   67. Klene, *Southwell-Sibthorpe Commonplace Book*, 76–84.

"yeelding to the serpents toongg" ("Adooltery," 25–28) but also argues that because Adam also ate the fruit, he is "the slaue to evill" while Eve was merely "commanded to obey his will" ("Adooltery," 37–38). Turning her ire toward the contradictions of conventional masculinity— "The man that for gods cause forbears to kill / to sweare, lye, steale, or ^(droune his soll) <be made drunck w^(th)> in wine," she notes, is "scornde and calde a femynine" ("Adooltery," 43–46)—she complains that those who subvert God's will in defending these behaviors have no grounds to criticize women. On folio 48v, she appears to revise a stanza about how men and women alike will be redeemed:

> Thou onely strongg in ill: thy lost renowne
> the second Adam will agayne repayre
> take houlde of it and with it take thy crowne
> that sinne pulls off and le<f>ues thy forehead bare
> so shall ^the <a> female as be^(fits her) ^(<in> duti)<hioues a wife>
> houlde thee hir lord ^hir <and> comforte < of this lyfe>
>
> croune and beutie
>
> ("Adooltery," 67–72)

To clarify what is happening here: Southwell has revised the final couplet from "so shall a female as behioues a wife / houlde thee hir lord and comforte of this lyfe" to "so shall the female as befits her duti / houlde thee hir lord hir comforte croune and beautie." We know, thanks to Jean Klene's editorial eye, that Southwell made these corrections with her own hand. Further down on the same page appears another revision at the end of another stanza. Here, Southwell seems to have reconsidered the same rhyme she replaced in the stanza above:

> <wherfore the anchor houlde of a good life>
> in this presept woulds thow liue fre from blame
> <is to be Ioyned to a vertuous wife>
> in holy wedlocke tacke sum uertious fame
>
> ("Adooltery," 83–84)

Recovering the rationale for revisions like this is always speculative, but in this instance, the Commonplace Book offers a substantial clue in the margin of folio 49r (figure 4.2).

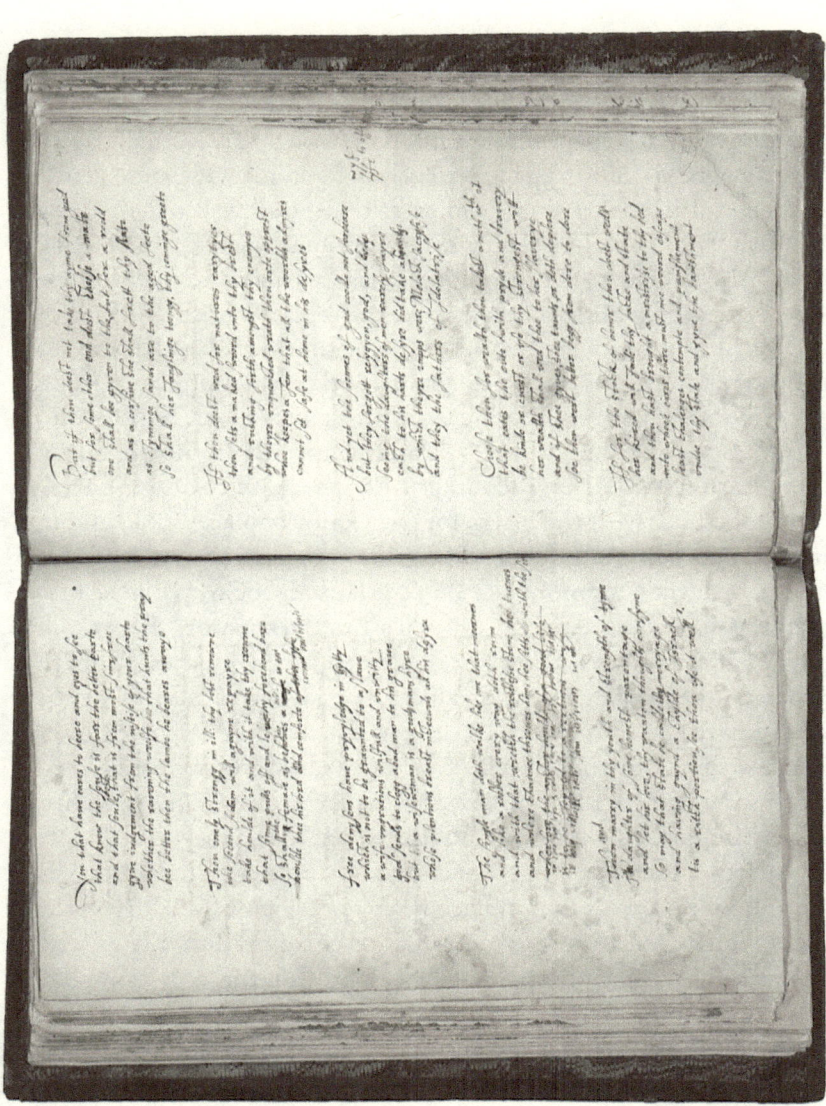

FIGURE 4.2. Lady Anne Southwell (1573–1636), *Miscellany of Lady Anne Southwell* (ca. 1587–1636), folios 48v–49r. Call # V.b.198. Used by permission of the Folger Shakespeare Library.

This marginalia, written in Henry Sibthorpe's hand, reads,

wyf
   to ofte
lyfe

Alongside a draft of a poem about virtuous marriage as a mutually nourishing partnership, Sibthorpe apparently offered his wife some gentle constructive criticism. His note indicates that Southwell was rhyming "wife" with "life" too often (she was), a note that she apparently took in stride—the evidence of her revisions, discussed above, appears on the facing page. Setting aside the irony that she replaces "wife"/"life" with "duty"/"beauty"—another rhyming pair that she arguably deploys "to ofte"—the revisions underscore a view of poetry as an opportunity to improve one's work through conference with trusted eyes. While we do not know much about Southwell's relationship with Sibthorpe, it is at the very least clear that he encouraged her poetic activities. He originally supplied her with the leaves for the Commonplace Book, and in addition to his editorial suggestions, appears to have been responsible for the state of the Commonplace Book as it exists today. While he may or may not have been Anne Southwell's first "resonator," he was, in more formal respects, the first editor of her collected "workes." Later in the poem, Southwell describes idealized marriage in terms of Christ's relationship to the church, lines that may also describe a generous editor and teacher: "Christ doth not curse, sweare, rayle, at spouses error / but with softe voyce, with humble woords and teares / and his good life, becomes hir gratious myrror" ("Adooltery," 133–35).

At this point, it is perhaps necessary to properly introduce the Southwell-Sibthorpe Commonplace Book, or Folger MS. V.b.198—the name of which identifies it as a product of collaboration. Klene, who diplomatically transcribed the entire volume for the only complete print edition, supposes that its present state reflects Captain Sibthorpe and Lady Anne Southwell's "attempts to gather her compositions and favored selections into an existing volume."[68] Moving through the manuscript, readers witness poetic writing situated alongside prose letters, copies of sermons, and documents of early modern household affairs.

---

68. Klene, introduction, xxxiv.

Danielle Clarke suggests that the book is more a "table book" than a "commonplace book" because of its eclectic mix of poems, letters, notes on reading, and household records.[69] Also included are an inventory of the family's library of 110 volumes, prose writings, and epitaphs written for her after her death.

Jonathan Gibson, taking issue with the seeming coherence suggested by Klene's print edition, argues that her printed presentation makes it "hard for readers to appreciate the shifts in structure and function through which the manuscript passed."[70] His scrutiny reveals that the book first functioned as the account book of John Sibthorpe, Captain Henry's father, at the end of the 1580s. After Henry's marriage to Lady Anne nearly forty years later in 1626, a scribe entitled the volume "The workes of the Lady Ann Sothwell/Decemb. 2° 1626."[71] Gibson avers that these additions show that "the function of the manuscript changed, from (a) a paper book in use by Southwell, gradually accumulating material by way of blank casting-off, into (b) a full collection of texts by Southwell."[72] Where Gibson would prefer editions that present manuscripts like Southwell's "less as single, coherent texts and more as a sequence of disjunct forms," Clarke sees the volume as possessing a "kind of coherence" as "a gathering, an anthology" that represents "an attempt to create a specific textual locus for a series of writings identified purposely as those of Lady Anne Southwell."[73] The book itself may consequently be understood as a coherent testament to the incoherent and often collaborative nature of textual production in the early modern manuscript system.

A poem inscribed in a commonplace book necessarily participates in a polyvocal view of poesy. Transcribing another's poem often introduces accidents and interventions, and these changes, however small, index the movement of poesy within a community of witness and participation. The title, "workes," implies to modern eyes a kind of authorial possession—but such possession is belied by the fact that the very first poem, transcribed under the title "Fly from the world, o fly, thou poore distrest," which is labeled "Sonnett 1.a," is a transcription of one of Alphonso Ferrabosco's *Ayres* (1609). The volume's second poem,

---

69. Clarke, "Gender," 115.
70. Gibson, "Synchrony and Process," 89.
71. Klene, *Southwell-Sibthorpe Commonplace Book*, 1.
72. Gibson, "Casting off Blanks," 221.
73. Gibson, "Synchrony and Process," 95; Clarke, "Gender," 117.

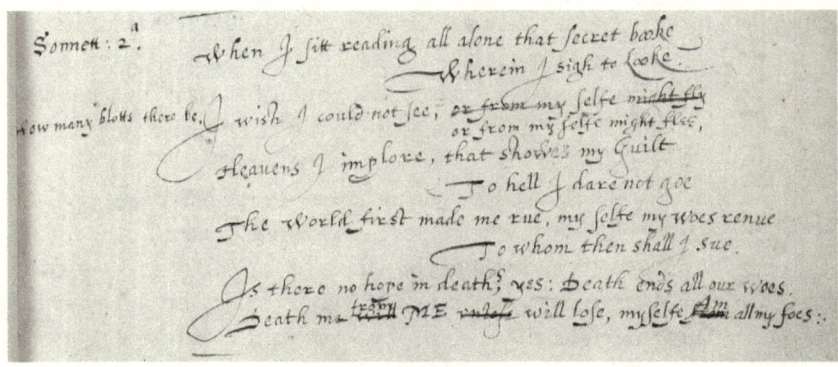

FIGURE 4.3. Lady Anne Southwell (1573–1636), *Miscellany of Lady Anne Southwell* (ca. 1587–1636), detail of folio 1r. Call # V.b.198. Used by permission of the Folger Shakespeare Library.

"Sonnett: 2ª" (figure 4.3), affords a close look at the Commonplace Book's fundamental polychrony and polyvocality.[74]

> Sonnett: 2ª.   When. I sitt reading all alone that secret booke
> Wherein I sigh to Looke
> ^{How many blotts there be.} I wish I could not see, <or from my selfe might fly>
> Or from my selfe might flee.
> Heauens I implore, that showes my Guilt
> To hell I dare not goe
> The World first made me rue, my selfe my woes renue
> To whom then shall I sue.
> Is there no hope in death^e, yes: Death ends all our woes.
> Death me ^{from} <will> ME <vnlose> will lose, myselfe ^{Am} <from> all my foes:.

Like the opening poem, "Sonnett: 2ª" is also a copy of an earlier song, this time one that appeared in Robert Jones's *A Musicall Dreame* (1609)—but there are some differences between Southwell's copy and the original in terms of both layout and language.[75] Perhaps misremembering the

---

74. Klene, *Southwell-Sibthorpe Commonplace Book*, 1.
75. Here is the poem as it appears in Jones, *Musicall Dreame*, sig. K1r–K2r:

> When I sit reading all alone that secret book
>
> Wherein I sigh to looke
> How many spots there bee
> I wish I could not see

song, Southwell or her scribe first wrote "or from my selfe might fly" before dashing this out and cramming "How many blotts there be" in the margin. It is ambiguous whether this insertion should be read before or after "I wish I could not see," because both phrases are metrically equivalent and share a rhyme. In Jones's version, the lines read, "How many spots there be / I wish I could not see / Or from myself might flee," implying that the reviser did want "How many blotts there be" to be placed *before* "I wish I could not see." The effect of these corrections, especially coupled with the amendments in the last line, "Death me ^{from} <will> ME <vnlose> will lose, myselfe ^{Am} <from> all my foes," creates a presumably inadvertent material metaphor: Jones's "spots" become Southwell's "blotts." As if reflecting briefly on the very apparent contents of the very book being compiled, the author—Southwell, or the scribe, or both—appears to regret the imperfections the process itself has wrought. It is most likely that "how many blotts there be" was introduced before the scribe ever arrived at transcribing the final line, but from a retrospective vantage—noticing the blots before the words—the association is difficult to shake.

The Commonplace Book's blots indicate a poet navigating her own creative impulses, her aesthetic and formal touchstones, her religious fervor, and a desire for recognition. Danielle Clarke argues that for this volume, "it is the process of textual creation that is the point, not solely or exclusively the production of a finished text." Such "open-ended fluidity is obviously a feature of manuscript culture more generally," Clarke continues, adding that, for Southwell, such fluidity was also a "logical extension of the minute engagement with the word that [her] faith prescribed and encouraged."[76] Southwell obviously wrote poems that she wanted people to read, and her reckoning with what it

---

    Or from myself might flee
    ....

Heauens I impore, that knowes my fault, what shall I doe,

    To hell I dare not goe,
    The world first made me rue,
    My selfe my griefes renew,
    To whome then shall I sue.

Alasse, my soule doth faint to draw this doubtfull breath,

    Is there no hope in death,
    O yes, death ends my woes:
    Death me from me will lose,
    My selfe am all my foes.

76. Clarke, "Gender," 118.

would take to achieve that goal comes through in the traces of her self-reflection. Her poetics attempt to reconcile questions of faith with literary activity, and one way she does this is to consider the interrelations of blots as signs of missteps in faith and as totems of the continual labor of self-reformation. Clarke observes that "in her insistence that she will not sell God's grace cheap she effectively elevates her work above earthly preoccupations with 'wealth or fame.' She insists throughout her work that poetry should be a pure, uplifting medium—not least because of its link to God's imprint—and that it shouldn't be pulled down by 'amorous Idiotts' (l. 310) by sloppy or hypocritical phrasing (again, perhaps one explanation for her revisions upon revisions). The poetic process is central."[77] Within "Sonnett: 2a," blots analogize instances of the pious soul losing control over her own will, leading her to desire being cleansed only by the death of worldly doubts. Yet, as discussed in the previous chapter, blots also evince writers trying to distance themselves from their errors by amending them (just as pressing the delete key is not the mistake but the remedy). Southwell's revised final line thus reflects the blot's twofold function as evidence of both error and correction.

As it sits in the Commonplace Book, "Sonnett: 2ᵃ" records an encounter between Jones, Southwell, and her scribe, provoking our own reflection on how the practice of composition leads to deliberation, to other books, and to other witnesses. To even begin to recover the process that led to the creation of this artifact, we must imagine ourselves in the room with them, see them transcribing Jones's poem, see them pausing, changing the transcription, and maybe even smiling at the incidence of blots that this supposedly private practice has generated. Reading a tidied-up version of this poem—or even a page that puts Jones's version alongside Southwell's—inevitably restricts this opportunity for such imaginative exercise. What would it take to "give out" the *poesy* or *process* of this artifact, to show not the final poem but the *activity* of those who participated in making it?

Klene's diplomatic transcription, she explains, "concentrated primarily on the textual content of the original, reproducing as closely as possible the exact spelling, punctuation, and capitalization of the document."[78] Throughout, deletions and cancellations are marked by angle brackets (< >), which results in documents that collapse the

---

77. Clarke, "Gender," 121.
78. Klene, introduction, xxxviii.

Sonnett: 2ᵃ.
    When I sitt reading all alone that secret booke
        Wherein I sigh to Looke.
How many blotts there be,
    I wish I could not see, <or from my selfe might fly>
        or from my selfe might flee,
[5]   Heauens I implore, that showes my Guilt
        To hell I dare not goe
    The World first made me rue, my selfe my woes renue
        To whom then shall I sue.
    Is there no hope in death? yes: Death ends all our woes.
[10] Death me <will> ⁽ᶠʳᵒᵐ⁾ ME <vnlose> will lose, myselfe<from>⁽ᴬᵐ⁾ all my foes:.

FIGURE 4.4. "Sonnett: 2ᵃ," from *The Southwell-Sibthorpe Commonplace Book: Folger MS. V.b. 198*, ed. Jean Klene (Tempe, AZ: Medieval & Renaissance Texts & Studies, 1997), 1.

turbulent nature of these drafts into considerably more legible texts. Figure 4.4 shows what "Sonnett: 2ᵃ" looks like in Klene's edition.

Every effort has been made to enable those without a talent for paleography to decipher the original manuscript page. These efforts make the edition incomparably useful to researchers (this chapter would not have been possible without it) and evince a tremendous amount of care and effort—attentiveness that characterizes academic study in general. Klene's edition is the only edition of Southwell's complete "workes" currently available in print, though some of her poems have been printed in *Early Modern Women Poets* (2001), edited by Jane Stevenson and Peter Davidson, and in *Early Modern Women's Manuscript Poetry* (2005), edited by Jill Seal Millman and Gillian Wright. In both volumes, only a handful of poems appear; in the latter, Southwell's offerings are edited by Jonathan Gibson. Both anthologies endeavor to create accessible texts by women writers from the period, putting to rest any doubts that women were not actively involved in early modern literary production. The former modernizes spelling and punctuation, while the latter does not; both separate critical apparatus and annotations from the text itself. Reading Southwell's poems in this way thus makes them considerably more accessible to lay readers—they look like poems by Donne or Marvell one might encounter in the *Norton Anthology*—but this format also reduces the reader's ability to access the traces of poetic labor.

How would something like "Sonnett: 2ᵃ" even make it into a modern edition of her poems, given the fact that we cannot really attribute it, or even the corrections made to it, to her? A tidied-up version that modernized spellings, accepted all revisions as final, and regularized formatting would erase the negotiations visible here between Jones's poem and this transcription. Klene's edition tries to show some of the messiness of this negotiation, but Gibson's complaint about the linear progression of the edition in general stands. This complaint extends, of course, to his own editorial renderings. This is not to critique either of them, but to recognize that the work of editing early modern manuscripts like Southwell's involves continuously making decisions about intention, audience, and even authorship. The rhetorical situation of a modern edition is both informed by and distinct from that of the original text. Whatever "text" we end up reading has necessarily been produced via collaborative endeavor. The page cannot help but be a static artifact, and there are consequently few options for editors who wish to render poesy's lively activity; a critical edition must pause the circulatory energy of poetic activity into a provisionally stable form.

Textual scholars and bibliographers who prepare early modern texts for modern readers engage with questions of materiality, intention, and reception when deciding what to include. They also, inevitably, face the complication of having to disentangle their own material situatedness, desires, fears, and technical limitations from those of the original authors. Critical editions are, like the original texts they are working with, often also made possible only by funding structures, technologies of production, and cultural contexts. The predominant strain of early twentieth-century textual scholarship, following the work of W. W. Greg and Fredson Bowers, prioritized the ideal "copy text" representative of an author's final intentions.[79] Such approaches met a challenge from D. F. McKenzie, who took into account the ways in which authorial intention both collides and aligns with historical conditions and technologies of production in order to promote a perspective organized around the "sociology of texts."[80] Jerome McGann pressed this perspective further, arguing that a fixation on authorial intentions produced an "underdetermined concept of literary work."[81] In the wake of these debates about editorial practice, textual criticism began attending to each individual text as an "event" representative of a plenitude of historical and material forces. McGann argues that "every text, including

---

79. See, for starters, Greg, "Rationale of Copy-Text"; Bowers, *Textual and Literary Criticism*.
80. McKenzie, *Bibliography*.
81. McGann, *Critique*, 122.

those that may appear to be purely private, is a social text," and that a "text" is "not a 'material thing' but a material event or set of events, a point in time (or a moment in space) where certain communicative interchanges are being practiced."[82] G. Thomas Tanselle would respond to McGann by insisting that an author's intentions cannot be erased from the rooms in which a text was composed, and that the same applies for the *editor's* intentions when he or she decides to produce a new edition.[83] Even edited texts are always reflections of historically contingent theorizations of authorship and collaboration.[84]

As technologies of production evolve, the possibilities for representing texts to readers also evolve. "In a hypertext edition," Tanselle envisions, "one can have as many full texts as one wishes, regardless of the length of the work involved, and one can easily switch from a given word in one text to the variant at that point in another text, having the whole context available in each case."[85] Such digital editions may also make it possible for readers to access different perspectives toward the same object—versions, for example, that reconstruct poems in different ways to show "what editorial emendations should be made to produce other critical texts besides the one presented as a full reading text."[86] This fantasy tracks with Gibson's recommendations for editing the Southwell-Sibthorpe Commonplace Book. At first, Gibson imagines "a very unwieldy sort of edition presenting successively a number of different 'versions' of the manuscript, providing the reader with a clear sense of the evolution of the manuscript as a whole," but he discards such a proposal as unlikely to materialize ("Would the Renaissance English Text Society ever sponsor such an edition?"). A more likely electronic edition, he reasons, might be "designed in such a way as to allow users to click to change the view on their screen from one version or state of the manuscript . . . to another." With an edition wherein a user might "watch the successive stages of copying unfold before her or his very eyes," volumes like Southwell's Commonplace Book would appear

---

82. McGann, *Textual Condition*, 21.
83. See Tanselle, "Textual Instability."
84. Gary Taylor proposes that, in response to recognizing the impossibility of "unediting" historical texts and divorcing them from editorial mediation, editors "begin by re-conceptualizing editorial theory as a specialized subset of translation theory" and recognize that such an approach may help bridge the chasm between "foreignizing" and "domesticating" approaches to textual editing. Taylor, "In Media Res," 98.
85. Tanselle, "Textual Instability," 53–54.
86. Tanselle, "Textual Instability," 54.

"less as single, coherent texts and more as a sequence of disjunct forms, a text (or, more accurately, a number of texts) in constant process."[87]

Recent born-digital editions of early modern women's writing serve as models for making collaboration—and editorial creativity—central to the way the texts are apprehended. This ethos informs the Digital Cavendish project, started by Shawn W. Moore and codirected by Moore, Jacob Tootalian, and Liza Blake. An "edition" that is also a meeting ground, Digital Cavendish aims to "build a collaborative space for Cavendish scholars and students" and "become a space for those who wish to share their work to build and continue to analyze the multitudinous networks of Cavendish scholarship."[88] A feature of the project is a digital edition of Margaret Cavendish's *The Blazing World*, annotated using Hypothes.is, a plugin for web browsers that allows editors to unobtrusively mark variants in the text via highlighting that can be turned off. In the first annotation, the project leaders encourage users to "collaborate in this editorial process, replying to these notes or adding annotations of their own."

A similar emphasis on editing as a collective practice is fundamental to The Pulter Project: A Poet in the Making, spearheaded by Leah Knight and Wendy Wall. Convening an international team of scholars in the production of a modern edition of Hester Pulter's collection of manuscript poetry, the Pulter Project places images of Pulter's original manuscripts alongside both legible "elemental" transcriptions and "amplified" editions that draw attention to each editor's choices about what features of the text they wish to emphasize. Effectively making the mediation of Pulter's text central to its attempts to put the text out into the world, the Pulter Project is as much about editing as it is about Pulter's verses. "Owing to the relatively recent discovery of Pulter's work after centuries of silence upon it," the project leaders explain, "Pulter's manuscript affords scholars of literary history the rare opportunity to reflect on the creation of a writer's profile in the making." Bearing witness to the creation of a writer's profile, the website explicitly acknowledges, is also a participatory act: "*The Pulter Project* makes Pulter's poetry public while publicizing the making of Pulter as a poet: a creative process being carried out on an ongoing basis by a collaborative crew of contributors, editors, advisors, and readers." On the site's home

---

87. Gibson, "Synchrony and Process," 94–95.
88. Shawn Moore and Jacob Tootalian, "Welcome!," Digital Cavendish Project, April 16, 2019, http://digitalcavendish.org/welcome/.

page, the editors state their hope that this work will not stop with their edition: "We invite you," they say, "to continue the making."[89]

Projects like these emphasize that scholars have come to think about the material conditions of composition, authorship, and publication as far more complicated than just the way in which writing is presented to undergraduates. The editorial maneuvers they employ are, in this way, closer to the writing habits of early modern authors themselves; they are attempts, sometimes self-consciously, to join with and empower the original authors as a continuation of the coterie. In an article reflecting on her own contributions to the Pulter Project, Fran Dolan links Pulter's "dunghill poetics"—one that recognizes an affinity between poetic composition and the way that dunghill compositing is "a process as much as a thing, a collective described as a discrete entity"[90]—to her own editorial practice: "I lay up in a kind of parallel operation to Pulter's, which does not aspire to reproduce her process but rather to model a virtual version of it, imagining and practicing a creative, open-ended collection and construction process, a labor that is grubby but purposeful. Like Pulter, I might go back later to tweak and add.... Rather than what precedes poetry, the dunghill is poetry; dunghill poetics invites dunghill editing as a similarly creative act, a process of making and mucking that attaches one to this dunghill earth, to the future, and to one's co-muckers."[91]

Dolan's reflection recognizes how, at the core of textual scholarship, perhaps as a function of the wealth of specialized historical and bibliographical knowledge that it demands, is an awareness of the limitations of knowledge. Academic writers are all, in effect, "co-muckers"—not just with those who help process one's rubbish into something productive, but with those who came before, the genealogy of names we know only from our reading but with whom we come to feel a continual bond. Susan L. Greenberg describes editing as *"the art of seeing a text as if it is not yet finished"* (emphasis in the original),[92] which is, by implication, also an art of recognizing one's own limitations and the imperfections of the work at hand. Such humility not only recalls Southwell's blend of conviction and caution, but also reveals how the experience of editing, like

---

89. "The Pulter Project: Poet in the Making," accessed July 22, 2021, https://pulterproject.northwestern.edu/.
90. Dolan, "Hester Pulter's Dunghill Poetics," 19.
91. Dolan, "Hester Pulter's Dunghill Poetics," 34.
92. Greenberg, *Poetics of Editing*, 14.

authorship, can be a laborious process that may nevertheless yield its own intellectual rewards. "All editors," Tanselle notes in a telling aside, "have recognized that their own experience was richer, as a result of working with primary records, than that of the readers of their editions, who were generally limited to what was presented in those editions."[93] The richness of this experience is one of discovery, corroboration, and collaboration; its value lies in the process of searching, confirming, and reconfirming.

What would happen if students in an early modern literature course were challenged to edit a piece of manuscript verse—to decide, for themselves, what it would mean to "give it out" to future readers? One example they might be presented with is the second recto of the Southwell-Sibthorpe Commonplace Book: a transcription of some verses of Sir Walter Ralegh's "The Lie." Ralegh's poem very frequently appears within commonplace books from the era, though what is notable about this iteration is not only that Southwell appears to have selected only certain verses (or had only certain verses available to her to select *from*), but also that she added some of her own. Figures 4.5 and 4.6 show what the page looks like in the Commonplace Book.

In rendering this manuscript, Klene's print edition makes some very pointed interventions. It adds an attribution to Ralegh at the top, though it signals, with an *S* in the right-hand margin in square brackets, which changes were made by Southwell's own hand. It does not, however, suggest which of the verses were *not* composed by Ralegh—these are the final three lines at the bottom of the page. These were not inscribed in Southwell's own hand, however, so they do not even receive the marginal attribution of the [S], as her signature does.

Most obviously, the edition also loses the compositional symmetry created on Southwell's page, in favor of rendering the poem's stanzas in one vertical line rather than as two columns. What Klene's framing gains in legibility, it loses in terms of capturing the complex dynamics of authorship represented on the manuscript page. Southwell's treatment of the poem, as Gillian Wright observes, is "largely typical of most contemporary compilations [in] remaining close to the 'core' version at the beginning and end of the poem, while varying her satirical targets in the middle stanzas." But it is also, Wright joins Gibson in observing, "almost unique among contemporary copies in representing the

---

93. Tanselle, "Textual Instability," 57.

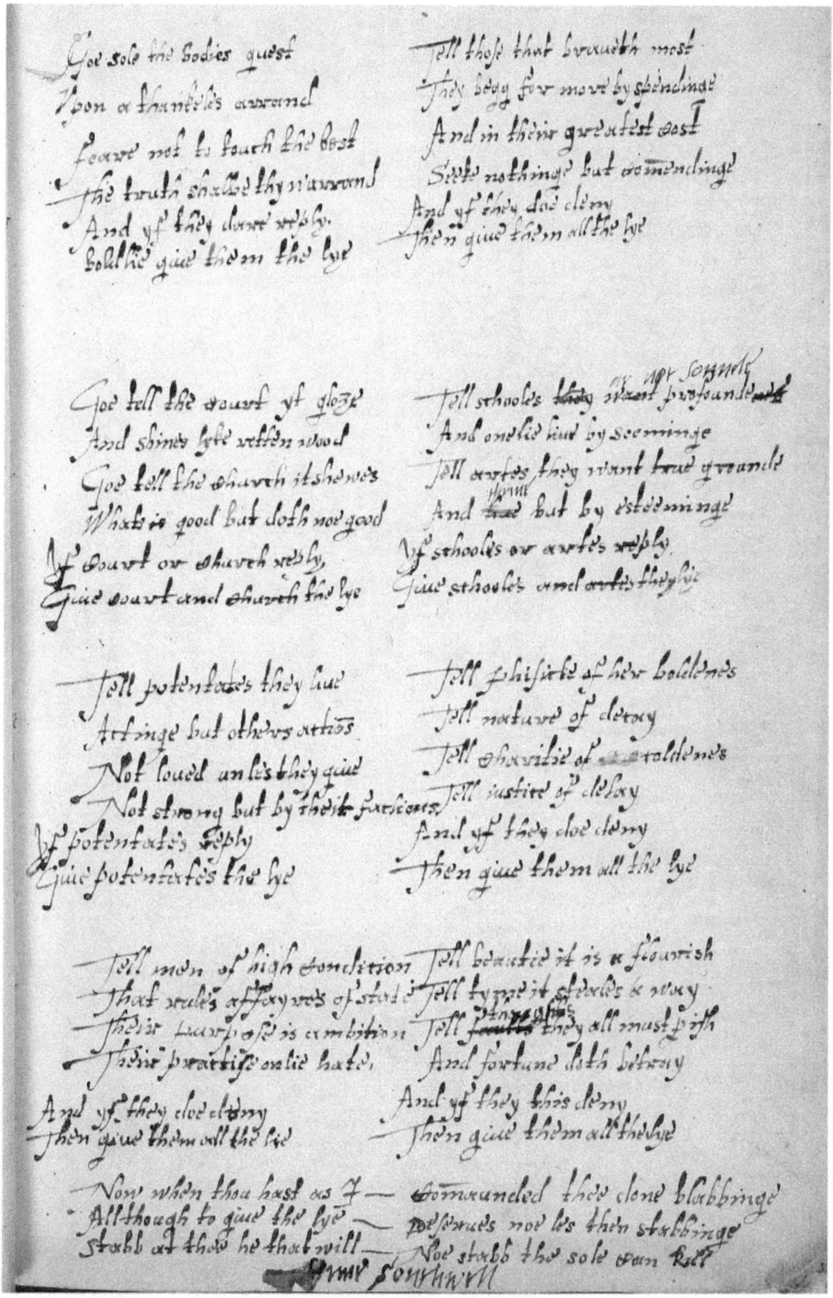

> Goe soule the bodies guest
> Vpon a thanklesse arrand
> feare not to touch the best
> The truth shalbe thy warrant
> And yf they doe reply,
> Boldlie giue them the lye

> Tell those that brauith most
> They begg for more by spending
> And in their greatest cost
> Seeke nothinge but comending
> And yf they doe deny
> Then giue them all the lye

> Goe tell the court yf glose
> And shines like rotten wood
> Goe tell the church it showes
> Whats is good but doth not good
> Yf court or church reply,
> Giue court and church the lye

> Tell schooles they want profundnes
> And onelie liud by seeminge
> Tell artes, they want true grands
> And that but by esteeminge
> Yf schooles or artes reply
> Giue schooles and artes the lye

> Tell potentates they liue
> Acting but others actions
> Not loued vnles they giue
> Not strong but by their factions
> Yf potentates reply
> Giue potentates the lye

> Tell phisicke of her boldnes
> Tell nature of decay
> Tell charitie of coldnes
> Tell iustice of delay
> And yf they doe deny
> Then giue them all the lye

> Tell men of high condition
> That rules affayres of state
> Their purpose is ambition
> Their practise onlie hate,
> And yf they doe deny
> Then giue them all the lye

> Tell beautie it is a flourish
> Tell type it should be away
> Tell them all must perish
> And fortune doth betray
> And yf they this deny
> Then giue them all the lye

> Now when thou hast as I
> Allthough to giue the lye
> Stabb at thee he that will
> Commanded thee done blabbinge
> Deserues not les then stabbinge
> Noe stabb the sole can kill

> Anne Southwell

FIGURE 4.5. Lady Anne Southwell (1573–1636), *Miscellany of Lady Anne Southwell* (ca. 1587–1636), detail of folio 2r. Call # V.b.198. Used by permission of the Folger Shakespeare Library.

[1ᵛ is blank]
[2ʳ]

[Ralegh, "The Lie"]
Goe sole the bodies guest
Vpon a thankeles arrand
feare not to touch the best
The truth shalbe thy warrand
[5] And yf they dare reply
boldlie giue them the lye

Goe tell the Court yt gloze
And shines lyke rotten wood
Goe tell the Church it shewes
[10] Whats <is> good but doth noe good
If Court or Church reply
Giue Court and Church the lye

Tell potentates they liue
Actinge but others actions
[15] Not loued unles they giue
Not strong but by their factions
If potentates reply
Giue potentates the lye

Tell men of high Condition
[20] That rules affayres of state
Their purpose is ambition
Their practise onlie hate,
And yf they doe deny
Then giue them all the lie

[25] Tell those that braueth most
They begg for more by spendinge
And in their greatest Cost
Seeke nothinge but Commendinge
And yf they doe deny
[30] Then giue them all the lye

            ar not sounde
Tell schooles <they want> profounde<nes>   [S]
And onelie liue by seeminge
Tell artes they want true grounde
        thriue
And <liue> but by esteeminge   [S]
[35] Yf schooles or artes reply
Giue schooles and artes the<y> lye

Tell phisicke of her boldenes
Tell nature of decay
Tell Charitie of < > Coldenes
[40] Tell iustice of delay
And yf they doe deny
Then giue them all the lye

Tell beautie it is a flourish
Tell tyme it steales a way
        thoughts
[45] Tell <faults> they all must perish
And fortune doth betray
And yf they this deny
Then giue them all the lye

Now when thou hast as I—Commaunded thee done blabbinge
[50] Allthough to giue the lye—Deserues noe les then stabbinge
Stabb at thee he that will—Noe stabb the sole Can kill
            Anne Southwell   [S]

FIGURE 4.6. "The Lie" as transcribed in *The Southwell-Sibthorpe Commonplace Book: Folger MS. V.b. 198*, ed. Jean Klene (Tempe, AZ: Medieval & Renaissance Texts & Studies, 1997), 2–4.

text not as a legacy but as an answer poem."[94] Southwell did not just transcribe Ralegh's poem; she made space for herself within it. Examining how the couplet closing the first stanza changes the context of the soul's journey to one in which the speaker remains alive, Wright suggests that Southwell's version "depicts the poem as a conversation, which she herself initiates and dominates and in which she awards herself the triumphant last word." She "explicitly claims it as her own" by "adding her own distinctive signature at the end of the scribal copy."[95] Yet this conversation, if understood *as* a conversation, does not and cannot end with Southwell's manuscript. Klene's version (of Southwell's version of Ralegh's version) can offer only so much in the form of context and information about what is happening here. Readers of Southwell need an editor's willingness to make some decisions about what to show and how to show it, and only in the process of making such decisions might they trace the dynamics of Southwell's own exchanges with Ralegh, her scribe, and herself.

The way this manuscript leaf and its diplomatic transcription exposes the complexities of authorship and challenges of editing makes them extremely useful for teaching. I have presented students with Ralegh's "original" (it usually appears in the anthology assigned as a class textbook), an image of Southwell's manuscript leaf, and Klene's transcription—and then challenged the class to edit Southwell's work for inclusion within their textbook. What would they want it to look like? What might be gained and lost by making this poem appear to be a "collaboration" between Ralegh and Southwell? Is Southwell authoring, appropriating, plagiarizing, stealing? What would be gained and lost by presenting only Southwell's added lines, isolated in the anthology, perhaps dozens of pages away from Ralegh's poem? More simply: how would they format the page? Would they acknowledge the scribal hands as well as Southwell's hand? Would they indicate the corrections and amendments to the parts Ralegh wrote? At the center of this discussion is a metapedagogical question: what would they want readers of their anthology—other students—to *think about* during their encounter with a text like this? I followed this exercise with an examination of how, in *Reading Early Modern Women* (2004), Victoria Burke edited this leaf by transcribing it, adding Ralegh's poem as an appendix, and

---

94. Wright, *Producing Women's Poetry*, 40.
95. Wright, *Producing Women's Poetry*, 41.

situating it alongside another answer to Ralegh by Anne Bowyer.[96] As Burke observes in her commentary, Southwell's engagement with "The Lie" reveals her to be "one of many people who personalized, rewrote, even 'improved' existing poems, since when texts entered the realm of manuscript transmission, contemporaries often interacted with this material as they recorded it in their volumes."[97] Upon recognizing how participatory engagement was pervasive within the manuscript system, some students have even been inspired to add new verses of their own to their editions of "The Lie," continuing Southwell's method and "lay[ing] up in a kind of parallel operation," to borrow Dolan's phrase, with her model.

The goals of this exercise are (1) to share with students the different ways in which the texts on the syllabus have been edited and designed, and (2) to introduce the Southwell-Sibthorpe Commonplace Book less as an editorial problem to be solved than as an invitation to modify our relationship not just to literary texts but to what it means to author a text. Radically destabilizing the different ways in which students think about what they have been asked to read then creates the possibility of destabilizing more familiar early modern texts, like those by Donne or Shakespeare. There are affinities between appropriating Southwell's poetics through re-presenting her words in our own hands and adapting Shakespeare's plays into the constrained theatrical space of a classroom. What would happen if we approached texts in the same way we approach plays during those days when we shuffle the seats around to make a makeshift stage? What signals do we give our students about how writing works if we treat written work as necessarily finished? Why must our students' writing be something that aspires toward a state of completion, as opposed to something they might approach as a platform for thinking with others?

---

96. Burke, "Lady Anne Southwell."
97. Burke, "Lady Anne Southwell," 338.

Reflection: Generous Thinking

"Writing is a technologically displaced form of conversation," writes Kenneth Bruffee, adding that "we internalize conversation as thought; and then by writing, we re-immerse conversation in its external, social medium."[98] Promoting the virtues of collaborative work in the classroom, Bruffee borrows Richard Rorty's categories of "normal discourse" and "abnormal discourse" to explain the internal dynamics of communities of writers and readers. Normal discourse describes the nature of conversation within "a community of knowledgeable peers," a community such as an academic field (or a cohort of regular theatergoers). Abnormal discourse, by contrast, "occurs between coherent communities or within communities when consensus no longer exists with regard to rules, assumptions, goals, values, or mores." In an educational setting, conversations first aspire to consolidate a normal discourse, but the virtue of allowing students to collaborate and converse with one another—such as in seminar discussions or small groups—is that this also enables abnormal discourse, which "sniffs out stale, unproductive knowledge and challenges its authority, that is, the authority of the community which that knowledge constitutes." Like quick capacity, like rhetorical *kairos*, like restless fantasy, like humility, abnormal discourse, Bruffee says, "cannot be directly taught"—but it can be given space to flourish.[99]

It is through exposure to abnormality that conversation may become generative. It is when students do not know what they are supposed to do, when routinized interactions grow discomposed, that they contribute most to the construction of knowledge. While one of our goals as teachers may be to help students internalize the discursive expectations of our discipline, having this be the only goal absolves us from being receptive to what students may have to offer. It also prevents our discipline from extending the conversation at its core—the debates about method, about inclusivity, about canonicity, about affect—to students who may find the conversation invigorating and who may, themselves, reinvigorate it. What would it mean, then, to genuinely become our students' interlocutors, rather than their evaluators? How might we become for them the kind of readers Anne Southwell sought for her own verses: readers who take writing, and not just writers and things written, seriously? Here we

---

98. Bruffee, "Collaborative Learning," 641.
99. Bruffee, "Collaborative Learning," 648.

might take Carolyn Matalene's cue and imagine the "teacher as editor": a figure who is "the writer's best and most helpful reader."[100]

We might reframe our approach to student writing in terms of our own approach to the writings at the heart of our profession. For professors of early modern literature, editing encompasses a host of domains: we teach with (and sometimes create) scholarly editions, work with (or as) scholarly press or journal editors, rely on heroic copyeditors, take advice from peer reviewers, and, of course, help students revise their papers. We might even say that by supplementing literary texts with our own expertise through lectures, discussions, and curricular juxtaposition with other texts, the literature classroom itself is predicated on seeing texts as if they are "not yet finished." Our classes are consequently places that might robustly connect the unstable workings of invention, drafting, and revising to both the evidentiary instability of fragmentary textual artifacts and the instability of manuscript poesy. The early modern literature classroom, in other words, might become a space that elucidates not only how perfect mastery is itself a fantasy, but also how perfect mastery is often a historically, epistemologically, and politically motivated construct. Recognizing that criticism and correction are strange bedfellows, we might then reconsider the gap between the sort of reading we encourage students to do during their encounters with poems—exploratory, imaginative, attentive, close—and the sort of reading to which we often subject their writings.

When we read a poem, according to Louise Rosenblatt, we do not read it as "an object or an ideal entity." For the reader, a poem "happens during a coming-together, a compenetration, of a reader and a text." Poetic events stimulate the reader's memory of "past experiences" via "concepts linked with verbal symbols." Then, as the reader "seeks a hypothesis to guide the selecting, rejecting, and ordering of what is being called forth, the text helps to regulate what shall be held in the forefront of the reader's attention."[101] Read without any context, the first line of a poem might call forward a network of associations, some of them indicative of shared discursive patterns and touchstones and some of them particular to the reader's life experiences and expectations. A reader may find, in utterly misreading "Goe, sole the bodies guest," the beginnings of a poem about how footwear (soles) might be treated hospitably by a body, and may contrive a hypothesis that the poem will examine the reciprocal service

---

100. Matalene, "Teacher as Editor," 11.
101. Rosenblatt, *Reader*, 17.

that humans and material objects offer to one another. Or the reader may get hung up on the spelling and punctuation and begin to wonder whether "bodies" is plural, or possessive, or both. For the attentive and humble reader, the subsequent elements of the poem will hopefully correct such wayward associations—but they will not necessarily fully eradicate the role the false starts played in the poem as an event. The reading of the poem may ultimately prove even richer for these false starts, because while soles or plural bodies may not be anything near what Southwell intended, the elevation of questions concerning materiality, hospitality, and plurality by happenstance may well lead the reader to think about embodiment and identity within "The Lie." A failure of apprehension may in this way become the *beginning* of the process of critical reading, rather than its end.[102]

The process of peer review in literary studies, the collaborative crux of academic discourse, continues the dialectic of stimulation and regulation by treating new critical arguments as avenues for intellectual exchange. Ideally, peer review both affirms and expands the discursive terrain of an academic field. There are many ways to be "right" in one's reading of a poem (just as there are many ways to be wrong), and one can certainly imagine a persuasive reading of "The Lie" that interrogates how its treatment of embodiment and materiality relates to the theme of hypocrisy. New readings are meant to broaden a field's horizon of expectations, after all; writers of criticism want, hopefully, to teach their reviewers something—even as they seek the advice and instruction of those reviewers. Speaking on behalf of journal referees, Ramón Saldívar observes that "[a]s we read, we perform the thought experiment of testing the aims, methods, and conclusions presented in the article by comparing them with our own understanding of the textual, historical, or analytical problem. This doubly reflective process—the self-conscious reflection by the referee, who also examines the level of self-consciousness in the article being assessed—requires a degree of self-reflexiveness that resembles nothing less than Schlegel's notion that '[t]hinking that reflects on itself in self-consciousness is the basic fact.'"[103] Saldívar's account of the "basic

---

102. Rosenblatt's understanding of transactional poetic reading draws on John Dewey and Arthur F. Bentley's account of knowledge making, which she summarizes in a manner reminiscent of Jonson's discussion of poesy: "a 'known' assumes a 'knower'; a 'knowing' is the transaction between a particular individual and a particular environment." Rosenblatt, *Reader*, 15. As McGann puts it, a work of art "is fundamentally an action" that "tries to call out in the reader/viewer/audience a reciprocating response." McGann, *Literature of Knowledge*, 13.

103. Saldívar, "Work of Criticism," 965.

fact" of humanistic inquiry lying in self-consciousness recalls the "doubling up of points of view" that Greenberg places at the core of professional editing. It also recalls Annette Federico's definition of close reading as "the cultivation of self-consciousness about the reading experience," which was discussed in the introduction.

What literary scholars are best at is thinking *together* about reading and writing *together*. We are our best selves in seminar rooms that spin single metaphors around in the air for half an hour, at Q&A sessions after paper presentations that lead to follow-up emails and schemes for future collaboration, and when we are enthusiastically commenting on one another's work. How might we build, model, and affirm this sort of community in our classrooms? If we want to cultivate the intellectual terrain of the disciplinary fields we call "Shakespeare" and "early modern literature" rather than simply defend them, our classrooms might take lessons from writers like Anne Southwell and study the collaborative, conversational, uncertain work of writing itself. The more people who take writing seriously, I believe, the more interest there may be in confronting the so-called greatest writers ever to have lived on their own terms, and on their own turf.

Consider what might change in students' relationships to their own writing if they trusted that their first readers were there primarily to help them. Consider how such generosity might provoke them to think more broadly about the practices of education in general, and what sorts of policies they might support after graduation, for their own future children. Such generosity toward student writing, however, must not mean that professors exhaust themselves with individual conferences and comments on essays. To reclaim not just our labor but our pedagogy from the imperatives of competition, productivity, and individualism that stifle poesy, we must model the labor conditions and expectations we would want our students to see as worth defending. If we spend as much time in class focusing on students' writing as we do on the texts on the syllabus, we must create time for this work. We might reclaim that time from *coverage* and instead focus on specific problems pertaining to critical writing. We might ask ourselves, what are the educational benefits of requiring students to write three essays in a semester, rather than producing, over several weeks of sustained attention, revision, and discussion, one thoroughly revised paper? This project may involve the teacher's input every few weeks and may become something like a directed study in which both teacher and student have a stake.

If we strive to care about the student writers in our classrooms as much as we do the field we represent, the students may also come to care about the field. Like Southwell reaching out to Lady Ridgeway to connect her to the "streame of all mankind," our task is to extend to our students an invitation to conversation. The modern academy, forced to professionalize to survive, has come to prioritize competitiveness and condescension in ways that undermine the most important service it provides to the public: a space to think slowly and carefully with others. In *Generous Thinking*, Kathleen Fitzpatrick argues that cultivating "a mode of engagement that emphasizes listening over speaking, community over individualism, collaboration over competition, and lingering with the ideas that are in front of us rather than continually pressing forward to where we want to go" may be one of our last hopes in orienting the university that can model and support "generous thinking as a way of being in and with the world."[104] One of the most (the only?) potent forms of civic agency that Shakespeare professors wield *as* Shakespeare professors lies in our ability to show the hundreds of thousands of students we collectively teach every year that the study of literature is worth defending—and funding—because it believes in tethering the hard work of intellectual inquiry to practices of collective generosity and care. We can make our classrooms spaces where soliciting and acquiring feedback is the point and profit of the study of writing, where students feel secure in seeking out challenges to their habits of thinking, where the aim is to provoke conversation by asking new questions rather than to reassert old answers. The slow, collective study of poesy might in this way become practice for the slow, collective labor required to remake this far-from-golden world, and to keep our chain of pearls from breaking.

---

104. Fitzpatrick, *Generous Thinking*, 5–6.

Chapter 5

Performance Anxiety
William Shakespeare's "Perfectness"

Even if, as Heminges and Condell suggest, his "mind and hand went together" such that he confidently produced unblemished sheets, William Shakespeare knew what it was like to be anxious and indecisive.[1] For example, he memorably dramatizes nervousness in his twenty-third sonnet:

> As an unperfect actor on the stage
> Who with his fear is put besides his part,
> Or some fierce thing replete with too much rage
> Whose strength's abundance weakens his own heart,
> So I, for fear of trust, forget to say
> The perfect ceremony of love's rite,
> And in mine own love's strength seem to decay,

---

1. Heminges and Condell, "Great Variety of Readers," A2\. Lucrece blots her lines for being either "too curious good" or "too blunt and ill," and because her inventions throng "like a press of people at a door" (lines 1300-1301). The speaker of the sonnets repeatedly complains about the uncontrollable nature of readers' responses: "If I could write the beauty of your eyes," he conjectures in Sonnet 17, "The age to come would say, 'This poet lies'" (lines 5-7). In Sonnets 76 and 105, he openly addresses his own repetitiveness and lack of inventive variation, and in Sonnet 103 (line 5) he defends his verse's impotence in comparison with its object: "Oh, blame me not, if I no more can write."

O'ercharged with burden of mine own love's might.
Oh, let my books be then the eloquence
And dumb presagers of my speaking breast,
Who plead for love and look for recompense
More than that tongue that more hath more expressed.
　Oh, learn to read what silent love hath writ!
　To hear with eyes belongs to love's fine wit.[2]

Overburdened and overprepared, the performance implodes before it begins. The sonnet's speaker (or rather, writer) first likens himself to "an unperfect actor on the stage / Who with his fear is put besides his part," explaining that he fails to deliver his lines "for fear of trust." He discovers himself "unperfect" not because he has forgotten what to say (he has the "perfect ceremony" memorized), but because doubts about his beloved's reciprocity have made him incapable of saying anything at all. Recalling, once more, Sidney's account of the poetic *"idea,"* the "excellency" of which is discernible only if readers choose to "learn aright" why and how its maker made it, the speaker's sense of perfection reveals itself to be contingent on the audience's response.[3] Recognizing this, the sonnet ends by turning to written performance as compensation for his failed recitation. As the poet makes this turn, he again rests his fate on the beloved's response: if only the beloved will "learn to read what silent love hath writ" and so find in his writing the excessive outpouring that a tongue might express, these "dumb presagers" may seem appropriately eloquent. Thus the poem recognizes that authors, like actors, eventually put themselves at the mercy of responses that they cannot fully control. Even the poet who supposedly never blotted a line apparently knew that perfection must be granted and may not be claimed.

At some point, all authors must relinquish control over their work, because they cannot control what their readers will do with it. Balking at such disempowerment, they may prolong their labor and resist the stresses of publication by subjecting themselves to a taskmaster with a deceptively amiable name: "perfectionism." Understood by psychologists as, in Joachim Stoeber's words, "a multidimensional personality disposition characterized by striving for flawlessness and setting exceedingly high standards of performance accompanied by overly critical evaluations of one's behavior," perfectionism counterproductively

---

2. Greenblatt et al., *Norton Shakespeare*, 2258.
3. Sidney, *Sir Philip Sidney*, 217.

endeavors to completely satisfy productivity's inexhaustible demands.[4] Striving (a condition of lack) after exceedingly high standards (a condition of excess), chasing after perpetually shifting goalposts, being ready to abandon a project near its completion—these perfectionist behaviors confuse work with toil.

Perfectionism, as Elizabeth Tallent puts it, is "a love letter the psyche sends to an unresponsive Other."[5] Riffing on the conceit of Sonnet 23, Shakespeare wrote an entire play preoccupied with the problem of winning love through writing. Set in and around the "little academe" of the French court of Navarre, *Love's Labor's Lost* (1594–96) is riddled with patchwork erudition, blocked speeches, frustrated revisions, and rejected appeals for collaboration. Beyond its scenes of both writerly and actorly failure, the play itself fails at the level of genre: it is a comedy that does not satisfy convention by ending in reconciliation or marriage. Moreover, the text of the play may also be read as fundamentally "unfinished."[6] The title page of its first quarto announces itself as "Newly corrected and augmented," but it is unclear, H. R. Woudhuysen suggests, what the prior text it purports to have revised might have been.[7] Even if a reprint, however, the play's composition betrays many signs of authorial uncertainty and indecision.[8] Grace Ioppolo specifically notes the "compelling evidence of second-thought revisions" in the play, going so far as to observe that in his special attention to revising Biron's speeches, "Shakespeare revised his hero, his play, and his own artistic role, function and method. In other words, Shakespeare revised himself."[9] The play's composition glimpses its playwright's uncertainties, and its title page lays bare the false starts the play underwent in its life as a public document.

Reading *Love's Labor's Lost* as a finished, authored text falls into a trap the play itself sets; by prioritizing reciprocal, live exchanges over the written word, it challenges readers to recognize the interpretive limitations of solitary reading. Scholars have long seen the play as emphasizing

---

4. Stoeber, "Psychology of Perfectionism," 3. Also see Frost and Marten, "Perfectionism and Evaluative Threat."
5. Tallent, *Scratched*, 10.
6. Bevington, "'Jack Hath Not Jill,'" 4, 9.
7. Wouldhuysen, taking cues from Paul Werstine's work, supposes that Q1, the first quarto, may have been reprinted based on a print copy original, "Q0." See Woudhuysen, "Appendix 1," 302–7.
8. See Woudhuysen, "Appendix 1," 307–17, for a full summary of the different forms of authorial revision visible in Q1, especially with respect to character names and speech prefixes.
9. Ioppolo, *Revising Shakespeare*, 98.

the "folly of loving by the book," with the term "book" metonymically extending across styles of discourse derived from courtly etiquette manuals, the Petrarchan tradition of courtly love, and the humanist curriculum.[10] Each context against which the interpersonal exchanges of the play may be read—the spaces of courtly love, legal property disputes, the latter-day humanist academy, the modern Shakespeare classroom—finds it prompting a reconsideration of the means by which judgments are made, conclusions are drawn, and knowledge is discovered.[11] I argue that by rejecting a conception of "perfection" rooted in bookish adherence to conventional wisdom, the play dislocates perfectionism with a practice of trust. In this way, it can help us conceive a critical and poetic pedagogy that requires students and teachers, readers and writers, and actors and audiences to construct an environment wherein failure is seen not as a conclusion but as a prompt for further conversation.

Following Shakespeare's lead, in this chapter I conflate the submission of written work with the staging of live theater, and in so doing recognize that the perfectionist anxieties that authors face may be understood as a form of performance anxiety. Psychologists such as Glenn D. Wilson and David Roland tell us that performance anxiety names "an exaggerated, often incapacitating fear of public performance," a fear that Ariadna Ortiz Brugués observes as preconditioned on the existence of "high ego investment and evaluative threat."[12] In actors, it derives from a fear of rejection, making one of its signal manifestations

---

10. Colie, *Shakespeare's Living Art*, 47. David Bevington compares the play to how Lyly's *Sappho and Phao* undermines "hoary formulas from the *Ars Amatoria*" for counseling "self-assurance" in male lovers. Bevington, "'Jack Hath Not Jill,'" 4. William C. Carroll observes that "the lovesick Petrarchan wooer afflicted with melancholy and heart-burn requires a certain rhetoric and vocabulary." Carroll, *Great Feast of Language*, 77. Eric C. Brown compares *Love's Labor's Lost* to *Doctor Faustus*, arguing that it "dramatizes the complications of learned authority, dependence, and influence." Brown, "Shakespeare's Anxious Epistemology," 21. Mark Breitenberg observes how "[t]he play offers more than just a comic exaggeration of [the Petrarchan] literary convention: Petrarchism underwrites the economy of masculine desire that structures the play and shapes its action." Breitenberg, "Anatomy of Masculine Desire," 434. These readings corroborate Carla Mazzio's sense that, in the play, "idealist conceptions of texts clash again and again with materialist conceptions of the physical book in the social world." Mazzio, *Inarticulate Renaissance*, 161.

11. Lorna Hutson finds that "the language of love in this play is bound up at every turn with the terminology of *good faith* and of *making bargains*" in a way that entwines the love plot with the play's marginal but serious negotiations over land and paternity. Hutson, *Invention of Suspicion*, 298. As Katherine Eggert suggests, Navarre's courtly practices resemble a form of experimentation akin to the "sloppiness and imprecision" and "characteristically improvisational style" of alchemy. Eggert, *Disknowledge*, 193.

12. Wilson and Roland, "Performance Anxiety," 47; Brugués, *Music Performance Anxiety*, 1.

stage fright: what Donald M. Kaplan describes as a "state of morbid anxiety disturbing the sense of poise," where poise "depends upon our anticipations of others' receptions of how we are hoping to represent ourselves."[13] In writers, whose scenes of writing become "public" performances only at the threshold of submission, performance anxiety may blend concerns about demonstrations of skill with concerns about social and affective relationships. Academic writers who subject their work to peer review know this experience well. As Ronald Britton suggests, their publication anxiety "emanates from fear of criticism by third parties who are regarded as authoritative and from fear of disaffiliation from colleagues with whom the author feels the need to be affiliated."[14] While actors may be more likely to freeze up and become incapable of performing at all, writers, according to Britton, may produce "a superficial and complacent text" designed explicitly to please their imagined audiences.[15] These wires can be crossed too: writers may experience blockage, and anxious actors may start pandering and hamming it up.

Throughout this book, I have suggested that experiences of discomposition are fundamental to the activation of poetic and critical insight. To promote these experiences, I have advocated for a pedagogy rooted in license, transparency, generosity, and a spirit of genuine collaboration between teachers and students. At the point of finally sharing their work with others, however, all writers—be they students or Shakespeare—confront the fearsome heart that animates all discomposition: the shame of failure. How do writers countenance "evaluative threat" in ways that are generative rather than paralyzing? How can we help students approach writing, if not with confidence, then at least with a conviction that failure, too, is an acceptable outcome? It may help, I propose, to think about writing as Shakespeare must have when he set about writing his plays: as something that invites, rather than fears, readers' responses. Seen in this light, a piece of writing may fail only when it regards itself as having no need of further discomposition.

The primary form of failure dramatized in *Love's Labor's Lost*—awkward and disjointed conversation between lords and ladies—was an

---

13. Kaplan, "On Stage Fright," 60.
14. Britton, *Belief and Imagination*, 199–200.
15. Britton, *Belief and Imagination*, 200. As Anne Lamott puts it, perfectionism "will ruin your writing, blocking inventiveness and playfulness and life force." Lamott, *Bird by Bird*, 28.

educational problem in early modern England.[16] Continuing the previous chapter's examination of poesy as a social and conversational process, the first section of this chapter tracks the parallels between *Love's Labor's Lost* and Stefano Guazzo's *The Civile Conversation* (first translated into English in 1581). I argue that by repeatedly dramatizing scenes of failed delivery—of speech, of letters, of theatrical performance—the play launches a sustained critique of verbal self-assuredness and unilateral social discourse. Relating the failures of the lords of Navarre to the play's own depictions of theatrical failure, the second section then locates early modern playwrights in the moments prior to the first performances of their plays. What did they worry about? How did they conceive of the challenge of winning the audience's love? Taking cues from Sara Jane Bailes's account of the "poetics of failure" and its relationship to amateur theater, I connect metatheatrical depictions of actors going "out" of their parts—scripted scenes of actors forgetting or flubbing lines, losing their place, standing amazed—to the early modern construction of theatrical authorship as an exercise in imperfectness. The chapter's third section then studies how twinned depictions of amateur theater and fractured conversation in *Love's Labor's Lost* index a conception of what it meant to write texts destined to be shared with potentially unreceptive audiences.[17] At its anticlimactic close, the play encourages actors and audiences, authors and readers, speakers and listeners alike to reflect on what allows social interactions with the potential to be mutually beneficial—be they conversations, theatrical events, or any kind of written work—to fail.

In the reflection that closes this chapter—and this book—I take the revised image of failure offered by Shakespeare and train it on the unstable ground on which the early modern literature classroom currently stands. What would it mean, in practical terms, to let Shakespeare fail in the way we hope to encourage our students to fail—to risk something, to embrace possibility, to disaffiliate with the status quo and the institutions that prop it up? Doing so, I propose, requires professors to reckon with the limitations of their own hard-won expertise. Even though, as agents of professionalization, we cannot realistically play any role in the classroom other than that of the expert, we might remember that our students will always have new things to show us simply by virtue of being students. It is for this reason that Derek Attridge, championing

---

16. See also Erickson, "Failure of Relationship."
17. Bailes, *Performance Theatre*, 13.

amateurism as a breeding ground for critical insight, suggests that the "best hope for a new emphasis on the amateur impulse in literary studies . . . lies in the classroom."[18] To this, I add that the best hope for Shakespeare to evade prescriptive declarations of his perfectness—declarations that threaten to make him more irrelevant, because they suggest that he no longer has any work left to do—is to allow him to interact with readers who have not yet been professionalized.

Giving the Occasion

When the Princess of France and her retinue—Rosaline, Katherine, and Maria—first arrive in Navarre, they are immediately asked to play along with a prewritten script. On an embassy to settle a longstanding land dispute over the region of Aquitaine, the princess learns that the king of Navarre and his attendant lords—Biron, Longueville, and Dumaine—have vowed an oath to cloister themselves in study for three years and shun any interactions with women. Indeed, their anxieties about women are so great that their oath includes the provision that any woman who comes within a mile of the court will be punished by "losing her tongue" (1.1.122)[19]—and that any man seen speaking with a woman will be shamed by his peers.[20] The princess's prescheduled arrival forces the lords to make some immediate exceptions, and so, minutes after making their oath, they breach it. Despite granting themselves this accommodation, however, they do not extend any to the princess herself: they do not let the women physically enter the court of Navarre. As a result, the first encounter between the lords and ladies takes place "in the field" where the princess is to be lodged not as a guest, but "like one that comes here to besiege his court" (2.1.86-87). Despite this treatment, the king's first words to the princess are a flatly ceremonial performance of mock hospitality: "Fair Princess, welcome to the court of Navarre" (2.1.91). Spotting the facetiousness of these terms, the princess refuses to keep up the pretense, replying, " 'Fair' I give you back again, and 'welcome' I have not yet" (2.1.92-93). She immediately perceives that the king's unselfconsciously reflexive greeting

---

18. Attridge, "In Praise of Amateurism," 42.
19. All references to *Love's Labor's Lost* will be to Greenblatt et al, *Norton Shakespeare*, and indicated in-text by act, scene, and line numbers.
20. Wendy Beth Hyman pointed out in comments on this chapter that such antisocial vows are a recurring plot device in Shakespeare's plays. Olivia makes one against men in *Twelfth Night*, as do the votaries of St. Clare in *Measure for Measure*.

betrays an inability either to think about what he is saying or to take his own words seriously.

Shortly after this encounter, Boyet, a lord accompanying the princess's retinue from France, offers her an unnecessary explanation of the semiotics of masculine affection. The gist of it is that the princess does not know how to read the behavior of men. Boyet says that he immediately perceived the king to have fallen in love with the princess because the king's "face's own margent did quote such amazes / That all eyes saw his eyes enchanted with gazes" (2.1.245-46). Despite the king never actually confessing such affection, Boyet suggests that the princess soften her disposition toward him (2.1.247-48). Over the course of the next three acts, the king and the other lords affirm Boyet's suspicion, and believe themselves to have fallen in love with the visiting ladies. They send love tokens and attempt to court the ladies with a masquerade, but the princess, fearing their insincerity, orders her masked retinue to swap their love tokens and confuse the approaching lords. Thwarted and confounded, the men then attempt to convey that their affections had been in earnest—Dumaine asserts that their letters "showed much more than jest," to which Longueville adds, "So did our looks"—but Rosaline responds that the women "did not quote them so" (5.2.771-73).[21] The lords might thus be understood as complaining that the ladies are misreading the text of their courtship, while the ladies might be understood as responding that the lords had miswritten it.[22]

A prevailing conceit of *Love's Labor's Lost* is this clumsy imbrication of "penned speech"—letters, speeches, tokens, habituated gestures—and live conversation. As we saw in chapters 1 and 2, the rhetorical education that humanist students received in grammar school armed them with techniques for discovering arguments, organizing them, embellishing them with ornamentation, and reciting them with proper pronunciation. Lynn Enterline suggests that this "constant demand for the performance of eloquence and socially sanctioned affect under the threat

---

21. As Douglas Bruster explains, in Elizabethan England "quoting" could call to mind a range of the *OED*'s definitions: the textual practice of marking books with marginal annotations "to give reference to other passages or texts" and, as is now more common, the practice of "reproduc[ing] or repeat[ing] a passage from (a book, author, etc.)." Bruster for this reason places quotation "midway between imitation and citation," noting that it refers "to both the borrowed matter of texts and the activity of borrowing itself." Bruster, *Quoting Shakespeare*, 4, 16; *Oxford English Dictionary*, s.v. "Quote, v., Def. 1," accessed June 25, 2021, http://www.oed.com/view/Entry/156908.

22. Rosaline's "quote," it is worth noting, appears as "cote" in the 1598 quarto and "coat" in the 1623 folio.

of punishment" reverberated in the mature writings of schoolboys who had to endure "the drama, fears, and desires of their own schoolroom performances." One way this manifested was in students' fascination with "the hallmark Ovidian moment of vocal failure"—moments "when characters like Philomela, Orpheus, Echo, Io, and Actaeon try, in vain, to *do* something with words, only to find that their own tongues betray them."[23] Shakespeare's schoolroom, organized around students "taking the institutional scene of judgement inside, as their own," offered practice in avoiding vocal failure via staged debates and theatrical productions.[24] These supervised encounters with classmates could not really substitute for real-world interactions, however, because forensic rhetorical training was fundamentally antagonistic.[25] This shift in emphasis correlated with an extension of eloquence beyond the domain of learned men. When women, the vast majority of whom were not permitted the excessively textual humanist education given to the men, joined men in courtly conversations, performances of book learning proved even less socially useful.

This is something Biron even anticipates, prior to signing his oath: "Small have continual plodders ever won, / Save base authority from others' books" (1.1.86-87). Biron's lesson, itself delivered aphoristically within the formal logic of a sonnet, does not appear to resonate with his peers or change his own disposition. When the king responds that Biron has only shown how "well he's read to reason against reading" (1.1.94), this foreshadows how the sunk costs of the lords' education overpower their ability to adapt to novel experiences. The comic scenes that follow largely dramatize how their pretensions repeatedly obstruct their own desires. For the lords, performances of verbal skill function as a sort of game for which emulation, memorization, and recitation are the only form of training. Being well read suffices to win an argument. When they confront situations in which this learned discourse proves insufficient or inappropriate, however, the lords find themselves overexposed.

---

23. Enterline, *Shakespeare's Schoolroom*, 79.
24. Enterline, *Shakespeare's Schoolroom*, 44.
25. David Randall explains how the Renaissance recovery of Ciceronian *sermo*—"the private discussion of equal noblemen in their country villas" that served as a complement to *oratio*'s "address to a mixed multitude in the forum"—saw humanists begin to employ conversation itself as a metaphor for the rhetorical encounter. This not only promoted an education in "familiarity" and sociability (the general meaning of *conversatio*), but also worked to counteract rhetoric's perceived affiliation with deceptive manipulation. See Randall, *Concept of Conversation*, 5. For more on *conversatio*, see 30-32.

It is one thing to fail at performing eloquence by misremembering the topics of invention or misquoting a witty commonplace, they learn; it is another entirely to fail to make a good impression.

The lords fail to make their intentions clear in part because they approach communication primarily via ceremonial and scripted declarations. They are, as Carla Mazzio observes, "lovers full of text," a surfeited state attributable to the "proliferation of amatory discourses in printed texts" during the early modern period.[26] Noting the increasingly formulaic nature of courtly interactions in general, the ladies do not take the lords' words at face value (much less by virtue of whatever lies in the "margents"). As the men have already demonstrated through their lapsed oath, they do not take their own words either literally or seriously, despite publishing them broadly. Later in the play, when they each secretly write love poems and letters, they also do not commit to sharing their words openly or enthusiastically. Biron witnesses the king of Navarre contrive to drop the sonnet he had written for the princess rather than deliver it himself; both Biron and the king witness Longueville confess his fear that his "stubborn lines lack power to move" and that he will tear the verses and "write in prose" (4.2.50–51); Biron, the king, and Longueville observe Dumaine deciding to send Kate his poem alongside "something else more plain" (4.2.116); and, when Costard returns Biron's letter to Rosaline to him within view of his compatriots, Biron tears it up and rails at Costard, "You were born to do me shame" (4.2.198–99). The lords' anxieties about their writerly failure—anxieties determined in part by their self-appraisals, in part by the ladies' responses, and in part by their fear of what their peers might think of them—make them evasive, stubborn, and insincere. The written word somehow proves too final, too determinative, and too vulnerable to misapprehension—yet it also allows the lords to disavow meaning and shield themselves from direct criticism. These qualities of writing insinuate themselves into how the lords speak; the lords cannot help but sound, as Mazzio suggests, "as if they were reading and writing."[27] What they require, in a theme befitting the cultural moment in which the play was written, is an education in how to have a conversation.

The art of "civil conversation" arrived in early modern England in the sixteenth century by way of continental, and mostly Italian, treatises on etiquette and courteousness such as Baldessare Castiglione's

---

26. Mazzio, *Inarticulate Renaissance*, 143.
27. Mazzio, *Inarticulate Renaissance*, 145.

Il cortegiano (published in Italy in 1528), Giovanni Della Casa's *Il galateo* (1568), and Stephano Guazzo's *The Civile Conversation* (1574). Before long, aspiring gentlemen courtiers attempted to emulate the sparkling social skills fictionalized in these books, and they practiced at places where young gentlemen gathered. As discussed in chapter 3, such places were increasingly institutions of higher learning such as Oxford, Cambridge, and the Inns of Court.[28] Lynne Magnusson makes a persuasive case for the influence of the festival events at Gray's Inn during the 1594–95 season on *Love's Labor's Lost*, noting how, during that season, students at the revels were assigned to "read and peruse *Guizo*, the *French* Academy, *Galiatto* the Courtier, *Plutarch*, the *Arcadia*, and the Neoterical Writers, from time to time" to bolster their social tact.[29] Seeing the play amid this heightened preoccupation with conversational sociability reveals the plot closely tracking Guazzo's text in particular. The first three books of Guazzo's *The Civile Conversation* were translated by George Pettie in 1581 (from a French translation), with the fourth book translated by Bartholomew Young and added for a reprinting in 1586. *The Civile Conversation* is largely a dialogue between the author's infirm and solitary brother, William, who wishes to spend all his time in his library, and the worldly Annibal, an esteemed physician who happens to be William's neighbor. The fourth book shifts the frame of their dialogue, allowing William to witness the "conversational games" played by a cadre of six lords and four ladies at a banquet.[30]

---

28. Bruce Smith notes how, along with being law schools for aspiring statesmen, the Inns were engines of socialization. Smith, "Night of Errors."

29. Magnusson, "Scoff Power," 197. For the revelers' reading list, see Davison, *Gesta Grayorum 1688*, 29–30. At the neighboring Middle Temple in 1597–98, the reading list expanded, especially with respect to textbooks on amorous courtship. There, revelers were charged with contemplating the art of love and defending what they perceived as its foundational texts: "If any man deprave the books of *Ovid de Arte amandi*, *Euphues* and his *England*, *Petite Pallace*, or other laudable discourses of Love; this is loss of his Mistris favor for half a year." Rudyerd, *Le prince d'amour*, 57. This syllabus corroborates Gabriel Harvey's account to Edmund Spenser that students at Cambridge no longer read Aristotle and other classic works, in favor of "outlandish braveryes" in order to "helpe countenaunce owte," such as "Philbertes Philosopher of the Courte, Castiglioes fine Cortegiano, Bengalassoes Civil Instructions to his Nephew, Guatzoes new Discourses of curteous behaviour." Harvey, "Third Letter," 137. Also see Stamatakis, "'With Diligent Studie.'"

30. For another reading of the links between this play and Guazzo, see Larson, "Conversational Games." Randall attributes to Guazzo a reconception of classical "*conversatio* in secular terms as the realm of society and manners intermediate between the *oikos* and the political world." Randall, *Concept of Conversation*, 12. As Jennifer Richards observes, Guazzo's text "allows the rules of conversation to emerge from its representation of the speech form"; the text recognizes that its dialogic form creates knowledge through

Guazzo begins the dialogues with William complaining that he would rather hole himself up to "reade or write" (1.3r) than grow "acquainted with the course of the worlde" (1.5v).³¹ Explaining himself to Annibal, William proceeds like a dutiful scholar and cites biblical, philosophical, and literary passages affirming the value of reading and maligning the superficiality and crass immorality of society. Observing that public life is "full of suspitions, deceites, lasciuiousnesse, periuries, detractions, enuy, oppressions, violences, and other innumerable mischiefes" (1.6v)—not to mention boring small talk—he resolves that conversation is simply not as worthwhile as studying. William's show of citational learnedness leads Annibal to remark, "[Y]ou haue here co[m]mended solitarinesse, partly by reasons deriued from your owne good wit, & partly by ye doctirine you haue learned of some famous writers" (1.8r). In this compliment, he identifies William as a compiler of *sententiae* adhering to Seneca's widely reproduced recommendation to follow "the example of bees, who flit about and cull the flowers that are suitable for producing honey, and then arrange and assort in their cells all that they have brought in."³²

To counterpoint William buzzing through his library, however, Annibal twists the "example of bees": "[C]onuersation is not onely profitable, but moreouer necessary to the perfection of man, who must confess that hee is lyke the Bée which cannot liue alone.... [M]an is created for the vse of man, to the intent that following nature as their guide and Mistres, they haue to succour one another, to communicate together common profites, in giuing and receiuing, vniting and binding themselues together by artes, occupations, and faculties" (1.12r). For Annibal, the introverted work of scholastic reading must eventually transform into the extroverted work of testing one's ideas out in order to refine them. Study without disputation is barren, he argues, and learning how to productively engage with those different from oneself is both a necessary and a rewarding skill. Sometimes, Annibal suggests, he must embark in vessels "wherin there are sometime men, women, religious,

---

the incidence of contradictions, interruption, and changing perspectives. Richards, *Rhetoric and Courtliness*, 30.

31. Guazzo, *Civile Conversation*. References will appear in-text and indicate book, page number, and recto/verso.

32. Pervasive throughout the humanist curriculum—Erasmus renders it as "So our student will flit like a busy bee through the entire garden of literature, collect a little nectar from each, and carry it to his hive"—the "example of bees" was a commonplace about making commonplace books. Erasmus, quoted in Crane, *Framing Authority*, 59.

seculer, Souldiours, Courtiers, Almans, Frenchmen, Spaniards, Iewes, and other of diuers nations and qualities" (1.5r). While he was at first upset about being in such mixed company, he eventually learned to derive pleasure from framing himself "to the humours of others" and departing "being verie well thought of by the companie when I was gone" (1.5r–v).[33]

The hallmarks of the good conversationalist were awareness of the context and of the disposition of one's interlocutors, creativity, and open-mindedness.[34] A bad conversationalist, by contrast, was identifiable by egotism, rigidity, and a propensity to cow others into silence.[35] Agreeable interlocutors, Annibal observes, "frame themselves to doe, to leave, to chaunge, to correct many things according to the judgement of others" (2.4v). The amiable companion gets goodwill "by giuing eare curteously, as by speaking pleasantly" because "wée thinke, they thinke wel of vs, which are attentiue to our talke, and wée sée our pleasant spéeche serueth vs to no purpose, if it bee not hearde of others" (2.7v).[36] Additionally, when speakers encounter correction of their own

---

33. This strikingly tolerant perspective complicates historical narratives about the development of civility in European society. Whereas Norbert Elias (*Civilizing Process*) tracks the transformation of "courtesy" into "civility" as a function of elite moral codes permeating and homogenizing European society in the late middle ages, and Jorge Arditi (*Genealogy of Manners*) sees "civility" decoupling from moral ideals and arrogating distinction for aristocrats by becoming "etiquette" in the eighteenth century, Guazzo's text sits in murky in-betweenness, charting an emerging and pluralistic discursive public sphere. Guazzo's civil conversation, Anna Bryson observes, produces an "intermediary ideal" that requires a "science of sociability" attentive to one's integration within a "whole social world." Bryson, *From Courtesy to Civility*, 55.

34. Cicero, *De officiis*, 137, 139.

35. Annibal's account of conversation anticipates Michael Oakeshott's sense of conversation as an "unrehearsed intellectual adventure." He goes on to affirm that conversation "is impossible in the absence of a diversity of voices: in it different universes of discourse meet, acknowledge each other and enjoy an oblique relationship which neither requires nor forecasts their being assimilated to one another." Oakeshott, "Voice of Poetry," 198–99. For Oakeshott, human conversation is "the meeting-place of various modes of imagining" by individual subjects, one where there is "no voice without an idiom of its own," because, in the space of conversation, "voices are not divergencies from some ideal, non-idiomatic manner of speaking, they diverge only from one another" (206). Oakeshott's "conversation of mankind" is one concerned not simply with practical application ("the voice of a self among selves") or making knowledge ("essentially a co-operative enterprise"); the voice of science began as "a conversible voice, one speaking in an idiom of its own but capable of participating in the conversation" (208).

36. Cicero similarly advises that it is proper to express anger and reproach others when they misstep, but even in such circumstances, those doing so must be attentive to how they themselves are being perceived: "For what is done under some degree of excitement cannot be done with perfect self-respect or the approval of those who witness it." Cicero, *De officiis*, 141.

behavior, it is imperative that they take the note in stride and not grow defensive. In the same vein, being overly desirous of praise would lead to bad habits like repetitiveness, tedium, and defensiveness. In his essay "Of Discourse," likely inspired by familiarity with texts like Guazzo's, the notable Gray's Inn alumnus Francis Bacon writes, "Some in their discourse desire rather commendation of wit, in being able to hold all arguments, than of judgment, in discerning what is true, as if it were a praise to know what might be said, and not what should be thought." The worst of this lot "have certain common places and themes wherein they are good, and want variety; which kind of poverty is for the most part tedious, and when it is once perceived, ridiculous."[37]

Annibal points out to William that only active conversation—within which the possibility of discomfort always looms—may also provide the affective education of demonstrating what *not* to do:

> These are thinges whiche are learned, not so muche by readyng, as by using company, for when an other speaketh, wée marke what liketh and what disliketh, and by that wée knowe what we ought to auoyde and what to followe: as when wee our selues speake, and that wee sée some of the hearers litle attentiue, or some other way to vse some yll behauiour, wée learn by his inciuilitie how we ought to behaue our selues in hearing others. It shall suffice then to say for this time, that touching this action, wee must frame all the bodie in suche sort, that it séeme neither to bée of one whole immooueable lumpe, neither yet to bee altogether loosely disioynted. (2.12r-v)

To train yourself in the art of conversation, you must listen to how others speak and remember what you disliked about their demeanor. The goal of a conversation is for all participants to gain something from the encounter.[38] If you attend a conversation with the goal of trotting out what sounds smart, of playing a zero-sum game of esteem and self-aggrandizement, you risk boring your company and—as happens to the lords of Navarre—leading them to laughter or disdain before departing from you.

---

37. Bacon, "Of Discourse," 191. Della Casa makes the same point: "Most people are so infatuated with themselves that they overlook other people's pleasures; and, in order to show themselves to be subtle, intuitive, and wise, they will advise, and correct, and argue, and contradict vigorously, not agreeing with anything except their own opinions." Quoted and discussed in Miller, *Conversation*, 54–55.

38. Bacon recommends sticking to asking questions, because "he that questioneth much, shall learn much, and content much." Bacon, "Of Discourse," 193–94.

Forms of conversational failure like these were most damning, the etiquette guides insist, when courtly gentlemen attempted to converse with ladies.[39] During the 1594-95 festival season at Gray's Inn, revelers were rewarded with a broad license for mirth but warned (in the characteristically conceited copiousness then in vogue) that excepted from the general pardon were "All such Persons as have, or shall have any Charge, Occasion, Chance, Opportunity, or possible Means to entertain, serve, recreate, delight, or discourse with any vertuous or honourable Lady or Gentlewoman, Matron or Maid, publickly, privately, or familiarly, and shall faint, fail, or be deemed to faint or fail in Courage, or Countenance, Semblance, Gesture, Voice, Speech, or Attempt." In other words, if a member were to "stand mute, idle, frivolous, or defective, or otherwise dull" or broadly "different from the Profession, Practice and Perfection of a compleat and consummate Gentleman or Courtier," he would be soundly mocked.[40] Being a good courtier meant being nimble and charming in mixed company; it meant somehow exchanging what Magnusson terms the "scoff power" conditioned by institutions like Gray's for gentleness and solicitousness.[41] In practice, this process involved going outside, talking to people, and learning how it felt to be spoken *with* rather than *at*. In the spirit of this sentiment, the organizers of the Gray's Inn revels insisted that in addition to their reading, the young gentlemen "also frequent the Theatre, and such like places of Experience; and resort to the better sort of Ord'naries for Conference, whereby they may . . . become accomplished with Civil Conversations, and able to govern a Table with Discourse."[42] Going to the theater—not only to see fluent actors deliver eloquent dialogue and portray characters in strange and surprising circumstances, but also to think about one's own public presentation by engaging in discussion, interpretation, and argument—was one of the ways that young men supposedly learned how to converse.

---

39. Thomas Gainsford's *The Rich Cabinet* describes courtiers as "companions with Schollers" because "vnlesse they study and read histories, they will faile in discourse & conuersation, the principall end of a courtiers life." Even with such preparation, however, courtiers could fail in their "principall end": those "of the vainer sort" were still predisposed to being "puzzeld in amorous encounters" because "a crosse answer of their Mistres crosseth their armes, hangs downe the head, and puts a willow branch in the hat-band" (20-21).

40. Davison, *Gesta Grayorum 1688*, 16.

41. See Magnusson, "Scoff Power."

42. Davison, *Gesta Grayorum 1688*, 30.

Failing Out

As we observe the young men from the Inns at Court filing into London's playhouses to develop their social skills, we might also consider the players therein, anxiously awaiting them. It was not just with other auditors that these city gallants practiced conversation; they were also known to talk back to, or over, the actors on stage as well.[43] While *Love's Labor's Lost* depicts the arrogant lords forced to confront the limitations of their "penned speech," what must it have been like for its author, anticipating the opening performance, penning those speeches? Imagine our poet, working through issues of plot, theme, character, and style at his writing desk. The scene of writing buzzes with a host of real and imagined voices: those of his collaborators, who may need him to have finished certain scenes according to the agreed-on plot structure; those of the actors, who would suit his parts to their personalities and particular skills; and finally, those of the imagined audience, who may turn against the derivative, the tedious, the unskillful, and the outlandish. In *Love's Labor's Lost*, Shakespeare positions courtly conversationalists alongside amateur theatrical performers, exposing continuities between their experiences of sociable discourse. While I am certainly far from the first person to suggest affinities between early modern actors and aspiring courtiers, I emphasize that these figures were aligned not just in terms of their capacities for "self-fashioning" but also in terms of how their self-conscious artificiality left them vulnerable to performance anxiety.[44]

Lynn Enterline observes that professional players in Elizabethan England proceeded on a "trajectory from one institutional scene of performance and judgment (the schoolroom) to another (the commercial theater)" as the rite of passage into social maturity.[45] Their humanist training, she argues, produced "divided, rhetorically capable, yet emotionally labile speakers for whom language learning and self-representation entailed the incessant dislocations of the theater." These dislocations were associated with "the constant internal movement in [Shakespeare's] characters between seeming and being, *persona* and person, address and self-representation; between assuming, whether successively or simultaneously, the positions of writer, actor,

---

43. See Preiss, *Clowning and Authorship*, esp. 18–59.
44. See Greenblatt, *Renaissance Self-Fashioning*; Gaylard, *Hollow Men*; Whigham, "Interpretation at Court."
45. Enterline, *Shakespeare's Schoolroom*, 40.

and audience."⁴⁶ Enterline's account of the schoolboy's crisis resembles what Donald M. Kaplan calls "blocking," which he identifies as the "split between a functioning and an observing self" that is symptomatic of stage fright.⁴⁷ Early modern theatrical culture anticipated this experience, and made much of it, through a metaphorical dislocation: one of the most common expressions actors used for the experience of stage fright was of being "out."⁴⁸

To be out was to experience the breakdown of the theatrical event as a collaborative endeavor. Erving Goffman, developing his famous sociological study of "everyday life" by analogizing it with theater, observed that when an individual "projects" a situation onto others that others are responsible for "protecting," they aspire to build something analogous to Guazzo's civil conversation: a "working consensus."⁴⁹ If a projection is disrupted and a consensus broken, however, "the interaction itself may come to a confused and embarrassed halt" and "the individual who has been discredited may feel ashamed while the others may come to feel ill at ease, nonplussed, out of countenance, embarrassed, experiencing the kind of anomy that is generated when the minute social system of face-to-face interaction breaks down."⁵⁰ Anticipating Goffman's account, early modern Londoners deployed terms such as being "out," "at *non plus*," "out of countenance," or "without a prompter" to describe everyday interactions. By the end of the sixteenth century, theatrically going "out" had become a resonant shorthand for the disorientation that caused performances of all kinds to fail: those of schoolchildren before their masters, gentlemen at court speaking with social superiors, and lovers before their beloveds.⁵¹ Jonson, for

---

46. Enterline, *Shakespeare's Schoolroom*, 47–48.
47. Kaplan, "On Stage Fright," 64. Nicholas Ridout suggests that stage fright emerges because of "the absence of reciprocity in the encounter between professional and consumer." Ridout, *Stage Fright*, 29. While Ridout associates the phenomenon with "urban modernity," and while the term "stage fright" was apparently coined by Mark Twain, early modern players often alluded to how they could swoon, freeze, or, turn "wooden." For studies of stage fright and early modern actors, see Nardizzi, "Wooden Actors"; Skura, *Shakespeare the Actor*, 9–28.
48. For more on actors going "out," see Palfrey and Stern, *Shakespeare in Parts*, 84–88.
49. Goffman, *Presentation of Self*, 9–10.
50. Goffman, *Presentation of Self*, 12.
51. For example, when Simon the mayor in Thomas Middleton's *Hengist, King of Kent; or, The Mayor of Queenborough* encounters some cheaters promising to put on a play, he warns, "Have you audacity enough to play before so high a person? Will not my countenance daunt you?" (5.1.81–87). In *A Midsummer Night's Dream*, Theseus overrules Philostrate's warning that the performance by Athens's "rude mechanicals" (3.2.9) will be a stammering failure by recounting how "great clerks have proposèd / To greet me with premeditated welcomes" but ended up having to "[t]hrottle their practiced accent in their fears" (5.1.93–99).

example, describes courtiers as akin to "neophyte players" because they are "daunted at first presence or interview" with those of higher social station.[52] Robert Greene's *Greene's Groatsworth of Wit* (1592) recounts a character who "had a good meaninge to utter his minde" to a beautiful courtesan, but upon seeing her "want[ed] fit wordes" and so "stood like a trewant that lackt a prompter, a plaier that being out of his part at his first entrance, is faine to have the book to speake what he should performe."[53] As the theater grew to be an increasingly popular cultural touchstone, early modern popular culture began employing its conventions and protocols for describing everyday life. Every social performance carried with it some theatricality, and its failures could be rendered in terms of theatrical failure.

As conversational breakdown grew metonymically linked with theatrical implosion, this analogy also began to work in reverse: players, composing themselves and their plays for public performance, began envisioning the encounter as a potentially tense conversation. Players deployed representations of their own theatrical incompetence to remind audiences that putting on a show was embodied, physical labor that could be applauded on merits distinct from the merits of the written play alone. In analogizing stage fright with scenes of abjection such as the schoolboy before his master, a subject before royalty, or the lover before a beloved, players implied that the presence of spectators was partly responsible for their mistakes. In so doing, they encouraged spectators to perceive themselves as collaborators in the success of a theatrical event. After all, a play, especially a new commercial play, had to court audiences and persuade them of its charms. By the end of the sixteenth century, according to Jeffrey S. Doty, players—a category of professional that includes poets, actors, and businessmen shareholders—were confronting "mass audiences who essentially voted on what they liked or did not like."[54] To sustain their business, players needed and attempted to fashion what Paul Menzer calls a "cultivated crowd."[55] In this sense, plays like *Love's Labor's Lost* aimed at a shifting target, one that they would need the audience's trust to even attempt striking.[56] Audience

---

52. Jonson, "Cynthia's Revels," 174 (3.1.3–5).
53. Greene, *Greenes, Groats-Vvorth of Witte*, sig. C3r.
54. Doty, *Shakespeare*, 21.
55. Menzer, "Crowd Control," 21.
56. Mark Bayer identifies a fundamental problem recognized by players: "that part of their challenge was to appeal to multiple and stratified audiences simultaneously." Bayer, "Curious Case," 57–58. Matteo Pangallo summarizes how "playgoers and playmakers in the

members would interrupt performances, write their own revisions and original plays, and publicize their critiques, drawing on their experiences from other venues. Facing such crowds almost certainly gave poets and their professional companies pause.

As if to combat this likelihood by openly acknowledging it, players across early modern drama began to *perform* their stage fright. Actorly failure would be scripted into performances, confusing the player's professional occupation with the audience's interpretation of characters' emotional lives. This happened most conspicuously through prologues and epilogues, which came to emblematize the ways in which both the composition and performances of plays were vulnerable to audiences.[57] As Tiffany Stern observes, the prologue and epilogue materialized onstage the ambivalences and contradictions of authorship on the early modern stage because "a prologue or epilogue heralded a play in its freshest and so most fluid state."[58] Theatrical prologues offered plays up for revision and correction, and so the actors who would deliver the prologues grew stereotypically associated with weak knees and pale faces. These figures perform a kind of worry that sheds light on playwrights' own worries about the difference between theatrical and compositional "perfectness." Thomas Middleton and Thomas Dekker, for example, have a prologue complain that "[a] play (expected long) makes the audience look / For wonders—that each scene should be a book, / Composed to all perfection; each one comes / And brings a play in's head with him."[59] In trying to address the varied and unknowable whims of audiences, play producers took on an impossible task; rather than making confident compositional decisions, they made guesses about what the audience might want and how they would react.

While writers and printers in Shakespeare's time used "perfect" to suggest that a text was complete or no longer needed correction

---

period understood the audience's relationship with the stage to be fluid, open, and dialogic, in which playgoers' creative input could be just as authoritative as that of professional playmakers." See Pangallo, *Playwriting Playgoers*, 27, 52–60.

57. Douglas Bruster and Robert Weimann explain how early modern prologues ushered playgoers over "an imaginary threshold" and performed a "differentiating function" that "helped isolate dramatic form from non-verbal types of performances." Bruster and Weimann, *Prologues to Shakespeare's Theatre*, 37.

58. Stern, *Documents of Performance*, 82.

59. Middleton and Dekker, "Roaring Girl," 727 (prologue.3). As Stern observes, during the initial performances of new plays, what players were testing was not the actors' ability to perform, "for they can put on another play if this one is damned"—the trial was of "the playscript itself." Stern, *Documents of Performance*, 88–89.

with reference to an original, the term had a broader range of associations.[60] Players often used the term to indicate the "word-perfect" memorization of their parts—when Letoy in Brome's *The Antipodes* (1638) declares that his players "[a]re all in readinesse; and I thinke all perfect," he renders "perfect" synonymous with flawless memorization and recitation.[61] But John Marston's *Jack Drum's Entertainment* (1601) clarifies some of the subtleties that attended the term: it begins with a mock prologue explaining that the playwright snatched the book of the play away from the players both because he had not finished writing it—"he was loth, / Wanting a Prologue"—and because the players were not ready to put it on: "& our selues not perfect, / To rush vpon your eyes without respect."[62] Perfect might have meant "completed," but it also suggested an actorly disposition.[63] Evelyn Tribble describes this disposition as comprising "the skills behind the skills": "memory, vigilancy, and pregnancy of wit." Vigilancy, the cognitive glue of the actor's onstage practice, accounts for an "alertness and attentiveness" and "flexible mindfulness" that underlie an "ability to perform whilst monitoring and appraising audience reaction, all the while adjusting on the fly."[64] Vigilancy was not easily acquired, however, even though it was partly promoted by schoolroom performances as the acquisition of "audacity."[65] Thomas Gainsford's account of early players captures the affective and emotional dimensions of "perfectness," revealing that players are "at the first very bashfull, as strucken with a maze at the

---

60. See Massai, *Shakespeare*, 5–10; Zurcher, "Deficiency and Supplement."

61. Brome, *Antipodes a Comedie*, sig. D2v. The same may be said of when Bottom, in *A Midsummer Night's Dream*, instructs his company, "Take pains; be perfect" prior to their rehearsal (1.2.90), or when Tharsalio, in George Chapman's *The Vviddovves Teares a Comedie*, asks of his nephew preparing to perform, "Is he perfect in's part? has not his tongue learn'd of the *Syluans* to trip ath' Toe?" (sig. Gv).

62. Marston, *Iacke Drums Entertainment*, sig. A2r–v.

63. As Richard Preiss points out, actors could be "prepared" for a performance without having memorized their parts at all. In the same speech from *The Antipodes* quoted above, Letoy explains that despite not being perfect in his part, the clown Byplay could "frible through" his lines by making "shifts extempore." See Preiss, "Undocumented," 76–77.

64. Tribble, *Early Modern Actors*, 125–26. Tribble suggests that the ability to cope with interruptions is a salient distinguishing mark between pros and amateurs. Tribble, *Cognition in the Globe*, 117–50. When Viola in *Twelfth Night* observes what it takes to be "wise enough to play the fool" (3.1.53), the labors she documents account for some of this invisible theatrical skill.

65. Thomas Heywood notes that universities saw acting as "necessary for the emboldening of their junior scholars to arm them with audacity again when they come to be employed in any public exercise." Heywood, "Apology for Actors," 227. Acting, he adds, "not only emboldens a scholar to speak, but instructs him to speak well" and "fit his phrases to his action, and his action to his phrases, and his pronunciation to them both" (227).

multitude, which being of various dispositions, will censure him accordingly, but custome maketh perfectnesse, and emboldeneth him sometimes to be shameless."⁶⁶ The perfectness alluded to here has little to do with the part the actor would be playing and relates more to experientially earned boldness—to the extent that perfectness could mean dangerous impudence.⁶⁷ Perfectness thus becomes roughly synonymous with both "completeness" and "readiness": something finished in that it knows itself to be potentially unfinished. Its degree of completion can be discovered only through exposure to its own limitations—sufficient to seem successful, but free to fail.

The self-consciously failed text knows that an agreement has yet to be reached.⁶⁸ This allows it to be more responsive, and potentially more creative, because a potential breakdown, Sara Jane Bailes suggests, "indexes an alternative route or way of doing or making."⁶⁹ Her paradigmatic example of vulnerable performance is an unperfect actor:

> The order in which, for example, a line of playtext must be remembered and recited produces one solution. Forgetting that line produces the possibility of a number of versions (the ways of coping with forgetting and making-do as well as alternative versions of the line itself) that might stand in for the forgotten words, such as paraphrasing, improvising text that leads in another direction, standing in silence, reinventing the text through gesture, and so on. In this sense, strategies of failure in the realm of performance can be understood as generative, prolific even; failure *produces*, and does so in a roguish manner.⁷⁰

If failure is an outcome of evaluation, it is also a provocation to closer analysis, because it registers an intrusion on the evaluator's horizon of expectations.⁷¹ For Bailes, this means that failure "enables us to perceive

---

66. Gainsford, *Rich Cabinet*, 117r–v.
67. Tribble points out how early modern players accommodated a "range of levels of fidelity to the author's words"; see Tribble, *Cognition in the Globe*, 75. Richard Preiss discusses how the threat posed by improvisatory clowning, from the perspective of the playing company, was "not the sheer fact of deviation from the script, but the surrender of institutional autonomy thereby." Preiss, *Clowning and Authorship*, 186.
68. Bailes, *Performance Theatre*, 2.
69. Bailes, *Performance Theatre*, 2.
70. Bailes, *Performance Theatre*, 2–3.
71. Alison Carr makes a similar point, noting that "when failure causes *notice*—when it provokes fits of shame, anxiety, tears, loss of confidence, paralyzing fear and isolation—it exposes the bones and sinews, the unique and messy and sometimes improvised structure of the thing we're trying to create." Carr, "In Support of Failure."

the processes of refinement expressed by mechanisms of choice and control" and the "disavowed workings of power and exclusion."[72] Forgetting a line during performance disarticulates the script, even if momentarily, by revealing it to be a script. It draws notice to the contingency and constructedness of success, making practice itself a referendum on the possibility of mastery.[73] Bailes's view of failure echoes that of Jack Halberstam, who argues that failure may be read "as a refusal of mastery" and as "a critique of the intuitive connections within capitalism between success and profit."[74] Julietta Singh develops these ideas to propose a method of "vulnerable reading" that deprioritizes conclusiveness, suggesting that "in failing to master, in confronting our own desires for mastery where we least expect or recognize these desires, we become vulnerable to other possibilities for living." To accompany Singh's championing of "vulnerable reading" as an "an open, continuous practice that resists foreclosures by remaining unremittingly susceptible to new world configurations that reading texts—literary, artistic, philosophical, and political—can begin to produce,"[75] we might imagine a pedagogy of vulnerable writing: writing confident only in the knowledge that it will not end a conversation.

Not Generous, Not Gentle, Not Humble

Love's Labor's Lost itself memorably concludes with a performance reduced to unexpected silence—or, more precisely, it concludes with cascading failures of performance. Near the beginning of its final scene, Boyet reports to the princess that the men are planning to disguise themselves to "parley, court and dance" as they advance their "love suits" (5.2.122-23). To announce their arrival, they have enlisted Mote, "a petty knavish page" who "well by heart hath conned his embassage" as the prologue to their masque (5.2.97-98). Though Mote had received instruction in "[a]ction and accent" and in how to bear his body, the lords still worried—playing to the stereotype of the quaking prologue—that the princess's "[p]resence majestical would put him

---

72. Bailes, *Performance Theatre*, 34.
73. Bailes, *Performance Theatre*, 109.
74. Halberstam, *Queer Art of Failure*, 11-12.
75. Singh, *Unthinking Mastery*, 21-22. For Singh, these alternative possibilities represent an embodied resistance to colonialist fantasies of domination; failures of mastery reveal ways to imagine "being together in common" and *"feeling* injustice and refusing it without the need to engage it through forms of conquest."

out" (5.2.99–102). The lords could not have anticipated, however, that after hearing Boyet's report, the princess would interpret their play as an attempt to mock the ladies with more superficial flattery. Preempting their performance, the princess advises the other ladies to turn away their faces and pay no attention to the lords' "penned speech" (5.2.147). When Boyet warns that this may "kill the speaker's heart" and "divorce his memory from his part" (5.2.149–50), she replies that this is precisely her goal, thereby making the men the recipients rather than the imparters of mockery.

The princess's plan works perfectly. Figure 5.1 shows how the scene is presented in the 1598 quarto.

Mote (identified above as "Page" and "Pag." in the speech prefixes, "Boy" in the stage direction, and "Moth" in the first folio, and whose name evokes the French for "word," *mot*) enters alongside the masked

> *Enter Black-moores with musicke, the Boy with a speach, and the rest of the Lordes disguysed.*
> Page. All haile, the richest Beauties on the earth.
> Berow. Beauties no richer then rich Taffata.
> Page. A holy parcell of the fayrest dames that euer turnd their backes to mortall viewes.
>   *The Ladyes turne their backes to him.*
> Berow. Their eyes villaine, their eyes.
> Pag. That euen turnde their eyes to mortall viewes.
> Out
> Boy. True, out in deede.
> Pag. Out of your fauours heauenly spirites vouchsafe Not to beholde.
> Berow. Once to beholde, rogue.
> Page. Once to beholde with your Sunne beamed eyes, With your Sunne beamed eyes.
> Boyet. They will not answere to that Epythat, You were best call it Daughter beamed eyes.
> Pag. They do not marke me, and that bringes me out.
> Ber. Is this your perfectnes? begon you rogue.
>   *Rosa.*

FIGURE 5.1. William Shakespeare, *Loues Labors Lost* (London: William White, 1598), sig. G3v. Used by permission of the Folger Shakespeare Library.

courtiers of Navarre. As he begins to deliver his speech, which he has apparently brought in with him as a prop, the princess and her retinue turn their backs to him. The way the quarto is printed suggests this happens after he says, *"turnd their backes to mortall views."* The logic of the scene suggests this happens just before he speaks this line, however, because as Biron prompts him, Mote was supposed to say, "their eyes." I share the scene in its original published form because the bare evidence of the page elucidates the limitations of integrating "speeches penned" with live performance. Any actors performing this moment would need to make the adjustment to capture the way the ladies' behavior inflects Mote's delivery—the page makes it impossible for audiences to witness two things simultaneously. As a function of being ignored and heckled, Mote falls "out" of his part just as the word *"Out"* falls out of his mouth and hangs in the "margent" of the quarto, its italic typeface collapsing the distinction between stage direction and speech.[76] "They do not marke me, and that bringes me out," he reflects, providing Biron the cue to literally pull Mote out of the production, yelling after him, "Is this your perfectnes?"

"Perfect" appears three times in *Love's Labor's Lost*, each time in relation to expectation and execution. Its first appearance is at the very start of the second act, when Boyet describes King Ferdinand of Navarre as "the sole inheritor / Of all perfections that a man may owe," after describing the princess herself as "held precious in the world's esteem" (2.1.4–6). In reply, the princess tactfully rejects Boyet's flattery of her own beauty and, by implication, conveys skepticism about Navarre: "Beauty is bought by judgment of the eye, / Not uttered by base sale of chapmen's tongues" (2.1.15–16). Like beauty, a courtier's supposed perfections were to be demonstrated in person rather than simply claimed, and as we saw above, reports of Navarre's supposed perfection immediately prove overblown. The second instance in which "perfect" appears is Biron's lamentation about Mote's "perfectness" (5.2.174), which extends the first usage by indexing the discrepancy between a presumed role and its embodied execution. The word's final instance appears at the end of the play, during the performance of the Nine Worthies put on by Costard, Mote, and Armado. After flubbing one of his lines by calling himself "Pompey surnamed the Big" (5.2.547), Costard appears to laugh off his error: "'Tis not so much worth; but I hope I was perfect:

---

76. For a compelling reading of this scene's bibliographical theatricality, see Bourne, "Typography after Performance," esp. 208–9.

I made little fault in 'Great'" (5.2.556–57). Ironically hoping that he was "perfect" while also recognizing his own "little fault," he effortlessly liberates perfectness from flawless recitation. Despite literally failing to play the role he was assigned, Costard, encouraged by the princess's kind gratitude—"Great thanks, great Pompey" (5.2.555)—takes his imperfections in stride. The inability to laugh it off, to adjust, to reciprocally engage with the audience constitutes failure for theater just as it constitutes failure for a conversationalist—an analogy the play makes overt by repeatedly juxtaposing the lords' conversational awkwardness with scenes of stage fright and theatrical implosion.

Once the ladies buffet the lords with wordplay and mockery, each of them suffers, like Mote, an experience of disturbed poise. Boyet gleefully remarks, as they depart, that they appeared as "[t]apers . . . with your sweet breaths puff'd out" (5.2.267). The princess similarly notes that Biron was "out of count'nance quite" (5.2.272), and Maria reports that Dumaine "straight was mute" (5.2.277). Later, once the ladies disclose their bait-and-switch of exchanging favors and masks, Biron appears so "[a]maz'd" that Rosaline worries that he may faint (5.2.391–92). By shunting these men from their prepared performances, the princess, to borrow Matteo Pangallo's description of how audiences influenced early modern theatrical production, "reverses the conventional producer-consumer relationship" and puts "active consumers in control over responsive producers."[77] By insisting on collaborating in the "mocking merriment" and not just being subjected to it, the ladies expose the lords' failure to treat the women as interlocutors. Concertedly provoking amazement, the ladies offer precisely the kind of education that Annibal recommends in *The Civile Conversation*: firsthand experience of what it is like to confront a bad conversationalist.

The inexperienced lords repeatedly demonstrate that they have no idea what they sound like when they speak, or of how their words sound to the people who must listen to them. When the king returns unmasked to face the princess, again opening with a hollow pleasantry—"All hail, sweet madam, and fair time of day!"—she twists his clearly forced words once more by pointing out that hail is foul rather than fair weather (5.2.340–41). This prompts the end of the exercise, for once the flustered king replies, "Construe my speeches better, if you may," the princess explains, "Then wish me better" (5.2.342–43). This

---

77. Pangallo, *Playwriting Playgoers*, 42.

disagreement precedes Rosaline mocking Biron's "superfluous case" (5.2.388), indicating that she saw through his mask. At this, the gentleman renowned for his quick wit stammers in response, "Where? When? What visor? Why demand you this?" (5.2.387). The game now fully exposed, the lords recoil in embarrassment. The king blurts out, "We are descried! They'll mock us now downright," and Dumaine proposes to "confess and turn it to a jest" (5.2.390-91). They each proceed through the symptoms of stage fright, as the princess remarks on how they appear "amazed" (5.2.392), and Rosaline notices of Biron, "Help! Hold his brows! He'll swoon. Why look you pale?" (5.2.392-93). Once he gathers himself, Biron claims to have learned his lesson:

> Oh, never will I trust to speeches penned
> Nor to the motion of a schoolboy's tongue,
> Nor never come in visor to my friend,
> Nor woo in rhyme, like a blind harper's song.
> Taffeta phrases, silken terms precise,
> Three-piled hyperboles, spruce affectation,
> Figures pedantical—these summer flies
> Have blown me full of maggot ostentation.
> (5.2.403-10)

Finally sensing that it is his rehearsed language, encrusted with affectation and rote learning, that keeps getting him into trouble, Biron declares, "Speak for yourselves. My wit is at an end" (5.2.431). The princess's deception pressed the courtiers into an experience of conversational failure, exposing their mechanical commitment to "speeches penned," "taffeta phrases," and "figures pedantical" as making them worthy of ridicule. Biron's recognition of his own ostentatious speech directly affiliates him and the other lords with the broadest caricature of pedantic academics within the play: Holofernes and Nathaniel. Holofernes's fundamental gesture in his conversations is to adapt occasions into opportunities to demonstrate his learnedness. His first lines capture the flavor of his pedantic performance: "The deer was, as you know, *sanguis*, in blood, ripe as a pomewater who now hangeth like a jewel in the ear of *caelo*, the sky, the welkin, the heaven, and anon falleth like a crab on the face of *terra*, the soil, the land, the earth" (4.2.1-6). Complimented by Nathaniel for how his "epithets are sweetly varied, like a scholar" (4.2.8), Holofernes represents the copiousness of the humanist orator taken to its ludicrous limit. Deploying Latin interchangeably with English and parsing it with three translations, Holofernes blathers on, pleased by the sound of his own speech.

Even though Biron's speech suggests that the lords have learned their lessons, there are over five hundred lines left in the play. These largely consist of the theatrical performance of the Nine Worthies, put on by Mote, Holofernes, Nathaniel, Costard, and Don Armado. Before these amateur players are about to enter, the king fears that they will shame the court of Navarre through their incompetence. In response, the princess explains that "sport best pleases that doth least know how" (5.2.514), and that zeal, even when coupled with ineptitude, generates harmless mirth. Biron then suggests that the "confounded" performance in fact may resemble the courtiers' own masque (5.2.519), but despite having been exposed to what it feels like to confront "liberal opposition" (5.2.719) as performers, the men prove as poor spectators as they had been actors. In fact, they labor at length to ruin the amateur performance. They ridicule Costard for his "little fault," "dismay" Nathaniel out of his part as Alexander the Great until he is "afraid to speak" (5.2.574), insult Holofernes as Judas Maccabeus until he declares himself "out of countenance" (5.2.615), and heckle Armado as Hector until he appeals directly to the princess, "Sweet royalty, bestow on me the sense of hearing" (5.2.654). Before departing, Holofernes stops serving as a satirical target and becomes, like Mote, pitiable. He storms offstage, attesting, "This is not generous, not gentle, not humble" (5.2.623).

While a theatrical catastrophe, as a work of amateur theater the pageant of the Nine Worthies complicates the conditions by which a performance may be regarded as a failure. Bailes, taking cues from Walter Benjamin and Bertolt Brecht, articulates the distinction between amateur and professional theater in terms of the former's capacity for soliciting aesthetic flexibility:

> Amateur theatre was intriguing to both theorists [Brecht and Benjamin] for the way in which it could reveal the conditions of theatre and the potential for change in the world. Professional theatre, on the other hand, could not achieve such a revelation because of its slick façade which rendered most if not all of its labor invisible, presenting the ideology and values of bourgeois society as universal and unchanging. According to Brecht, professional theatre, founded on bourgeois aesthetic and cultural values, could learn from the "image of the world" presented by amateur theatre

with its "rudimentary, distorted, spontaneous efforts"; for the ways, then, in which the inability to do something might overwhelm ability and instead radiate different values and beliefs.[78]

While the princess and her ladies receive the pageant amiably, the lords, with Boyet in tow, behave boorishly; they try, conspicuously, to reaffirm the class distinctions between their own failed performances and those of the amateur actors. We might read the closing pageant, then, less as a play within a play than as two simultaneous performances: amateur and courtly. The amateur performers, lacking polish, skill, and technique, nevertheless manage to please the princess because of their earnest zeal. Costard, at least, manages to have a good time. The courtiers, however, in attempting to surpass one another's scoff power, disclose the caustic rigidity of performances that yearn only to reassert preconceptions of ability and mastery.

The play's final moments then reiterate the lords' inability to adjust from their own conceitedness in the most awkward fashion: like a broken record, the king, to console a princess who has just learned of her father's death, continues ornate and verbose attempts at courtship. The princess can only respond, "I understand you not; my griefs are double" (5.2.738). The ladies then decide to depart for France, leaving behind some final bits of advice. The king, who began the play by issuing hollow pleasantries to mask a failure of hospitality, concludes it with the princess asking him to live the life of a solitary hermit for a year. Biron, who began the play with a reputation for self-serving wit, concludes it by being tasked with learning how to translate others' pain into their pleasure. Rosaline explains, "A jest's prosperity lies in the ear / Of him that hears it, never in the tongue / Of him that makes it," and so her concluding request to Biron is that he "never rest" and "[v]isit the speechless sick and still converse / With groaning wretches" (5.2.807, 836–37). This echoes one of Annibal's points to William: "For you cannot goe to visite the sicke, to reléeue the poore, to correct and admonishe your brother, to comfort the afflicted, if you remain alwaies mewed vp" (1.8r). The lords who decided in their solitariness to deprive women of speech now must learn the value and virtues of conversation. Dramatizing poor spectatorship as of a piece with the lords' poor conversational skills, the play serves as an object lesson to its own audience on how not to behave at a theatrical performance.

---

78. Bailes, *Performance Theatre*, 33.

I conclude my reading of *Love's Labor's Lost* by returning to the scene discussed at the beginning of this section, in which the lordly actors prepare for their performance with Mote the page. As mentioned, prior to sending Mote out as their prologue, the lords were worried that the princess would put him out of his part and thereby spoil their whole production. I return to this passage now to observe how these players mustered the courage to get themselves out onstage:

> And ever and anon they made a doubt,
> Presence majestical would put him out.
> "For," quoth the King, "an angel shalt thou see.
> Yet fear not thou, but speak audaciously."
> The boy replied: "An angel is not evil.
> I should have feared her had she been a devil."
> With that, all laughed and clapped him on the shoulder,
> Making the bold wag by their praises bolder.
> One rubbed his elbow thus, and fleered, and swore
> A better speech was never spoke before.
> Another with his finger and his thumb
> Cried "*Via!* We will do't, come what will come!"
> The third he capered and cried, "All goes well!"
> The fourth turned on the toe and down he fell.
> With that, they all did tumble on the ground,
> With such a zealous laughter, so profound,
> That in this spleen ridiculous appears,
> To check their folly, passion's solemn tears.
> (5.2.101–18)

Mote, we are told, protested the king's warning that he would not be flustered because the princess is "[a]n angel" and not "a devil." This response elicited such good cheer from the others that they ended up tumbling over themselves into a heap of "zealous laughter." Their anxieties about the performance were sublimated into a "spleen ridiculous" because Mote's reply, gently reversing the king's hyperbolic declaration, made fun of how severely the lords had been taking their own idolatry. This moment, presented to the audience entirely through Boyet's reporting, captures in miniature what the play never manages to portray onstage: a failure that does not turn into a conclusion. Read in this light, the lords' "come what will come" attitude and their resolution that "all goes well" foresee the comic resolution that *Love's Labor's Lost* as a whole refuses to supply. Its actors know what the script should say—"our wooing doth not end like the old play"—but the play itself cannot deliver it: "Jack hath not Jill" (5.2.860-61). Instead of finding ways to laugh at themselves, they stammer, freeze, and swoon as the play careens toward a confused and embarrassed halt.

Reflection: Ars Amateuria

"When we ask our students to be original—and we do ask that of them," Kara Wittman cautions, "we ask them to occupy two positions at once."[79] If our assignments say things like, "Your thesis should be original," should be "imaginative, authoritative, with original insight," or "original, interesting, and relevant," Wittman argues, these assignments are asking students "to walk the line between expert and tyro; professional and amateur: to be enough of a naif to experience the wonder of 'first-ness' and knowledgeable enough to recognize that first-ness as such."[80] Suspended between their own apparent amateurishness and the exemplary professionality displayed by their teachers, many student writers will come to distrust their own responses to course readings. Becoming a professional, they have come to learn, means rejecting the part of themselves that approaches texts naively. When trying to produce an original argument or to develop a critical insight, however, these students invariably find that following the instructions will get them only so far. In the empty space between perfectible instructions and open-ended interpretation yawns, to borrow a phrase from Constantin Stanislavski, an "awful hole."[81] Perfectionism, performance anxiety, and frustration emanate from it, and the fearful student writer vacillates between what feels like recklessness or automation.[82]

How can we help our students learn that not knowing how to address a text need not lead to either blockage or canned arguments; that although the challenge to say something original may be discomposing, it need not be debilitating? We might start by recognizing that students *do* genuinely have insights to offer about the texts we have assigned them to read—even if these insights strike us as rudimentary, banal, or even wrong. Students approach early modern texts as amateurs, and as Derek Attridge points out,

> [an] amateur reading, no matter by whom, involves an openness to whatever the work, on a particular occasion, will bring—a readiness to have habits and preconceptions challenged and a willingness to be

---

79. Wittman, "Epilogue," 244.
80. Wittman, "Epilogue," 244.
81. Stanislavski, *Actor Prepares*, 7.
82. As Peter Elbow observes, these conditions do not apply to just our students: "Have you ever noticed that when we write articles or books as academics, we often have the same feeling that students have when they turn in papers: 'Is this okay? Will you accept this?'" Elbow, "Being a Writer," 82.

changed by the experience. A professional reading in the narrowest sense of the word, by contrast, will approach the text instrumentally, scrutinizing it for such things as evidence of some historical trend, an insight into the psychology of the author, signs of the influence of a precursor, or examples of a stylistic device. Both kinds of reading, no doubt, bring pleasure, but the pleasure of the scholar who has added to a bank of data is different from the pleasure generated by a reading of the work as literature, which is to say as the product of an author's (or authors') creativity.[83]

The professional knows how to make use out of the reading experience, but the amateur does not necessarily intend to put the reading to any specific use, at least not yet. An unperfect actor, the amateur inspired to be attentive and given leave to speak what he or she feels may well say something surprising. The amateur may even see things that professionals do not yet see or have trained themselves to stop seeing.

Recognizing this, the Shakespeare classroom may become one in which students are empowered by the fact that their responses have access to insights and experiences that their professors do not—that their readings, done with attention and care, are valuable. The classroom must be structured, in this light, to give students the occasion—to allow them to enter the dance without fear of being judged or laughed out of the room. Building this structure requires us, their teachers and interlocutors, to fully embrace and even lay bare the limitations of our own professional authority.

Discomposing a discipline, discomposing literary studies, discomposing Shakespeare all demand that we challenge ourselves to practice imperfectness. This does not mean that professors must aspire toward amateurism. Pretending not to know something is a masquerade; pretending that we do not know better than our students about some things makes our presence in the classroom trivial. The allure of presenting oneself as an amateur is the allure of shirking responsibility, and such performances of self-repudiation allow academics to disavow their complicity within the professional structure they inhabit. Only one person in the room is being paid to produce literary criticism, so try as we might, we will not become amateur Shakespeareans. Even so, the only way to improve our art as teachers, Shakespeare himself labors to teach us, is to recognize it as imperfect.

---

83. Attridge, "In Praise of Amateurism," 39.

CHAPTER 5

What does the art of teaching a text like *Love's Labor's Lost* involve? In one sense, it involves providing students with context and information: a teacher may direct students' attention to topics such as courtesy and etiquette, illuminate how the play manipulates the contours of comedy's generic conventions, or point out that it was potentially written concurrently with Shakespeare's sonnets. In another sense, teaching the play may also involve offering close readings of it as models of interpretation. In yet another sense, teaching the play may involve curating an encounter between the play and other texts, such as *The Lover's Discourse* or a modern romantic comedy, with the idea that these other texts will render the play more approachable. These forms of teaching rely on helping students reach some sort of elucidation about a difficult text; they shine a beam of light through an obscure tangle of language. These forms of teaching (which, to be clear, I have practiced and will continue to practice) proceed, simply put, via different forms of explanation: here is why this line is important, these are some things that the play is about, here is how to think about what you are seeing.

In a heartening article exploring the obscure and potentially "unteachable" words of *Love's Labor's Lost*, however, Adam Zucker reflects on the pedagogy of explanation in the Shakespeare classroom as at once inevitable and potentially undermining what students will learn:

> The moment when a student clearly cannot understand something that I myself know; the moment when I say something like, "well, what Shakespeare means here is …" or "Actually, there's a joke about sixteenth-century animal husbandry here" or something along those lines; that "teaching moment" is crucial, but it enacts over and over again the process that Rancière critiques in *The Ignorant Schoolmaster*. It is a moment that reminds everyone in the room that I know things that they do not. Our relative intelligences are created in those moments, no matter how often I let them know that I, too, rely on marginal glosses and past classroom lessons to guide me through semantic problems as I wend my way through *Hamlet* for the 700th time. Horrifyingly, the practical conversations I use to put my students at ease about ignorance simply reinforce the point: I know a lot about how to learn Shakespeare.[84]

---

84. Zucker, "Antihonorificabilitudinitatibus," 140.

Zucker zeroes in on something elemental to teaching and learning with literature: acknowledging experiences of incapacity and failure as fundamentally constitutive of how readings of complex texts take shape. "We might perform Shakespeare's unteachable words in ways that permit them to be just that," Zucker proposes. "We might hold up their incomprehensibility not as something that always needs to be squashed out of existence in an edition or explicated into sense, but use them rather as the tools they are, use them to animate comic scenarios in which teachers and students share in the pleasure of befuddlement."[85] To give students facility with Shakespeare's work, failures of understanding might become part of our pedagogy. We must try to help students prioritize the value of not knowing the answer, the value of failure as the first step toward discovery.

Explaining a joke often ruins it. *Love's Labor's Lost* works very hard to make this clear. If explained, Mote's quip to Costard—"They have been at a great feast of language and stolen the scraps" (5.1.35–36)—would not only render the joke lifeless but, in the expenditure of language meant to serve as an explanation, miss the very ironies the joke relies on. If explained, Dull's reply to Holofernes's remark that he has "spoken no word all this while"—"Nor understood none, neither, sir" (5.1.132)—would lose entire dimensions of comic effect. These moments are funny because the characters tap into something that the audience, the reader, and the actors themselves also perceive: there is a lot of confusing gibberish in here. Trusting that the audience is more akin to Dull than to Holofernes, the players allow the unlearned to get one over on the pedants. The joke here is not simply that Dull is dull, but that the scholars' prolix posturing is visible even to someone like Dull. Winking at every corner of its audience, the play plays with the paradox that only a pedant would fully understand the polyglot errors being made by the conceited pedants; everyone else, it knows, can laugh at pedantry without falling into the crossfire. By satirizing such failed performances of erudition, a play replete with puns for the learned suggests that confessing one's befuddlement can create opportunities for different sorts of pleasure: the pleasure of turning failure into fun, of robbing authoritativeness of its authority, of denying the bourgeois polish of professional performance its representational claims.

What kind of performance are we soliciting when we ask students to produce critical writing? To approach the question from another direction: in what ways are we inviting our students to fail? These questions hinge

---

85. Zucker, "Antihonorificabilitudinitatibus," 149.

on the double meaning of performance as "the competence or effectiveness of a person or thing in performing an action" and as "an individual performer's or group's rendering or interpretation of a work, part, role."[86] The former definition affiliates performance with proficiency, with the capacity to perfectly hit an implicit or explicit standard: were the singers able to reach the high notes, just like they do on the record? The latter definition, by contrast, invites affective and interpretive engagement: a singer's voice cracking may be the most moving and memorable part of the concert. A performer committed to sounding exactly like the record while also endeavoring to generate spontaneous affective responses from the audience risks metastasizing perfectionism, because, like keeping too many plates spinning, perfectionism renders uncertain the terrain on which labor must be undertaken.[87] How might a student's failure to match the terms of a discipline's expectations become not a marker of writerly failure but the beginning of a conversation? What would it take to restructure a course, and the timeline whereby students undertake the work of writing, so that experiences of failure appear early and often, and are welcomed by both students and teachers alike? How might "failure" in a literature class be redefined not as an inability to meet tacit or explicit terms of engagement, but as a failure to listen and to share, a failure to see oneself as a work in progress?

Partway through writing this book, I realized that the feeling of suspended, thrilling uncertainty I have tried to locate at poesy's scene of writing most closely evokes one of my favorite feelings: the feeling of the night before the first day of classes. I may have printed out the syllabuses and carefully drafted assignment prompts, but really, I know that how the class will go will not be entirely up to me. A new crop of readers, with predilections, histories, and attitudes of their own will meet Hamlet, or Viola, or Iago, or yes, even Costard. These readers will not arrive to class knowing

---

86. *Oxford English Dictionary*, s.v. "Performance, n., Definitions 1b. and 4c.," accessed June 25, 2021, http://www.oed.com/view/Entry/140783.

87. The perfectionist performer thus recalls Sianne Ngai's account of the theatrical "zany," a figure whose excessively unproductive work happens at the "politically ambiguous intersection between cultural and occupational performance, acting and service, playing and laboring." Ngai, *Our Aesthetic Categories*, 182. In a similar vein, Richard Schechner observes that in the world of business, "to perform means doing a job efficiently with maximum productivity," but the ways in which efficiency relies on routinization, optimization, and best practices reveal how performance in this context is, like all performance, a collection of "twice-behaved behaviors." Self-consciously attentive to the material conditions of the present as well as to the residual influence of past performances, performances both take up and render obsolete the behaviors that gave birth to them; in this way, Schechner suggests, performances "resist that which produces them." Schechner, *Performance Studies*, 34, 30.

which John Davies is the better poet or assume that Lady Anne Southwell has less of a claim to literary authority than Sir Walter Ralegh. My preparation, my prompts, my lesson plans will never fully anticipate what they will think, or say, or write upon reading these texts.

A class in literature is not like a how-two guide; we are not presenting students with a blueprint for enlightenment. We are, when we are at our best, inviting them to a conversation—a conversation often mediated through writing but hardly limited to the page. I wrote this book as a work of literary criticism and not as a how-to guide because I also wanted to participate in a conversation. I wanted to write back to the scholars I cite throughout it; I also wanted to write forward, to any scholars who happen across it in the future. At this late juncture, I resign myself to knowing that my ability to participate in a conversation means giving up some control. The perfectionist in me wants to work on it for just a few days more, but I know that I will never really be ready to find out whether what I have written clearly represents what I wanted to say. I must trust that I will learn as much from my failures as I have learned from the process of writing. The next part of the conversation is not mine; it is yours. I accept this just as I accept that my best teaching happens when I treat my students' work with the same curiosity, critical attentiveness, and generosity that I grant to the poetry I love most.

Bibliography

Acheson, Katherine. *Early Modern English Marginalia*. New York: Routledge, 2018.
Adorno, Theodor W. *Aesthetic Theory*. Translated by Christian Lenhardt. London: Routledge, 1984.
Alexander, Gavin. *Writing after Sidney: The Literary Response to Sir Philip Sidney, 1586–1640*. Oxford: Oxford University Press, 2010.
Arditi, Jorge. *A Genealogy of Manners: Transformations of Social Relations in France and England from the Fourteenth to the Eighteenth Century*. Chicago: University of Chicago Press, 1998.
Aristotle. *Art of Rhetoric*. Translated by J. H. Freese and Gisela Striker. Loeb Classical Library. Cambridge, MA: Harvard University Press, 2020.
———. *Metaphysics*. Translated by Hugh Tredennick. Loeb Classical Library. Cambridge, MA: Harvard University Press, 1933.
———. *On Rhetoric: A Theory of Civic Discourse*. Translated by George A. Kennedy. Oxford: Oxford University Press, 1991.
Armstrong, E. *A Ciceronian Sunburn: A Tudor Dialogue on Humanistic Rhetoric and Civic Poetics*. Columbia: University of South Carolina Press, 2006.
Ascham, Roger. *The Scholemaster*. London: John Daye, 1570.
Attridge, Derek. "In Praise of Amateurism." In *Introduction: Criticism for the Whole Person*, edited by Saikat Majumdar and Aarthi Vadde, 31-48. New York: Bloomsbury Academic, 2020.
———. *Well-Weighed Syllables: Elizabethan Verse in Classical Metres*. Cambridge: Cambridge University Press, 1974.
Aune, M. G. "Thomas Coryate versus John Taylor: The Emergence of the Early Modern Celebrity." *Cahiers Élisabéthains* 101, no. 1 (2020): 85-104.
Austen, Gillian. *George Gascoigne*. Cambridge: Cambridge University Press, 2008.
Bacon, Francis. "Of Discourse." In *The Works of Francis Bacon*, edited by James Spedding, Robert Leslie Ellis, and Douglas Denon Heath, 12:191-94. Boston: Houghton Mifflin, 1900.
———. *The Works of Francis Bacon*. Vol. 6. Edited by James Spedding, Robert Leslie Ellis, Douglas Denon Heath, and William Rawley. Boston: Houghton Mifflin, 1900.
Bailes, Sara Jane. *Performance Theatre and the Poetics of Failure*. New York: Routledge, 2011.
Bajetta, Carlo M. "The Authority of Editing: Thoughts on the Function(s) of Textual Criticism." *Textus* 19 (2006): 305-22.
Baker, Christopher. "Hamlet and the Kairos." *Ben Jonson Journal* 26, no. 1 (2019): 62-77.

Baldwin, T. W. *William Shakspere's Small Latine & Lesse Greeke*. 2 vols. Urbana: University of Illinois Press, 1944.
Barthes, Roland. *Image-Music-Text*. Translated by Stephen Heath. New York: Hill & Wang, 1977.
———. *The Neutral: Lecture Course at the Collège de France (1977-1978)*. Translated by Rosalind E. Krauss and Hollier Denis. New York: Columbia University Press, 2005.
Bartholomae, David. "Inventing the University." In *Writing on the Margins*, 60–85. New York: Palgrave Macmillan, 2005.
———. "Living in Style." In *Writing on the Margins*, 1–16. New York: Palgrave Macmillan, 2005.
———. "The Study of Error." *College Composition and Communication* 31, no. 3 (1980): 253–69.
Bastard, Thomas. *Chrestoleros Seuen Bookes of Epigrames Written by T B*. London: Richard Bradocke, 1598.
Bate, Jonathan. *The Genius of Shakespeare*. 10th anniv. ed. Oxford: Oxford University Press, 2008.
Bates, Catherine. *On Not Defending Poetry: Defence and Indefensibility in Sidney's Defence of Poesy*. Oxford: Oxford University Press, 2017.
Bayer, Mark. "The Curious Case of the Two Audiences." In *Imagining the Audience in Early Modern Drama, 1558–1642*, edited by Jennifer A. Low and Nova Myhill, 55–70. New York: Palgrave Macmillan, 2011.
Bean, John C. *Engaging Ideas: The Professor's Guide to Integrating Writing, Critical Thinking, and Active Learning in the Classroom*. 2nd ed. San Francisco: John Wiley & Sons, 2011.
Beau Chesne, Jean de, and Joseph Baildon. *A Booke Containing Divers Sortes of Hands*. London: Thomas Vautrouillier, 1571.
Beehler, Sharon A. "'Confederate Season': Shakespeare and the Elizabethan Understanding of Kairos." In *Shakespeare Matters: History, Teaching, Performance*, edited by Lloyd Davis, 74–88. Newark: University of Delaware Press, 2003.
Bender, Daniel. "The Whip Hand: Elite Class Formation in Ascham's *The Schoolmaster*, Shakespeare's *Love's Labour's Lost*, and the Present Academy." In *Shakespeare and the 99%: Literary Studies, the Profession, and the Production of Inequity*, edited by Sharon O'Dair and Timothy Francisco, 57–78. Cham: Palgrave Macmillan, 2019.
Berry, Edward. *The Making of Sir Philip Sidney*. Toronto: University of Toronto Press, 1998.
Bevington, David. "'Jack Hath Not Jill': Failed Courtship in Lyly and Shakespeare." *Shakespeare Survey*, no. 42 (1990): 1–13.
———. Review of *Shakespeare, "A Lover's Complaint," and John Davies of Hereford*, by Brian Vickers. *Renaissance Quarterly* 60, no. 4 (2007): 1463–66.
Birk, Lara Blakiston. "The Sounds of Silence: A Structural Analysis of Academic 'Writer's Block.'" PhD diss., Boston College, 2013.
Bishop, Wendy. "Crossing the Lines: On Creative Composition and Composing Creative Writing." *Writing on the Edge* 4, no. 2 (1993): 117–33.

———. "The Literary Text and the Writing Classroom." *Journal of Advanced Composition* 15, no. 3 (1995): 435–54.

———. "Places to Stand: The Reflective Writer-Teacher-Writer in Composition." *College Composition and Communication* 15, no. 1 (1999): 9–31.

———. *Released into Language: Options for Teaching Creative Writing*. Urbana, IL: National Council of Teachers of English, 1990.

Bizzaro, Patrick. "Writers Wanted: A Reconsideration of Wendy Bishop." *College English* 71, no. 3 (2009): 256–70.

Blum, Susan D. *"I Love Learning, I Hate School": An Anthropology of College*. Ithaca, NY: Cornell University Press, 2017.

———. *My Word!: Plagiarism and College Culture*. Ithaca, NY: Cornell University Press, 2011.

———. *Ungrading: Why Rating Students Undermines Learning*. Morgantown: West Virginia University Press, 2020.

Bond, Garth. "'Rare Poemes Aske Rare Friends': Ben Jonson, Coterie Poet." *Modern Philology* 107, no. 3 (2010): 380–99.

Bourdieu, Pierre. *Distinction: A Social Critique of the Judgement of Taste*. Translated by Richard Nice. New York: Routledge, 2010.

Bourne, Claire M. L. "Typography after Performance." In *Rethinking Theatrical Documents in Shakespeare's England*, edited by Tiffany Stern, 193–215. London: Arden Shakespeare, 2020.

Bowers, Fredson. *Textual and Literary Criticism*. Cambridge: Cambridge University Press, 1966.

Brannigan, John. *New Historicism and Cultural Materialism*. London: Macmillan, 1998.

Breitenberg, Mark. "The Anatomy of Masculine Desire in *Love's Labor's Lost*." *Shakespeare Quarterly* 43, no. 4 (1992): 430–49.

Brink, Jean R. "Literacy and Education." In *A New Companion to English Renaissance Literature and Culture*, edited by Michael Hattaway, 27–37. Malden, MA: Blackwell, 2010.

Brinsley, John. *Ludus Literarius: or, The Grammar-Schoole*. London: Humphrey Lownes, 1612.

Britton, Ronald. *Belief and Imagination: Explorations in Psychoanalysis*. New York: Routledge, 1998.

Britzman, Deborah P. *A Psychoanalyst in the Classroom: On the Human Condition in Education*. Transforming Subjects: Psychoanalysis, Culture, and Studies in Education. Albany: State University of New York Press, 2015.

Brodkey, Linda. *Writing Permitted in Designated Areas Only*. Minneapolis: University of Minnesota Press, 1996.

Brome, Richard. *The Antipodes a Comedie*. London: I. Okes, 1640.

Brooks, Douglas A. *From Playhouse to Printing House: Drama and Authorship in Early Modern England*. Cambridge: Cambridge University Press, 2006.

Brown, Eric C. "Shakespeare's Anxious Epistemology: *Love's Labor's Lost* and Marlowe's *Doctor Faustus*." *Texas Studies in Literature and Language* 45, no. 1 (2003): 20–41.

Brown, Georgia. *Redefining Elizabethan Literature*. Cambridge: Cambridge University Press, 2004.

Brown, Richard Danson. *"The New Poet": Novelty and Tradition in Spenser's "Complaints."* Oxford: Oxford University Press, 1999.
Browne, David. *The New Invention, Intituled, Calligraphia*. Saint-Andrews: Edward Raban, 1622.
Bruffee, Kenneth A. "Collaborative Learning and the 'Conversation of Mankind.'" *College English* 46, no. 7 (1984): 635–52.
Brugués, Ariadna Ortiz. *Music Performance Anxiety: A Comprehensive Update of the Literature*. Newcastle upon Tyne: Cambridge Scholars, 2019.
Bruster, Douglas. *Quoting Shakespeare: Form and Culture in Early Modern Drama*. Lincoln: University of Nebraska Press, 2000.
Bruster, Douglas, and Robert Weimann. *Prologues to Shakespeare's Theatre: Performance and Liminality in Early Modern Drama*. New York: Routledge, 2004.
Bryant, John. *The Fluid Text: A Theory of Revision and Editing for Book and Screen*. Ann Arbor: University of Michigan Press, 2002.
Bryson, Anna. *From Courtesy to Civility: Changing Codes of Conduct in Early Modern England*. Oxford: Oxford University Press, 1998.
Burke, Victoria E. "Lady Anne Southwell, Commonplace Book Entry on Ralegh's 'The Lie' (after 1592)." In *Reading Early Modern Women*, edited by Helen Ostovich and Elizabeth Sauer, 336–39. New York: Routledge, 2004.
———. "Medium and Meaning in the Manuscripts of Anne, Lady Southwell." In *Women's Writing and the Circulation of Ideas: Manuscript Publication in England, 1550–1800*, edited by George L. Justice and Nathan Tinker, 94–120. Cambridge: Cambridge University Press, 2002.
Burwick, Frederick. "Shakespeare and the Romantics." In *A Companion to Romanticism*, edited by Duncan Wu, 553–60. Malden, MA: John Wiley & Sons, 2017.
Bushnell, Rebecca W. *A Culture of Teaching: Early Modern Humanism in Theory and Practice*. Ithaca, NY: Cornell University Press, 1996.
Calhoun, Joshua. *The Nature of the Page: Poetry, Papermaking, and the Ecology of Texts in Renaissance England*. Philadelphia: University of Pennsylvania Press, 2020.
Calvin, Jean. *Institutes of the Christian Religion*. Translated by Henry Beveridge. Peabody, MA: Hendrickson, 2008.
Carr, Allison. "In Support of Failure." *Composition Forum* 27 (2013): http://compositionforum.com/issue/27/failure.php.
Carroll, William C. *The Great Feast of Language in "Love's Labour's Lost."* Princeton, NJ: Princeton University Press, 2015.
Carter, Michael. "Stasis and Kairos: Principles of Social Construction in Classical Rhetoric." *Rhetoric Review* 7, no. 1 (1988): 97–112.
Certeau, Michel de. *The Practice of Everyday Life*. Translated by Steven Rendall. Berkeley: University of California Press, 1984.
Chapman, George. *The Vviddovves Teares a Comedie*. London: William Stansby, 1612.
Charlton, Kenneth. *Education in Renaissance England*. Toronto: University of Toronto Press, 1965.
Chartier, Roger. *The Author's Hand and the Printer's Mind: Transformations of the Written Word in Early Modern Europe*. Translated by Lydia G. Cochrane. Malden, MA: Polity, 2014.

Cheney, Patrick. "'The Forms of Things Unknown': English Authorship and the Early Modern Sublime." In *Medieval and Early Modern Authorship*, edited by Guillemette Bolens and Lukas Erne, 137-60. Tübingen: Narr, 2011.
Christen, Richard S. "Boundaries between Liberal and Technical Learning: Images of Seventeenth-Century English Writing Masters." *History of Education Quarterly* 39, no. 1 (1999): 31-50.
Cicero. *De officiis*. Translated by Walter Miller. New York: G. P. Putnam's Sons, 1928.
——. *On the Orator, Books 1-2*. Translated by E. W. Sutton and H. Rackham. Loeb Classical Library. Cambridge, MA: Harvard University Press, 1948.
[Cicero]. *Rhetorica ad Herennium*. Translated by Harry Caplan. Loeb Classical Library. Cambridge, MA: Harvard University Press, 1964.
Clark, Donald Lemen. "The Requirements of a Poet: A Note on the Sources of Ben Jonson's *Timber*, Paragraph 130." *Modern Philology* 16, no. 8 (1918): 413-29.
Clark, Mark Edward. "Quintilius' Ethos as Critic of the Poet: Horace, AP 438-44." *Classical World* 85, no. 3 (1992): 229-31.
Clarke, Danielle. "Animating Eve: Gender, Authority, and Complaint." In *Early Modern Women's Complaint: Gender, Form, and Politics*, edited by Sarah C. E. Ross and Rosalind Smith, 157-81. Early Modern Literature in History. Cham: Palgrave Macmillan, 2020.
——. "Gender, Material Culture, and the Hybridity of Renaissance Writing." In *Renaissance Transformations: The Making of English Writing, 1500–1650*, edited by Margaret Healy and Thomas Healy, 112-27. Edinburgh: Edinburgh University Press, 2009.
Clarke, Danielle, and Marie-Louise Coolahan. "Gender, Reception, and Form: Early Modern Women and the Making of Verse." In *The Work of Form: Poetics and Materiality in Early Modern Culture*, edited by Elizabeth Scott-Baumann and Ben Burton, 144-61. Oxford: Oxford University Press, 2014.
Clarke, Elizabeth. "Anne, Lady Southwell: Coteries and Culture." In *The Intellectual Culture of Puritan Women, 1558–1680*, edited by Johanna Harris and Elizabeth Scott-Baumann, 57-70. London: Palgrave Macmillan, 2010.
——. "Anne Southwell and the Pamphlet Debate: The Politics of Gender, Class, and Manuscript." In *Debating Gender in Early Modern England, 1500–1700*, edited by Cristina Malcolmson and Mihoko Suzuki, 37-53. New York: Palgrave Macmillan, 2002.
Clegg, Cyndia Susan. *Press Censorship in Elizabethan England*. Cambridge: Cambridge University Press, 1997.
Clement, Francis. *The Petie Schoole*. London: Thomas Vautrollier, 1587.
Colie, Rosalie Littell. *Shakespeare's Living Art*. Princeton, NJ: Princeton University Press, 2015.
Collier, John Payne. *Rarest Books in the English Language*. 2 vols. London: Joseph Lilly, 1865.
Coolahan, Marie-Louise. "Ideal Communities and Planter Women's Writing in Seventeenth- Century Ireland." *Parergon* 29, no. 2 (2012): 69-91.
Corbett, Edward P. J. *Classical Rhetoric for the Modern Student*. Oxford: Oxford University Press, 1965.

———. "The *Topoi* Revisited." In *Rhetoric and Praxis: The Contribution of Classical Rhetoric to Practical Reasoning*, edited by Jean Deitz Moss, 43–57. Washington, DC: Catholic University of America Press, 1986.

Crabb, George. *Crabb's English Synonymes: Revised and Enlarged by the Addition of Modern Terms and Definitions Arranged Alphabetically, with Complete Cross References Throughout*. New York: Harper & Brothers, 1917.

Craik, Katharine A. "John Taylor's Pot-Poetry." *Seventeenth Century* 20, no. 2 (2005): 185–203.

Crane, Mary Thomas. *Framing Authority: Sayings, Self, and Society in Sixteenth-Century England*. Princeton, NJ: Princeton University Press, 1993.

Crawford, Julie. *Mediatrix: Women, Politics, and Literary Production in Early Modern England*. Oxford: Oxford University Press, 2014.

Crawforth, Hannah. *Etymology and the Invention of English in Early Modern Literature*. Cambridge: Cambridge University Press, 2013.

Cressy, David. *Literacy and the Social Order: Reading and Writing in Tudor and Stuart England*. Cambridge: Cambridge University Press, 1980.

Crosby, Christina. "Writer's Block, Merit, and the Market: Working in the University of Excellence." *College English* 65, no. 6 (2003): 626–45.

Crowley, Sharon. *Composition in the University: Historical and Polemical Essays*. Pittsburgh: University of Pittsburgh Press, 1998.

Davies of Hereford, John. *The Complete Works of John Davies of Hereford (15..–1618)*. 2 vols. Edited by Alexander B. Grosart. Edinburgh: Edinburgh University Press, 1878.

———. *The Writing Schoolemaster, or The Anatomie of Faire Writing*. London: Printed for Michaell Sparke, 1631.

Davison, Francis. *Gesta Grayorum 1688*. Malone Society Reprints. Oxford: Oxford University Press, 1914.

Daybell, J. *Early Modern Women's Letter Writing, 1450–1700*. London: Palgrave Macmillan, 2001.

Dejoy, Nancy. *Process This: Undergraduate Writing in Composition Studies*. Logan: Utah State University Press, 2004.

Derrida, Jacques. *Aporias*. Translated by Thomas Dutoit. Stanford, CA: Stanford University Press, 1993.

———. "Force of Law: The 'Mystical Foundation of Authority.'" In *Deconstruction and the Possibility of Justice*, edited by Drucilla Cornell, Michel Rosenfeld, and David Gray Carlson, 3–67. New York: Routledge, 1992.

Dewey, John. *How We Think*. Boston: D. C. Heath, 1910.

———. "My Pedagogic Creed (1887)." In *The Essential Dewey: Pragmatism, Education, Democracy*, edited by Larry A. Hickman and Thomas M. Alexander, 1:229–35. Bloomington: Indiana University Press, 1998.

Dieter, Otto Alvin Loeb. "Stasis." *Speech Monographs* 17, no. 4 (November 1, 1950): 345–69.

Dobson, Michael. *The Making of the National Poet: Shakespeare, Adaptation, and Authorship, 1660–1769*. Oxford: Oxford University Press, 1992.

Doelman, James. "Circulation of the Late Elizabethan and Early Stuart Epigram." *Renaissance and Reformation/Renaissance et Réforme* 29, no. 1 (2005): 59–73.

Dolan, Frances E. "Hester Pulter's Dunghill Poetics." *Journal for Early Modern Cultural Studies* 20, no. 2 (2020): 16–42.

———. "Reading, Writing, and Other Crimes." In *Feminist Readings of Early Modern Culture: Emerging Subjects*, edited by Valerie Traub, M. Lindsay Kaplan, and Dympna Callaghan, 142–67. Cambridge: Cambridge University Press, 1996.

Dolven, Jeff. *Scenes of Instruction in Renaissance Romance*. Chicago: University of Chicago Press, 2008.

———. *Senses of Style: Poetry before Interpretation*. Chicago: University of Chicago Press, 2018.

Donne, John. *Complete Poetry and Selected Prose of John Donne*. Edited by Charles M. Coffin. New York: Modern Library, 1994.

Doty, Jeffrey S. *Shakespeare, Popularity and the Public Sphere*. Cambridge: Cambridge University Press, 2017.

Dubrow, Heather. *Echoes of Desire: English Petrarchism and Its Counterdiscourses*. Ithaca, NY: Cornell University Press, 1995.

Duncan-Jones, Katherine. *Sir Philip Sidney, Courtier Poet*. New Haven, CT: Yale University Press, 1991.

Dunn, Kevin. *Pretexts of Authority: The Rhetoric of Authorship in the Renaissance Preface*. Stanford, CA: Stanford University Press, 1994.

Eggert, Katherine. *Disknowledge: Literature, Alchemy, and the End of Humanism in Renaissance England*. Philadelphia: University of Pennsylvania Press, 2015.

Eklund, Hillary. "Shakespeare, Service Learning, and the Embattled Humanities." In *Teaching Social Justice through Shakespeare: Why Renaissance Literature Matters Now*, edited by Hillary Eklund and Wendy Beth Hyman, 187–96. Edinburgh: Edinburgh University Press, 2019.

Elbow, Peter. "Being a Writer vs. Being an Academic: A Conflict in Goals." *College Composition and Communication* 46, no. 1 (1995): 72–83.

———. *Writing with Power: Techniques for Mastering the Writing Process*. 2nd ed. Oxford: Oxford University Press, 1998.

Elias, Norbert. *The Civilizing Process: Sociogenetic and Psychogenetic Investigations*. Translated by Edmund Jephcott. Malden, MA: Blackwell, 2000.

Ellinghausen, Laurie. *Labor and Writing in Early Modern England, 1567–1667*. New York: Routledge, 2018.

———. "University of Vice: Drink, Gentility, and Masculinity in Oxford, Cambridge, and London." In *Masculinity and the Metropolis of Vice, 1550–1650*, edited by Amanda Bailey and Roze Hentschell, 45–66. New York: Palgrave Macmillan, 2010.

Elliot, Norbert. *On a Scale: A Social History of Writing Assessment in America*. New York: Peter Lang, 2005.

Enterline, Lynn. *Shakespeare's Schoolroom: Rhetoric, Discipline, Emotion*. Philadelphia: University of Pennsylvania Press, 2012.

Enzensberger, Hans Magnus. *Mediocrity & Delusion*. Translated by Martin Chalmers. New York: Verso, 1992.

Erasmus, Desiderius. "A Cento from Homer, to the Most Illustrious Prince Philip, upon His Return." In *The Collected Works of Erasmus*, edited by

Harry Vredeveld, translated by Clarence H. Miller, 85:139. Toronto: University of Toronto Press, 1993.

———. *De conscribendis epistolis*. In *Opera omnia Desiderii Erasmi Roterodami*, edited by Jean-Claude Margolin, 1.2:154–580. Amsterdam: North-Holland, 1971.

———. *De copia: Foundations of the Abundant Style*. In *The Collected Works of Erasmus*, edited by Craig R. Thompson, translated by Betty I. Knott, 24:279–660. Toronto: University of Toronto Press, 1978.

———. *Dialogvs Ciceronianvs*. In *Opera omnia Desiderii Erasmi Roterodami*, edited by Pierre Mesnard, 1.2:581–710. Amsterdam: North-Holland, 1971.

———. *On the Writing of Letters*. In *The Collected Works of Erasmus*, edited by J. K. Sowards, translated by Charles Fantazzi, 25:1–254. Toronto: University of Toronto Press, 1985.

———. *The Ciceronian*. In *The Collected Works of Erasmus*, edited by A. H. T. Levi, translated by Betty I. Knott, 28:323–448. Toronto: University of Toronto Press, 1986.

Erickson, Peter B. "The Failure of Relationship between Men and Women in *Love's Labor's Lost*." *Women's Studies* 9, no. 1 (January 1, 1981): 65–81.

Eskew, Doug. "Shakespeare, Alienation, and the Working-Class Student." In *Shakespeare and the 99%: Literary Studies, the Profession, and the Production of Inequity*, edited by Sharon O'Dair and Timothy Francisco, 37–56. Cham: Palgrave Macmillan, 2019.

Estill, Laura. "*Richard II* and the Book of Life." *SEL: Studies in English Literature, 1500–1900* 51, no. 2 (2011): 283–303.

Ezell, Margaret J. M. "Afterword: 'Her Book' and Early Modern Modes of Collaboration." In *Gender, Authorship, and Early Modern Women's Collaboration*, edited by Patricia Pender, 245–58. Early Modern Literature in History. Cham: Palgrave Macmillan, 2017.

Fahnestock, Jeanne. *Rhetorical Style: The Uses of Language in Persuasion*. Oxford: Oxford University Press, 2011.

Fahnestock, Jeanne, and Marie Secor. "The Rhetoric of Literary Criticism." In *Textual Dynamics of the Professions*, edited by Charles Bazerman and James Paradis, 76–96. Madison: University of Wisconsin Press, 1991.

Fall, Rebecca L. "Popular Nonsense According to John Taylor and Ben Jonson." *SEL: Studies in English Literature, 1500–1900* 57, no. 1 (2017): 87–110.

Fallon, Samuel. *Paper Monsters: Persona and Literary Culture in Elizabethan England*. Philadelphia: University of Pennsylvania Press, 2019.

Federico, Annette. *Engagements with Close Reading*. New York: Routledge, 2015.

Fenstermaker, John J. "Literature in the Composition Class." *College Composition and Communication* 28, no. 1 (1977): 34–37.

Finkelpearl, Philip J. "Davies, John (1564/5–1618), Poet and Writing-Master." In *Oxford Dictionary of National Biography*. Oxford University Press, September 23, 2004. http://www.oxforddnb.com/view/10.1093/ref:odnb/9780198614128.001.0001/odnb-9780198614128-e-7244.

Fitzpatrick, Kathleen. *Generous Thinking: A Radical Approach to Saving the University*. Baltimore: Johns Hopkins University Press, 2019.

Flaccus, Aulus Perseus. *The Satires of A. Persius Flaccus*. Translated by John Conington. Oxford: Clarendon, 1874.

Flaherty, Kate. "Shakespeare and Education: The Making of an Unlikely Marriage." In *The Shakespearean World*, edited by Jill L. Levenson and Robert Ormsby, 361–76. New York: Routledge, 2017.
Fleming, Juliet. *Graffiti and the Writing Arts of Early Modern England*. London: Reaktion Books, 2001.
Fleming, Paul. *Exemplarity and Mediocrity: The Art of the Average from Bourgeois Tragedy to Realism*. Stanford, CA: Stanford University Press, 2008.
Florio, John. *A Worlde of Wordes*. London: Arnold Hatfield, 1598.
Fox, Adam. *Oral and Literate Culture in England, 1500-1700*. Oxford: Oxford University Press, 2000.
Frost, Randy O., and Patricia A. Marten. "Perfectionism and Evaluative Threat." *Cognitive Therapy and Research* 14, no. 6 (1990): 559–72.
Fuller, Thomas. *The Worthies of England*. Edited by John Freeman. London: George Allen & Unwin, 1952.
Furey, Constance M. *Poetic Relations: Intimacy and Faith in the English Reformation*. Chicago: University of Chicago Press, 2017.
Gainsford, Thomas. *The Rich Cabinet*. London: John Beale, 1616.
Gascoigne, George. *The Glasse of Governement*. In *The Complete Works of George Gascoigne*, edited by John W. Cunliffe, 2: 1–90. Cambridge: Cambridge University Press, 1910.
———. *A Hundreth Sundrie Flowres*. Edited by G. W. Pigman. Oxford: Oxford University Press, 2000.
Gaylard, Susan. *Hollow Men: Writing, Objects, and Public Image in Renaissance Italy*. New York: Fordham University Press, 2013.
Gibson, Jonathan. "Casting off Blanks: Hidden Structures in Early Modern Paper Books." In *Material Readings of Early Modern Culture: Texts and Social Practices, 1580–1730*, edited by James Daybell and Peter Hinds, 208–28. New York: Palgrave Macmillan, 2010.
———. "Synchrony and Process: Editing Manuscript Miscellanies." *SEL: Studies in English Literature, 1500–1900* 52, no. 1 (2012): 85–100.
Gitelman, Lisa. *Paper Knowledge: Toward a Media History of Documents*. Durham, NC: Duke University Press, 2014.
Goffman, Erving. *The Presentation of Self in Everyday Life*. New York: Anchor Books, 1959.
Goldberg, Jonathan. *Writing Matter: From the Hands of the English Renaissance*. Stanford, CA: Stanford University Press, 1990.
Gosson, Stephen. *The School of Abuse*. London: Shakespeare Society, 1841.
Grafton, Anthony, and Lisa Jardine. *From Humanism to the Humanities: Education and the Liberal Arts in Fifteenth- and Sixteenth-Century Europe*. Cambridge, MA: Harvard University Press, 1986.
Greenberg, Susan L. *A Poetics of Editing*. Cham: Palgrave Macmillan, 2018.
Greenblatt, Stephen. *Renaissance Self-Fashioning: From More to Shakespeare*. Chicago: University of Chicago Press, 1980.
———. "What Is the History of Literature?" *Critical Inquiry* 23, no. 3 (1997): 460–81.
Greenblatt, Stephen, Walter Cohen, Suzanne Gossett, and Jean E. Howard, eds. *The Norton Shakespeare*. 3rd ed. New York: W. W. Norton, 2016.

Greene, Robert. *Greenes, Groats-Vvorth of Witte.* London: [J. Wolfe and J. Danter], 1592.

Greene, Roland. *Five Words: Critical Semantics in the Age of Shakespeare and Cervantes.* Chicago: University of Chicago Press, 2013.

Greg, W. W. "The Rationale of Copy-Text." *Studies in Bibliography* 3 (1950): 19–36.

Grosart, Alexander B. "Dedicatory Sonnet to George H. White, Esq." In *The Complete Works of John Davies of Hereford (15..–1618),* edited by Alexander B. Grosart, 1:vii. Edinburgh: Edinburgh University Press, 1878.

———. "Memorial-Introduction." In *The Complete Works of John Davies of Hereford (15..–1618),* edited by Alexander B. Grosart, 1:ix–lix. Edinburgh: Edinburgh University Press, 1878.

Guazzo, Steeven [Stefano]. *The Civile Conversation.* Translated by George Pettie. London: Richard Watkins, 1581.

Guillory, John. *Cultural Capital: The Problem of Literary Canon Formation.* Chicago: University of Chicago Press, 1993.

Hackel, Heidi Brayman. *Reading Material in Early Modern England: Print, Gender, and Literacy.* Cambridge: Cambridge University Press, 2005.

Hackett, Helen. "'He Is a Better Scholar Than I Thought He Was': Debating the Achievements of the Elizabethan Grammar Schools." *Journal of the Northern Renaissance,* no. 9 (2017). http://www.northernrenaissance.org/he-is-a-better-scholar-than-i-thought-he-was-debating-the-achievements-of-the-elizabethan-grammar-schools/.

Halberstam, Judith [Jack]. *The Queer Art of Failure.* Durham, NC: Duke University Press, 2011.

Halpern, Richard. *The Poetics of Primitive Accumulation.* Ithaca, NY: Cornell University Press, 1991.

Harington, Sir John. "An Answer to Critics." In *Elizabethan Critical Essays,* edited by G. Gregory Smith, 2:194–222. London: Oxford University Press, 1904.

Harris, Joseph. "Revision as a Critical Practice." *College English* 65, no. 6 (2003): 577–92.

———. *Rewriting: How to Do Things with Texts.* Logan: Utah State University Press, 2006.

———. "Undisciplined Writing." In *Delivering College Composition: The Fifth Canon,* edited by Kathleen Blake Yancey, 155–67. Portsmouth, NH: Heinemann-Boynton/Cook, 2006.

Hart, John A., Robert C. Slack, and Neal Woodruff. "Literature in the Composition Course." *College Composition and Communication* 9, no. 4 (1958): 236–41.

Harvey, Gabriel. "Letters on Reformed Versifying." In *Elizabethan Critical Essays,* edited by G. Gregory Smith, 1:123–26. London: Oxford University Press, 1904.

———. "A Third Letter of Harvey to Spenser." In *The Works of Gabriel Harvey, D.C.L.,* edited by Alexander B. Grosart, 1:136–40. London: Huth Library, 1884. http://archive.org/details/worksofgabrielha01harvrich.

Hawhee, Debra. *Bodily Arts: Rhetoric and Athletics in Ancient Greece.* Austin: University of Texas Press, 2013.

Hawkins, Gary. "The Irrational Element in the Undergraduate Poetry Workshop: Beyond Craft." In *Teaching Creative Writing*, edited by Heather Beck, 44–50. London: Palgrave Macmillan, 2012.
Heath, John. *Two Centuries of Epigrammes*. London: John Windet, 1610.
Helgerson, Richard. *The Elizabethan Prodigals*. Berkeley: University of California Press, 1976.
———. *Self-Crowned Laureates: Spenser, Jonson, Milton, and the Literary System*. Berkeley: University of California Press, 1983.
Heminges, John, and Henry Condell. "To the Great Variety of Readers." In *The Norton Shakespeare*, 3rd ed., edited by Stephen Greenblatt, Walter Cohen, Suzanne Gossett, and Jean E. Howard, A25. New York: W. W. Norton, 2016.
Hetherington, Michael. "Gascoigne's Accidents: Contingency, Skill, and the Logic of Writing." *English Literary Renaissance* 46, no. 1 (2016): 29–59.
Heywood, Thomas. "An Apology for Actors." In *Shakespeare's Theatre: A Source Book*, edited by Tanya Pollard, 213–54. Malden, MA: Blackwell, 2004.
Hirschfeld, Heather. "Early Modern Collaboration and Theories of Authorship." *PMLA* 116, no. 3 (2001): 609–22.
hooks, bell. *Teaching to Transgress: Education as the Practice of Freedom*. New York: Routledge, 1994.
Horace. *Odes and Epodes*. Translated by Niall Rudd. Loeb Classical Library. Cambridge, MA: Harvard University Press, 2004.
———. *Satires. Epistles. The Art of Poetry*. Translated by H. Rushton Fairclough. Loeb Classical Library. Cambridge, MA: Harvard University Press, 1991.
Howard, Rebecca Moore. "A Plagiarism Pentimento." *Journal of Teaching Writing* 11, no. 2 (1992): 233–45.
———. "Plagiarisms, Authorships, and the Academic Death Penalty." *College English* 57, no. 7 (1995): 788–806.
Hughes, Felicity A. "Gascoigne's Poses." *Studies in English Literature, 1500-1900* 37, no. 1 (1997): 1–19.
Huisman, Rosemary. *The Written Poem: Semiotic Conventions from Old to Modern English*. London: Cassell, 1998.
Hull, Glynda, and Mike Rose. "Rethinking Remediation: Toward a Social-Cognitive Understanding of Problematic Reading and Writing." *Written Communication* 6, no. 2 (1989): 139–54.
Huloet, Richard, and John Higgins. *Huloets Dictionarie*. London: Thomas Marsh, 1572.
Hunt, Maurice A. *Shakespeare's "As You Like It": Late Elizabethan Culture and Literary Representation*. New York: Palgrave Macmillan, 2008.
Hutson, Lorna. *The Invention of Suspicion: Law and Mimesis in Shakespeare and Renaissance Drama*. Oxford: Oxford University Press, 2007.
Hyman, Wendy Beth, and Hillary Eklund. "Introduction: Making Meaning and Doing Justice with Early Modern Texts." In *Teaching Social Justice through Shakespeare: Why Renaissance Literature Matters Now*, edited by Hillary Eklund and Wendy Beth Hyman, 1–26. Edinburgh: Edinburgh University Press, 2019.

Iliffe, Robert. "Author-Mongering: The 'Editor' between Producer and Consumer." In *The Consumption of Culture, 1600–1800: Image, Object, Text*, edited by Ann Bermingham and John Brewer, 166-92. New York: Routledge, 1995.

Inoue, Asao B. *Labor-Based Grading Contracts: Building Equity and Inclusion in the Compassionate Writing Classroom.* Boulder: University Press of Colorado, 2019.

Ioppolo, Grace. *Revising Shakespeare.* Cambridge, MA: Harvard University Press, 1991.

Isaacs, Emily. "Teaching General Education Writing: Is There a Place for Literature?" *Pedagogy* 9, no. 1 (2009): 97-120.

Jackson, MacDonald P. "Shakespeare's Sonnet CXI and John Davies of Hereford's *Microcosmos* (1603)." *Modern Language Review* 102, no. 1 (2007): 1-10.

Jackson, Phoebe. "Connecting Reading and Writing in the Literature Classroom." *Pedagogy* 5, no. 1 (2005): 111-14.

Jacobson, Jean Alice. "How Should Poetry Look? The Printer's Measure and Poet's Line." PhD diss., University of Minnesota, 2008.

Jacobson, Miriam. *Barbarous Antiquity: Reorienting the Past in the Poetry of Early Modern England.* Philadelphia: University of Pennsylvania Press, 2014.

Jardine, Lisa, and Anthony Grafton. "'Studied for Action': How Gabriel Harvey Read His Livy." *Past & Present*, no. 129 (1990): 30-78.

Jones, Emrys. *The Origins of Shakespeare.* Oxford: Clarendon, 1977.

Jones, John. *Shakespeare at Work.* Oxford: Clarendon, 1995.

Jones, Robert. *A Musicall Dreame.* London: J. Windet, 1609.

Jonson, Ben. *The Complete Poems.* Edited by George Parfitt. New York: Penguin, 1988.

———. "Cynthia's Revels: Or, the Fountain of Self-Love." In *The Complete Plays of Ben Jonson*, edited by Ernest Rhys, 1:149-232. New York: E. P. Dutton, 1946.

Kaplan, Donald M. "On Stage Fright." *Drama Review: TDR* 14, no. 1 (1969): 60-83.

Kempe, William. *The Education of Children in Learning.* London: Thomas Orwin, 1588.

Kerrigan, John. "The Editor as Reader: Constructing Renaissance Texts." In *The Practice and Representation of Reading in England*, edited by James Raven, Helen Small, and Naomi Tadmor, 102-24. New York: Cambridge University Press, 1996.

Kinneavy, James L. "Kairos: A Neglected Concept." In *Rhetoric and Praxis: The Contribution of Classical Rhetoric to Practical Reasoning*, edited by Jean Dietz Moss, 83-94. Washington, DC: Catholic University of America Press, 1986.

Klene, Jean. Introduction to *The Southwell-Sibthorpe Commonplace Book: Folger MS. V.b.198*, edited by Jean Klene, xi-xliii. Tempe, AZ: Medieval & Renaissance Texts & Studies, 1997.

———, ed. *The Southwell-Sibthorpe Commonplace Book: Folger MS. V.b.198.* Tempe, AZ: Medieval & Renaissance Texts & Studies, 1997.

Knights, Ben. *Pedagogic Criticism: Reconfiguring University English Studies*. London: Palgrave Macmillan, 2017.
Knights, Ben, and Chris Thurgar-Dawson. *Active Reading: Transformative Writing in Literary Studies*. London: Bloomsbury, 2008.
Kramnick, Jonathan. "Criticism and Truth." *Critical Inquiry* 47, no. 2 (2021): 218–40.
Lamb, Edel. *Reading Children in Early Modern Culture*. New York: Palgrave Macmillan, 2018.
Lamb, Julian. *Rules of Use: Language and Instruction in Early Modern England*. London: Bloomsbury, 2014.
Lamott, Anne. *Bird by Bird: Some Instructions on Writing and Life*. New York: Anchor Books, 1994.
Lanham, Richard A. *The Economics of Attention: Style and Substance in the Age of Information*. Chicago: University of Chicago Press, 2006.
Larson, Katherine R. "Conversational Games and the Articulation of Desire in Shakespeare's *Love's Labour's Lost* and Mary Wroth's *Love's Victory*." *English Literary Renaissance* 40, no. 2 (2010): 165–90.
Lauer, Janice M. *Invention in Rhetoric and Composition*. West Lafayette, IN: Parlor, 2004.
Leader, Zachary. *Writer's Block*. Baltimore: Johns Hopkins University Press, 1991.
LeFevre, Karen Burke. *Invention as a Social Act*. Carbondale: Southern Illinois University Press, 1987.
Lerer, Seth. *Children's Literature: A Reader's History, from Aesop to Harry Potter*. Chicago: University of Chicago Press, 2009.
Lesser, Zachary, and Peter Stallybrass. "The First Literary Hamlet and the Commonplacing of Professional Plays." *Shakespeare Quarterly* 59, no. 4 (2008): 371–420.
Levao, Ronald. "Sidney's Feigned Apology." *PMLA* 94, no. 2 (1979): 223–33.
Lilley, Kate. "Fruits of Sodom: The Critical Erotics of Early Modern Women's Writing." *Parergon* 29, no. 2 (2012): 175–92.
Lipari, Lisbeth. "Ethics, Kairos, and Akroasis." In *Philosophy of Communication Ethics: Alterity and the Other*, edited by Ronald C. Arnett and Pat Arneson, 75–93. Madison, NJ: Fairleigh Dickinson University Press, 2014.
Liu, Yameng. "Aristotle and the Stasis Theory: A Reexamination." *Rhetoric Society Quarterly* 21, no. 1 (1991): 53–59.
Longfellow, Erica. *Women and Religious Writing in Early Modern England*. Cambridge: Cambridge University Press, 2004.
Longinus. *On the Sublime*. In *Aristotle: Poetics. Longinus: On the Sublime. Demetrius: On Style*, translated by W. H. Fyfe, 143–308. Loeb Classical Library. Cambridge, MA: Harvard University Press, 1995.
Love, Harold. *Scribal Publication in Seventeenth-Century England*. Oxford: Clarendon, 1993.
Lyly, John. "Iohn Lyly to the Authour His Friend." In *The EKATOMPATHIA, or Passionate Centurie of Love*, by Thomas Wilson, 7–8. Manchester: Charles S. Simms, 1869. Originally published in 1582.

Lynch, Jack. *Becoming Shakespeare: The Unlikely Afterlife That Turned a Provincial Playwright into the Bard*. New York: Walker, 2007.
Mack, Peter. *Elizabethan Rhetoric: Theory and Practice*. Cambridge: Cambridge University Press, 2002.
Macray, William Dunn, ed. *The Pilgrimage to Parnassus: With the Two Parts of "The Return from Parnassus."* Oxford: Clarendon, 1886.
Magnusson, Lynne. "Scoff Power in *Love's Labour's Lost* and the Inns of Court: Language in Context." *Shakespeare Survey* 57 (2004): 196–208.
Mandel, Barrett John. "Teaching without Judging." *College English* 34, no. 5 (1973): 623–33.
Mann, Jenny C. "Aporia." In *The Princeton Encyclopedia of Poetry and Poetics*, 4th ed., edited by Roland Greene, Stephen Cushman, Clare Cavanagh, Jahan Ramazani, and Paul Rouzer, 60. Princeton, NJ: Princeton University Press, 2012.
———. *Outlaw Rhetoric: Figuring Vernacular Eloquence in Shakespeare's England*. Ithaca, NY: Cornell University Press, 2012.
Marotti, Arthur F. *Manuscript, Print, and the English Renaissance Lyric*. Ithaca, NY: Cornell University Press, 1995.
Marston, John. *Iacke Drums Entertainment*. London: [Thomas Creede], 1601.
Maruca, Lisa. "Bodies of Type: The Work of Textual Production in English Printers' Manuals." *Eighteenth-Century Studies* 36, no. 3 (2003): 321–43.
Massai, Sonia. *Shakespeare and the Rise of the Editor*. Cambridge: Cambridge University Press, 2007.
Masten, Jeffrey. *Textual Intercourse: Collaboration, Authorship, and Sexualities in Renaissance Drama*. Cambridge: Cambridge University Press, 1997.
Matalene, Carolyn. "The Teacher as Editor." *Journal of Teaching Writing* 5, no. 1 (1986): 3–16.
Matz, Robert. *Defending Literature in Early Modern England: Renaissance Literary Theory in Social Context*. Cambridge: Cambridge University Press, 2000.
Mazzio, Carla. *The Inarticulate Renaissance: Language Trouble in an Age of Eloquence*. Philadelphia: University of Pennsylvania Press, 2009.
McCabe, Richard. *"Ungainefull Arte": Poetry, Patronage, and Print in the Early Modern Era*. Oxford: Oxford University Press, 2016.
McCarthy, Erin A. *Doubtful Readers: Print, Poetry, and the Reading Public in Early Modern England*. Oxford: Oxford University Press, 2020.
McCoy, Richard C. "Gascoigne's 'Poëmata Castrata': The Wages of Courtly Success." *Criticism* 27, no. 1 (1985): 29–55.
McGann, Jerome J. *A Critique of Modern Textual Criticism*. Chicago: University of Chicago Press, 1983.
———. *The Textual Condition*. Princeton, NJ: Princeton University Press, 1991.
———. *Towards a Literature of Knowledge*. Oxford: Oxford University Press, 1989.
McKenzie, D. F. *Bibliography and the Sociology of Texts*. Cambridge: Cambridge University Press, 1999.
McRae, Andrew. "The Literary Culture of Early Stuart Libeling." *Modern Philology* 97, no. 3 (2000): 364–92.
Menzer, Paul. "Crowd Control." In *Imagining the Audience in Early Modern Drama, 1558–1642*, edited by Jennifer A. Low and Nova Myhill, 19–36. New York: Palgrave Macmillan, 2011.

Meskill, Lynn S. *Ben Jonson and Envy*. Cambridge: Cambridge University Press, 2009.

Middleton, Thomas. "Hengist, King of Kent; or, The Mayor of Queenborough." Edited by Grace Ioppolo. In *Thomas Middleton: The Collected Works*, edited by Gary Taylor and John Lavagnino, 1448-87. Oxford: Oxford University Press, 2010.

Middleton, Thomas, and Thomas Dekker. "The Roaring Girl; or, Moll Cutpurse." Edited by Coppélia Kahn. In *Thomas Middleton: The Collected Works*, edited by Gary Taylor and John Lavagnino, 721-78. Oxford: Oxford University Press, 2010.

Miller, Anthony. "Ben Jonson and 'the Proper Passion of Mettalls.'" *Parergon* 23, no. 2 (2006): 57-72.

Miller, Carolyn R. "Aristotle's 'Special Topics' in Rhetorical Practice and Pedagogy." *Rhetoric Society Quarterly* 17, no. 1 (January 1, 1987): 61-70.

———. Foreword to *Rhetoric and Kairos: Essays in History, Theory, and Praxis*, edited by Phillip Sipiora and James S. Baumlin, xi-xiii. Albany: State University of New York Press, 2002.

Miller, J. Hillis. "Nietzsche in Basel: Writing Reading." *Journal of Advanced Composition* 13, no. 2 (1993): 311-28.

Miller, Stephen. *Conversation: A History of a Declining Art*. New Haven, CT: Yale University Press, 2007.

Miller, Susan. *Textual Carnivals: The Politics of Composition*. Carbondale: Southern Illinois University Press, 1993.

Millman, Jill Seal, and Gillian Wright, eds. *Early Modern Women's Manuscript Poetry*. Manchester: Manchester University Press, 2005.

Mitchell, Dianne. "'Or Rather a Wyldernesse': The Changing Works of Dudley, Third Baron North." *Studies in Philology* 114, no. 2 (2017): 368-94.

———. "Shakespeare's Several Begetters." *Modern Philology* 118, no. 4 (2021): 515-36.

Morrow, Nancy. "The Role of Reading in the Composition Classroom." *Journal of Advanced Composition* 17, no. 3 (1997): 453-72.

Moss, Jean Dietz. "'Godded with God': Hendrik Niclaes and His Family of Love." *Transactions of the American Philosophical Society* 71, no. 8 (1981): 1-89.

Moxon, Joseph. *Mechanick Exercises on the Whole Art of Printing*. New York: Dover, 1978.

Murray, Donald M. *The Craft of Revision*. 5th ed. Boston: Wadsworth, Cengage Learning, 2013.

Nadeau, Ray. "Classical Systems of Stases in Greek: Hermagoras to Hermogenes." *Greek, Roman, and Byzantine Studies* 2, no. 1 (1959): 51-71.

Nardizzi, Vin. "Wooden Actors on the English Renaissance Stage." In *Renaissance Posthumanism*, edited by Joseph Campana and Scott Maisano, 195-220. New York: Fordham University Press, 2016.

Nashe, Thomas. "Pierce Penniless His Supplication to the Devil." In *The Unfortunate Traveller and Other Works*, new ed., edited by J. B. Steane, 49-145. New York: Penguin, 1985.

———. *Strange Newes, of the Intercepting of Certaine Letters*. London: John Danter, 1592.

Nelson, Victoria. *Writer's Block and How to Use It*. Cincinnati, OH: Writer's Digest Books, 1985.

Nelson, William. "The Teaching of English in Tudor Grammar Schools." *Studies in Philology* 49, no. 2 (1952): 119–43.

Newberry, Thomas. *A Booke in English Metre, of the Great Marchaunt Man Called Diues Pragmatics*. London: Alexander Lacy, 1563.

Ngai, Sianne. *Our Aesthetic Categories: Zany, Cute, Interesting*. Cambridge, MA: Harvard University Press, 2012.

———. *Theory of the Gimmick: Aesthetic Judgment and Capitalist Form*. Cambridge, MA: Harvard University Press, 2020.

Nicholson, Catherine. *Uncommon Tongues: Eloquence and Eccentricity in the English Renaissance*. Philadelphia: University of Pennsylvania Press, 2013.

Niclaes, Hendrik. *All the Letters of the A.B.C. by Euery Sondrye Letter Wherof Ther Is a Good Document Set-Fourth and Taught in Ryme*. [Cologne, Germany?: N. Bohmberg?], 1575.

North, Joseph. *Literary Criticism*. Cambridge, MA: Harvard University Press, 2017.

Oakeshott, Michael. "The Voice of Poetry in the Conversation of Mankind." In *Rationalism in Politics, and Other Essays*, 197–247. London: Methuen, 1962.

O'Callaghan, Michelle. *The English Wits: Literature and Sociability in Early Modern England*. Cambridge: Cambridge University Press, 2007.

Olive, Sarah. *Shakespeare Valued: Education Policy and Pedagogy, 1989–2009*. Chicago: Intellect Books, 2015.

Osborn, James Marshall. *Young Philip Sidney, 1572–1577*. New Haven, CT: Yale University Press, 1972.

Ostovich, Helen, and Elizabeth Sauer, eds. *Reading Early Modern Women: An Anthology of Texts in Manuscript and Print, 1550–1700*. New York: Routledge, 2003.

Palfrey, Simon, and Tiffany Stern. *Shakespeare in Parts*. Oxford: Oxford University Press, 2007.

Palmer, Philip S. "'The Progress of Thy Glorious Book': Material Reading and the Play of Paratext in *Coryats Crudities* (1611)." *Renaissance Studies* 28, no. 3 (2014): 336–55.

Pangallo, Matteo A. *Playwriting Playgoers in Shakespeare's Theater*. Philadelphia: University of Pennsylvania Press, 2017.

Parker, Lindsay, and James Gifford. "Rethinking How Humanities Think: Daring and 'Do/Make/Think.'" *ESC: English Studies in Canada* 38, no. 1 (2012): 89–113.

Parker, Patricia. *Shakespeare from the Margins: Language, Culture, Context*. Chicago: University of Chicago Press, 1996.

Paul, Joanne. "The Use of Kairos in Renaissance Political Philosophy." *Renaissance Quarterly* 67, no. 1 (2014): 43–78.

Peltonen, Markku. *Rhetoric, Politics and Popularity in Pre-revolutionary England*. Cambridge: Cambridge University Press, 2012.

Pendarves, Robert, and Job Weale. "Robert Pendarves His Booke Amen, Written by Me . . . Anno Domini 1652 [V.a.629]." Manuscript, 1645.

Pender, Patricia. *Early Modern Women's Writing and the Rhetoric of Modesty*. New York: Palgrave Macmillan, 2012.
———. ed. *Gender, Authorship, and Early Modern Women's Collaboration*. Early Modern Literature in History. Cham: Palgrave Macmillan, 2017.
Pender, Patricia, and Alexandra Day. "Introduction: Gender, Authorship, and Early Modern Women's Collaboration." In *Gender, Authorship, and Early Modern Women's Collaboration*, edited by Patricia Pender, 1–19. Early Modern Literature in History. Cham: Palgrave Macmillan, 2017.
Phillippy, Patricia, ed. *A History of Early Modern Women's Literature*. Cambridge: Cambridge University Press, 2018.
Pickering, Andrew. *The Mangle of Practice*. Chicago: University of Chicago Press, 1995.
Pigman, G. W. "Textual Introduction." In *George Gascoigne: A Hundreth Sundrie Flowres*, edited by G. W. Pigman, xlv–lxv. Oxford: Oxford University Press, 2000.
Plato. *Laches. Protagoras. Meno. Euthydemus*. Translated by W. R. M. Lamb. Loeb Classical Library. Cambridge, MA: Harvard University Press, 1924.
Plett, Heinrich. "Rhetoric and Humanism." In *The Oxford Handbook of Rhetorical Studies*, edited by Michael J. MacDonald, 377–86. New York: Oxford University Press, 2017.
Potter, Ursula. "'No Terence Phrase: His Tyme and Myne Are Twaine'; Erasmus, Terence, and Censorship in the Tudor Classroom." In *The Classics in the Medieval and Renaissance Classroom*, edited by Juanita Feros Ruys, John O. Ward, and Melanie Heyworth, 365–89. Turnhout: Brepols, 2013.
Poulakos, John. "The Logic of Greek Sophistry." In *Historical Foundations of Informal Logic*, edited by Douglas Walton and Alan Brinton, 12–24. New York: Routledge, 1997.
Preiss, Richard. *Clowning and Authorship in Early Modern Theatre*. Cambridge: Cambridge University Press, 2014.
———. "Undocumented: Improvisation, Rehearsal, and the Clown." In *Rethinking Theatrical Documents in Shakespeare's England*, edited by Tiffany Stern, 68–88. London: Bloomsbury Academic, 2019.
Probyn, Elspeth. *Blush: Faces of Shame*. Minneapolis: University of Minnesota Press, 2005.
Prouty, Charles Tyler. *George Gascoigne: Elizabethan Courtier, Soldier, and Poet*. New York: Columbia University Press, 1942.
Puttenham, George. *The Art of English Poesy: A Critical Edition*. Edited by Frank Whigham and Wayne A. Rebhorn. Ithaca, NY: Cornell University Press, 2016.
Pye, Christopher. "The Betrayal of the Gaze: Theatricality and Power in Shakespeare's *Richard II*." *ELH* 55, no. 3 (1988): 575–98.
Pye, David. *The Nature and Art of Workmanship*. Cambridge: Cambridge University Press, 1978.
Quintilian. *The Orator's Education, Vol. IV: Books 9–10*. Edited and translated by Donald A. Russell. Loeb Classical Library. Cambridge, MA: Harvard University Press, 2002.

Rancière, Jacques. *The Ignorant Schoolmaster: Five Lessons in Intellectual Emancipation*. Translated by Kristin Ross. Stanford, CA: Stanford University Press, 1991.

———. "Un-What?" In *The Pedagogics of Unlearning*, edited by Aidan Seery and Éamonn Dunne, 25–46. [Santa Barbara, CA]: Punctum Books, 2016.

Randall, David. *The Concept of Conversation: From Cicero's Sermo to the Grand Siècle's Conversation*. Edinburgh: Edinburgh University Press, 2019.

Rebhorn, Wayne A. "Outlandish Fears: Defining Decorum in Renaissance Rhetoric." *Intertexts* 4, no. 1 (2000): 3–26.

Relle, Eleanor. "Some New Marginalia and Poems of Gabriel Harvey." *Review of English Studies* 23, no. 92 (1972): 401–16.

Rescher, Nicholas. *Aporetics: Rational Deliberation in the Face of Inconsistency*. Pittsburgh: University of Pittsburgh Press, 2009.

Rhodes, Neil. *Common: The Development of Literary Culture in Sixteenth-Century England*. Oxford: Oxford University Press, 2018.

———. *Shakespeare and the Origins of English*. Oxford: Oxford University Press, 2004.

Richards, Jennifer. *Rhetoric and Courtliness in Early Modern Literature*. Cambridge: Cambridge University Press, 2003.

Richardson, Brian. *Print Culture in Renaissance Italy: The Editor and the Vernacular Text, 1470–1600*. Cambridge: Cambridge University Press, 1994.

Ridout, Nicholas. *Stage Fright, Animals, and Other Theatrical Problems*. Cambridge: Cambridge University Press, 2006.

Ringler, William A. *The Poems of Sir Philip Sidney*. Oxford: Clarendon, 1962.

Robbins, Bruce. *The Beneficiary*. Durham, NC: Duke University Press, 2007.

Rose, Mike. *Writer's Block: The Cognitive Dimension*. Carbondale: Southern Illinois University Press, 1984.

Rosenblatt, Louise M. *The Reader, the Text, the Poem: The Transactional Theory of the Literary Work*. Carbondale: Southern Illinois University Press, 1994.

Rosenfeld, Colleen Ruth. *Indecorous Thinking: Figures of Speech in Early Modern Poetics*. New York: Fordham University Press, 2018.

Ross, Sarah C. E. *Women, Poetry, and Politics in Seventeenth-Century Britain*. Oxford: Oxford University Press, 2015.

Ross, Trevor. *The Making of the English Literary Canon: From the Middle Ages to the Late Eighteenth Century*. Montreal: McGill-Queen's University Press, 1998.

Roychoudhury, Suparna. *Phantasmatic Shakespeare: Imagination in the Age of Early Modern Science*. Ithaca, NY: Cornell University Press, 2018.

Rudenstine, Neil L. *Sidney's Poetic Development*. Cambridge, MA: Harvard University Press, 1967.

Rudyerd, Sir Benjamin. *Le prince d'amour; or The Prince of Love*. London: William Leake, 1660.

Rule, Hannah. *Situating Writing Processes: Physicality, Improvisation, and the Teaching of Writing*. Fort Collins: University Press of Colorado, 2019.

Runco, Mark A. "'Big C, Little c' Creativity as a False Dichotomy: Reality Is Not Categorical." *Creativity Research Journal* 26, no. 1 (2014): 131–32.

Russ, Joanna. *How to Suppress Women's Writing*. Austin: University of Texas Press, 1983.

Salamon, Linda Bradley. "A Face in 'The Glasse': Gascoigne's 'Glasse of Governement' Re-examined." *Studies in Philology* 71, no. 1 (1974): 47-71.
Saldívar, Ramón. "The Work of Criticism in Journal Refereeing." *PMLA* 127, no. 4 (2012): 963-67.
Scaliger, Julius Caesar. *Select Translations from Scaliger's Poetics*. Translated by Frederick Morgan Padelford. New York: Henry Holt, 1905.
Schechner, Richard. *Performance Studies: An Introduction*. 2nd ed. New York: Routledge, 2006.
Schmidgall, Gary. *Shakespeare and the Courtly Aesthetic*. Berkeley: University of California Press, 1981.
Schoeck, R. J. "'Nosce Teipsum' and the Two John Davies." *Modern Language Review* 50, no. 3 (1955): 307-10.
Schulz, Herbert C. "The Teaching of Handwriting in Tudor and Stuart Times." *Huntington Library Quarterly* 6, no. 4 (1943): 381-425.
Scodel, Joshua. *Excess and the Mean in Early Modern English Literature*. Princeton, NJ: Princeton University Press, 2009.
S[egar], F[rancis]. *The Schoole of Vertue*. London: Wyllyam Seares, 1557.
Shakespeare, William. *Loues Labors Lost*. London: William White, 1598.
Sheavyn, Phoebe. *The Literary Profession in the Elizabethan Age*. New York: Manchester University Press, 1967.
Shenk, Robert. "Deliberative Stasis According to the Ancients, as Illustrated from Shakespeare's *Henry IV*." *Ben Jonson Journal* 23, no. 2 (2016): 192-211.
Sherman, William. *Used Books: Marking Readers in Renaissance England*. Philadelphia: University of Pennsylvania Press, 2008.
Sidney, Philip. *The Countess of Pembroke's Arcadia*. Kent, OH: Kent State University Press, 1970.
———. *Sir Philip Sidney: The Major Works*. Edited by Katherine Duncan-Jones. Oxford: Oxford University Press, 1989.
Simonova, Natasha. *Early Modern Authorship and Prose Continuations: Adaptation and Ownership from Sidney to Richardson*. New York: Palgrave Macmillan, 2015.
Sinfield, Alan. "Give an Account of Shakespeare and Education . . ." In *Political Shakespeare: New Essays in Cultural Materialism*, 2nd ed., edited by Jonathan Dollimore and Alan Sinfield, 156-81. Ithaca, NY: Cornell University Press, 1994.
Singer, Jerome L., and Michael V. Barrios. "Writer's Block and Blocked Writers: Using Natural Imagery to Enhance Creativity." In *The Psychology of Creative Writing*, edited by Scott Barry Kaufman and James C. Kaufman, 225-46. Cambridge: Cambridge University Press, 2009.
Singh, Julietta. *Unthinking Mastery: Dehumanism and Decolonial Entanglements*. Durham, NC: Duke University Press, 2017.
Sipiora, Phillip. "Introduction: The Ancient Concept of Kairos." In *Rhetoric and Kairos: Essays in History, Theory, and Praxis*, edited by Phillip Sipiora and James S. Baumlin, 1-22. Albany: State University of New York Press, 2002.
Sipiora, Phillip, and James S. Baumlin, eds. *Rhetoric and Kairos: Essays in History, Theory, and Praxis*. Albany: State University of New York Press, 2002.

Sirc, Geoffrey. *English Composition as a Happening.* Logan: Utah State University Press, 2002.
Skinner, Quentin. *Forensic Shakespeare.* Oxford: Oxford University Press, 2014.
Skura, Meredith Anne. *Shakespeare the Actor and the Purposes of Playing.* Chicago: University of Chicago Press, 1993.
Sloane, Thomas O. *On the Contrary: The Protocol of Traditional Rhetoric.* Washington, DC: Catholic University of America Press, 1997.
Smit, David W. *The End of Composition Studies.* Carbondale: Southern Illinois University Press, 2004.
Smith, Bruce. "A Night of Errors and the Dawn of Empire: Male Enterprise in *The Comedy of Errors.*" In *Shakespeare's Sweet Thunder: Essays on the Early Comedies,* edited by Michael J. Collins, 102–25. Newark: University of Delaware Press, 1997.
Smith, Emma. *This Is Shakespeare.* New York: Vintage, 2019.
Smith, G. Gregory. *Elizabethan Critical Essays.* 2 vols. London: Oxford University Press, 1904.
Smyth, Adam. *Material Texts in Early Modern England.* Cambridge: Cambridge University Press, 2018.
Sommers, Nancy. "Revision Strategies of Student Writers and Experienced Adult Writers." In *Concepts in Composition: Theory and Practice in the Teaching of Writing,* 2nd ed., edited by Irene L. Clark, 100–108. New York: Routledge, 2012.
Sontag, Susan. "On Style." In *A Susan Sontag Reader,* 137–55. New York: Farrar, Straus & Giroux, 1982.
———. *Where the Stress Falls: Essays.* New York: Picador, 2001.
Spiller, Michael R. G. *The Development of the Sonnet: An Introduction.* New York: Routledge, 2003.
Spingarn, J. E. "The Sources of Jonson's 'Discoveries.'" *Modern Philology* 2, no. 4 (1905): 451–60.
Spufford, Margaret. *Small Books and Pleasant Histories: Popular Fiction and Its Readership in Seventeenth-Century England.* Cambridge: Cambridge University Press, 1985.
Stamatakis, Chris. *Sir Thomas Wyatt and the Rhetoric of Rewriting: "Turning the Word."* Oxford: Oxford University Press, 2012.
———. "'With Diligent Studie, but Sportingly': How Gabriel Harvey Read His Castiglione." *Journal of the Northern Renaissance,* no. 5 (November 9, 2013). https://northernrenaissance.org/with-diligent-studie-but-sportingly-how-gabriel-harvey-read-his-castiglione/.
Stanislavski, Constantin. *An Actor Prepares.* Translated by Elizabeth Reynolds Hapgood. New York: Routledge, 1989.
Stephenson, Hunter W. *Forecasting Opportunity: Kairos, Production, and Writing.* New York: University Press of America, 2005.
Stern, Tiffany. *Documents of Performance in Early Modern England.* Cambridge: Cambridge University Press, 2009.
Stevenson, Jane, and Peter Davidson, eds. *Early Modern Women Poets: An Anthology.* Oxford: Oxford University Press, 2001.

Stoeber, Joachim. "The Psychology of Perfectionism: An Introduction." In *The Psychology of Perfectionism: Theory, Research, Applications*, edited by Joachim Stoeber, 3-16. New York: Routledge, 2017.

Stone, Lawrence. "The Educational Revolution in England, 1560-1640." *Past & Present*, no. 28 (1964): 41-80.

Sullivan, Dale L. "Kairos and the Rhetoric of Belief." *Quarterly Journal of Speech* 78, no. 3 (1992): 317-32.

Sullivan, Patricia A. "Writing in the Graduate Curriculum: Literary Criticism as Composition." *Journal of Advanced Composition* 11, no. 2 (1991): 283-99.

Sumillera, Rocío G. "Poetic Invention and Translation in Sixteenth-Century England." *SEDERI Yearbook*, no. 22 (2012): 93-114.

Tallent, Elizabeth. *Scratched: A Memoir of Perfectionism*. New York: HarperCollins, 2020.

Tanselle, G. Thomas. "Textual Instability and Editorial Idealism." *Studies in Bibliography* 49 (1996): 1-60.

Taylor, Gary. "In Media Res: From Jerome through Greg to Jerome (McGann)." *Textual Cultures* 4, no. 2 (2009): 88-101.

———. *Reinventing Shakespeare: A Cultural History, from the Restoration to the Present*. Oxford: Oxford University Press, 1991.

Taylor, Gary, and John Jowett. *Shakespeare Reshaped, 1606–1623*. Oxford: Clarendon, 1993.

Taylor, John. *The Praise of Hemp-Seed*. London: For H. Gosson, 1620.

Thadani, Simran. "'For the Better Atteyning to Faire Writing': An Analysis of Two Competing Writing-Books, London, 1591." *Papers of the Bibliographical Society of America* 107, no. 4 (2013): 422-66.

Thomas, Max W. "Eschewing Credit: Heywood, Shakespeare, and Plagiarism before Copyright." *New Literary History* 31, no. 2 (2000): 277-93.

Thompson, Ayanna, and Laura Turchi. *Teaching Shakespeare with Purpose: A Student-Centred Approach*. New York: Bloomsbury, 2016.

Tillich, Paul. *The Interpretation of History*. New York: C. Scribner's Sons, 1936.

Tribble, Evelyn. *Cognition in the Globe: Attention and Memory in Shakespeare's Theatre*. New York: Palgrave Macmillan, 2011.

———. *Early Modern Actors and Shakespeare's Theatre: Thinking with the Body*. New York: Bloomsbury, 2017.

Tucker, George Hugo. "From Rags to Riches: The Early Modern 'Cento' Form." *Humanistica Lovaniensia* 62 (2013): 3-67.

Valdivia, Lucía Martínez. "Mere Meter: A Revised History of English Poetry." *ELH* 86, no. 3 (2019): 555-85.

Van Dorsten, Jan. "Literary Patronage in Elizabethan England: The Early Phase." In *Patronage in the Renaissance*, edited by Guy Fitch Lytle and Stephen Orgel, 191-206. Princeton, NJ: Princeton University Press, 1981.

van Elk, Martine. *Early Modern Women's Writing: Domesticity, Privacy, and the Public Sphere in England and the Dutch Republic*. Cham: Palgrave Macmillan, 2017.

van Es, Bart. *Shakespeare in Company*. Oxford: Oxford University Press, 2013.

Vickers, Brian. *Shakespeare, "A Lover's Complaint," and John Davies of Hereford*. Cambridge: Cambridge University Press, 2007.

Viswanathan, Gauri. *Masks of Conquest: Literary Study and British Rule in India*. New York: Columbia University Press, 1989.

Vogl, Joseph. *On Tarrying*. Translated by Helmut Muller-Sievers. Kolkata: Seagull Books, 2011.

Wagoner, Brady. "Creativity as Symbolic Transformation." In *Rethinking Creativity*, edited by Vlad Petre Glăveanu, Alex Gillespie, and Jaan Valsiner, 16–30. New York: Routledge, 2014.

Wall, Wendy. *The Imprint of Gender: Authorship and Publication in the English Renaissance*. Ithaca, NY: Cornell University Press, 1993.

———. "Reading for the Blot: Textual Desire in Early Modern English Literature." In *Reading and Writing in Shakespeare*, edited by David Bergeron, 131–59. Newark: University of Delaware Press, 1996.

Warner, John. *Why They Can't Write: Killing the Five-Paragraph Essay and Other Necessities*. Baltimore: Johns Hopkins University Press, 2018.

———. *The Writer's Practice: Building Confidence in Your Nonfiction Writing*. New York: Penguin, 2019.

Watson, Foster. *The English Grammar Schools to 1660: Their Curriculum and Practice*. Cambridge: Cambridge University Press, 1908.

Werstine, Paul. "Narratives about Printed Shakespeare Texts: 'Foul Papers' and 'Bad' Quartos." *Shakespeare Quarterly* 41, no. 1 (1990): 65–86.

Whigham, Frank. "Interpretation at Court: Courtesy and the Performer-Audience Dialectic." *New Literary History* 14, no. 3 (1983): 623–39.

Wilder, Laura. *Rhetorical Strategies and Genre Conventions in Literary Studies: Teaching and Writing in the Disciplines*. Carbondale: Southern Illinois University Press, 2012.

Wilder, Laura, and Joanna Wolfe. "Sharing the Tacit Rhetorical Knowledge of the Literary Scholar: The Effects of Making Disciplinary Conventions Explicit in Undergraduate Writing about Literature Courses." *Research in the Teaching of English* 44, no. 2 (2009): 170–209.

Willis, Jonathan. "'By These Means the Sacred Discourses Sink More Deeply into the Minds of Men': Music and Education in Elizabethan England." *History* 94, no. 315 (2009): 294–309.

Wilson, Glenn D., and David Roland. "Performance Anxiety." In *The Science & Psychology of Music Performance*, edited by Edward Geldard, Richard Parncutt, and Gary McPherson, 47–62. Oxford: Oxford University Press, 2002.

Wilson, Hugh. "Anne Southwell, Metaphysical Poet." *Quidditas* 21 (2000): 129–48.

Wilson, Thomas. *The Arte of Rhetorique for the Vse of All Suche as Are Studious of Eloquence, Sette Forth in English, by Thomas Wilson*. London: Richard Grafton, 1553.

Winston, Jessica. *Lawyers at Play: Literature, Law, and Politics at the Early Modern Inns of Court, 1558–1581*. Oxford: Oxford University Press, 2016.

Wiseman, Rebecca. "A Poetics of the Natural: Sensation, Decorum, and Bodily Appeal in Puttenham's Art of English Poesy." *Renaissance Studies* 28, no. 1 (2014): 33–49.

Witmore, Michael. *Culture of Accidents: Unexpected Knowledges in Early Modern England*. Stanford, CA: Stanford University Press, 2001.

Wittman, Kara. "Epilogue: New, Interesting, and Original—the Undergraduate as Amateur." In *The Critic as Amateur*, edited by Saikat Majumdar and Aarthi Vadde, 243-64. New York: Bloomsbury Academic, 2020.
Wolosky, Shira. "Modest Claims." In *Poetry and Public Discourse in Nineteenth-Century America*, edited by Shira Wolosky, 1-13. Nineteenth-Century Major Lives and Letters. New York: Palgrave Macmillan, 2010.
Woolf, Virginia. *A Room of One's Own*. Hammersmith: Grafton, 1977.
Woudhuysen, H. R. "Appendix 1." In *Love's Labour's Lost*, by William Shakespeare, 298-338. Arden Shakespeare 3. London: Arden Shakespeare, 1998.
———. *Sir Philip Sidney and the Circulation of Manuscripts, 1558-1640*. Oxford: Oxford University Press, 1996.
Wright, Gillian. *Producing Women's Poetry, 1600-1730: Text and Paratext, Manuscript and Print*. Cambridge: Cambridge University Press, 2013.
Wright, Louis B. "Language Helps for the Elizabethan Tradesman." *Journal of English and Germanic Philology* 30, no. 3 (1931): 335-47.
Yarbrough, Stephen R. "Deliberate Invention: On the Motive to Create Novel Beliefs." *Rhetoric Society Quarterly* 33, no. 3 (2003): 79-94.
Zarnowiecki, Matthew. *Fair Copies: Reproducing the English Lyric from Tottel to Shakespeare*. Toronto: University of Toronto Press, 2014.
Zembylas, Tasos, and Martin Niederauer. *Composing Processes and Artistic Agency: Tacit Knowledge in Composing*. New York: Routledge, 2018.
Zucker, Adam. "Antihonorificabilitudinitatibus: *Love's Labour's Lost* and Unteachable Words." *Shakespeare Survey* 70 (2017): 135-45.
Zurcher, Andrew. "Deficiency and Supplement: Perfecting the Prosthetic Text." *SEL: Studies in English Literature, 1500-1900* 52, no. 1 (2012): 143-64.

Index

Page numbers in *italics* indicate illustrations. Authored works will be found under the author's name.

academia: as shared endeavor, 162; women and women's writing, modern scholarship on, 160, 167, 185, 193. *See also* pedagogy of English literature and composition
Adams, Bernard, 174–75, 176
Adorno, Theodor W., 32, 47
aesthetic versus historicist/contextualist discourse, 6–7
Alexander, Gavin, 87n45
amateurism and professionalism, 205–6, 226–27, 230–31
Aphthonius, *Progymnasmata*, 57
aporia, 74, 92–95, 98
aposiopesis, 11, 129
Arditi, Jorge, 212n33
Aristotle, 58, 77, 91, 92, 104, 210n29; *Art of Rhetoric*, 91n58, 91n60; *Metaphysics*, 92n63; *Nicomachean Ethics*, 139n74; *On Rhetoric*, 58n85
Arminianism, 161n19
Ascham, Roger, 43–44, 45; *The Scholemaster* (1570), 38
Attridge, Derek, 205–6, 230–31
authorship, concepts of, 166–68

Bacon, Francis, 11, 99, 213
Baildon, John, 122
Bailes, Sara Jane, 205, 220–21, 226–27
Bajetta, Carlo M., 158n9
Baldwin, T. W., 12, 29n8, 41, 46
Barker, Christopher, 49
Barrios, Michael V., 90
Barthes, Roland, 21, 48, 59; *The Lover's Discourse*, 232
Bartholomae, David, 64, 66
Bastard, Thomas, 129–30, 142n84; *Chrestoleros* (1598), 130, 136n66

Bate, Jonathan, 2, 5n17
Bates, Catherine, 89, 100
Bayer, Mark, 217n56
Bean, John, 117
Beau Chesne, Jean de, 122
Bedford, Lucy, Countess of, 123
Bender, Daniel, 45n60
Benjamin, Walter, 226
Bentley, Arthur F., 197n102
Berry, Edward, 87n44, 90
Bevington, David, 112n3, 203n10
Bialo, Caralyn, 162
Bishop, Wendy, 16, 26, 106–8
Bizzaro, Patrick, 106n95
Blake, Liza, 188
the blot: Davies of Hereford, emblematizing dissonance of composition process for, 116, 122, 126–29; in Southwell's "Sonnett 2.a," *182*, 182–84
Blum, Susan D., 16, 65–66
Bond, Garth, 166n34
botching/bodgery and patching, 35–36, 42–48, 51, 65, 66, 106, 130–131, 147, 164
Bourdieu, Pierre, 140
Bowers, Fredson, 186
Bowyer, Anne, 194
Brecht, Bertolt, 226
Breitenberg, Mark, 203n10
Brinsley, John, 35, 44–46, 60; *Ludus Literarius* (1612), 44, 112–13
Britton, Ronald, 204
Britzman, Deborah F., 94
Brodkey, Linda, 3
Brome, Richard, *The Antipodes* (1638), 219
Brown, Eric C., 203n10
Browne, David, 122n37
Bruffee, Kenneth, 195
Brugués, Ariadna Ortiz, 203

261

INDEX

Bruster, Douglas, 207n21, 218n57
Bryant, John, 120
Bryson, Anna, 212n33
Burke, Victoria, 175, 177, 193–94
Burlase, William, 129
Bush, Paul, *The Extirpation of Ignorancy* (1526), 33n19

Calvinism, 156, 161n18, 161n19, 171, 174, 177
Campion, Thomas, 100
Carey, Elizabeth, 123
Carr, Alison, 220n71
Carroll, William C., 203n10
Castiglione, Baldassare, *Il cortegiano* (1528), 4n12, 209–10
Cavendish, Margaret, *The Blazing World* (1666), 188
Certeau, Michel de, 48
Chapman, George, 146n92; *The Vviddovves Teares a Comedie* (1612), 219n61
Charles I (king of England), 159
Charlton, Kenneth, 114n12
Cheney, Patrick, 139n75, 140–41
Christen, Richard S., 112
Cicero (Tully), 38, 44, 45, 46, 48, 60, 208n25; *De officiis*, 139n74, 212n36; *De oratore*, 81n26
Clarke, Danielle, 156n3, 176, 181, 183
Clarke, Elizabeth, 161n18
Cogswell, Thomas, 142
Colet, John, 29, 35, 41, 44
collaborative nature of literary production, 3–4, 9, 108–9, 157–62, 198–99. *See also* editing; Southwell, Lady Anne
Combe, Thomas, 30
Condell, Henry. *See* Heminges, John, and Henry Condell
conversation, art of, 205, 210–14
Coolahan, Marie-Louise, 156n3, 169n47, 171n51
Corbett, Edward P., 77
Coryate, Thomas, *Coryats Crudities* (1611), 137n70
Cox, Roger, 175–77
Crabb, George, *Crabb's English Synonymes* (1816), 10
Craik, Katharine, 142–43nn85–86
Crawford, Julie, 167, 168
Crawforth, Hannah, 75n11
Cressy, David, 29n7, 114
Cullman, Leonhard, *Sententi Pueriles* (1543), 30n11

cultural hegemony of English literature, 5–7, 117, 149
Curtius, Ernst Robert, 139

Daniel, Samuel, 100, 136n66
Davidson, Peter, 185
Davies, Sir John, 114, 116, 137–38
Davies, Richard (brother of Davies of Hereford), 128
Davies of Hereford, John, 16, 110–48; the blot emblematizing dissonance of composition process for, 116, 122, 126–29; fame, pursuit of, 111, 114, 115, 116, 135–38; inditing and writing, relationship between, 113, 116, 118, 123–24, 127–32, 164; life and career as writing master, 112–14, 117–18, 121–22; mediocrity of, 111, 112, 114, 116, 121, 133–34, 138–41; poetics of revision and, 118–21; on revision/failure to revise, 110–11, 116; self-comparisons to other writers, 129–32, 136–45, 146n92; Shakespeare and, 112n3, 113, 146, 146n91; Sidney Psalter, commissioned copy of, 121, 127; student expectations regarding, 235; time/money/status, understanding of poets' need for, 113–15, 116, 132–35, 136, 145–48, 153–54
Davies of Hereford, John, works: *Microcosmos* (1603), 112n3, 116, 121, 128–29, 145–46; *Mirum in Modum* (1601), 125–26; "Of My Selfe," 110–11, 115, 127–28, 131, 135; "Of Myselfe," 132; *Paper's Complaint* (1611), 116, 146–48; *Wittes Pilgrimage* (1605), 110, 111, 115, 128; *The Writing School-master* (ca. 1620), 115–16, 121–25
Day, Alexandra, 167, 168
Day, Angel, *The English Secretary* (1586), 139n75
Dekker, Thomas, and Thomas Middleton, *The Roaring Girl* (1611), 218
Della Casa, Giovanni, *Il galateo* (1568), 210, 213n37
Derrida, Jacques, 92–94
Dewey, John, 8, 22, 197n102
Digital Cavendish Project, 188
digital text production, 187–89
discomposition in English poetics, 1–27; centrality to poetic and critical insight,

9, 10–11, 204; compromise between possibility and ingenuity as hallmark of, 164; concept of, 9–15; cultural hegemony of English literature and, 5–7, 117, 149; defined, 9; historicist/contextualist versus aesthetic discourse and, 6–7; imperfectness and, 231; literary epistemology and writing process, 15–27; myth of genius and "easiness" of composition, 1–9; pedagogy and, 8–9 (*see also* pedagogy of English literature and composition); specific writers and, 13–16 (*see also* Davies of Hereford, John; Gascoigne, George; Shakespeare, William; Sidney, Philip; Southwell, Lady Anne); writing process and, 13–16 (*see also* editing; invention; perfection, perfectionism, and failure; revision/failure to revise; style)
dissoi logoi, 83
Dolan, Fran, 189, 194
Dolven, Jeff, 13, 32–33, 46
Donne, John, 1, 18, 108, 116, 136–37, 151, 165–66, 169, 177, 185, 194; *Anniversaries*, 172; *Devotions upon Emergent Occasions* (1624), 10
Doty, Jeffrey S., 217
double translation, 30, 38, 45
Drayton, Michael, 113; *Poly-Olbion* (1612), 163n25
Dubrow, Heather, 86n43
Dyer, Edward, 100, 101

editing: authorial collaboration in, 164–67; composition process, as part of, 177–80; critical reading/writing, affinities with, 161, 195–99; defined and distinguished from revision, 157–58; historical emergence of editorial vocation, 158, 162–64; modern transcription and edition of collaborative works, 184–93, *185*, *192*; as pedagogy, 190–94, *191–92*; readers' participation in, 163; Southwell's inviting of, 157–61 (*see also* Southwell, Lady Anne)
education. *See* pedagogy of English literature and composition
Edward VI (king of England), 46
Eggert, Katherine, 12, 203n11
Eklund, Hillary, 6

Elbow, Peter, 149–50, 230n82
Elias, Norbert, 212n33
Elizabeth I (queen of England), 36, 49, 76, 90, 114, 137, 169
Ellinghausen, Laurie, 113–14, 143n86
English literature studies. *See* pedagogy of English literature and composition
Enterline, Lynne, 13, 207–8, 215–16
epigrams and epigrammatists, 111, 114, 127, 129–30, 132, 136–37, 142, 146–47, 165–66
Erasmus, Desiderius, 16, 29, 33–34, 35, 41–48, 51, 60, 66, 143, 211n32; *De conscribendis epistolis* (1528), 43n52; *De copia* (1512), 43, 71; *Dialogus Ciceronianus* (1528), 42
Eskew, Doug, 7
Estill, Laura, 126n50
Ezell, Margaret, 166–67

Fahnestock, Jeanne, 32n17, 104
failure, poetics of, 205, 220–21. *See also* perfection, perfectionism, and failure; revision/failure to revise
Fallon, Samuel, 136n65
Faulkner, William, 20
Featley, Daniel, 177
Federico, Annette, 21, 22–23, 198
Ferrabosco, Alphonso, *Ayres* (1609), 181
Finkelpearl, Philip J., 111
Fitzpatrick, Kathleen, 8, 17, 199
Flaherty, Kate, 5n18, 5n20
Fleming, Paul, 139–40, 141
Fletcher, Phineas, 163n25
Florio, John, *A World of Wordes* (1598), 9, 35n25
Foucault, Michel, 21
Freire, Paolo, 18
Fuller, Thomas, *Worthies of England* (1662), 121
Furey, Constance, 3–4

Gainsford, Thomas, *The Rich Cabinet* (1616), 214n39, 219–20
Gascoigne, George, 16, 28–63; *Certayne Notes* (1575), 34, 36–40, 56–61, 71; discomposition, commitment to, 34; early modern literary pedagogy and, 28–35, 38, 41–47; *The Glasse of Governement* (1575), 34–36, 40–41, 43, 47–56, 58–60, 63, 65, 68, 70; *A Hundreth Sundrie Flowres*

Gascoigne, George (*continued*) (1572/73), 37–40, 61–63; invention, understanding of, 57–59, 61; life and career, 34, 36–37, 38–39, 61–62; patching and botching, 35–36, 42–48, 51, 164; *The Posies* (1575), 37–40, 47, 55; on "quick capacity," 36, 55–63, 70; recommendations on style, 35–36, 66
Gibson, Jonathan, 175, 181, 185–88, 190
Gifford, James, 107–8
Gitelman, Lisa, 119
Goffman, Erving, 216
Goldberg, Jonathan, 118
Gorges, Arthur, 173
Gosson, Stephen, *The Schoole of Abuse* (1579), 76–77, 81n28, 87
Grafton, Anthony, 12, 46
Gray's Inn, 38, 61, 210, 213–14
Greenberg, Susan L., 157–58, 189, 198
Greenblatt, Stephen, 4n12
Greene, Robert, *Greene's Groatsworth of Wit* (1592), 217
Greene, Roland, 75
Greg, W. W., 186
Grosart, Alexander B., 113n8, 133–34
Guazzo, Stefano, *The Civile Conversation* (1581), 205, 210–14, 216, 224, 227
Guillory, John, 20
Guilpin, Everard, 142n84

Hackett, Helen, 13n43
Halberstam, Jack, 221
Halpern, Richard, 33, 34
Harington, Sir John, 137; *Orlando Furioso* (trans. 1607), 127
Harris, Joseph, 20–21
Harris, Sir Thomas, 169–70
Harvey, Gabriel, 32, 47, 100, 210n29
Hawhee, Debra, 84n40, 84n42
Hay, James, 111
Heath, John, 128, 131
Helgerson, Richard, 38, 73
Heminges, John, and Henry Condell, *Mr. William Shakspeares Comedies, Histories, & Tragedies* (1623), 1, 2, 4, 5, 200
Hendrick, Niclaes, *All the Letters of the A. B. C* (1575), 28–29
Henry, Prince of Wales (son of James I), 122–23, 164
Herbert, Mary Sidney (sister of Philip Sidney), 73, 76, 167, 168
Herbert, Philip, 111
Hermagoras of Temnos, 77, 91

Herrick, Robert, "Delight in Disorder," 10–11
Hershinow, David, 162
Hetherington, Michael, 39, 59
Heywood, Thomas, 219n65
Hirschfeld, Heather, 166
historicist/contextualist versus aesthetic discourse, 6–7
Homer, 42, 132, 151
hooks, bell, 19–20, 149
Horace, poetics of, 6n24, 13, 80n24, 100, 132, 139–40, 141, 144, 164–65, 166
Howard, Rebecca Moore, 36, 66
Hughes, Felicity, 40
Huisman, Rosemary, 117–18
Hutson, Lorna, 203n11
Hyman, Wendy Beth, 6, 162, 206n20

Iliffe, Robert, 163
inefficiency of writing process, 124–25
Inns of Court, 36, 61n92, 114, 137, 210. *See also* Gray's Inn
Inoue, Asao B., 16, 152
invention: change in meaning from discovery to conception, 75–76; deliberative versus forensic, 91; in early modern rhetorical composition, 70–71; forensic argument, *stasis* theory, and *topoi*, 73, 75, 77–79, 82–83, 85, 91; freedom and regulation, interplay between, 71–74, 79–82, 99–100; Gascoigne's understanding of, 57–59, 61; *kairos*, 74, 83–85, 106, 195; in modern literary pedagogy, 104–9; Sidney's view of, 70–74 (*see also* Sidney, Philip)
Ioppolo, Grace, 2, 202

Jacotot, Joseph, 60
James I and VI (king of England), 111, 114, 122, 128, 137, 159, 169–70; Declaration of Sports (1617/1618), 161n19; *Poetical Exercises* (1591), 32
Jardine, Lisa, 12, 46
Johnson, Samuel, 5n18
Jones, Emrys, 29–30n8
Jones, Robert, *A Musicall Dreame* (1609), 182–83, 184, 186
Jonson, Ben: annotation and commonplace books, use of, 3n10; courtiers compared to actors by,

INDEX

216–17; Davies of Hereford and, 113, 116, 118, 129, 136; on poetic discomposition, 13–15, 22, 72; Rosenblatt on transactional poetic reading and, 197n102; Shakespeare, critique of, 2, 14–15, 165; on social virtues of poetry, 22; Southwell's collaboration compared, 158, 164–66, 168–69, 177; Woolf on, 1, 2; *The Workes of Benjamin Jonson* (1616), 166
Joyce, James, 20
Julius Caesar, 45

kairos, 74, 83–85, 106, 195
Kaplan, Donald M., 204, 216
Kempe, William, 44, 46
Kerrigan, John, 163
King, Henry, 161n19
Kingra, Mahinder, 162
Kleist, Heinrich von, 141
Klene, Jean, 158n10, 178, 181, 184–86, 190–93
Knight, Leah, 188
Knights, Ben, 23–24, 25
Kolb, Laura, 162
Kramnick, Jonathan, 23

la Perriere, Guillaume de, *Theater of Fine Devices* (1614), 30
Lamb, Julian, 35
Lamott, Anne, 124
Languet, Hubert, 87
Lanham, Richard, 125
Lanyer, Aemelia, *Salve Deus Rex Iudaeorum* (1611), 175
Lasswell, Harold, 157
Lauer, Janice, 78
Leader, Zachary, 90n54, 95
Lefevre, Karen Burke, 82–83, 157, 166
Lerer, Seth, 33n19
Levao, Ronald, 89
Lilley, Kate, 168, 171n53
Lipari, Lisbeth, 84n42
Liu, Yameng, 91n58
Lodge, Thomas, *Works of Seneca* (1620), 163n25
Longfellow, Erica, 170
Longinus, *On the Sublime*, 140
Love, Harold, 160
Lyly, John, 164; *Sapphо and Phao* (1584), 203n10
Lynch, Jack, 4

Mack, Peter, 56–57
Macray, William Dunn, 136n69
Magnusson, Lynne, 210, 214
Mandell, Barrett John, 151–52
Mann, Jenny C., 93, 162
manuscript texts, 117–19, 158–60, 161, 172, 177–94, *179*, *182*, *185*, *191–92*
Marlowe, Christopher, 18, 113; *Doctor Faustus* (ca. 1588–1592), 203n10; *Tamburlaine* (1587–1588), 138–39
Marotti, Arthur, 119n24, 160
Marston, John, *Jack Drum's Entertainment* (1601), 219
Marvell, Andrew, 185
Matalene, Carolyn, 196
Matz, Robert, 6n24
Mazzio, Carla, 11, 203n10, 209
McCabe, Richard, 115
McCoy, Richard C., 49, 50n77
McGann, Jerome, 186–87, 197n102
McKenzie, D. F., 186
McRae, Andrew, 142n84
mediocrity, 111, 112, 114, 116, 121, 133–34, 138–41, 143n86
Menzer, Paul, 217
Middleton, Thomas: *Hengist* (1620), 216n51; *Roaring Girl* (1611), with Dekker, 218
Miller, Carolyn R., 84
Miller, J. Hillis, 20
Miller, Susan, 25–26
Millman, Jill Seal, 185
Milton, John, 1, 18
Mirandula, Octavio, *Flores Poetarum* (1480), 44–45
Mitchell, Dianne, 118–19n24, 162, 168n45, 175n60
Moore, Shawn M., 188

Nashe, Thomas, 47, 48, 113, 146
Nelson, Victoria, 97
Nevile, Alexander, 61
New Historicism, 6
Ngai, Sianne, 141n81, 234n87
Niederauer, Martin, 124
North, Dudley, Third Baron, 118n24
North, Joseph, 6

Oakeshott, Michael, 212n35
Olive, Sarah, 4n14
Overbury, Thomas, 170

INDEX

Ovid, 44, 45, 48, 208; *Ars Amatoria*, 203n10, 210n29
Owen, John, 137

Pangallo, Matteo, 217–18n56, 224
Panke, William, *Breefe Receite* (1591), 122n40
Pardi, Phil, 162
Parker, Lindsay, 107–8
Parker, Patricia, 35n25
patching and botching/bodgery, 35–36, 42–48, 51, 65, 66, 106, 130–131, 147, 164
pedagogy of English literature and composition, 8–9; attention, prioritization of, 59–60; critical reading/writing and editing, affinities between, 161, 195–99; cultural hegemony of English literature and, 5–7, 117, 149; destabilizing familiarity of texts, 194, 195; doubt and hesitation, cultivation of, 74, 104–9; early modern pedagogical programs, 12–13, 28–35, 38, 41–47; early modern writing masters and writing instruction, 112–13, 117–25; editing as frame for, 190–94, *191–92*; invention protocols and, 104–9; judging, teaching without, 151–52; labor-based grading contracts, 16, 152; literary epistemology and writing process, 17–27; patching and botching/bodgery, 35–36, 42–48, 51, 65, 66; perfection, perfectionism, and failure in, 204, 205–6, 230–36; plagiarism, problem of, 65–67; "quick capacity" and intellectual liberation in, 36, 60–61, 64–69; revision process and, 149–54; Shakespeare, teaching, 18–19, 20, 232–33; time/money/status affecting, 116–17, 149, 153–54. *See also* rhetoric
Pembroke, Mary, Countess of, 121, 123
Pendarves, Robert, 30–31, *31*, 33
Pender, Patricia, 167, 168
perfection, perfectionism, and failure: definitions, 201–2, 220; discomposition and imperfectness, 231; failed delivery, dramatizations of, 204–5, 206–14; in pedagogy, 204, 205–6, 230–36; performance anxiety/stage fright, 203–4, 216, 217, 230; poetics of failure, 205, 220–21; Shakespeare's *Love's Labor's Lost* on, 200–201, 203, 223–24 (*see also* Shakespeare, William); theatrical authorship and performance, imperfect experience of, 205, 215–21; twinned depictions of amateur theater and fractured conversation, 205, 221–29
Persius Flaccus, *Satires*, 98
Petrarchian tradition, 98, 203
Pettie, George, 210
Pickering, Andrew, 120–21, 124–25
plagiarism, 65–67, 136, 193
Plato, 78; *Meno*, 93n64
Plutarch, 210
pot poets, 142–45
Potter, Ursula, 49
Poulakos, John, 83
Preiss, Richard, 219n63, 220n67
printers and printing technology, 49, 115, 117–19, 158, 160, 163–64
Probyn, Elspeth, 88
Prouty, Charles Tyler, 49
Pulter, Hester, and *Pulter Project*, 188–89
Puritanism, 161n19
Puttenham, George, 93, 100
Pye, Christopher, 126n50

Quarles, Francis, 161n19
"quick capacity": Gascoigne on, 36, 55–63, 70; in pedagogy of English literature, 36, 60–61, 64–69
Quintilian, 112, 130n58
Quintilius Verus, 164–65, 166

Ralegh, Walter, 235; "The Lie," 161n19, 190–93, 197
Ramus, Peter, 71
Rancière, Jacques, *The Ignorant Schoolmaster*, 59–60, 232
Randall, David, 208n25, 210n30
Relle, Eleanor, 32n13
Rescher, Nicholas, 95
revision/failure to revise: the blot emblematizing dissonance of composition process, 116, 122, 126–29; Davies of Hereford on, 110–11, 116 (*see also* Davies of Hereford, John); editing distinguished, 157; inefficiency of process, 125; in pedagogy of English literature and composition, 149–54; poetics of, 118–21; psychology of, 112;

time/money/status, writer's need for, 132–33
rhetoric: *aporia,* 74, 92–95, 98; *decorum/indecorum* and, 11; deliberative, 91; dialectic and, 71; *dispositio,* 71; in early modern pedagogy, 29, 33, 58, 70–71; *elocutio,* 32, 71, 72; forensic, 73, 75, 77–79, 82–83, 85, 91; modern rhetoric and composition studies, 16, 25, 81, 104; poetics and, 71–72; *pronuntiatio,* 71; *stasis* theory, 73, 77, 79, 82, 83, 85, 104; style in, 32, 33; *topoi,* 77–78, 104–6. *See also* invention
Rhetorica ad Herennium, 78, 80, 91, 139n74
Rhodes, Neil, 12–13, 139
Richards, Jennifer, 210–11n30
Richardson, Brian, 163
Ridgeway, Cicely Mackwilliams, Lady, 155–56, 159, 170–74, 199
Ridout, Nicholas, 216
Ringler, William, 70n2, 73, 127
Robbins, Bruce, 7
Roland, David, 203
Rorty, Richard, 195
Rose, Mike, 89–90
Rosenblatt, Louise, 196, 197n102
Rosenfeld, Colleen Ruth, 11
Ross, Sarah C. E., 159, 169
Ross, Trevor, 115n15
Roychoudhury, Suparna, 125n49
Rudenstine, Neil, 100
Rule, Hannah J., 16
Russ, Joanna, 167

Salamon, Linda Bradley, 49
Saldívar, Ramón, 197–98
Sarkar, Debapriya, 162
Schechner, Richard, 234n87
Schlegel, Friedrich, 197
Schoeck, R. J., 137n71
Scodel, Joshua, 139n74
Secor, Marie, 104
Selden, John, 163n25
Seneca, 163n25, 211
Shakespeare, William, 17, 200–235; on botching and patching, 47–48; in composition studies, 25n81; cultural hegemony and, 5–9; Davies of Hereford and, 112n3, 113, 146, 146n91; destabilizing familiarity of, 194; on failed delivery, 204–5, 206–9; Jonson's critique of, 2, 14–15, 165; myth of genius and "easiness" of composition, 1–9, 200–201; pedagogy of, 18–19, 20, 232–33; on perfectness, perfectionism, and performance anxiety, 200–201, 203, 223–24; theatrical authorship and performance, imperfect experience of, 205, 215–21; twinning depictions of amateur theater and fractured conversation, 205, 221–29, *222*
Shakespeare, William, works: *Hamlet,* 48, 232; *Henry V,* 47; *A Lover's Complaint,* 112n3; *Love's Labor's Lost,* 17, 202–9, 215, 217, 221–29, *222,* 232–33; *Measure for Measure,* 206n20; *A Midsummer Night's Dream,* 216n51, 219n61; *The Rape of Lucrece,* 163n25, 200n1; *Sir Thomas More,* 3; Sonnets, 200–201, 202; *Twelfth Night,* 47–48, 206n20, 219n64; *Venus and Adonis,* 146
Shenk, Robert, 91n60
Sherman, William, 3n10, 163–64n25
Sibthorpe, Henry (husband of Anne Southwell), 159, 160, 170, 180, 181, 187
Sibthorpe, John (father), 181
Sidney, Henry (father), 87, 90
Sidney, Philip, 16, 69–103; *aporia* and writer's block, 69–70, 74, 89–90, 92–95, 97–98, 100, 102; *Arcadia,* 76, 210; *Astrophil and Stella* (ca. 1581), 69–74, 76, 86–88, 90–92, 95–100, 101, 102–3, 111; *Certain Sonnets* (ca. 1570s), 100–102; change in meaning of invention and, 75–76; *The Defense of Poesy* (1595), 16, 73, 76–86, 87, 88–89, 100, 111, 115, 124, 144, 145, 156; on doubt and shame in literary activity, 12, 73–77, 85–91, 102–3, 112; feminine rhymes, use of, 127; freedom and regulation, interplay between, 71–74, 79–82, 99–100; invention, understanding of, 70–74; on the poetic "idea," 81–82, 85, 100, 201; sister's role in editing of, 167
Sinfield, Alan, 6
Singer, Jerome L., 90
Singh, Julietta, 221
Sipiora, Phillip, 83, 84
Sirc, Geoffrey, 16, 64
Skinner, Quentin, 91
Sloane, Thomas O., 83
Smit, David, 16
Smith, Emma, 4
Smith, Nicholas, 137n70

Snodham, Thomas, 163n25
solitary activity, literary composition viewed as, 3, 9
Somerset, Countess of, 170, 173–74
Sommers, Nancy, 149
Sontag, Susan, 32
Southwell, Lady Anne, 17, 155–94; borrowings from other writers, 159, 161n19, 173, 181, 182, 186, 190–94; collaborative nature of poetic endeavor for, 157–58, 160–61, 168–69 (*see also* editing); composition process, editing as part of, 177–80, *179*, 181–86, *182*, *185*; defense of poetry by, 155–57, 168, 170, 173; life and career, 169–70; male readers, appeals to, 174–77; manuscripts of, 158–60, 161, *172*, 177–94, *179*, *182*, *185*, *191–92*; modern transcription and edition of collaborative works of, 184–93, *185*, *192*; religious convictions and poetry of, 156, 160–61, 171, 172, 174–77, 184; Lady Ridgeway and, 155–57, 159, 170–74, 199; Sidney compared, 156–57; social approach to writing in early modern manuscript culture and, 160, 170–77; student expectations regarding, 235; women and women's writing, ambivalence about, 161, 174–77; women readers, poems reaching for social connections to, 170–74, 199
Southwell, Lady Anne, works: "An Elegie written by the Lady A," 170–73; "An Epitaph vpon the Countess of Somerset," 173–74; "An: Epitaph vppon Cassandra MackWilliams," 173; "A Letter to Doctor Adam Bpp of Limerick," 174–75; "The Lie," 161n19, 190–93, 197; "Sonnett 1.a," 181; "Sonnett 2.a," *182*, 182–86, *185*; "Sr. giue mee leaue," 175–77; "Thou shalt not commit Adooltery," 177–80, *179*
Southwell, Thomas, 169–70, 177
Spenser, Edmund, 32, 76, 100, 210n29; *The Faerie Queene* (1590), 125
sprezzatura, 4
Stamatakis, Chris, 118–19n24
Stanislavski, Constantin, 230
stasis theory, 73, 77, 79, 82, 83, 85, 104
Stern, Tiffany, 219n59

"Sternhold and Hopkins" (*The Whole Booke of Psalmes Collected into Englysh Metre;* 1562), 29, 33n19
Stevenson, Jane, 185
Stoeber, Joachim, 201
style: defining, 32–33; Gascoigne on, 35–36, 66 (*see also* Gascoigne, George); inherent contradictions of, 32–34; non-style, 47
Suckling, John, 163n25

Tallent, Elizabeth, 202
Tanselle, G. Thomas, 187, 190
Taylor, Gary, 187n84
Taylor, John (the Water Poet), 116, 142–45; *The Praise of Hemp-Seed* (1620), 143; *Urania* (1615), 144
teaching English literature. *See* pedagogy of English literature
Terence, 48; *Eunuchus,* 135
Thadani, Simran, 122n40
theatrical performance. *See* perfection, perfectionism, and failure
Thomas, Max W., 136
Thompson, Ayanna, 18–19, 21
time/money/status, writers' need for, 113–15, 116–17, 132–35, 136, 145–48, 149, 153–54
Tootalian, Jacob, 188
topoi, 77–78, 104–6
total depravity, Calvinist doctrine of, 156
Tribble, Evelyn, 219, 220n67
Turchi, Laura, 18–19, 21
Twain, Mark, 216n47

Vickers, Brian, 111, 138n72
Virgil, 38, 42, 44–46, 52, 53, 60
Viswanathan, Gauri, 5
Vogl, Joseph, 25n80

Wagoner, Brady, 82n29
Wall, Wendy, 117, 126n50, 188
Warner, John, 16, 22–23, 65–67
Watson, Thomas, 164
Weimann, Robert, 218n57
Werstine, Paul, 119n25
Wilder, Laura, 16, 77n19, 78n23, 104–6, 108n103, 153
Willis, Jonathan, 29n4
Wilson, Glenn D., 203
Winston, Jessica, 61n92
Witmore, Michael, 11

Wittman, Kara, 230
women and women's writing: ambivalence of Southwell on, 161, 174–77 (*see also* Southwell, Lady Anne); collaboration and patriarchy, managing, 169, 177; Davies of Hereford on writing instruction for women, 123; modern scholarship on, 160, 167, 185, 193; Shakespeare's *Love's Labor's Lost,* anxiety about interactions with women in, 204–5, 206–9; social nature/treatment of, 167–68
Woolf, Virginia, 1–2, 20

Woudhuysen, H. R., 202
Wright, Gillian, 158–59, 160, 169, 170, 185, 190–93
writer's block, 69–70, 74, 89–90, 94–95, 97, 100, 102
Wroth, Mary, 167
Wyatt, Thomas, 118n24

Yarbrough, Stephen, 92

Zarnowiecki, Matthew, 119–20
Zembylas, Tasos, 124
Zucker, Adam, 232–33

www.ingramcontent.com/pod-product-compliance
Lightning Source LLC
Chambersburg PA
CBHW030119240426
43673CB00041B/1336